Born Singing

Annette Willoughby

Visit us online at www.authorsonline.co.uk

An Authors OnLine Book

ISBN 0-7552-0192-2

Authors OnLine Ltd
40 Castle Street
Hertford SG14 1HR
England

This book is also available in e-book format, details of which are available at
www.authorsonline.co.uk

About the Author

Annette Willoughby was born in the West Riding of Yorkshire, the eldest of five children. A Grammar School education led her into the Civil Service. After gaining a Dip.Ed, she entered Primary Education, then taught in a Boys Public School in Hertford, specialising in remedial English. She has two children from her first marriage.

In 1996 her partner Barrie was contracted to work in Lesotho, Southern Africa, on a hydro-electric construction project. She gave up a teaching post in Croydon to join him. Her new life in 'The Mountain Kingdom' inspired her to start writing. They were married in South Africa in 1997. Her books capture the atmosphere of life in Africa. Fascinated by traditional Basotho culture, their spontaneous displays of singing and dancing, the country's historic past; dinosaur fossils, San Bushmen, Sangomas….her spirit of adventure has taken her on a new and different journey.

The success of her first book, 'Innocent in Africa' has brought her into contact with other like-minded people who supported her ideals. She has campaigned for a small village in the Lowlands of Lesotho, which now has a fresh water supply and electricity. Currently, she arranges sponsorship enabling children to go to school. 'We cannot change their lives, but we can make a difference,' she says.
The people have built her a clay house with a tin roof and given her a Basotho name, 'Malimakatso' which means 'Mother of Miracles'. She has made three return visits to Lesotho and South Africa, adding yet more miles of vivid and colourful memories.

Annette is now enjoying retirement in a Bedfordshire village and cares for her disabled granddaughter, as well as working on her writing and her garden. Giving talks to schools and professional groups, she raises awareness of the plight of poorer families in the community, with whom she has forged links over the past seven years.

Celtic Blessing

May the road rise up to meet you,
May the wind always be at your back,
May the sun shine warm upon your face,
The rains fall soft upon your fields,
And until we meet again,
May God hold you in the palm of his hand.

Acknowledgements

Without Barrie, I could not have written 'Innocent in Africa' or this sequel, 'Born Singing'. I thank him from the bottom of my heart for giving me the opportunity to realise my dream. He is the civil engineer in our marriage, yet enabled me to build my own bridges. 'Born Singing' is intended as a memoir of our happy times in Africa.

This book was both easy and traumatic to write. I have tried to portray things as they seemed at the time, not to be guilt-edged by hindsight. I give my thanks to Liliane Pazuki, my friend and confidante. Together, we shared many journeys through South Africa and Lesotho, experienced moments both solemn and tragic, truly comical and simply hilarious. Her frequently-used French expression, *'dead of laughing'* will always inspire me with a fit of giggles. Priscilla Ripa-di-Meana has almost no need of introduction, her pages almost wrote themselves. She is just a wonderful person and helped us to appreciate wild animals in quite another dimension. She forgot to tell me about the scorpions. Betty Majoro will be fondly remembered, not only for keeping house for us at Leribe Camp but for educating me in Lesotho culture in our lunch breaks. I feel privileged that she allowed me to name her baby. My thanks to Anne Dungey, who brought her own brand of humour to Lesotho and proved to be a fine companion on our travels in Zimbabwe. To Amelia Masupha and Rose-Mary, many thanks for your hospitality and friendship.

I thank my sister Marje for providing a smooth transition to acceptable grammatical standards in my writing. She stayed up nights working on my comma-happy manuscript and her suggestions were always valuable. Thanks to my South African friend, Kim Masters, whose sparkling enthusiasm never diminished. She gave willingly of her free time to engage in the nitty gritty editing sessions, over many months of hard work and chocolate biscuits. After a long period of gestation, the book reached the pen of Jean Gardner, who, like a conscientious midwife, read the whole script and accurately delivered 'Born Singing'. Other supporting readers were Sheila Jones, Dorothy Clarke, Eddie Evans and Alex Olney in the final stages.

The final accolade is to Walter and all the Makibi family, to whom I owe a debt of gratitude for accepting me into their community. I felt so at home in Ha Simone. Without such generosity, caring and friendship I would not have discovered my own identity. The humour and laughter, the trauma of Walter's terrible illness, the miles we travelled together, have enriched my understanding of their country and their culture Sadly, I learned of the death of Charlotte, the Headmistress of Leribe School, whose memory I shall treasure. The people who populate these pages are all heroes. Their game is survival - their courage truly remarkable.

Links with Datchworth have continued. Funding started in 1999 to support the project of bringing fresh water to Ha Simone with an electricity link. This was achieved in January 2001. Reverend Makibi danced in the street when he received the message. Our goal then was education. I want to thank all those sponsors who have helped send Basotho children to school. The success of the scheme can be measured in kids who now proudly wear a school uniform. Emily, you are a star. Rose, I could not have known a finer friendship. Stephen, you are a man with a vision. Walter, thank you for finding me.

Acknowledgements and permissions

I acknowledge the source of material on dinosaurs from Professor David Ambrose MBE of the National University of Lesotho in Roma, whose Journal of Research on Lesotho palaeontology is a treasure trove of valuable information.

Thanks to Hilary Turnbull for taking the trouble to seek out Dr Ambrose in Roma, whose contact has been invaluable.

Source Material on Initiation from 'Vanishing Cultures of South Africa' by Peter Magubane, published by Struik Publishers in 1998, text by Associate Professor Andrew Spiegel.

Thanks to Angela Symonds for her patience in preparing photographs for use with the text.

I readily accept that my knowledge of the culture of the Basotho people is limited and I apologise for any misinterpretations which may be evident. All opinions expressed and of course, errors are entirely mine.

To Walter

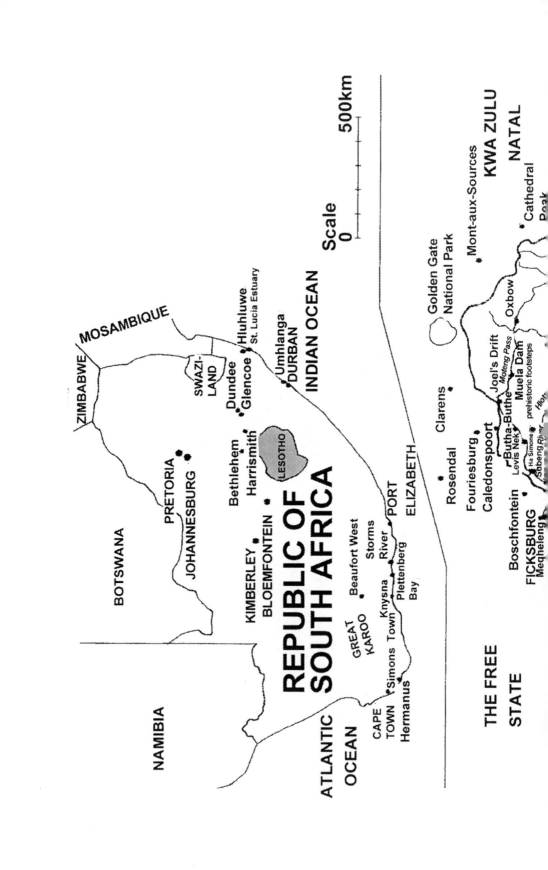

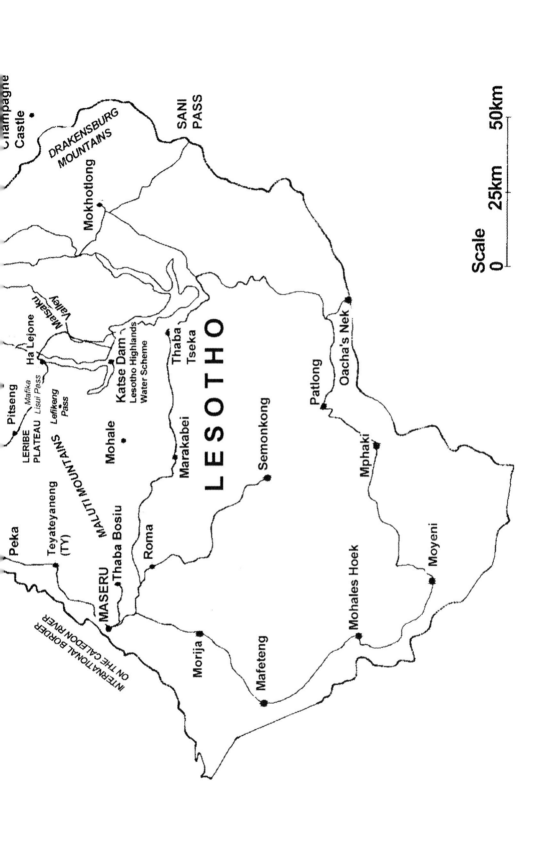

CONTENTS

Foreword

The political upheaval and civil disturbances in Lesotho, which took place in 1998 left Maseru, the capital, devastated. Since then the country has recovered, the political climate is healthy and the economy stable, though still fragile. Tourism numbers are rising. King Letsie III, crowned in 1997 as a bachelor, has since married. His Queen, Karabo, has become a very popular member of the Royal Family and they now have two daughters. Lesotho has settled down into a forward-thinking nation with a clear vision of its future, though unemployment is still a severe problem. Sadly the recent death of Mamohato, the Queen Mother, has been a great loss.

This new title, 'Born Singing' by Annette Willoughby, reflects the time shortly before the political uprising. Every book has an historical impact and I am privileged to have known the author personally, and have been privy to her many schemes which have been for the benefit of her Basotho family/community in particular and for the wider good of Lesotho as a whole .

We first met in connection with the Lesotho Diocesan Association (LDA) which meets every year at Partnership House in London, with the aim of improving links with Lesotho. We also share a common interest in the Lesotho Durham Link, which she supports avidly. Her faith in the people of Lesotho has never wavered and she has made many changes in the quality of life for the people of Ha Simone.

Her books describe her observations of Basotho culture during her time in Lesotho and the widespread poverty of ordinary people she encountered in the Lowland villages. She saw through the poverty into the hearts of the people. Something special happens when people from two different worlds begin to understand one another. Through her books, 'Innocent in Africa' and 'Born Singing' eyes have been opened and a learning process has begun. Our hope for the future lies in continuing this process and our traditional strong links with Britain.

Lebohang Ramohlanka
High Commissioner for the Kingdom of Lesotho,
London 2000 - 2005

Born Singing

Chapter 1

Child of Mine

October peach trees peppered the landscape like pink frilly skirts. The air filled with the song of morning. The bare earth heard their coming. Some of the women, their toes pressing the soft sandy gradients, gathered grasses as they approached. Round their skirts, children clung. Babies folded into blankets, some asleep, rocked against their mothers' backs. The women stopped singing and halted by the big gate. The guards looked on, roused from night duty, wondering what message this small chorus wanted to deliver.

They gathered like a flock of birds around the high wire fence, eyes peering through the bars like nervous sparrows. Then it began.

"White ladies, please listen to us. We look after de children, we cook for you…" voices pleading, striving to keep their dignity, called through the high wire fence.

"We are good maids. We clean de house and work for you, please give us now a job - we are hungry…."

The voices went on calling. One of them had jewellery to sell so I went down to the gate to buy trinkets. I liked the girl who made earrings made from copper wire (probably stolen from the site.) She and I had exchanged greetings several times in the past few months when she came with her clever pieces of crafted jewellery. These women faced dilemmas which we could not possibly understand. Poverty and sickness dictated their lives.

How could we say to them, " It will be better when the dam is built. You will have electricity in your homes. Your farmers will have irrigation for their crops. The people will have jobs."

A mist of silver dew spread along the lower slopes and dazzled like jewels in the grass. In the far distance snow still lingered on the highest peaks. The mountains listened, hearing the pain of their womenfolk. In October families must have seed for the next harvest. If they have no money there is no seed. Sometimes the people are so hungry they eat the seeds and there are none to plant. Sometimes the seed vanishes into the thin soil and is washed away by the heavy rains. Their men folk are probably away working in the gold mines in South Africa. The Mosotho woman must do the best she can – alone. She waits for months, sometimes years, for her man to come home.

My husband Barrie and I had moved to a house on the slopes of the Lowlands of Lesotho, and domestic help had not been on our agenda. But this was Africa. Expatriate wives were expected to have one - if not two - cleaning ladies. And perhaps a garden boy.

Betty was employed on the basis that I didn't need a maid but she needed the money. On the day we hired her, Mrs Mojoro explained that she had three children and was expecting baby number four, promising to work throughout her pregnancy and continue after the birth. That was the deal. Betty's deal.

This new reality had hit me like a kick from a bad tempered mule. Maids and garden boys had never before been part of my vocabulary. Desperately, I tried to make sense of the things which were the very bedrock of South African society in 1997. I had stumbled into a history book and the pages fell open before me.

Betty was large and lovely. Wearing a blue dress and scarf to match, sporting frizzy hair which refused to be brushed, she stepped inside the door, arms akimbo, and radiated a smile as wide as the Orange River. Her bright eyes sparkled with determination. We agreed to pay her the going rate. She would start on Monday.

Betty's grasp of cleaning and polishing was simple. Make dust. Madam pleased. Patting her belly proudly and stretching wide apron twice round midriff, my new maid harnessed herself to the vacuum cleaner as in frigate pulling yacht out to sea.

"*Lumela 'M'e.* Today I will make you as clean as a pin. I will take the bedrooms first. My work is very fast."

We had three bedrooms off a central hall which was wide enough for an elephant to pass through. A tin of Brasso at the ready and polishing rags stuffed down every pouch and pocket – Betty hitched up her abdomen and launched into the attack. A small framed charcoal print hanging opposite the kitchen was the first to fall off the wall. A cloud of dust rose into the air and set off the smoke alarm. Clearly she was happy, as chair after chair was swung across the hall and polished to the tune of some illuminating gospel song.

"White ladies like shiny furniture," she chorused, as with gusto the beeswax was ladled onto the top of my already polished dining room table, in ice-cream cornet scoops. Betty had no idea why we needed so many pieces of paper, known as letters or bills, sitting on the sideboard. Nor could she possibly know that Barrie was a tidy person and liked things in date order. Papers were for collecting together and filing behind the sofa out of sight. There was a slight blip in domestic harmony, when bills were not paid on time due to Betty's filing system.

Cheerfully, she washed the dishes with the same amount of water other people used to hose down their cars. In her village there were no taps and water had to carried in buckets from a stand pipe - and it was cold. Hot water, a sink and 'Fairy Liquid' was Betty's washing heaven.

It took us a while to get used to each other. From Betty I learned my first Sesotho phrases. She taught me what a *Sangoma* was, how the women planted vegetables and how to barter for fruit in the market. Her spoken English improved by the week On hot days during the long months of her pregnancy, she would finish the ironing on the *stoep* where it was cool and there she would hum softly to herself while straightening the clothes..

"Can you tell me de English name for my baby *'M'e?* I will practise saying it. The name must be *not common.*"

This went on for months. Her stomach grew large and most days she suffered from hiccups. We went through all the names: David, Edward and Christopher. Daniel, John and Richard.. Betty repeated them over and over again to herself, pressing the name rhythmically into Barrie's shirts.

"No *'M'e* - it is not the right one."

It was Easter Saturday. Petros, our Chief Engineer and Director of Infestations (to give him his full title) came running to tell me there was a lady at the security gate who would not leave until she had seen me. She was a Mosotho lady and wanted to hand me a note. Consumed with curiosity, Petros hung about until I read it to him.

The note read: '*Miss Glen I will not be at wok, my child is born. Betty.*'

"It is from Mrs Mojoro, Petros – her time has come."

A look of genuine concern fell over his face. He was very fond of my maid. The staff always loved to hear of the birth of a baby; for them it was a time for celebration.

Early the next morning, carrying a parcel of cotton wool, blankets, soap and a bunch of cosmos, I walked across the field leading to the hospital, past the large tree where people were gathering – for it was Easter Day. From the hospital building I could hear the hum of voices. Tiptoeing inside the entry door to the maternity ward, I was greeted by a sea of black faces. Patients and visitors alike were sitting on the ground. They filled the whole corridor. Pregnant girls who looked ready to drop their babies any minute, old ladies, men in wheelchairs, small children wearing frothy organza dresses snuggled against adults in bible black cloaks, all singing their hymn of Easter morning: '*Christ is risen, Christ will come again*' in English.

Faces turned to stare at me and children whispered. A white stranger making for the maternity ward would have seemed unusual. A sudden tide of homesickness pressed against my chest. African voices sang loudly, praising God for his love. I was unable to swallow. Tears pricked my eyes. My thoughts sprang to another Easter four years ago. Easter 1993, when Barrie and I first met. A village churchyard in Hertfordshire, where, during every spring, petals of blossom cling round the mossy trunks of the old cherry trees like pink coronets. *Our* place. Six thousand miles away. Together we had come to Africa ….and now The Mountain Kingdom was our home.

In the next bed to Betty was a women whose baby had been born dead. Scenes of torment and misery were acted out in the same room in the hours which followed. Privacy was not catered for. While one mother glowed with pride at her healthy baby son, another was wracked with pain and cried pitifully for most of the night.

The plain grey walls of the hospital corridors stared down as I hurried to find her. In the grim recesses of the maternity wing, Betty's child had been born. A child weighing 2.6 kilograms - a child to whom I had been asked to give a name. Inside the rough blanket, a tiny scrap of life screwed up his face and turned a velvet head to his new world.

"Look *'M'e....* my baby son.," whispered Betty, as I bent to see inside the folds of cloth beside her. My heart was thumping. "He is alive....I prayed he would be born before you came.....it was one o'clock in the night. His name will be *Oliver* – it is the one I liked the best of all the names. The nurses - they were kind to me *'M'e* because you paid for my delivery. Thank you and Mr Barrie." Her head went down and her words soaked into the pillow. For a few moments a bond of silent weeping engulfed us. It was a promise kept.

"Betty, he was born on Easter Day. He's a really special baby...mm...Oliver... I like it. Come on, wipe your eyes."

Large tears splashed onto her brown hands and I saw the lines of exhaustion on her strong face. She looked pale. But there was still that spark of determination to make the best of everything – money or no, husband or no husband. Oliver, the brother of four-year-old Margaret would be taken to the tin shack up in the shanty village. So long as he didn't take an infection in the first two weeks, he should survive.

"…. I will go to see my mother in Maputsoe today. She will look after me…. I will come back to work soon *'M'e*. I can send my cousin to do the work if you need a maid."

"Don't worry Betty, when you are well, come back to us. Your job is safe. Now let me hold Oliver and see how tiny he is. Do you want me to bring the baby clothes this afternoon?"

"No *'M'e*," she hesitated and lowered her voice to a whisper, "new clothes will be stolen in the hospital. Please, I only like one blanket."

The news filled me with dismay. Levels of poverty were so extreme, that stealing was commonplace. Even here. That Betty had an English visitor to her bedside would have already been noticed. Jealousies arose between womenfolk when favours became known. Women who could not pay were not given a hospital confinement. They must do the best they can in their own homes.

Straw hard mattresses and no bedding to speak of, dysfunctional taps and toilets, insufficient nursing staff, all indicated a lack of money in the system. The burden of Betty's problems had just been staved off for a few days. Soon she would be out there facing the world. No one supported her financially. Like thousands of other African women, my maid was caught in the poverty trap. Her job on camp was her only salvation.

"Betty, how will you manage at home with baby Oliver?"

It will be okay '*M'e* he will sleep with Margaret and me. In our country a mother helps her daughter. The men – they drink too much," she answered with a dismissive wave of her hand.

Her man of was one of those, but she would not name and shame.

*   *   *   *

I had never planned to come to Africa. It was the last place on earth I had ever expected to find myself. My roots were well and truly in England. There was no hidden traveller in me. Foreign countries existed in my mind as places where other people went. The sun fried my skin and multiplied my freckles. Funny insects bit me.

Slogging happily away at our chosen future, my partner's new appointment had come like a bolt from the blue. A move from our base in South London could not have been further from our thoughts. Cemented into mortgage repayments, family commitments and a suburban garden which demanded nothing less than a course in grave digging before planting, we were putting down roots for the next ten years. Somewhere between the galloping Russian vine and laying a concrete base for a garden shed, the earth under our feet moved. A kind of divine intervention had scalded us, something sharp and painful – yet exhilarating, disturbing. It was our first parting, our first emotional prod.

Barrie and I had taken out our first late-in-life loan in March 1996 and acquired an elegant Victorian flat in an elegant Victorian street in Beckenham, Kent. After investing in new garden chairs and a concrete mixer, we spent hours discussing prospective gin and tonic evenings sitting on the south facing veranda, which we hadn't built yet. When, two months later, my other half was sent his marching orders to drop everything and go build a dam in Lesotho as part of his international status agreement, he took the first available flight to Johannesburg and left me clutching a wet hanky in one hand and a copy of 'Romantic Herb Gardens' in the other.

"For Heaven's sake" said my sister, "he's only gone for three weeks!"

A sense of pure loneliness engulfed me and like the gas boiler in our kitchen, everything shut down. There didn't seem any point in cooking for one. On the windowsill, unwatered seedlings shrivelled in their infancy and plastic wrapped roses were left to wilt. My children took to ringing me up every day - a sure sign that all was not well.

Exactly twenty one days after Barrie's departure, something approaching insanity propelled me onto a flight to South Africa. Me and a small bag of unsuitable clothes. And maybe a very small miracle. Without a backward glance at sunken garden or worried bank manager, I embarked on my first real life adventure. Beckenham to South Africa in three days with no forward planning and the wrong clothes, has to be a record of some sort.

5

Aboard the flight to Johannesburg, my emotions still dangling in the free fall position, feeble thoughts of my school geography lessons chased through my mind - images of elephants in the bush, crocodiles and swamps …..leeches, scorpions, snakes. What *was* I doing? This sudden surge of adventure in mid-life had nothing to do with Miss Beale's geography lessons at the Percy Jackson Grammar School in Doncaster, and everything to do with hormones. My man had been sent on a job and that's where I wanted to be. I knew absolutely nothing about Africa and even less about The Kingdom of Lesotho.

Leaving a warm rosy summer in England, carried out with my usual brand of optimism and lack of planning, was probably the most painful way of being introduced to an African winter. Travel guides are helpful if you have time to read them, but in three days flat, with a buttock full of typhoid and tetanus and a frenetic farewell to friends and family, not even a passing 'Lonely Planet' reached my brain. Booking myself onto a flight with South African Airways, carrying a small suitcase containing a few pairs of shorts, a bottle of Factor 30 sun cream and little else, galvanised me into a whole new cycle of energy which confounded even my closest friends.

After the shock of my arrival ("God, Nettie, I know you're spontaneous, but this is crazy…..yes of course I'm pleased to see you!") and the teary joyful reunion in Johannesburg Airport Arrivals' lounge, Barrie's company phoned to offer us a solution. A rented house in the nether regions of Fouriesburg, a small town in the Free State. What we could not have known was that an unexpected snowfall – the worst in twenty seven years – was imminent and would completely cover the mountains.

For six days we were marooned in the icy grip of winter. All the power in the region had gone off. Six foot snow drifts were all we could see from our window and candles were in extremely short supply. There was only one thing to do – make an igloo in the garden. An engineer's igloo, built to scale. This housed our food rations, which were slowly deteriorating without a fridge. Our house was icy cold and a visit to the bathroom in the middle of the night was the equivalent of a mad dash to the North Pole. Had it not been for Baden Powell's survival techniques, casually learned at Caterham5th Scout Camp during a previous summer, we would have been perilously close to disaster. Hilarity and a supply of good humour threw us together in the teeth of the storm.

Next door's Alsation dog was frozen into his kennel. His pathetic howls could be heard during the night like wolves across the prairie. Like a scene from Dr Shivago, Fouriesburg Jail on the opposite side of the road must have been the only safe house where prisoners were happy to be locked up.

As soon as main roads were passable, we received instructions from the company to move from Fouriesburg to a new home in Lesotho, which meant we would be nearer to Barrie's job. With ice on the road and more snow forecast, we embarked on a dangerous journey across the South African border complete with entire possessions packed into the boot of our car. This journey was to be my initial introduction to Lesotho, the Mountain Kingdom.

At snail's pace, we made our way across the Caledon River Bridge, in the dazzling afternoon sun, feasting our eyes for the first time on the majestic peaks of the Maluti Mountains. We stopped at the side of the road to take a long look.

I had never seen anything so beautiful. There were hardly any trees, no fences, no towns, just open vistas of pure dazzling whiteness rolling away to a rim of hills and then higher peaks in the distance. Nothing could have prepared us for this dramatic landscape. The purple streak of a pine forest showed on the horizon like a piece of driftwood on white sand.

"Isn't it stunning… magnificent. The snow is actually blue," I gasped.

"But where are the people?"

Herd boys with their goats were out on the slopes, seeking the few patches of grass where the snow had melted. They waved at us from underneath woolly hats. Miniature dwellings, higher up, looked like silver thimbles threaded together along the ledges of rock. The sky was ice-pink. It was love at first sight

We were travelling through a silent world, the only beings alive on this planet or so we felt. The road dipped and rose in front of us. Homesteads stood along the low slopes, grouped together under traditional thatch, a horse or a donkey tethered in the yard. Some of the houses were square with tin roofs. After a time, the translucent pearly twilight which precedes night descended onto the mountain. A few women passed us carrying water pots on their heads.

Our progress was slow and slippery. Only another ten kilometres to go My excitement grew with every bend in the road. The temperature was dropping fast. No vehicles passed going the other way. Rubbing the ice off the car window, I peered out. On the outskirts of Leribe, families who lived in villages near the road were preparing their evening fires. Every now and then a fountain of live embers showered the frosty night. The sky was damson. Daylight had almost gone.

"Look at that sky full of snow Barrie," I said softly, drawing my blanket closer. "They must be so cold cooking outside on a night like this."

Our journey had taken three hours. We pulled up outside the main gate of Leribe Camp. Someone stepped out of the darkness and shone a torch in our faces.

"Come in folks, we're expecting you.." said an English voice. "The electricity's gone off, sorry about that – often happens here. Come this way. I'll show you to your house."

Life on camp had been an enigma at first. Living at a height of 1,700 metres, initially we were a little breathless, but quickly readjusted to breathing pure air and revelled in our new- found love of the Mountain Kingdom. The fact that the electricity supply crashed every few days, phones didn't work, and hardly anyone spoke English was a little disconcerting. Having to travel in convoy was new to me. Gossip and rumours circulated wildly about hijacks and company cars being stolen. But the construction work had to go on.

The engineers were here to build dams so that water from the Highlands of Lesotho could flow into South African reservoirs to alleviate the problem of drought in the exploding industrial city of Johannesburg. Where the Senqu River rose, high in the Maluti Mountains would be the source of that water and in future years, the installation of electricity supplies with the added bonus of stable employment, would be the reward.

Katse Dam, the largest in the scheme, had already been built. Our contribution was to bring about the impounding of a second dam at Muela in the north, the new water transfer system with an underground hydro-electric power station that would generate electricity to supply the entire needs of Lesotho.

Barrie's job was in the underground powerhouse at the Muela site. His involvement in planning the future programming of the power station was challenging work and often necessitated long journeys and tight schedules. Seeing him off at the crack of dawn with a hard hat and a packet of sandwiches became a regular routine. For him, it would be a twelve hour day. He would arrive home after sundown, tired and caked in white dust from the site, with a raging thirst. I could contribute nothing towards hydro-power and transfer tunnel deadlines, but I made it my business to organise early evening swims before a hearty supper, keep the wine cupboard well stocked and plan for leisurely Sundays – Barrie's only day off.

*   *   *   *

It was four weeks since Oliver was born - or one moon. Betty had counted her pregnancy in moons. Her illnesses came in moons and she counted her money in moons. Three moons to a new pair of shoes. Time doesn't get any more specific than this in Africa.

I saw her approaching the verandah steps one hot afternoon.

"*Lumela'M'e*, I have brought my new son....he is now ready to greet you."

"Hello Betty, come on in. Let me look at Oliver. It's good to see you well again."

Her beaming maternal smile told me everything.

"Wait there one moment." I ducked under the vines around the verandah and went inside the house. There in the drawer lay the gift. I took it out of its paper and felt the softness against my cheek.

A shy smile came over Betty's face. Her dark eyes shone. Slowly, she bent forward, her legs planted comfortably apart on the wooden floor. She picked up Oliver and placed him face down on her back. Skilfully she drew the soft

8

blanket around herself, taking him expertly into the folds and then, tying the corners of the cloth firmly in a knot on her stomach. She stood up.

"Today I have de gold coin and I am singing de song of happiness. My baby will be warm, even in cold winter night. In Sesotho we call this thing *mohlolo 'M'e."* (a miracle) Betty had come to ask if she could have her old job back. "Oliver will come with me." As she rocked to and fro a tiny cry came from within the folds of the blanket. "For feeding, I will sit outside on the *stoep 'M'e*," she murmured, "in case I am not agreeing with you."

It was settled. Oliver would visit us three times a week and I would watch him grow. She had no income other than from her jobs on the camp. Her partner offered her neither financial nor emotional support and she spent her life trying to avoid him. This was the only solution for Betty. She needed to keep her job. And her pride. Her two older children lived with their grandmother. She only saw them once every moon.

"If you like Oliver can have his bath every day in our sink. He must begin life with a clean face," I suggested .

"Yes, *'M'e* I would be glad of it."

We walked together towards the camp entrance where the duty guards opened the big gates to let her out. We parted agreeably and the liquid brown eyes of her baby peered out of the blanket at his new world. The grinding poverty the child had been born into was no fault of his.

"Khotso 'M'e Ke le boha", (peace and Blessings)

"Come soon," I replied gently.

She walked away down the dusty track and across the tussocky grass where the cows were tethered. A patch of cosmos caught the breeze and fluttered pink and white by the high wire fence which marked the perimeter of our camp. The afternoon was hot and the mountains glimmered blue in the distance. The May wind was picking up and in less than an hour the afternoon storms would lash into the eucalyptus trees and the rains would fill the hard - baked dykes around the camp until the road became a yellow swamp.

She didn't come the following day. Or the next. No word came from her. Then on the night of the new crescent moon, she came walking to the gate of the camp. Beams of silver lay on the ground as she came swiftly across the lawns. The small shape of Oliver lay close to his mother as she passed by the window. Hercule, our neighbour's large black wolfhound, waved a ghostly tail as the moonlight caught his shadow. His bark was silent as our visitors disappeared into the *rondavel* where the maids always slept.

Betty came back to work fresh and in good spirits, carrying Oliver with her. I would hear him cry every now and again when she sat on the *stoep* to feed him.

Most days after lunch, we would have our language lessons at the big table under the green baize roof where the sun fell in bright shafts onto the floor. With Oliver on my lap - tightly bound in his cloth, I felt sure that he would come to know me a little. His fingers clung onto mine. They were tiny and plump and black. The inside of his palm was a pale milky colour and the dimple on the back showed a little hollow which would change when he grew. I looked into his chubby face and loved him with all my heart.

The phone in the house rang; an unusual sound - I almost ignored it. I gave Oliver to Betty and went to answer it. The call was from Barrie.

"Nettie, Thabo is coming soon to deal with the tree. He's got to go up on the roof. Make sure he has the long ladder."

"Yes, okay, I'll be going out with Betty soon. I'll leave everything ready. Does he know what to do?"

I went outside again and spoke to Betty. "*U tsoha ka nako mang?*" (what time are you going?) I asked her, " I'm going down into Leribe, do you want a lift home?"

"*Ke hantle 'M'e*, I will come."

"I want *moroho* (vegetables) from the market, can you help to translate for me?"

She laughed, knowing that I paid more than the price I should. White ladies with a purse always got charged more if they couldn't speak the language.

"There is cow meat at the butchery, do you want sausages – or liver?" I questioned, knowing that she loved the offal to cook for her children.

"*Kea leboha 'M'e.*"

She picked up Oliver who was growing into a sturdy weight now. He had inherited her dancing eyes. Her dry unruly hair stuck out from underneath the sides of her scarf which was tied attractively around her head. It perfectly matched her blue dress.

" *'M'e* I am ready." She hitched up Oliver and without a whimper, he settled into a comfortable bulge on her back.

Most weeks, I would drive into our local town to buy fruit from the market. Leribe is not a big town by English standards. It used to be known as Hlotse (pronounced *Shlotsie*) and recently changed its name. Founded by Reverend John Widdecombe, an Anglican missionary in 1876, it gradually became a town of some importance. The District Commissioner's Office built of sandstone, situated on the main street must have been very imposing in its day and still has an air of civic grandeur about it. The kneeling figure of a soldier carved by a local sculptor is still there but the flagpole has sadly gone. Major Bell's Tower, the old monument built in 1879, is the only reminder of the days of the Empire.

I know my town well now after living here for almost a year. Its faded run-down ambience with crumbling pavements and decaying buildings, is anything but modern, but I like it. The noise and bustle of the main street, filled with jostling crowds and shouting traders; its smiling faces and loud funky music is now my home. Many stalls sell fascinating cure-all medicines and herbal remedies in packets. The customer describes a symptom of illness and the trader knows exactly which colour medicine to use as the solution to the problem. Instant spiritual guidance, looking dangerously seductive in jars of bright red and blue powder, is handed over for a few maloti. Nowadays, there is a Standard Bank in the main street, which has changed the way people think about organising their money. Plastic and neon have arrived in the form of garish shop signs, flashing incongruously next to corrugated sheeting and wooden planks of home made stalls.

"*Lumela 'M'e,*" called out the ladies from the butcher's shop, in unison, "how is your Queen?" I would smile and wave.

"She is well!"

This was the regular greeting if I went to buy meat, from the only butcher in town who possessed a fridge. It was assumed Her Majesty and I were on serious nodding terms. The queue inside the shop gyrated to Radio Lesotho's thigh slapping music which came in waves over the loudspeaker. The lady butcher with arms akimbo peered over a blood-spattered apron and waved her cleaver in recognition of our friendship.

"Will you have the ox-tail today?"

"No, only liver for my maid and some fillet of beef from your freezer please."

We could buy a whole fillet for the equivalent of two pounds sterling. Nothing excited the locals so much as when the 'offal man' came to town. Long queues would form on both sides of the main high street. Tons off it came in fortnightly from the abattoirs in South Africa, driven in huge container lorries.

"*Kea Leboha* Alice, see you next week."

As a lone shopper I was illiterate and invisible. In the presence of my maid bargaining was much more fun. I walked across to the pavement stalls. Fresh supplies of *litapole, sepinichi* and enormous *tamati* – were bought under Betty's eagle eye.

Feeling pleased with my purchases I drove back up the hill to the camp. As I unloaded the boxes from the car later in the afternoon I stepped over a spade lying in the grass. Thabo, the head gardener, was in the process of digging yet another trench. He was trying to save the roots of our weeping willow tree. Without rain its leaves shrivelled up. With too much rain the water ran away quickly from the hard baked soil and no moisture reached its roots. Only one of Thabo's trenches could save it now.

The sight of a blue boiler suit and a hose pipe reassured me that the job would be done today. When Thabo said the word 'soon' it could mean anything from 'tomorrow' to 'next week'.

" '*M'e* I am cutting wood from branches. De tree – it grows too much in de roof. Do you want I look for rats also?" Thabo, who was very fond of tips, looked pleased to see me.

Our willow tree dropped its dead branches onto the roof and filled the loft with seething insects, which clung in orange patches under the eaves. Lately, we had also experienced rat noises on the ceilings in the early morning. We had a feeling they had taken up residence.

"Thanks Thabo," I shouted, carrying my bags into the house and reaching urgently for the kettle. Barrie's long ladder leaned perilously close to the drainpipe. It would not be a good idea to watch Thabo climb skywards. He wasn't good with ladders. And with the added hazard of the tree cutters it could be a disaster. I went indoors. Esther, one of my regular pupils, had just arrived and wanted to tell me about her school examination results.

"Esther do you want a cup of tea? I will make one for Thabo."

Esther didn't usually stop to drink tea. She liked to get on with her lesson. She had done better than all my other pupils. And that was without an English teacher at her school.

"My mother say thank you '*M'e* for giving me the lessons. She say she is very grateful."

"Tell her that I hope one day you will be a famous doctor. You will make a good doctor Esther...." my voice trailed off at the sound of metal scraping metal in the direction of my bathroom.

"Heavens above - what was *that*?"

Thabo had come to rest in a pile of lopped branches. The ladder had slid crazily away from its moorings. I stared at the devastation. The fronds of my willow would no longer weep. Its wonderful flowing foliage had been shaved off and only bald tentacles stuck out at rakish angles ten feet from the ground. Sheepishly Thabo raised himself from the leaves and smiled his beautiful smile.

"'*M'e* I did not see any rat."

Chapter 2

Life on Camp

Barrie and I had a house with a large garden, looking onto wide open views and the sculpted peak of Qoqolosing, the volcanic mountain. From my kitchen window the shining road to Pitseng wound its way up towards Katse Dam; the good tarmac road up to the Highlands, which had taken clever engineers eight years to build, even before the dam could be realised. There were hardly any trees or vegetation. Every morning on the lower pasture, laden ox carts driven by herdsmen, lumbered peacefully to the hollow tune of cowbells - almost like a scene from the Bible. Young shepherds wearing bright red cloaks and blankets slipped silently between thin grazing cows, moving at a pace slower than their animals. They leant on their sticks, then glided over the ridge, fading into the rosy light where they changed into faint dots among tall aloes.

The Basotho are a nation of horsemen and for many years it has been their only mode of transport. Riders sitting astride their sturdy ponies, wearing traditional red and brown patterned blankets pinned high across their shoulders, are proud and dignified. Their greeting of *'Khotso'* always comes as a surprise, as they pass by on the side of the track near our camp. Only the men ride. The women walk, carrying empty water carriers on their way to the *setibeng.* Taps are available in every village and the people gather and wait until it is their turn to draw water. Between tap and bucket, the juiciest bits of gossip and scandal are picked over. They turn to the nearest hillside, bracing themselves to push heavy wheelbarrows full of water jars home for their families. It is the social event of the day.

Nelson Mandela Road runs down the hill past the camp to Leribe village. Nowadays, minibuses and small trucks ferry passengers around and the business of driving has taken hold. Not every driver will have passed a road test Not every vehicle will have a clean bill of health. Driving under the influence of *joala* is a common occurrence. It did nothing to stop me from venturing out in the villages on my own.

Journeys out of the camp were the highlight of my week. When the sky was as blue as my willow pattern china and the phosphorescent clouds floated over the land like swans, I was at my happiest in my Volkswagon Fox driving out to Maputsoe or Butha-Buthe. This was my new country and I felt at home. The wild splendour of the Malutis and the granite-grey monolithic shapes resembling those prehistoric monsters that once roamed the *highveld,* stared down at me and accompanied me on my journeys. Ponies with flying tails galloped alongside. If the rider wore a blanket you might guess he was going on a long journey up into the Highlands. The Basotho pony is strong and sure footed – the result of cross breeding between short Javanese horses and European mounts.

"*Lumela 'M'e!*" shouted a young man one morning, travelling in the direction of Leribe near St Monica's Mission. I had slowed down to let a herd of goats cross in front of me. We both stopped by the roadside. He was white and that was a good reason for exchanging pleasantries. He was a member of the American Peace Corps.

It was strange to see a white man dressed in a blanket and riding bareback like a Mosotho. He was able to speak fluently in Sesotho and we had an interesting exchange. When he realised I was English he was keen to stay and talk. He told me he was a teacher and travelled every day by horse to a school near Mafeteng. I discovered he wanted to return to America where he could study medicine so that he could come back and work with the people up in the mountains.

"I love these people God dammit, they're so poor but they have big hearts."

"Have you lived here for a while?"

"Yes Ma'am – almost two years and enjoyed every minute. Got struck by lightning a few days ago. Hell of a surprise - ended up clean across the yard!"

"Call and see us when you're passing," I invited. "We live at Leribe Camp."

"Sure will Ma'am, we could do with a teacher up at my school. My name's Matt by the way. Perhaps you'll come and spend some time with the kids. They'd appreciate an English teacher."

He clicked his heels at the pony and trotted away. I noticed he had a guitar slung across his back. From time to time I saw him again, always in the distance.

I had been out that morning to buy shirts from the clothing factory in Maputsoe. At the junction with the Maseru road., I stopped to offer a lift to a lady with a little girl and a baby, who were standing by the roadside. She was travelling to Leribe to see her mother and had no money for a taxi. Her name was Sylvia. Being offered a lift by a white lady rendered her speechless and she didn't say a word until I set her down at the bus stop near her destination.

"Thank you *'M'e,*" she said as she alighted nervously, "I will pray for you."

I wasn't sure if that meant I was hopelessly incompetent as a driver, or if she felt I needed extra assistance from the Almighty to obtain my entry to paradise. She and the child stood waving as I drove on.

As I drew into the gates of the camp, Sophie's voice hailed me loudly. Her white apron appeared at the doorway of the canteen, elbows working like steam paddles beating something in a metal bowl.

"Hello Mrs Glenn. How is Mr Barrie? We wish to cook for you tonight."

Meals for the engineers were served in the canteen. With steam billowing from the windows and a tremendous rattling of a large assortments of pans and cook pots, Sophie and her ladies always dished up a good simple menu. Engineers' stomachs were serious business. A dam could not be built without food and plenty of it. Sophie hadn't heard of pasta. But she knew about potatoes, pies and pastry - the kind that lined the bottom of your stomach - as in tunnels back-filled with cement. When raising themselves from the table after one of her three course meals, guests moved as if afflicted by some dire medieval penance.

Her wide smile spoke volumes. A meal in Sophie's kitchen followed by dancing, and a glass or two of Stellenbosch, could turn out to be an enjoyable evening. She turned and let out one of her famous cackles of laughter and I could still hear her as I drove down the gravel road to our house.

LHPC construction camp consisted of about twenty houses, all with large well stocked gardens. There was a central canteen, bar and swimming pool. Four or five wives were resident at that time and several unmarried engineers occupied single accommodation. The staff office building was very pleasant and occupied a large plot, butting onto a gravel car park, where lorries and *bakkies* clattered in and out all day long. Every morning, the flags of five countries involved in the joint venture, were ceremoniously raised by one of the guards. Management and administration staff were off to a swinging start at 7.00am. Barrie's desk was only a few minutes from home.

There was only one English family, other residents were French, Afrikaner, Thai, Vietnamese and South African. Even though the site was rather bleak and functional, the views in contrast were ecstatic and the air was like wine. The distant peaks of the Malutis changed from pale yellow in the early morning, to brilliant blue during the afternoon and deep purple by nightfall. The sun slid from the sky about five thirty and darkness fell quite suddenly.

One of the French families, the Pazukis, helped us to settle in and our friendship with them flourished. Liliane and I felt as though we had known one another all our lives. We discovered similar interests in history, reading and classical painting; my feeble attempts at describing a Renoir or a Monet reached an impasse when I could not get past the third word in a sentence. Liliane's English was superb and we regressed to laughing a lot and speaking only in my language. My failings in schoolgirl French did not prevent us from trying out ambitious painting mornings in my little studio at the back of the house. It usually involved a sharing of limited knowledge, a few tubes of aquamarine and burnt umber, a dip of turps and lashings of Rooibos tea.

On our wish list was losing weight. Convinced that we might reduce our extra inches if we started our own keep-fit routine, we acquired an ancient video of the 'Jane Fonda Fight the Flab' routine, and a television set programmed for when our husbands had gone off to work. Her maid Agnes thought we were completely mad. Shocked at the sight of two ladies in moth-eaten leotards rolling on the nylon carpet and groaning in time to music, she quickly made herself scarce. (well-nourished moths were *de rigeur* in camp wardrobes)

"Are you well, Mrs Pazuki?" she asked Liliane , her eyebrows in a question mark.

"Yes Agnes, I am fine – we are exercising."

Changed into our walking gear we ventured outside the boundary fence. During the days, the mountain air felt clean and crisp. Together Liliane and I explored the local lanes and alleyways around the camp on the hillside, intertwined around sunflower groves and houses with little tin toilets with chimneys sprouting up through the greenery - the sign of a well ordered household.

We sometimes borrowed Hercule, who would pull us along and bark furiously at anything that moved, especially sheep tethered in the lane. The whole of Lesotho is common land, so animals wander everywhere. There are no fences between properties, only boundaries of wire netting or piles of dried cattle dung laid in readiness for winter fires. Liliane stoically held onto Hercule's lead, and I heaved him back from near death whenever other dogs bared their teeth. Some properties had guard dogs of their own, tied to long chains, who very nearly strangled themselves to get to Hercule, who graciously pee-ed on every stick and gate post. Sometimes we walked for miles. Nobody with a grain of sense would rob us with the hound from hell attached to our wrist. Jane Fonda would have been proud of us.

Later on we caused a stir when one of the engineers loaned us a set of weights and we took to waving arms like windmills in Liliane's back garden for ten minutes every morning. The guards smiled and looked at us sideways, obviously deciding that we must be a few pence short of a shilling. Aerobics was plainly not something the Basotho understood.

Uniformed guards with guns were stationed in a hut not far from my kitchen window. An eight foot fence, regularly patrolled, surrounded the entire project area. Any international venture of this nature had to engage in high security. All traffic was screened and visitors reported to the main office, so it was with slight trepidation that I approached the guard hut one afternoon and offered up my plate of home baked scones. I noticed the man had no dentures but his smile was no less radiant for all that. He had been on duty all day in the hot sun and looked jaded.

Visibly delighted, he took the plate of scones and I was treated to a rare sight of hollow gums. Dark eyes squinted from under the brim of his hat. He laid his gun on the grass verge as if it were a truncheon. I winced.

"Madam, Gabriel no English - *Kea Leboha.*" His hat had slid comically to one side. Brown hands were extended to first shake mine and then held together in a prayerful gesture. In one movement he deftly slid all the cakes into the cavernous depths of his coat pocket, pointed towards his open mouth and handed me back the plate. "Gabriel, no eat."

After that any time I drove past the guard hut, there would be my friend waving and pointing to his stomach reminding me that he was hungry for more cakes.

The houses were separated from the main yard by a six foot hedge and we could hear the crunch and clatter of lorries on gravel and the shifting of heavy equipment. Daily camp noises became very familiar. The squealing of brakes. Sophie banging a gong for mealtimes or shouting greetings to truck drivers who delivered our provisions. Every month a helicopter landed on the field outside the camp bringing wages to the men. No amount of security patrol in cars would be enough to guarantee that the staff pay day arrived safely and on time. A metal case would be lowered from the hovering machine and then with a terrific whine, the helicopter blades would flatten all before it and it would disappear upwards.

The men were due to four days holiday every four weeks. On pay weekends, the mood on camp was high. After delivering the staff sandwiches which were balanced precariously on tin trays on her head, as far as the main office block, Sophie usually broadcast a retiring dinner in the canteen. As the engineers filed in to dine, a flamboyant. Sophie, in full voice, would dish up a 'last supper' accompanied by the orchestrated sounds of cutlery and crashing plates from the serving hatch.. Enormous portions of beef pie and vegetables would come steaming from the ovens, needing a block and tackle kit to lift it off the plate. The ideal trigger for a week's indigestion..

"Don't go swimming in de ocean Sir, or you'll be eaten by de shark!"

"I don't think I'll be able to swim ever again!" replied the pale voice of the site manager, wearing a floppy shirt with parrots down the front, in anticipation of a beach holiday by the Indian Ocean Families disappeared to different parts of South Africa during the break and the Basotho staff went off-duty to their respective homes. Only the guards remained. Some of the young engineers would escape to Sun City or across to Swaziland for a taste of night life, others to a safari trip in Kruger Park. There was so much to see in South Africa's vast country. Our four day holiday periods were most precious.

Thirty nationalities in all made up the entire engineering work force which spread across three construction sites. Butha-Buthe was the main camp, ours was much smaller and Ha Lejone was much higher up the mountains towards Katse. Between tankards of beer and doorstep sandwiches, the men talked in the bar of an evening and arguments about blasting, geological rock formations, ventilation systems, intake towers and surge chambers were thrashed out in many different languages. My husband and I were *uitlanders* for sure and could only listen in awe. Engineers would arrive from other camps with stories of this crisis or that. Tunnel-related news, excavation statistics and completion dates were often debated well into the night.

"Christ man did you hear about the sacred cow at Katse!" growled a visiting site manager, holding a glass handle with huge rough hands and taking a half pint gulp.

"What cow?"

"The four legged one found floating in the Intake Tower - blocked up every orifice for miles. Completely boshed up the bloody system. Filters packed up. Bloody mess when they got it out."

Noisily, he drew on his pint of cane lager, white foam forming on his upper lip. He slid the glass towards the bartender and ordered another with a nod of his head.

"Bloody kids! Can't they bloody read!"

Quite often, young herd boys managed to climb fences and gain entry to prohibited construction sites – a wire fence did not deter them from pasturing their animals where they thought there was some good grazing, nor a 'Notice of Restrictions' written in English on a piece of board above their head..

"Might have been worse I suppose. Could have been the kid who fell in."

Barrie and I felt we had pitched up in an exciting powerhouse of politics and progress. Engineers told us that engineering is a challenging job in normal circumstances but with electric storms, in-house power cuts, surprise snowstorms and local riots, it becomes construction work with knobs on..

The separation from our families was the bond which united us. Frenchmen drank beer with Swiss, German with Italian, South African with English, and it seemed the whole world was here in our small smoke-filled bar room. By eight o'clock most nights, the pool table had become a life and death competition, where those who lost the shot, paid for the beer.

It was a good month if the camp communication system was linked to the rest of the planet, but when the telephones didn't work, a kind of war-time camaraderie enveloped us, with Lesotho Telecom the bogey man. Evening *braai*s turned into feasts of grilled meat and fish and the winelands of Stellenbosch replaced Napoleon's vineyard as the gastronomic favourite. Musical evenings on the terrace were a great learning curve. A Welshman who lived at Butha-Buthe had a talent for the guitar and even more of a talent for singing in colloquial Sesotho and used to entertain us at weekends. Our rowdy evenings round the fire, when everyone was winding down after a hard day, soon became a form of impromptu nightly entertainment.

Ficksburg was our local small town which provided most basic commodities. This meant a trip into South Africa – a journey which could be brief or intolerably long-winded - depending on the mood of the border guards. Police road blocks were frequent; impervious to hurrying drivers, emergency situations and urgent appointments. Within weeks, we had both changed down a gear. I soon learned to drive myself there and back for weekly supplies from chemists, newsagents, wine merchants and cash machines. The Hoogland Hotel provided decent meals to suit all pockets. It was a nice town.

Our camp had no food shops so once a week, the ladies, in a state of high anticipation, boarded the *kombi* and drove ninety six kilometres to Bethlehem to restore main supplies. Loaded with umpteen cool boxes, and enough ice to freeze a vat of hot coals, we would embark on a day at the Pick n' Pay Supermarket. By now I was used to buying groceries in kilos and rands. The language of supermarket labels came in English and Afrikaans. Strips of biltong (dried meat) hung like flags along the supermarket shelves, tasting of unthinkable flavours, and the aroma from the fruit department was mango exotica. You could buy boxes of twelve for about one pound sterling and cherries to die for.

Our driver Kenneth, would organise our day so that we could stop off at the café for toasted sandwiches and ice-cream or cram in a visit to the hairdressers or Woolworths fashion store. New clothes were not really essential to life on a mountain plateau but female spending habits were hard to break. A trip into town also meant that you could get in a decent telephone call overseas, with a connection which didn't sound as though you were in a sawmill. South African telephone lines were far superior to those in Lesotho.

Putting money in a coin box in Bethlehem Post Office felt good as I dialled my son in England. My heart lurched as it always did, as I recognised a familiar voice.

"Hello James. How's life in St Albans? How's Claire?..."

"Hello Mum , ...yes, my car's broken down again. It needs a new gear box – the garage said it's on its way out. We're both fine apart from that. The weather's lousy ....." My heart sank. The familiar saga of my son's constantly changing old bangers was par for the course these days. ...a bit of healthy cash was usually the answer.

"Well keep your chin up, we both send you our love." In three minutes the phone cut out. Difficult to exchange news properly. South Africa Telkom rules were so unfair. I walked away from the booth blinking away my tears. My children's voices always bit into my maternal sympathies and reduced passionate resolve to paper hankies.

Leaving Bethlehem's crowded car parks, where shoppers were seen piling ever more cool boxes into car boots, Kenneth drove us back to Caledonspoort and the questioning border guards.

"Today - new rules," announced the inspector of rubber stamps. An indelible inky smile crossed his lips. Our driver gave in our passports. There was a long wait. Government strategies of dubious origin often held us up. The temperature was soaring. Perspiration was running down the back of my neck into my shirt. Short on humour, the officer returned to survey our heavily loaded *kombi.*

"How long are you staying in South Africa?"

"We are in transit to Lesotho. We are staying at L.H.P.C."

19

"Okay, you go through. No problems."

Kenneth drove slowly across the Caledon River and slowed to a halt at the Lesotho side.

"How much have you spent in South Africa?" the guards asked. "Are you carrying alcohol, eggs or tobacco?"

The Immigration Form tells you in Sesotho and English that a permit is required for maize, livestock and poultry, eggs, habit forming drugs, firearms and ammunition. With a pang of guilt I remembered Barrie's small bottle of gin and decided silence was the better part of valour.

At last we were away and rounding the curve of the river to the grasslands on the other side of the border, where young herd boys urged on their donkeys under the weight of heavy sacks of mealie. From an upturned cart by the side of the road, young children tending their goats, waved to us. These days were such memorable journeys with the sun beating down on sweaty sticky passengers, much laughter in the kombi and Kenneth telling us funny stories. Driving slowly, traversing the countryside, we tried to learn about the lives of the people living in the villages…and would ask many questions.

At Levis Nek, a few kilometres before the South African border, we passed a group of young girls sitting by the roadside, their faces and bodies smeared in white clay. They wore strange beaded tunics and bracelets on their arms and ankles. A *sangoma,* also dressed in tribal costume and decorated in purple body paint with a ghoulish face, sat in the middle. All of them carried sticks.

"What are they doing Kenneth?" I asked curiously.

"Its all very secretive. They go to school up in the caves somewhere, miles from anywhere."

"Do they have any choice? " I questioned.

" If their family says they must go, they have to."

*Like many other African countries, *Initiation* for males and females is still practised in Lesotho, though certainly not by everybody. Before the times of the missionaries, education for girls took place during their initiation, marking the passage to adulthood. The missionaries objected to initiation and for a time it fell from favour. In recent years it has come back and is seen as necessary. Not every family accepts it although it is seen as a desirable prelude to marriage - sometimes believed to encourage fertility. In some cases, when a wife is infertile, a husband might send her to be initiated.

The Basotho initiates wear masks and straw costumes and decorate themselves with other adornments associated with fertility and motherhood. During the many rituals the girls are trained to be wives and mothers. They are taught to endure all the harsh realities of growing crops and planting, carrying heavy burdens from lodge to lodge, replacing fences, re-plastering walls and floors with mud and grinding beans into sorghum.

Music and dance plays a large part in their lives, so initiation teaches them songs and dances, depicting their historic past. Their dances also symbolise status and power and prestige; it gives the woman a sense of importance or wisdom and endows her with special knowledge – this in turn enables her to attend women's meetings and ceremonies. During their strenuous physical activities, they learn how to recognise important characteristics such as honesty, loyalty, courage, humility, respect for parents and to respect their ancestors.

At the termination of their period of seclusion, the initiates set fire to their makeshift shelters (*mophato*) which they have built from twigs and leaves. They smash their clay pots, which held their food. All their clothes are burnt and each member will wear a red skirt or dress. They must walk away without looking back, symbolically turning their backs on childhood. The girls cover themselves in red clay from the river, which they rub onto their skin with animal fat. Beads, bracelets and anklets are worn proudly.

For every initiate, a coming-out ceremony is planned in her own village. Everyone will celebrate her transition to womanhood. She receives gifts from all her friends; beads, combs, mirrors, belts, new blankets or anything that will be useful in her new life. The chief of the village will come and welcome her. Sometimes a beast is slaughtered so that a public feast can be held. What we in the west think barbaric, Southern Africa regards as an important part of their heritage.*

Kenneth often let us stop to give drinks and sweets to the children playing by the roadside. Faces lit up in expectation. Squabbles ensued. The kids soon sorted out who got what and after a minor scrum, they would smile and rub their stomachs in appreciation. Blessed with the most amazing white teeth, they demonstrated an impressive array of dentures.

"Heh, Mister! Thank you Mister! Thank you white lady," they shouted through the window in best English. Regular journeys resulted in regular scrums on our homeward route.

Leaving the main tarmac road just outside Leribe, on the approach to the camp, Kenneth did his best to avoid rocks, ditches, small children and the tangled ropes of tethered cows. Both children and animals would stare at us with tolerant amusement. The track was immensely treacherous and spelled death to the springs of any vehicle. It used to baffle me that engineers who could build dams were a little reluctant to design good roads on their home patch. By the end of the day's shopping trip, the severe discomfort in my lower back had increased well beyond my pain threshold. Around five o'clock, tired and soaked with perspiration, bearing enough food to replenish the pantry for one week, we arrived home. And the husbands thought it was they who should take the credit for building dams.

* Source from 'Vanishing Cultures of South Africa' by Peter Magubane.

Chapter 3

White Gold

Barrie and I knew that the separation from our homeland had already crossed a barrier into a new world. It was more than a boundary of distance and time.

Africa attacks your soul. It shakes you until your teeth rattle. It sucks you dry. You become hooked into the risk factor, the feeling that nothing is as it seems......the not knowing what life will throw at you those, its breathtaking landscapes. You cannot escape its glory and its passion. Waking up every morning to the canary yellow glow in the sky above our mountain, watching it spread like fire towards the lower slopes, gradually touching house windowsills, scattering dazzling rainbows onto bedroom walls. The sweetness of mornings made us feel glad to be alive. Barrie loved his job. I loved teaching my students from the mountain villages, meeting new people Earlier this year on the road near the tiny village of Ha Simone, between Butha-Buthe and Leribe, something else had happened; something which was to become a turning point in my life.

I had been teaching English to the ladies at Butha-Buthe Camp and was driving home. It was getting dark and I was alone. My trusty vehicle had come to a halt on the main tarmac road somewhere between Butha-Buthe and Leribe, and refused to budge. I had been warned about people who were left stranded beside the road. Without wheels and only enough daylight to see clearly for one more hour, I was scared to death. I was also lucky. A gallant young Mosotho boy came to my rescue. He sat on the road beside me for an hour and stayed until help arrived, in the form of my panic-stricken husband with a pick-up truck.

Walter was the eldest son of Reverend Stephen and Rose Makibi and he took the trouble to assist a white lady in great distress. If it had not been for Walter, I could have been robbed or worse. I have since wondered exactly what it was that guided me to the village of Ha Simone, when I might have stopped anywhere on that twenty mile stretch of road.

With Betty as my interpreter, I returned the following day with a box of groceries and my gratitude, hardly able to recognise the place where I had broken down. Not many engineers' wives strayed into the villages by the Subeng River. My gut feelings had been right. The Basotho were very hospitable folk. I was invited into their home.

"We have nothing to offer you but water from our spring.....," said Walter's mother., with a look of real pleasure on her fine sculptured features. "We have never had a white lady in our house – you are the first.. You are a most welcome."

Within those first few weeks, I had become their most frequent visitor, a guest in their house, in their church and their busy community. Like the lens of a camera I saw into the lives of this family, met Walter's five brothers and sisters, saw how each day, they coped with desperate problems which we, in our world, could not begin to understand. They had no running water, no electricity, very few possessions and only maize to eat. And yet there was so much love in the way they cared for one another – of the kind which lifted your spirits. The day their cow had a baby calf, everybody sang. They praised God in their little church and their voices reached down inside me and brought my tears sharply to the surface. Their strong spiritual faith held them together .

Lesotho the country, was fascinating enough and my learning curve since leaving England had risen steeply. To meet with a real Basotho family presented me with opportunities of learning like no other. I soaked up events at Ha Simone like a sponge. My friendship with Rose, Stephen and the whole family grew quickly and the realisation dawned that perhaps in a small way, I could help them.

One drowsy sunny afternoon while watching the ladies do their washing in the river and carry up their wet clothes into the yard, Stephen and I were in deep discussion about the heavy work they had to cope with. It felt a good time to ask my question.

"If you could have help that would benefit your community at St John's Church, what would it be?" I said.

Stephen looked long and hard into the far distance before answering. His eyes looked serious and I believe in that moment, he was offering up a prayer. He turned to look at me and a moment of great happiness passed between us. I hardly knew myself what made me say the words. My attention was on Rose and Emily who were manfully wringing out wet blankets before hanging them on the barbed wire fence to dry in the sun. They laughed together - perhaps from happiness – perhaps exhaustion. Rose rested her arm on a wooden post and stood looking across the river. Emily went off to fetch more wet clothes.

"Nettie, if we could ever have some help for St John's we would wish for a well, electricity and decent toilets – in that order."

Knowing that I faced an uphill struggle even if I found a way, a glimmer of excitement rose in my throat. By some miracle, I managed to sound optimistic.

"Then that is the request I shall give to my church when I go back to England," I replied. "but Stephen – no promises."

One small problem intervened in my master plan. It was a recurrence of the pains in my own body. On a quiet evening at home with Barrie, engrossed in the ritualistic sending of photographs to every corner of the globe, I felt a touch on my shoulder. Our music was playing softly in the darkening room.

Barrie took my hand and pulled me over to the other side of the room, where the curtain was pulled back.

"Come here my wife…." he said jokingly, " What do you see?"

The moon had risen like a giant pearl. It shone from the heavens like a galleon on the high seas. A million stars twinkled in a black sky.

Sensing he wanted to say something important, I stalled... "I think I can see the Southern Cross. It's so bright - brighter than the rest."

"Do you want to go back to England?" he said gently, nudging me - knowing my old worries had once again re-surfaced. The question was deliberate. A shadow flickered across his eyes. I noticed his beard was growing rather too long, but it still looked nice. It suited him. It was time we took a trip into Bethlehem to find a hairdresser..

"No, I want to stay here with you…but the pain in my back is getting worse. I should go and see Dr Nettleton again. I know what he'll say….an operation."

We sat close together, staring out at the night sky.

"Shall we go to Bethlehem at the weekend?" he asked.

"Yes, it's our long weekend off. What about a meal at that nice restaurant we found last time? ….and I *would* like to go up to Katse Dam. Can we go up on Saturday….then go to the restaurant?"

It had been a long time since I had seen my children and the prospect of pushing my granddaughter in her wheelchair through the park was a heavenly thought. Homesickness was never far away. Barrie had read my thoughts.

"Yes, it's a good idea to go up to Katse. We haven't been right to the top. Last time we went it was snowing and we only got half way up…..remember?"

Coming from the green hills of Kent the extent of my knowledge of dams was not impressive. We left early on Saturday morning with a feathering of mist on the road to Pitseng. The air was as pure as silk. Our journey by car from Leribe should take two and a half hours. We climbed steeply. The landscape opened out. A winding tarmac road cut through spectacular cliff formations, dotted with waterfalls. A few years ago, this road did not exist.

We were overwhelmed by the beauty and grandeur of green slopes rising steeply around us. There was a point when the light seemed to acquire a new quality. Turning to look below, the hills were outlined with a startling clarity, razor sharp as though formed by the hand of a great sculptor. Greens and blues looked greener and bluer. The ridges of geological formations sparkled with definition.

One could easily sympathise with the engineers who had built this serpentine highway up into the highlands. It was difficult to imagine transport trucks and lorries bulldozing their way up to this height. You would need more than some rope and a prayer book to climb these mountains. After an hour we passed Ha Lejone Camp, one of the construction sites belonging to

LHPC, the home of other ex-pats. Ha Lejone housed many engineers, designers, planners and drill and blast tunnellers, who worked on the Highlands Water Scheme. The camp was often cut off by snow and ice in bad weather when the road became impassable. Stories about *kombis* getting stuck overnight were fairly frequent. It takes a certain kind of wife who will live up at this level and keep adding to her family. Babies born at Ha Lejone did not have the easiest time coming into the world, as anxieties were felt by the mothers about getting to a hospital in time for the birth. It was four hours to Bethlehem (where babies were normally delivered) on a clear road.

Across the Malibamat'so River, a new viaduct, eighty five metres high spans the wide river bed stretching through this most beautiful valley. The new tar road then climbs slowly over the Mafika Lisui Pass at 3,000 metres, continuing dizzily in hairpin bends until it reaches Katse village. The distance is a hundred and twenty two kilometres from Leribe.

Clutches of brown huts sprinkled the mountains. Women carrying water jars walked along the unmade tracks by the side of the road. Herd boys with their skinny cows, peered inquisitively from beneath tattered blankets. As visitors, we weren't entirely at ease about our reception. There are not many white people here in the mountains. A few American Peace Corps volunteers in remote villages, some church workers and the only other white presence is the engineer or tunneller from the Highlands Water Project, like ourselves.

Across the Malibamat'so valley, villagers whose homes have been flooded, now look across to see the wall of Katse Dam. Water has risen high up the sides of their ravine. Who knows what goes through the mind of the herd boy as he sleeps in his *motebo* high in the mountains, as he questions where his cows will graze and how his family will plant their crops? He does not think like a fisherman yet. Progress has taken away his land and given him a cemetery. He is a small voice on the mountain pass, telling his brothers about the white tribe who took away the territory where his ancestors once lived.

We unfolded our legs from a hot vehicle. Ice-cold drinks poured down parched throats. Under the burning expanse of sky, the sight of the dam wall is awesome. It almost takes your breath away. Add to this, a sense of reverence at man's engineering prowess. At the peak of construction, a work force of about two thousand men had been employed here.

Standing on top of this double curvature concrete arched dam, you experience a feeling of near weightlessness. At a hundred and eighty five metres, your eye cannot take in the proportions of this colossal architectural animal with foundations which go deep into the surface of the earth. It ranks among the highest dams of its kind in the world, certainly the highest in Africa.

As I looked downwards, my feet seemed to detach themselves from my brain and want to do things by themselves, at different speeds. A kind of dizzy vertigo took over. We felt as if we were being pulled forwards into the great reservoir below.

Millions of tons of water cascaded into underground tunnels beneath our feet - like the veins of a giant heart, releasing energy and power enough to feed a creature the size of Johannesburg. The concept of such an immense achievement was mesmerising. My fingers locked onto the safety bar and wouldn't let go.

"Isn't it incredible!" I whispered to Barrie who was also captivated by the feeling of standing close to the edge.

"Nettie, now can you see what a double curvature dam looks like?"

"Where does all the water go?"

"Through miles of tunnels down to Muela Reservoir."

"You have to admit, even though the vision of Katse was created years ago, the lake does blend in with the hills. I'm trying to imagine what the views will look like when the reservoirs are full."

"Yes, it'll be so dramatic. Think of all that fishing," Barrie mused.

To make use of Lesotho's otherwise wasted natural water resources, South Africa, with the backing of the World Bank, have agreed to pay the cost of this international venture. The whole scheme will take thirty years to complete. A significant source of income will be generated and, more importantly, much needed employment will be created. An annual income of twenty five million rands a year will be paid in revenue to the Lesotho Government. Little wonder that water in these parts is called 'White Gold'.

Standing on the bank high above the dam wall, we looked out across the shining waters of the reservoir, reaching out to the mountains. A warm breeze caressed our faces. Birds called over turquoise hills. This was more than a bridge across a valley; it represented our journey from England to South Africa. It spoke of another journey of trust and commitment and time. That we should be here at all seemed impossible. That we should have been married here, was totally unbelievable. Hands locked together for a time, holding the moment, I allowed my tears to fall unchecked and felt Barrie's fingers tighten on mine. Words were not enough to tell of such a day of beauty, adventure and most of all – the sharing of it.

We left early before the light had gone. As I dozed in the car, on the fringe of sleep, the steep helter-skelter drive down the mountain, completely scrambled my brain. Whether Katse was a monument to madness or a testament to human endeavour seemed a difficult question to answer. Bits of the dam tumbled endlessly round in my mind. Suddenly the car pulled up sharply as we turned in through the camp gates and I lurched awake… and felt a grinding pain somewhere at the bottom of my spine.

"Two hours coming down," muttered the driver who was almost asleep.

We had grown into the ordinariness of daily life. We loved our house on the mountain. A temperamental generator kept the electricity going when all the lights went out and progress at Muela became our evening meal agenda. During our after-supper evening stroll, when bullfrogs croaked and *cicadas* shrieked, our minds would fill with serious thoughts and family worries.

"I wonder how Abigail is. No news from Lizzie for quite a while. I hope they're okay," I said, as we walked silently on the grassy bank alongside the perimeter fence around our compound.

"She would phone if anything was wrong."

Barrie tried to allay my fears, but something in the back of my mind bothered me. My daughter was good at keeping quiet when things were not as they should be. Her letters had become irregular. Abigail's pretty face suddenly came into my mind. Lizzie had a difficult task ahead dealing with the medical problems by herself. Hospitals, doctors and therapists filled her diary every week. Abigail's condition, microcephaly, meant that she was going to need constant monitoring and we were very much in the hands of the professionals. But my daughter was a tough cookie, although not past hiding the truth from me. Fiercely independent for her twenty four years, she coped extremely well with the difficulties of caring for a handicapped daughter.

"No letters for six weeks. I have a feeling something's wrong."

There's bound to be an explanation, she would tell us if…" said Barrie unconvincingly.

There had never been a father in Abigail's life. Somewhere in the world there is a handsome soldier who would rather not know about this little girl; a child who makes others stop and smile. She is tall for her age with a shock of dark auburn hair; her skin as pale as a lily; those pale blue eyes, unable to focus on her Mummy's face. Although her sight is poor, both hands reach involuntarily towards familiar objects; her toys are most precious - her smiles serene and beautiful. Something about Abigail brings out the best in others. She engenders rare moments from the ether. She possesses a quality which fazes people – undeniably one of heaven's special children.

Barrie held my hand tightly as we walked on through the wet grass, seeing the dark shapes of resting cattle on the other side of the wire. We heard their chewing and their breathing. The peaks which towered above us, Sebothoane and Ha Mokhethi were lost in impenetrable blackness. Now and then, red embers from a fire flared up in the darkness. There was a special kind of hush at night - occasionally the hollow sound of dogs barking. The air was cool and still.

Bright light from the perimeter arc lamps shone for several yards then fizzled out. The moon rose up white and milky, glowing like ivory. From somewhere out in that other blackness beyond, came a flashback of me holding my father's hand when I was a child. He was tall and I was being pulled off my feet. We were running to catch a bus ….down a wide cobbled street in a Yorkshire village. In the uncanny way that a three-year-old knows, I knew that a new baby was coming to live at my house…..I can still see my father in a soldier's uniform. It was a puzzle to me why my mother wasn't there. The bright stars stayed in my head all that night.

From time to time that vision of my father came rushing into the forefront of my mind. That surreal sensation was with me at this moment. Strangely, the stars now were reminding me of something. As a child it had always been my father who had inspired me with a feeling that I could achieve *anything* I wanted. Now I had met someone …that special someone, who understood my need to be challenged, when certain things had to be strived for - and straight reason did not come into it….

Suddenly a voice broke into my thoughts..

"Well Nettie – do you want me to book you a flight tomorrow?"

"Yes honey, I *will* go back to England. The doctor says I ought to get treatment in London …*and* I can spend time with Lizzie and Abigail.." Then, thinking out loud, I spluttered, "and there is something else I must do."

Holding Barrie's hand, gazing up at the night sky and thinking of home - it came to me. A trip to England. Perhaps this was a chance?

Chapter 4

The Makibis

My claustrophobia probably saved me from facing a surgeon's knife. It was June 1997. I had returned from three weeks in England where I had been to visit a doctor in London. Nothing could be done for my painful back. An operation had been suggested, but surgery was not for me. The scanner and I fell out. A million galloping horses would not get me back inside one of those long metal tubes, so basically nothing could be done. Professional medical advice suggested a long period of rest. It was left to the African sun to produce a cure.

Barrie came to meet me at Johannesburg Airport in a blizzard. Because of treacherous roads, it had taken him five hours to drive from Lesotho. After a hasty breakfast at the nearest eating house, we set off on the long haul. Not the kindest situation for someone wearing a lumbar surgical body brace (a sort of re-designed liberty bodice). Despite the weather and the whalebones, it was a pleasure to be back in Africa. We made it to Leribe in four hours.

In the intervening weeks our garden had taken a battering. The trenches were full of water. The thatch on our *rondavel* looked completely storm blitzed and my peach trees were withered and fruitless. Water dripped down our necks from the tangled greenery which hung down from its moorings under the eaves.

"It's been the weirdest kind of weather," Barrie said, as he helped me up the steps of the verandah. My legs seemed to have gone into spasm after sitting so long in the car. "Lesotho has had so much rain in the last three weeks, the farmers are really struggling – *mealie* crops are ruined in some places."

"The bluebells are out in England," I said jauntily. "Bramfield Wood is a mass of blue. I wanted to bring you some back. How's baby Oliver?" I suddenly remembered Betty was coming back to work tomorrow.

"Oh, Betty's got a beetle in her leg – she's been to see a *Sangoma*. Nettie you'll have to talk to her. I think it's post natal depression or something. She's so unhappy. I think it's that man of hers."

"Yes, he's a waste of time if you ask me – I'll have a go, but I can't cope with a *thokolosi.*"

A *thokolosi* is a kind of malevolent hairy dwarf which means bad luck to the black people; they think if something bad happens, the thokolosi has come into their lives.

"Yes, I'll speak to her tomorrow, but I must go and see Rose first – she's going to…"

Barrie pulled me towards him with that special gentleness I had grown used to. As if in slow motion, my words hung in the air.

"Heh, it's great to be home love - really home I mean….Lesotho and you and ….I've got so much to tell you."

A bunch of flowers on the dining room table caught my eye - and a note propped beside it.

"Nettie, I missed you….they're for your first homecoming - as my wife."

"I can't believe I've been gone three weeks. Now look I must sit down or I'll fall down. This thing is so tight! "

Clutching the flowers so that I could smell them and with my arm round his waist, I said brightly, "I told all our friends about our African wedding – they were highly amused about the storm and when we got stuck in the swamp. The kids couldn't stop laughing - want us to have a 'do' in England so that we can celebrate again. Shall we have a church blessing when we go home?"

"Where's home - England or Lesotho? " he said facetiously, pulling up a chair, "as long as you take me with you."

"Barrie …I went to see Reverend Syms…..I made a special appointment to meet him at his home…..played him my tapes of Walter's family – he heard their voices." I gulped with excitement. "He's agreed to try and start a link with St John's at Ha Simone – he actually *listened* to my story. He says there's hope."

Those blue eyes looked at me quizzically. He worried about things and it showed.

"I know you Nettie when you get a bee in your bonnet. What did you tell him?"

"That I hoped Datchworth Church would be interested in learning about this country. No one I spoke to had ever heard of Lesotho. I tested people – nobody knows anything about where we live. This is a matter of cultivating friendship between people who don't know each other."

My young pupils who came to the house for lessons each week knew that England and Queen Victoria were an important part of their country's history. They knew that Lesotho had been a British Protectorate. Queen Elizabeth was known to them and associated with friendship. Walter was always talking about England.

"Wait a minute - these things can't happen overnight." Barrie gave me his most warning tone. He was always the one who pulled back on the reins when I wanted to gallop. "Well, don't give them any false hopes, it would be a bad thing."

"Yes, that would be unfair - but I *could* tell them that a meeting of the Datchworth Parochial Church Council will take place in July. Richard Syms promised to let me know the result as soon as he knew. I have a good feeling about it. Just think what it would mean – if we could make it work." I sat down stiffly with ten inches of whalebone poking into my ribs. "Darling we must have faith; success never comes without trying. It would be a sad day for posterity if we never tried. If we fail, then we fail."

"Nettie, I wish I had your faith."

The house phone rang and he went to answer it. With his hand over the receiver, he whispered, "It's Liliane asking us out for supper tomorrow night. She and Ali are going to the Karoo Desert next week. They want us to go with them."

*   *   *   *

In my suitcase, wrapped in tissue paper and carefully folded into my clothes was a special gift for Walter's mother. It was a present from St Albans Abbey. How I wished I could describe St Albans Abbey to Rose. She would never be able to imagine it. Her church, the Church of St John's of the Apostolic Faith Mission, the one which she and Stephen had built themselves on the riverside at Ha Simone and the Abbey – were worlds apart. Once I had tried to explain the magnificence of those glorious stained glass windows in the cathedrals of our big cities but Rose could not take it in.

My first opportunity to drive over to Ha Simone came a few days later while Barrie was at work. Mimosa trees with their pale delicate blossom grew along the pastures where children played and cattle grazed. I loved this road to Butha-Buthe. It made me want to sing out loud. The sky was clear and blue. As I turned left onto the dirt track which led down towards the river, Fred, the young lad who lived with his mother next to St John's Church, came flying up the track to meet me. I stopped the car and he leapt like a spring into the front seat.

"Hello Fred, how are you?" His dirty face and bright little eyes were a welcome sight. Nothing had changed. Fred did not speak one word of English and didn't reply – but clung to the dashboard and shouted loudly at every animal along the path, so that I would know he was an important person – as far as the cows were concerned anyway.

It was lovely to see the family again. Walter looked thinner than I remember. His two younger brothers, Justice and Petros came to shake hands and Rose gave me a welcoming hug. A new member of the family, a Makibi Auntie from Maseru, had arrived to seek advice from Stephen. The lady looked worried and drawn and sat on the stairs up to the living room drying her eyes. Stephen wasn't in.

"Welcome back Nettie. We've missed you," said Rose warmly. "Barrie came here last week. I think he was missing you too. The boys took him walking up the mountain. Emily, go and fetch your father. He's in the church."

Rose's long capable fingers unwrapped the tissue paper and took hold of the fragile glass angel, which seemed to come alive when it filled with light. She held it gently. As it hung there, twirling on its nylon thread sending rainbows everywhere, I saw that her smile was full of tears.

31

"Oh, it's so beautiful Nettie, I would love to have it in my house. We never had anything like this in the whole of Ha Simone."

But in my haste I had forgotten something vitally important. The window in Rose's kitchen was fashioned from clay. It had neither frame nor glass. It was just an opening which was stuffed with polythene bags in the winter and left open to the sky in the summer. The crafted angel would not work properly.

I stared at the empty space in the wall that passed for a window. Beyond I could see the outline of the first range of mountains which stretched towards South Africa.

"If Walter will come with me we'll go to see a glazier in Ficksburg. It was thoughtless of me." I muttered lamely.

No tape measure could be found but a piece of twine from a *mealie* sack was produced and placed across the opening in the wall. The next day Walter and I made a special journey over the border into Ficksburg to find the right person to do the job. There was one general store which was most obliging. Our piece of string was laid across the counter. The glass pane was cut to the correct size. Carefully we carried it back to Ha Simone. It fitted the window perfectly.

The following Saturday morning, having walked the three kilometres from Ha Simone., Walter knocked on our door. The guards were used to the Makibi family calling to visit and usually showed them across to our house.

"Nettie, you must come quickly, we're going to hang the angel! Dad says this morning they will do it. We have the glass in the window and it has something called putty round it. The people will be here soon."

"Which people Walter?"

"All the people who are coming to see the angel."

"Okay, I'll come."

We arrived just as the ceremony was about to begin. Stephen was standing on the *stoep* with outstretched arms towards the house. Though very short in stature, Stephen's jaw was set in determination. I knew that look of his when something important occupied him. Everyone who was gathered there had been told there was to be a hanging. Dazzling with the rainbows of early morning sun, the piece of glass received its blessing.

"Today part of St Albans Abbey in England is hanging in the window of our home," shouted Stephen. "An angel has come to live with me and my family. We have been blessed."

This was repeated in Sesotho for the benefit of the watchers. There were several women, including the new auntie whom I had seen, plus the rest of the family. A song followed. Then a moment's silence. Heads bowed and one of the cows moo-ed stolidly in approval from behind the low wall. The glass angel was given its place of honour – forever to grace the window of the Makibi house. Every evening Rose would watch it dance and sparkle with reflected light from the setting sun. She came over and took hold of my hand. Her white headscarf covered her hair and I noticed her blue church dress was patched and frayed at the elbows. She looked jaded and worn out. Not surprising since she had been up most of the night with Walter who had been suffering from night sweats. In the cool early dawn his mother had gone to fetch water from the spring to cool him.

"Nettie we in Lesotho will dream that we are looking at that cathedral in your country where the windows tell stories that are taken from the Bible. I will pray so much to see one of these windows."

We adjourned to the house. My bulging haversack spilled out onto the floor.

"Walter, I think you'd better come and help me unpack."

"Why?"

"I've brought a few presents from home...." The strap of the bag fell to the floor. "I know how much you all like reading... and how badly Augustinus wants to paint.... people have been so kind...."

There was a book of Shakespeare's plays, paintbrushes for Augustinus (an adopted son) a teddy bear for Bernice, dresses for Emily, pens for the boys and an old brass bell for the church door. Candles for the altar had been wrapped in yards of lace for Rose's kitchen - given by those amongst my friends who had heard about our friendship with the Makibis. Rose was a good seamstress. Stitching and sewing were her forte. Her timeworn hand machine with a bandage around its middle, always sat on the big table in the house. For Stephen there was a new Bible written in English.

There was great excitement in the house with the giving of gifts as the youngsters tore open parcels and envelopes. Never before had the family known such a moment.

"What is a teddy bear?" asked Bernice, their youngest daughter.

Outside in the yard, things Shakespearean were hotting up. Walter was testing his Richard Burton voice on the cows. His version of a Hamlet soliloquy sounded impressive. The ox cart on which he was standing was a fine platform for the rendition of tragic verse. From a cardboard box labelled 'paraphernalia' I tipped a pile of spectacles, rounded up from forgotten corners of English sideboards and spilling mantelpieces, onto Rose's table. My sister-in-law Maria had extracted at least twenty pairs from the members of her church in Knebworth. My short sighted English friends would have laughed at Stephen's discovery.

"Good gracious I can see the words plain as anything! The congregation will like my sermon next Sunday. The names of the twelve Apostles have become very clear." He laughed his big laugh and peered comically through his new bifocals.

"No excuses now Stephen," I teased.

"They can judge me by my good strong voice and my prayers of thanksgiving."

"You have no opticians in Lesotho, Stephen?"

"No Ma'am – we could never have any money to visit one of those people."

Rose looked up quietly from behind a pair of rimless specs. "Emily I can see my small stitches."

I looked round the table. Every member of the family was wearing glasses.

After the mad half hour I decided to tell them my good news.

"Stephen, I went to see Reverend Richard Syms when I was in England. He's a priest. I told him about you – about the Community at St John's. I told him everything."

Immediately, he came over to sit down. "You mean you told him about us – the Makibis?"

"Yes and what's more he listened. I asked if his church could start a link with Ha Simone, so that people will know about you. But it's not his decision. It's up to the Parochial Church Council."

I looked at Rose who was nervously twisting her fingers into the cloth she was sewing. I sat down next to her.

"It will take two months before they decide anything definite."

"What is a Parochial Church Council?" she asked.

"It's a committee; a group of people who have to agree on things. Richard will tell them about our conversation and then they will decide."

"What will they decide?"

"I don't know. It will mean you must have a lot of patience. In England things take a long time. People don't have any idea how you live. They only know what I told them. Stephen, you and Rose must write a letter so that they will understand more."

Close to my heart was this dream of mine; a link with the Church of All Saints in Datchworth, rural Hertfordshire. It was where Barrie and I planned to have our wedding blessing later this year. It was where our paths had first crossed. The village had a very special meaning for us.

"Nettie we are very grateful. I cannot find the good words to say." The priest looked at me very hard. "Rose and I will write a letter to your Minister."

"Stephen, they know that you and Rose help sick people here; people who walk for many days to come to St John's. They know you try to live as best you can with no money and they know how hard you work. I told them how you have to fetch water from the spring every day; that everything stops when the sun goes down… about your children and your community."

"Do they know us?" he insisted. "Do they know our country is poor and the people are hungry?"

"In England only a few people have heard of Lesotho. They only know South Africa. They know about apartheid and Nelson Mandela and that South Africa operated a system which segregated blacks and whites. They do not realise that the Kingdom of Lesotho belonged to England for a hundred years - that it is now a monarchy. "

There was a fine dignity about Rose. She handled every situation with grace and poise, which put everyone in their place. When she had anything to say, people listened.

"Our prayers tonight will be prayers of thanksgiving to the people in this English village. God will help us to be patient. The spirit of our Lord will bless us."

That evening Rose and Stephen lit candles for the hope that was in them.

St John's Community was situated about three kilometres from Leribe, along the main road to Butha-Buthe. Since that fateful meeting in February when my car had broken down outside Walter's village and Ha Simone had offered me such hospitality, it had become my second home. I felt with such certainty that it was some kind of new beginning. I didn't feel like a visitor - in no time their friendship had overwhelmed me. The point had long past when I needed to be asked to come into their house. Whatever Rose was doing - baking bread, scouring the *stoep* on her knees or sewing at the table - she would make certain I was given a hug, a cup of water and a chair. Together we had been to the river to wash clothes, but it was Rose who carried the tin bucket on her head up the steep rocky path to the house. Her boys all wore white shirts. Stephen wore a clean white shirt for every church service, pressed by a flat iron – heated on a kerosene stove.

My admiration for the family grew with each visit. During the weeks and months which followed, Rose and I developed a very special relationship. We talked while sitting on the stones by the river and the seeds of our friendship blossomed. She wanted to hear about England. I wanted to count as someone to whom she could turn, on dark days; those days when Stephen had to go away and she had to feed the children from an empty purse.

The day I brought them 'Jungle Oats' from the store in Ficksburg was of immense significance. The arrival of this special brand of cereal on the kitchen table at Makibis, made history in the yard. It was the first time I had witnessed real hunger. Obsessed as most parents are with making sure their children eat breakfast, Rose poured out bowl after bowl of thick steamy porridge straight from the pan on the primus stove.

"There's more," said Emily who ladled a second helping to her brothers. Walter's eyes grew as big as his plate. Petros, the fifteen year old, got up and left the room, smiling widely - openly showing the gap in his front teeth - wide enough to accommodate a Churchill cigar.

"That was good Nettie, how did you know we loved the Jungle Oats so much?"

"I guessed." I answered. "But what I didn't know, Petros, was how many dishes you can empty in five minutes. If I were your mother I wouldn't feed you again for a week."

He laughed, hitched worn trousers over skinny hips and went off towards the *kraal*, whistling.

The Silver Fox almost found its own way from Leribe to Ha Simone. Food from my own kitchen somehow found its way onto their table. After the last spell of wet weather the boys had made me a new bit of road where the track ended and the field dipped down towards the river. With rocks and stones they banked up the hollows where previously tyres sank and exhaust pipes clanged. The first time I drove over it I couldn't believe the difference. No more getting stuck in the ruts and having to be pulled out.

"Thanks you lot," I shouted to the kids as the car swung into the yard, "that's great. I've never had a road built in my honour before. It was enough to break my car to pieces. I thought you wanted me to end up in the river."

"Dad's building us a new toilet," they yelled. "He's right down in the bottom of the pit. Come and look."

I walked over. On a patch of land down below the house, a pile of new earth had appeared and clods of mud somersaulted through the air landing in a heap.

"Good morning Stephen, what's this I hear?"

"Morning Nettie, This is David – he's helping me dig a new latrine for the family."

A young man whom I had not met before, grinned and kept on digging. The two of them were standing in a pit some six or seven feet below ground.

"Let me take a photograph. This isn't the sort of job you generally see a priest doing – how's it going?"

"We are in desperate need of another toilet so we have started today – would you like a spade Nettie?"

"No thanks," I laughed, "I've come to see Emily. She and I have a lesson booked for today. Thanks for the new road Stephen – I am honoured."

"No Ma'am. You are part of our family – we started it when you were in England. You see, we want you to keep visiting us."

Stephen Makibi was a man with a passionate message. He provided a sanctuary for homeless people, took them in and cared for them when there was no hope in their lives. Sick people came to his door and they were welcomed. He never turned anyone away.

Rose was the one who fed them. She had little to offer but what they had they shared. Sometimes she made bread with maize flour or simply boiled the *mealies*, adding enough water so that it would swell and make enough to fill every plate. When the peas were fully grown in the lower field, she would collect them and add them to the *mealie* - pods and all. Cabbage was another luxury. They seldom, if ever, ate meat.

Their small three-roomed house with a tin roof had neither electricity nor running water. It was as clean as a new pin and smelled of polish. In the evenings Rose sewed by the light of a candle and made clothes for the girls. She often sang as she worked. Her voice was deep and mellow. Sometimes she and Emily sang together. When Emily sang you could imagine you were listening to a powerful contralto in a famous choral requiem. The richness of Emily's voice could easily bring a lump to the throat. Had she been born into another place, into another class, another time, her rare talent might have projected her into the realms of a top class soloist. There is no doubt that Emily would have been destined for a music scholarship in some fine university. With some professional training her voice may have earned her a living.

Walter was twenty four and Emily, nineteen. The next eldest was Justice who was seventeen, then there was Petros at fifteen and lastly Bernice, who was nine years old. Augustinus had come to live with them when he was seven. Rose had brought him up as one of her own sons. He and Walter attended the same school and after that they were inseparable.

Augustinus was the artist, the thinker and the poet. He owned nothing but what he stood in. He shared a hut with the brothers and took his share of the work in the family. He adored Rose and was Stephen's right hand man, doing all that he could to justify his place in the family. His parents had gone far away and he hardly saw them in his growing up years. His school work was exemplary.

Walter used to say, "One day Augustinus will leave us and travel the world. He knows too much and he fights for what is right. But he will always be my brother."

Justice was the quiet sensible member of the family. He was the peaceful one; always smoothing the waters; never complaining. He was only seventeen but the head on the shoulders was of one much older, with the soft gentle eyes of a wounded animal. Justice was born to be like his name. Whenever a problem arose, Justice seemed instinctively to know what to do.

Petros was the naturalist. He didn't like people much. He preferred cows. They recognised him from half a field away and came when he whistled. He was cheeky and clever, could run and jump like a gazelle and now and then he would take off into the mountains alone and not return for days. There was a wild streak in Petros. He could defy his father, be careless at his lessons. To redeem himself, he would write lines of poetry and draw stunning pictures of animals. He was one of the gang who organised rat races with the other herd boys. By digging a furrow, the boys would get the rats to run, then bet on which one would get to the end first. Yet, in Petros's young eyes, there was nothing closer to heaven than the arrival of a new calf. A healthy cow was a valuable commodity, rated highly in a Basotho family.

The Makibi's wealth boasted three cows. No more cows could be acquired by the family until the day that Emily got married. When daughters marry their bridegroom must present 'lobola' which is a bride price given in cows to the father-in-law before a marriage can take place. Emily was almost twenty and not yet bespoken.

Bernice the youngest daughter was very shy. She and I made friends quickly. We often walked together down to the river while the older ones were at school and she would show me how to jump across on the wide flat stones and laughed at me when I fell in. I didn't know the neighbourhood well but felt quite safe going off down the deserted valley with Bernice with only our hands to converse.

Walter was the charmer in the family. From the day we met, our friendship was cast in stone. He was extremely handsome, intelligent and versatile. He was the rock his mother leant on when his father was away at the big church in Durban He would assume the role as head of the family with ease. Somehow he commanded respect from everyone who met him. You could take Walter and put him in the London Stock Exchange or in the Royal Box at Ascot – and he would fit. He spoke about seven languages and could recite oceans of poetry by heart. In all the time I knew him I didn't come across one word of English he didn't know. I often wondered where he picked up all his knowledge. And yet he was a most sensitive character.

It was difficult taking Walter down any street in Maseru or Ficksburg or anywhere – he just seemed to attract a crowd. He was as charismatic with the border guards and the storekeepers as with pretty girls, the latter wasting no time in throwing themselves at his feet.

During the beautiful autumn days, we travelled many miles together in my little car. It was Walter who named it the 'Silver Fox'. He took me to meet all his relatives who lived in Levis Nek, Butha-Buthe and Maseru. We visited his Auntie who lived in a small tin house up a muddy track full of potholes in Butha-Buthe.

To enter the labyrinth of roads in a black village would have been unthinkable for a white lady alone. With Walter's presence it was a place of friendly faces, open doorways and crowds of curious children. Narrow lanes twisted through patches of *mealie* and sunflower groves – and the occasional bevy of plastic gnomes. Fences made from corrugated tin and bits of vintage wrecked vehicles lined the way. The road was more suitable for a donkey than a car. My stalwart Silver Fox defied all forces of gravity as it three-wheeled its way over the diametrically opposed tracks, its resilient powers of suspension battling against all odds.

Walter's Auntie had organised a welcome crowd, most of whom came inside her little house with us. I wondered how, without work or wages, these people survived. The children looked healthy, if a little thin, their garb from t-shirt-land – with holes. Shyly, they hid behind one another whenever I looked in their direction. Silently, they slid away after they had had a good stare at me.

Our host dispelled my anxieties in one go and bade me sit down at the table. She offered us food but we settled for water from a plastic bottle and a good chat. Several brown feathers on the floor gave my stomach a few warning signals as she offered chicken for lunch. Instead Auntie and I engaged in a steady exchange of Sesotho and English driven by mutual curiosity.

"How is your Queen of England? Does she have many cows?" I had heard these kind of questions many times.

"How is your employment? In Lesotho our people are poor – there is too much families starving. Some families cannot even light their homes. They try to borrow one candle and no one will help them."

Her gestures were cheerful as if resigned to the fact that everyone in Lesotho was poor.

"Our culture is very different," was all I could feebly mutter in reply.

"Nettie is a teacher in an English school," interrupted Walter.

The effect on Auntie was staggering. She showered me with compliments and asked me to reconsider the chicken lunch. As we spoke a brown speckled hen wandered out from underneath the sideboard and hoovered the floor.

"Please stay and show my children the good English writing."

"I have to leave soon, I'm taking Walter to Butha-Buthe to the main post office. We are expecting a letter from England."

"Sala hantle," I said, shaking her hand.

"Tsamaea hantle 'M'e."

We rose to leave and Walter guided me back to the car through a throng of surging children, who had increased in number since we arrived. A little girl, dressed in her sister's church day frock, was holding the door open for me. Auntie dabbed her eyes with happiness and gestured a blessing for my journey. She pushed a small paper bag into Walter's hand.

"For your friend from England," she added.

The same crowd which had greeted us on the way in, reappeared as my car hit the potholes again. This time the back seat was full. I counted five pairs of feet as we lurched once more down the murderous track. Walter smiled at me as we went into a nose dive and the kids squealed with excitement.

"Thank you for coming Nettie," he said above the din coming from the rear seat. "They will always remember your visit. No person from England has ever been inside their house, and they have never had a visitor who arrives in a car."

"Walter I have to tell you that I will never forget!"

We continued our descent, while the steering wheel developed a mind of its own. My foot hovered over the brake.

"Have faith!" he yelled again as I veered to a standstill next to a barbed wire fence thrown at me by the curvature of the path. At the bus stop on the main road, I pulled to a halt and five pairs of feet tumbled out, their goodbyes following us as we took to the tarmac leading to the market place. Butha-Buthe was heaving with people. Loud groovy music blared from every doorway.

"What's in the bag Walter?"

He grinned. "Roast chicken's feet," he said, "would you like one?"

Walter kept his promise that I should see the harvest. When the *mealies* are ready for picking, it is a joyful time for the family and they wait for signs of good weather in the sky. A blue haze over the eastern Malutis means they will be able to work from early morning until sunset. Unfortunately this year, the rains had been heavy and the ground on their side of the river waterlogged. If they left the maize any longer it would become riddled with mildew, soggy and useless.

Emily and I walked a mile or two across the fields to investigate their flooded land, on which next year's food depended. It was some distance from the house. The paths were worn by the trail of many feet and difficult to walk on. The scene reminded me more of the paddy fields of China than an African harvest.

Walter, who was in charge of the pick, greeted me like a long lost friend. The priest, Desmond, who was there to bless the crop and shout prayers to the Almighty, stared in disbelief as Walter and I hugged each other and the hem of my long skirt got soaked in mud. My Marks and Spencer sandals hung round my neck like a brace of pheasants. Sluiced in mud, Petros, Justice, Augustinus and Bernice were all up to their knees in murky water trying to pull out a cow which had wandered into the field and got stuck. The poor animal stood there, eyes blank, not moving. I couldn't begin to think what to do. My good English education had not prepared me for this.

"We'll have to dig channels," yelled Walter, waving his stick at the others. "Let's go up to the corner of the field and start. Desmond – please tell God we've had enough rain."

The kids did as Walter bid them. Their spades made sucking noises in the mud. Behind me, a small quantity of *mealies* were thrown in a sodden heap on the cart.

"Walter, what will you eat if all the crop is saturated?"

He didn't answer. Emily whispered in my ear as we walked round the edge of the field.

"Some years the harvest is good Nettie – but this year it is very bad. It is hard to live in the mountains. We still have the dried peas from that other field. We make it into something with some wheat – it is called *lihobe* and it is nice. We have potatoes. My mother makes yeast bread but often the boys are hungry."

"I can't think how you survive Emily," I said. "Does every family eat as little as you?"

"Less than us. We are lucky. Because my father is a priest, people look up to him. Neighbours give us food sometimes when they come to the church. You should have seen my father yesterday. He was here up to his knees in mud. It is good when he is with us. He makes us do it, but it is heavy work."

Stephen was a man who loved God and loved his children. At times, he could be uncompromising, but his tenacity was what helped them to survive. I was soon to realise the measure of his brand of faith. He worked hard himself and expected every member of his family to do the same. He had no problem with that.

During the warm days, Barrie and I happily explored the mountains around Ha Simone, walking as far as Ha Ntsutsu and Ha Mamokoaqo, small villages built beside the Caledon River where the border of Lesotho meets South Africa. If my London Doctor could see me now he would have a fit. My condition had magically improved.. I did not really understand it myself. The only dodgy aspect was that I could not bend without pain. Doctor Nettleton himself was amazed at the halt in deterioration. Cod liver oil and sunshine suited me well.

We often passed people searching for brushwood for their evening fires. In the Subeng river bed we saw the clear imprints of dinosaur footprints, as recorded in archaeological study books; fossilised imprints of creatures which existed more than three hundred million years ago. On the Leribe Plateau, nine kinds of fossilised dinosaur footprints have been found.

The Lesotho landscape is challenging and exciting to the newcomer. We turned our backs on small villages and climbed upwards over table flat rocks, where erosion has exposed the underlying sedimentary layers. We had grown to love the tall aloes, always outlined on the horizon. They are well known for their medicinal purposes and are nutritious for cattle. Birds hovered among the succulent spikes searching for insects.

We explored gullies and *dongas*, covered in shallow lakes. Weaver birds flew up in a cloud if you disturbed their busy nesting sites. Long-tailed Widows hovered low in the grasslands, displaying their graceful sweeping brush tails. The males perform spectacular flight displays over their nesting territories. Golden Bishops hovered on the edges of water pools, looking like large yellow bumble bees. Once we surprised a *meerkat* which popped up quite cheekily in front of us, turned its head to look, then beetled off through the long grass. Apart from the fields which had been cultivated for wheat or maize, the remaining areas were used for grazing.

The only humans we passed were herd boys, their cattle straggling in front and behind. I longed to stop and speak to them, but was afraid to approach them with questions, spoken in English. Lesotho folk are genuinely suspicious of whites walking for pleasure. Their own journeys are essentially to fetch water or visit a town far away. They misunderstand our reasons for hiking and feel we suffer from a lack of geography and basic intelligence. In hindsight they must wonder about the size of our brains – to park a car then strike off with knapsacks up into the hinterland.

The locals in nearby homesteads began to recognise our strange band; Irish wolfhound on lead and two ardent ramblers wearing leather boots and carrying binoculars. First that look of mindful curiosity. With the realisation that we resembled neither a hostile tribe, nor a threat to their crops, loud greetings bellowed from every hillside.

"Will you sell me your dog?" they often asked.

"He is not for sale."

The concept of Hercule as a pet mystified everyone. The word 'pet' has no meaning in Lesotho; to own a cow or a goat adds to a man's social status, counts as a worker, provides milk or can be offered as a sacrifice at a ceremony. Veterinary organisations for the care of animals don't exist. Tins of 'Whiskers' and 'Pedigree Chum' don't feature in supermarket trolleys and domestic cats do not sit on mats in a Basotho home.

Every shepherd has an indeterminate breed of dog with him on his travels, surviving like the boy, on what he can scavenge. Hercule, always the instigator of interesting conversation with a stranger, was not terribly obedient and could leg it up the hillside a mile or more if he slipped his collar. But he was too well fed for his own good and attracted a lot of attention from would-be owners – if only they could catch him. He usually came back smelling of cow dung and covered in tics.

One afternoon with a wintry blue sky overhead and the smell of rain in our nostrils, we faced a gale force wind that swept across the river. Purple clouds raced in torrents to obscure the mountain tops and we ran for a hiding place underneath a granite slab to wait for the storm to abate. The lightning flared and the great melodrama raged like a theatrical replay of the *'Siege of Mafeking'*. Thunder receded beyond our range of hills. Soon ice cream clouds sailed gloriously towards us as if they were telling us to come out of our cave.

Rain in Africa comes swiftly with a vengeance, tears the sky apart and shifts the ground beneath your feet. When it subsides new rivulets spring from the earth and every plant and flower is reborn, brighter than you ever remember.

Basotho riders in their traditional hats

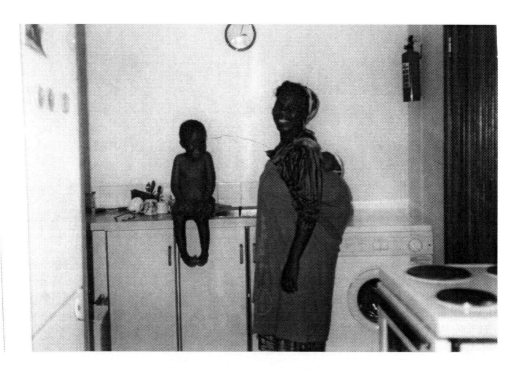

Betty, Margaret and baby Oliver

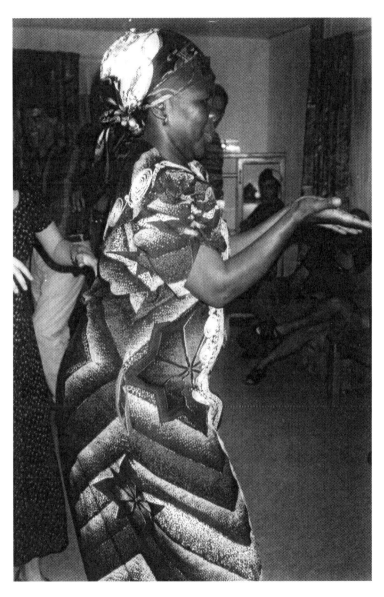

Betty dancing the Shosholosa

Liliane and the author at Leribe Camp

Basotho ladies going for water in the snow

Anna and Sophie in the canteen

Aloe growing on the road to Katse Dam

Herdboys tending the animals

Meeting Reverend Makibi in St John's Church, HaSimone

Liliane Pazuki with Walter Makibi

Rose winnowing

Rose and Stephen dressed for Church Service

Dinosaur fossil footprints in the Subeng River

Meeting village girls in the maize field

Chapter 5

The Great Karoo

The beautiful Eastern Cape and the Great Karoo Desert was one of the places we longed to explore and when Liliane and Ali suggested a visit to Graaff Reinet, we agreed to join them. Everyone wanted to see the Valley of Desolation.

In two powerful cars, we set off. The journey from Leribe would take seven hours. June was the middle of winter and a good time to go, although we were aware that it would be extremely cold at night. Extra blankets were a must. The climate there is dry, the land barren and the rainfall unpredictable. When it does fall, torrential hailstorms can cause destruction to both buildings and animals. The summer heat is fierce. They say it is dry enough to parch the throat of a desert lizard.

The vast empty plains of the Karoo Desert cast its fascination upon us; the solitude, the rocky angular beauty of the mountains, the extraordinary quality of light. Monotonous red and cobalt blue harsh layers of rock snaked on and on for miles except for a slash of sunlight now and then. The landscape contrasts strongly with the lush winelands and fertile valleys which you pass on the way to the Cape. Here nothing grows. At least nothing which leaves you with the meadow-sweet flavour of grass.

The timelessness of the Karoo seeps into your veins. Its uninhabitable barrenness has a unique kind of beauty, eerie with bird calls and sullen hills. You could drive a whole day and not see another living soul. The cool night air is refreshing after the heat of the day. At nightfall the sky turns paler, the mysterious grape-blue *kopjes* are seen in silhouette. Darkness comes, bringing with it a haunting almost magical quality. Night gazing in the Karoo soon becomes addictive. The wide African sky feels blacker and the stars brighter. Each solitary gem gleams with a special kind of radiance. Moonlight casts weird shadows on the ground. Farm gates and fences rise up like ribs of polished silver.

We passed through Ladybrand, to Zastron, then Aliwal North to Middleburg, where empty roads are punctuated only by creaking wind pumps which churn up water from underground, providing drinking troughs for livestock. The land is so barren that the farmer thinks in terms of how many hectares per sheep rather than sheep per hectare. One or two dignified old Cape Dutch farmhouses, hidden amongst brown parched hills, caught the late afternoon sun. On the horizon, dun-coloured merinos grazed on desert scrub. Thin stringy ostriches, the region's best known inhabitants, hovered on stick legs near the road, their feathers floating in the afternoon haze like grey mist.

We spotted no small mountain Zebra, known to breed in this part of the world, nor hovering black eagles. Claire and Axel, the two youngsters were on the look-out for tortoises and sure enough on an empty stretch of tarmac a sign appeared with the words, 'beware tortoises crossing'. Sadly all four legged creatures were invisible under their granite grey stones.

Our destination was a farm situated twenty-three kilometres off a dirt road on the main approach to Graaff Reinet. At nine o'clock with neither lights from the town nor signposts to guide us, we found the gate which would lead us to the farm. From here we could telephone the house. Our headlights lit the cattle grid. Out of the darkness emerged animals of all shapes and sizes. Barrie got out to search for the handset on the post Cattle, goats and deer with large antlers, rose from the ground in humped shadows, casting bizarre shapes in the moonlight. I shook with apprehension. The animals were neither wild nor dangerous, in fact they were afraid themselves. The gate clanged behind us. Five cattle grids later we arrived at the farm, having disturbed five gatherings of resting beasts, which must have felt as unnerved as we did.

The farmer, his wife and a herd of three hundred ostriches greeted us. The birds made a strange noise from their paddock behind the house, similar to the sound of hooting down a hollow tube. Late evening in the farmhouse meant the living room fire was lit. Bright cushions and easy chairs were in abundance and we immediately felt our hosts' warm hospitality. The house smelt of lavender and herbs. The couple welcomed us in English and Afrikaans. Liliane and the children spoke in French and Ali made his greeting in Persian. It was an unusual mix of languages and we ended up speaking English most of the time with the occasional attempt at first-year French for the benefit of the youngsters. Dishes of food kept arriving. The log fire threw showers of sparks from the hearth and the coals glowed red.

Our host was a very large man and more than filled his place at the table, while offering us hot spicy *bobotie,* slices of Karoo mutton and enormous measures of locally brewed beer. Gerry and Sheila Rose-Innes couldn't have been more welcoming.

We fell into bed, full of food and tiredness, despite unheated bedrooms and mattresses with steel sheets and frozen pillows. Central heating in South African farmhouses is extremely rare, possibly unknown. Outside, white moonlight shone on manicured lawns.

Before sunrise the trees outside our window seemed alive with birdsong. In my ignorance I had imagined Karoo farmers didn't go in for gardening. I was wrong. Next to the house, smooth lawns were laid out with grapevines, lemon groves, and pomegranate trees; yellow grapefruit and velvet peaches, glossy with dew. Turkeys and peacocks jostled amongst the avocado trees round the edge of the garden, and on the green roofed homestead, crested birds were out, strutting and clinging to the overhanging branches in a display of finery. The sun was up and felt warm even at this hour, dispelling all notion of the cold night. Like an oasis in the desert, this cultivated garden was a small paradise. In the middle distance, the snow-tipped peaks were just visible.

Breakfast was a banquet. We tucked into mountains of fruit and home made bread, pancakes made with turkey eggs, cheeses, conserves and jugs of steaming coffee.

"Do you know any French dinosaur stories?" asked Gerry, directing his gaze towards Claire and Axel who were busy filling their stomachs.

"Non Monsieur, nous n'avons pas de dinosaures en France," answered Axel, obviously surprised by the question.

"I can arrange for you to see some real dinosaur bones," said our host casually.

With that he picked up a nearby telephone and dialled a number.

"John, I've got some important visitors staying here. They would like to visit Wellwood this afternoon."

After a few minutes of loud friendly conversation, Gerry finished speaking, wiped his mouth on a large checked table napkin and turned to address the children.

"This afternoon you will see the oldest fossil collection in the world. John Rubidge is a famous palaeontologist. His museum is not open to the public, it's a private collection. Dr Broom himself will show you round. It is considered one of the best museums in the world."

He paused to pick up a large bunch of keys. "Now I must go and see to my sheep."

With a wave of his hand he strode from the house.

It was hard to imagine Wellwood Museum's collection of rarities. Dr Broom introduced himself. I was aware of a man with a very firm handshake. He was himself a palaeontologist with an outstanding knowledge of the collection.

"The items found at Wellwood are of international importance. Many of them are the subject of publications by scientists from all over the world. I'm sure you will find them interesting."

He showed us across a yard and into a small building at the back. As a rule visitors are only allowed near the Wellwood merino sheep and orange groves. This was indeed a special treat.

"This is the Rubidge family museum," he said proudly. "Look at whatever you wish. I am here to answer your questions. Remember these fossils represent the rarest forms of life anywhere in the world."

Inside the large well lit exhibition centre were the displays.

*'Millions of years ago, the Great Karoo was a vast swamp. In the low lying Karoo basin, rocks were formed from the mud, sand and clay of the deep rivers and marshland, giving way to layers of sandstone and shales. Millennia winds, erosion and eruption, has gradually exposed a geological

system known as the 'Karoo Supergroup' providing the perfect earth formation for preserving the fossilised remains of animal life. The hardened mud has become the Karoo shale of today, gradually exposing bones and skeletons of some of the earth's ancient reptiles after being entombed for around 230 million years. These fossil reptiles have provided a unique insight into animal life, long before the advent of birds, mammals and man.

Preserved within the sandstone and rocks of the Karoo basin, is an unbroken record of vertebrate evolution, from fishes, through amphibians and reptiles, including dinosaurs. By taking out specimens of rock from the shale, it has been possible to identify life forms 230 million years old.' *

*The Wellwood Collection Archives. Graaff Reinet.

We saw whole skulls of creatures totally unknown to our eyes – exhibits which looked like a mixture of two animals; perhaps a crocodile with the horns of a rhinoceros, or a creature which resembled a cross between a camel and an elephant - the skull of one and the jaw of another. Each item was dated and labelled with its own Latin name. One could imagine the dilemma when identification took place and we began to invent our own names for some of them *'frogafishausaurus'* or *'camelelephantulus'*. There were lots of teeth and jaw bones, horns, rib cages and tail bones; they could have been sinister artefacts out of a horror movie. Fossilised skulls of reptiles and mammals from the Permian period and mid Triassic period were displayed before us. We were mesmerized..

"The Rubidge family have collected everything here from their own land over many years. The first fossils were found by accident in 1923 by curious children who happened to be digging on a family picnic," explained Dr Broom, as we struggled with a wealth of information given in each of the glass display cases. Liliane translated his talk into French for the benefit of the children. Our kind host, knowing our combined knowledge was limited, kept his talk to an appropriate level, but he hinted at the extreme importance of the finds in relation to the emergence of humankind.

"It was then that the Rubidges realised the significance of the discoveries. Gradually more items were discovered and the collection attracted interest from scientists from all parts of the world. Many have come here to see them. Some of the exhibits are today documented in famous scientific manuscripts."

Although our little party only caught the tourist version of the Wellwood collection, it was enough to inspire us with excitement at the very nature of the creatures – or parts of creatures we were looking at. None of us would easily forget such a rare privilege.

That same evening, seated once again with Sheila and her husband at their farmhouse table, we prepared to eat. Kudu, springbok, and home-reared lamb had been prepared for us. Delicate aromatic smell of herbs rose from saucepans of steaming vegetables which accompanied the main dishes.

Bottles of chilled wine floated in ice buckets large enough to drown in. Gerry insisted we wouldn't leave without sampling some of the Cape's best reds and other alluring products of the wine farms of the Eastern Cape. Mouth watering dishes of sweet pumpkin, butternut squash, avocados, patés and terrines covered in olives, perfumed lychees and fresh pineapple followed us around the table. It was as tempting as any State banquet.

Then their son, a farmer of a mere six hundred and fifty acres, arrived in the doorway. His frame was so big he blocked out the light. We all shook hands and I felt as though my fingers had been through a pair of double rollers. Together at the table, father and son almost represented the complete brawn of the Welsh Rugby side.

Championed on by the hospitality and the wine, Barrie and I went all out to eat for England but our efforts were feeble beside the Afrikaner appetite. Like a starving army the two farmers waded into their meals like a chain saw devouring a forest. Liliane's gentle *'bon appetit'* was hardly appropriate. It wasn't quite the ambience of the delicate French cuisine. Punctuated by loud laughter and tales of South African cellars, thick slices of meat were passed around the table on large knife blades and the business of eating took hold. With complete disregard for our digestion, we all ate far too much. The final gastronomic assault came with sweet dumplings covered in a tangy sauce. As the brandy bottle appeared, I think that's when my husband slid quietly underneath the table. I had a blurred but happy memory of leading him to bed via the pantry.

The following morning Liliane and I drove out to see the 'Owl House', the now-famous home of the reclusive artist Helen Martins who lived in Nieu Bethesda, about twenty kilometres outside Graaff Reinet. Most people go to Nieu Bethesda to marvel or shudder at the artist's weird sculpted statuary in the Camel Yard.

Beyond a line of pepper trees we found a strange-looking house surrounded by an old wall with barbed wire on top. Stone owls stare down at the visitors who pay to come in. In the yard at the rear, stand more than three hundred life-size statues made entirely from crushed glass mixed with cement. Naked stone travellers rub shoulders with peacocks and lambs. Owls with huge glass eyes watch over mosaic mermaids, donkeys, snakes and strange birds. Groups of hooded shepherds and angels, Buddha figures, sphinxes, lions and collections of other small animals cover the Camel Yard area.

As you walk between them along the inter-connecting pathways, you feel they are watchful, almost breathing. Life sized camels and giraffe heads (on necks without bodies) all look in the same direction. Adam and Eve stare with hollow eyes. Hooded shepherds with their crooks look towards the east. A feeling of expectation hangs in the air. Stars are represented by mirrors fixed by pieces of wire to the perimeter wall.

It is believed Helen Martins worked on these figures mostly at night away from the prying eyes of her neighbours. They say she was a sad woman who hid herself away from society and eventually became blind. The walls of her house glitter with powdered glass and sharp enamel. Inside the house - flamboyant murals of suns, moons and stars are emblazoned on ceilings. Pieces of cut glass and scores of odd shaped mirrors hang at peculiar angles. The atmosphere is sombre, the furniture sparse. Inside her workshop are dozens of unused jars of powdered glass as though ready for her next piece of work.

Speculation about the person who created all this, grows increasingly as you walk about the place; a kettle on the hob, the only legacy of normality in the artist's daily life. It is written that the house belonged to Helen Martins' parents and that she grew up in Nieu Bethesda but in some way was rejected by the community because of her strange ways. Children were afraid of her. She was tormented by unkind stories about her work and over the years people avoided her. Few people saw her during her last years. Some say she was paranoid, even mad. At the age of seventy eight, then living the life of a recluse, she committed suicide by drinking caustic soda and died a horrible death. Her ashes were scattered in the Camel Yard.

Stories about Helen Martins continue to flourish and books have been written about her work. People have questioned the meaning of her figures – half real, half fantasy – created by one woman in the middle of a desert. When she died in 1976 she was virtually unknown. Twenty years after her death, thousands have visited the Owl House to see her artistry for themselves.

Athol Fugard, the renowned playwright, wrote a play in 1984 called 'Road to Mecca' which featured the life of Helen Martins. Her absorbing love of the Karoo, brought out her talent for this unique art form of stone and glass sculpture. As her creatures multiplied, she lost interest in human beings. Within the walls of the Camel Yard, her fertile mind became confused between reality and fantasy; plummeting her existence into one of total seclusion. In 1991, 'Road to Mecca' was turned into a film, which captured the intimacy and passion of Helen herself.

Koos Malgas is remembered as the craftsman who worked with Helen Martins for twelve years. He lived a remote life in the extreme isolation of Nieu Bethesda and assisted in the creation of many of the sculptures now displayed in the Camel Yard. His dream was to create his own garden of sculptures but he was the main breadwinner of a large family and never achieved his ambition. Malgas also suffered from damage to his lungs from grinding glass but continued to work for Helen Martins until she died. One wonders if things had been different, would he have become an artist in his own right. Poverty and much later alcoholism, prevented him from expressing his own talents.

Over chilled *rooibos* tea at the Village Inn, Liliane and I agreed the artist had touched on unusual creative forces. It was impossible to ignore the effect the figures had on the mind. For me, it was the fact that the statues were life size. They became believable – you had to remind yourself that they were made of cement. They contained emotion as well as expression, which is quite scary in a medium such as cement, which is not usually associated with warmth and humanity. No attempt had been made to place them artistically as in a gallery or museum. They sprang from the earth like living creatures, side by side with no semblance of order; the skills of an artist mixed up with dreams and half finished ideas, in search of coherence. There was a feeling of expectation – a searching for answers to the meaning of life. Perhaps the statues existed in Helen Martins' mind as figures of re-incarnation, forever seeking their eternal goal. I would not have missed the experience for all the *rooibos* tea in South Africa.

After such an intense morning, a ride out into wilderness of the Karoo Nature Reserve came as a welcome break. Sixteen thousand hectares of mountainous *veld* surrounds the Karoo where, in the heat of the afternoon, herds of wildlife leisurely strolled within a short distance of moving vehicles. Hartebeest and blesbok stared with soft eyes, graciously allowing us to share their parched grass and spiky thorn, while steenbok and springbok jumped and fled swiftly at the sound of our engines. Further away amongst the rocky boulders lurked buffalo and wildebeeste. Buzzards hung like drapes in low dusty branches – waiting for their turn to scavenge; still no sign of the small mountain zebra. The air was hot and still.

We waited. Nothing moved. Kudu and eland may have been there on the upper slopes and they too would have been waiting for the dry afternoon to pass. When dusk falls the silence changes between rock and pasture. Small creatures dart and squeal in pain. The buzzard resting on his branch opens his hooded eyes.

"Eh bien Papa, la prochaine fois, la Vallée de la Désolation." said Claire, "nous voulons pour chasser les lézards. Axel dit qu'ils ressemblent à des monstres gigantesques."

"Okay, let's go," said Ali.

The name itself fires the imagination, especially in children. After climbing slowly for fourteen kilometres through some of the most wild and remote scenery, along steep gradients and tortuous hairpin bends, the two of them had invented enough lurid dragon stories to frighten anyone. During the journey strange echoes rose to our ears and we realised our own voices were being thrown back from the depths of the crags and caves below. Our journey ended at the lip of a canyon which fell hundreds of feet in a sheer drop. We parked the car. The ravine beckoned..

"I daren't look," said Barrie, backing away from the edge. "It makes me want to jump."

I held onto his arm, knowing his fear of high places made him feel nauseous and some weird compulsion drew him. The children were quiet.

"Come away," I said pulling his sleeve, "it's menacing down there."

Only an eagle shadowing its prey would know this place. The oxide red columns carved by winds and weather, balanced one on top of the other like grotesque statues, leaned precariously as if they would topple at the slightest breeze.

Like layers of pastry, millions of ledges of rock provided thin platforms for the most beautiful birds. They soared from the valley floor and the late afternoon sun caught flashes of red and gold as they dipped and swooped. Bizarre shaped pinnacles emerged from the bottom of the canyon, touching yet not touching. Ochre dolomite towers erupted like dead fingers from silent depths. Ugly sinister shapes bulged from the sides of the ravine.

They say that when the wind whistles across these mountains, it is a place where dead souls walk. The children shrank back from the edge, as though from a warning bell. Large birds circling on air streams above our heads gusted away on a semi-circular path, then re-appeared as though drawn to the sides of the ravine for eternity. Shrill calls echoed. Behind us the plains of the Camdeboo fell away down the valley.

Walking by the edge of the ravine we experienced the desolation of this forgotten place. It presides over desert but feels nearer to the stars. Rock rabbits moved along the ledges like huge grey rats, eyeing us and sniffing the smells of humans. Only the lizards didn't seem afraid. They slid and slithered between rock and rock, darting quickly into the stony earth's holes where our feet passed by. Eventually we finished the looped walk along the canyon lip then made our way back to the cars as the sun left the sky. We felt the cold breeze around our faces and shivered.

"Rentrons chez nous Papa," said a small voice.

The following day was a Sunday and Gerry offered to take us up to the top of the farm in an open truck. But not before we had paid a morning visit to Reinet House in Murray Street, the old parsonage built for of the Dutch Reform Calvinist Minister of the Cape, Reverend Kicherer.

In 1786 the Dutch East India Company sent its Governor to establish an outpost on the eastern frontier of its territory, to ensure the maintenance of law and order in the region of the Sundays River. Near the bend in the river, where the soil was fertile and water plentiful, a new outstation was developed. This was the first settlement after leaving the Cape where a traveller could stop and rest. Being the outpost of white civilisation in a barren and untamed country, it became an important trading centre.

Graaff Reinet is one of the oldest towns in South Africa. The Governor named his new district after himself and his wife. As this was the only road from the Cape, many famous explorers and missionaries stopped off on their way through to the interior, including the great Dr Livingstone and Eugene Casalis, one of the first white missionaries to be encountered by the Basotho.

Graaff Reinet's architectural heritage includes many fine buildings built in the 1800s, which have been preserved as national monuments. Outside the town is a statue of Andries Pretorius the Voortrekker leader, taking his people to victory against the Zulus in the Battle of Blood River.

The town was given an official Mayor/Magistrate/Tax collector, known as a *landdrost* who was housed in The Drosty in Church Street, built in 1806, which nowadays is a rather fine hotel. It served as a courtroom as well as the family's living quarters. At the back of the house are small restored cottages comfortably furnished, which were originally built for freed slaves to live in.

In the early years the settlers were little more than brigands and there were plenty of skirmishes between the *Khoi Khoi* and the San Bushmen who came down from the Sneeuberg mountains to steal cattle. The *Xhosa* tribes to the east around the Great Fish River resented white-owned towns growing up and on two occasions the Khoisan and the Xhosa joined forces to fight the Europeans. Gradually the Drosty became accepted as a place where crime and punishment met. An attempt by the Cape Governor to establish law and order in a region never before harnessed to civilisation.

Reinet House was built in the graceful architectural style of Cape Dutch with six gables and a semi-circular staircase to the garden, to be used as a parsonage for the Dutch Reform Ministers who were sent out to Graaff Reinet in 1812.

The early Calvinist ministers came from the Netherlands but during British occupation, ministers from Holland refused to serve in a former Dutch Colony occupied by the arch enemy, Great Britain. Missionaries from the London Missionary Society were recruited and then later, Scots Presbyterian ministers. Reverend Andrew Murray, one of Scotland's most notable churchmen was the first minister to come and fill the empty pulpit in Graaff Reinet - a rather unenviable position. He was succeeded by his son Charles. The Murrays occupied Reinet House for almost a century.

The parsonage has been turned into a period museum, now restored to the full former glory of its Dutch origins, showing how life would have been more than a hundred years ago in a growing frontier town. The house is furnished with a mixture of eighteenth and nineteenth century furniture, austere and sad. Costumes of a bygone era left me feeling that every theologian's wife must have suffered near asphyxia beneath steel corsets and tight beaded collars. Glassy eyed dolls sat rigidly in glass cabinets; generations of needlecrafts and trinkets, old fashioned medicinal accoutrements laid out in a funereal way.

Highly glossed polished floors in the house, reflected the strict régime when Reinet House became a boarding house for girls in1904. Everything preached of high mindedness, discipline and self control. One could almost hear the pupils, with their stiff collars and long hair, chanting dreary poetry in unison, their voices echoing along chilly corridors.

In the Doctor's room, notices explained the family had lived through the evils of unspecified illnesses, spittoons and enamel kidney dishes, stethoscopes and rubber devices for strangulated hernias were laid on a canvas trolley. A set of false teeth, unsavoury and smiling were displayed beside body parts in a bottle, floating green and shrivelled in some dire liquid.

Caught by a sudden longing for fresh air we abandoned the lurid catheters and kidney stones for the dappled light of the courtyard.

The garden of the parsonage is known for its coach house, horse-drawn carriages and carts, a working mill-wheel surrounded by orange groves. The famous Black Acorn Vine, planted by Reverend Charles Murray in 1870, is now the largest living grapevine in the world. It has an eight foot girth and still bears fruit.

The streets outside were bathed in sunshine. From the sombre interior of Reinet House, our small party strolled along past terraces of neat Karoo cottages, feeling the heat of the pavements through the soles of our shoes. The children collected seed pods of bush willows from the pavement edge as we strolled towards towering date palms in the centre of the town with feather-like branches, bronzed and dry from the Karoo winds. This was a little too much for Ali. As he gazed skywards he was struck by an attack of homesickness for the desert palms of his childhood and it was all we could do to drag him away to the garden of the hotel, to recover with yet more cups of *rooibos* tea.

Graaff Reinet's most famous national monument is the Dutch Reform Church built in 1886, which is an exact replica of our own Salisbury Cathedral. It stands at the north end of Church Street. With pointed turret and tall pinnacle so delicately carved, the roof might have been piped from icing sugar. Its single spire shone slate white in the sun. Groups of singers on their way to the main door were easily recognisable; their platinum blond hair and blue eyes so like their Dutch ancestors. Everything about Graaff Reinet was well-ordered and trim. Pride was emblazoned from every building and doorway. Gardens were clipped and neat. Restoration of this town has become a success story of which Graaff Reinet should be justly proud. No wonder it has been named 'Gem of the Karoo'.

In the late afternoon with precious little of our holiday left, we eagerly sought Gerry as he was preparing for his daily visit up to the outposts of his territory. Dressed in our oldest clothes, we climbed on board the high sided truck. Sheila volunteered to come with us. The sun dipped below the hills and it was starting to get cold. Gerry was obviously used to driving in the tearing gravel and stone spitting ruts of the three mile track to the topmost point of the farm. Ali sat up at the front and the rest of us clung to the sides of the battered old roadster, as it made its way slowly upwards. A few yards of knotted rope would have been useful to tie ourselves to the rail, as the jolts became more violent with every incline. The wind tore at our hair and snatched words out of our mouths.

The *bakki* swayed, shook and rattled until we thought our teeth would fall out. Hanging onto the sides of a truck going vertically up a mountain does not come naturally to me and I swore my lunch was resting in the roof of my mouth.

"Are there any snakes?" asked the kids.

"Oh yes," shouted our host from the driving seat, "but they keep out of the way – they can hear our vibrations We don't see many. We often see birds migrating for the winter. You might be lucky - we get storks and eagles passing over. They navigate by the sun and the stars all the way to Europe."

The Rose-Innes family owned several thousand hectares of dry barren scrub on which they reared three hundred sheep and goats. Water was crucial for their survival. Pumps were placed every hundred yards or so all the way to the top. Gerry had to check to make sure his animals were getting as much feed and water as they needed. Tiny new born lambs were visible here and there and helpless voices bleated on the wind.

"I need one and a half hectares per animal. The edible pasture is so poor," he shouted, "and the pumps are always in need of repair." Jumping down he strode over to attend to one of the water sources. "You can't imagine what its like up here in the middle of winter when snow falls. Temperatures fall below zero."

He got back in the truck and revved the engine. We went on even higher up the mountain. In the back of the truck all exposed parts were becoming decidedly chilly. Finally we reached the top. Just enough light to make out the beads of perspiration on Gerry's forehead. Two huge hands let go the steering wheel and he turned to Ali.

"Now man - do you still want to be a farmer?"

"Yes, I am sure. But I think it will be for the grapes."

Ali's dream was to quit engineering and farm his own land. His ideas of grape growing had been in his mind for a very long time. For the present he would have to remain an engineer. "My children must first be educated," he answered with a careful look towards Liliane. "Then I will buy my land."

Sheila helped the kids down from the truck.

"Look underneath the camelthorn - there may be a few porcupine quills," she suggested.

Sure enough, they found a scattering of brown and white spiked knitting needles discarded by an obliging porcupine, their colours hardly distinguishable amongst the leaves. They were added to a collection of pine cones and skeletal snake skins.

The light was fading fast. A pale moon rose and the wind became fiercer. I wondered what made people like Sheila and Gerry do this for a living. Sheep, water and wind pumps ruled their lives. And a few terrifying snake incidents for good measure.

"I came in the house one day to find a huge snake coiled up under the television," said Sheila in a matter-of-fact voice. "That was a bad day. One of the lads on the farm came inside and took it away on a stick and put it back into the scrub."

"Was it poisonous?" I asked.

"Oh yes, very," came the reply.

Whatever you need here you have to either bring in or invent. It is a land which you have to make yourself. Resourcefulness is the key. We were full of admiration for the Rose-Innes family – and others like them.

It was almost dark as we came down into the ostrich paddock. Gerry drew to a halt outside the pen. Three hundred pairs of gawky legs ran awkwardly to greet us, heads all facing the same way. Their comical appearance was exaggerated as they ran in tiers like a crowd of footballers who have mislaid the goalposts. Gerry climbed down over the side of the truck and three hundred feather dusters flounced petulantly as he ran into the flock distributing food. One wrong move and the back kick of a male ostrich could be fatal to the farmer.

At the turn of the century ostrich farms were a way of making money in the Karoo and some farmers were known as the 'feather barons'. The industry boomed as feather trimmed hats and cloaks became fashionable across Europe. Sharp businessmen built ostentatious residences known as 'feather palaces' while the demands in fashion increased. It was not unusual in those days for the birds to change hands at one thousand pounds a pair. Ostriches occur in the wild in this part of South Africa but in the early years of the century, they were bred specially for the high class fashion industry, that in turn brought wealth.

Today, the ostrich farms still thrive but the feathers are used more for dusters than the hats and boas which were once so fashionable. Some farms are kept open for tourists or for the meat which can be dried to make *biltong.*

Gerry's prize bird was named 'Winston' a magnificent male who gave us the long necked stare with beady eye and lethal beak. He came close up to the truck expecting a special treat. The farmer gave him a handful of feed from a bucket. Giving his long curly eyelashes a saucy flutter and his feathers another flounce, Winston swanned off merrily to join his mates.

Our departure from Graaff Reinet was immensely sad. We knew that it was unlikely we would return to the farm. The packing and the farewells were fraught with forgetfulness and tears. The farmer and his wife had given us such generous hospitality. Claire and Axel went round wishing the animals *'au revoir'* in fond French, right down to the last ostrich. Adult farewells were affectionate for such a short stay.

South Africa is full of people like Gerry and Sheila – and yet its history cannot be remembered without thoughts of wars and segregation. This country is unique. Its complexities are momentous. Shaped by conflict. Bleak with terrible memories. For many, the stock image of the Afrikaner is the burly figure in khaki carrying a rifle against a marauding lion or a restless native. Stereotypes do not harm anybody but they are not the truth.

In this extraordinary tapestry of race and culture, one must understand the English speaking South African, the Dutch Afrikaner, the Coloured and the Black. One must think of the influx of Italian and Greek settlers, Portuguese and Chinese, Russian, French, English, Jewish - and others who have changed the face of South Africa. Include in that very circle, the personal heroism of one man, who as a young herd boy, had the makings of a president. The unstoppable Nelson Mandela, who has done more to change the shape of the twentieth century than any other human being. His humility, his determination and his Formula for Peace has won him his place as a world leader. The dynamic politics of the last decade has brought new substance to the meaning of democracy. Future generations of South Africans will add their voice to the international stadium of music, sport, education and personal challenge.

The newly elected government which represents seventy six per cent of the total population, has given equal status to eleven official spoken languages of its people. You can hear your favourite football team commentary in any of them, by switching on a radio or television. African music is becoming widespread, talented sportsmen and women are noticeable in the world arena. Fine universities offer scholarships for black students.

Our preconceptions may be one thing – reality is another. The feeling of being in South Africa as a newcomer is to compare an infant to a sage. It helps if you understand a little about historical grievances. It helps if you know what the word '*transition*' means to people here. To the ordinary farmer and his family, the last ten years have not been easy. Barriers have already come down, some slower than others. That is not to say that people are yet ready to cross them. One has to forget about key divisions of previous years, one must be impressed by what is 'now' and what is 'real'. To me the things which matter are kindness and goodwill not the years of a war-ravaged fatherland.

And so we took our leave of these good people knowing that we would probably never meet again.

Chapter 6

Home is a small village without water

A few hundred yards from Makibis' house, there is a spring which runs down from the high plateau. Sweet pure water trickles over the rock face into a collecting chamber. Each morning the inhabitants of Ha Simone village walk across the mountain to fetch their family's supply. The water trickles very slowly. In winter the spring has been known to freeze up altogether. The queue is often long.

Usually it was the two daughters who visited the spring, more difficult for Emily as she had further to walk to school than Bernice and the family duty often made her late. Apart from the physical effort of fetching and carrying water, the time spent waiting at the spring could be frustrating. On the days I was there, the meeting and greeting went on in high spirits around me. The selection of containers was comical; from plastic buckets to empty bottles to rusty old petrol cans. Fascinated, I watched as the women swung container onto head with a swift grace that comes from years of practice; shifting their stance to obtain a good balance, then with the flash of a smile to the waiting crowd, they glided onwards and upwards - as if wings were attached to their feet.

At the Makibi household, the big barrel by the back door has to be filled every morning before the children go off to school. Day-to-day water management is a complex matter. Heavy washing and cleaning is done using water from the Subeng River, which is just below their church, brought up in turn by all the members of the family in large containers. It used to take Rose fifteen minutes to walk up the steep incline with a full container on her head. Sometimes more than a dozen white shirts would be blowing from the line across the yard, as bright as in any television commercial.

Their bathroom is a large zinc tub. Towels are hung out to dry on a line at the back of the house and none of the family would dream of setting out for the day unless he or she has washed. Day to day water management dominates their lives. I was impressed by the boys' teeth-brushing routines which must be completed after prayers and before breakfast. Each morning's dishes are washed in a bowl and put on the *stoep* to dry.

On blanket-washing days, Rose, Emily and Bernice got up early to fill their largest tub; the business executed with immense dignity. The God of cleanliness was a packet of Omo, a special washing powder for use in cold water. As it was something the family could ill afford, Rose was the only one allowed to pour from the packet. One almost felt the event should have been accompanied by a chorus of the National Anthem. The marathon of fetching water from the river, followed by the lengthy back-bending slog in elbow-level suds, then the wringing out of clothes – was enough to exhaust the ladies completely for that day.

One morning in the yard the blanket wash was in progress and the goat had escaped. Petros was in deep trouble because his animal had eaten its rope and skipped off – yet again in the direction of the neighbours' crops. If there is anything that makes a Basotho mad it is somebody else's animal stealing his crops.

"Petros," yelled his mother, "go and fetch your tiresome goat. He brings us nothing but trouble from our neighbours. Tie him up before your father comes back."

The boy was not listening. He was still sleeping.

In the church, which was situated below the house, the congregation were gathered for Communion. Prayers had started and the sacrament prepared. Mid-*Jeremiah* Chapter 8, Reverend Makibi, Bible in hand, stepped momentarily outside the side door of the church. He was inclined to breathe deeply in preparation for the delivery of his sermon. From this position, he could hear Rose's urgent command to Petros. Quite suddenly he handed his Bible to a server, abandoned his waiting congregation and *ran* up the mountain. Somewhere between the Holy Sacrament and the Blood of Christ, the Minister disappeared on a divine mission to reclaim an erring goat. He also had to apologise to his neighbour.

After several minutes, Reverend Makibi reappeared over the ridge dragging a reluctant animal on a very short rope. With an extremely curt nod, he handed it over to Walter who had appeared from inside the church, perplexed at his father's sudden disappearance. One or two curious heads peered out of the doorway. Perspiration ran down Stephen's face and the sullen brow was enough to indicate the fury aimed at his number three son.

Ceremoniously Rose took her hands from the tub, dried her arms on her apron and went to look in the bottom hut. Petros could not be found.

"That boy will receive a *sjambok* from his father when he returns," admitted Rose as she climbed back up the stone stairs from the church. Emily, who was continuing to beat the daylights out of a sodden blanket, agreed with heavy heart. It wasn't really Petros's fault that his goat had escaped, the animal was always breaking his rope and running off. She had a soft spot for her youngest brother, but knew her father well enough not to interfere.

"Our neighbour will not respect us any more – this is not the first time that animal has stolen their food," said Rose, pulling the end of a blanket and tossing it over the barbed wire fence some feet away. "Petros must go and apologize."

From what I gathered the goat's remaining days were very few in number and the prodigal son did not return for supper.

On Sundays the church was always full. Worshippers either walked or came by taxi from many villages, some quite far afield. The babble of voices grew to a crescendo in the yard as more people arrived. The ladies used one of the huts as a changing room to don their church uniforms. Several nursing mothers sat down to feed their babies on the small area of grass near the church, in readiness for Morning Prayer. The blue dresses and white hats of the ladies looked fresh and sparkling. The men wore white coats with a blue sash across the shoulder. There did not seem to be an exact starting time for the service, more like a 'well when everybody's ready' kind of nod from the priest.

St John's Church of the Apostolic Faith Mission was founded in 1939 by Mother Christina Nku, a South African woman who had a vision which told her that a church should be built by donations from a small group of Christian men and women so that they could be baptised and receive the gift of the Holy Spirit. Through her divine inspiration and faith, the message of the vision was passed on to many people. As time went on money and help flooded in and the first Church of St John's was built. Mother Christina became the first Archbishop. Its origins grew from the ideology of Anglican missionaries, known here as the Church of Lesotho.

The Mother Church of St John's was established in South Africa during the 1940s. More have flourished on similar lines, faithfully following established traditions of baptism and worship. The present Archbishop, Dr P.J.Masango, lives in a house in Teyateyaneng near Maseru. There the sandstone church was built on a grand scale with fine architecture. Designed to hold hundreds of people, it has for many years hosted all their important festivals. By comparison Stephen Makibi's parish is a small 'branch line' and vital to those members of St John's who live in the Leribe and Butha-Buthe district.

St John's fellowship uses the same version of the Bible as the Anglican Church. Their hymns are the same. 'Jerusalem the Golden' sounds equally rousing sung in unison by fifty or sixty Basotho voices, as an English cathedral choir with organ accompaniment – only the words are different.

Rose was ordained in 1984 and Stephen a little earlier. They are both qualified to conduct services which can and do take place any day of the week. Travellers come from long distances and sometimes arrive in Ha Simone unexpectedly. Thursday is always 'Ladies Day' which is Stephen's official day off and means that his wife will officiate.

St John's Church also supports a healing ministry for those who are sick, which sadly is a provision of necessity in Lesotho. One could ask many questions about why the people here are so poor? The reality is that many families suffer from malnutrition, resulting from poverty and lack of medical care. Starvation is only a few feet away from where you are standing at any given time. There are virtually no hospitals for the poor – general infections and diseases are still treated by traditional *Sangomas* where plant medicine is rife. The birth rate is high and deaths in infancy extremely common.

The rural communities are by far the poorest. Poverty is not only lack of money. Some rural farmers can live by owning livestock, building good houses, having fields to cultivate and sending out their children to work. But the very poorest households lack almost everything that can make life comfortable, and those who are in this category have very few assets which can keep them alive. Some households will brew and sell traditional beer to make money, even though this is illegal in Lesotho. A small proportion of families exist on the government aid programmes, where there is no work whatsoever and no agriculture. The ability to grow food can be the difference between maintenance of life and collapse.

Destitute families arrive at Ha Simone from time to time to seek out St John's Community because they have heard about the help which awaits them. Their plight is pitiful. They arrive at any time of the day or night. I have seen families whose relatives are terribly ill, gather at the door of Stephen's house, having walked for days. They have heard that if they come here, this small community might offer food, shelter and spiritual guidance. No government department supports them. They have nowhere else to go. They de-camp in the yard, looking dejected and miserable until Stephen and Rose take over their decisions. Sometimes the area in front of the house is like a casualty ward.

Food is very scarce. Usually Rose can offer them *mealie* or sorghum porridge, albeit from their own meagre diet and water from the spring. If there is room, the family can stay in one of the huts situated close to the church. It is hoped that the visitors will take part in the worship and prayers and feel a sense of caring and belonging. The mission of St John's is to welcome people into their church, help them pick up the pieces of their lives, put their faith in the spirit of God and hope that a time will come when they find their own way out of the darkness. Stephen spends much of his time listening to problems and helping people to make decisions.

Subsequently, most families form friendships after a few weeks and share in the daily tasks of agriculture, weeding or harvesting. The looks of desperation which ravaged their faces on arrival, are replaced by a new vitality of spirit. It is a heartening sight to witness. I had seen it in the expression of Johannes, even though he was blind. Johannes had discovered that he could be useful in the church by tidying books and rearranging the benches every time there was a service, feeling his way around the building and the yard until they became familiar - knowing that the people here cared about him. Walter and his brothers saw to his clothes, his washing and dressing. Rose gave him supper every evening. How could one fail to feel that love? After several months Johannes was well enough to leave Ha Simone and face the world.

Many others have made that same journey over the years. A similar story accounts for the two young brothers Fred and George, now living in the first house next to the church. Fred has a long Sesotho name with '*clicks*' in it. My feeble attempts to utter this child's name correctly gave great amusement to the others. The Basotho are very sensitive about pronunciation. I christened him Fred because I was unable to pronounce it properly. The new label stuck.

His ragged outfit and carefree smile was what brought this five year old to my notice. And the fact that whenever there was any food about the boy always seemed to appear. His dog looked after him while his mother worked during the day – otherwise he played around the yard and generally got in everyone's way. He used to sit cross-legged on the ground watching everything with huge saucer eyes without saying a word and stare at the Silver Fox as though it were a heap of gold.

Fred had no chance of attending school. His education would be the mountains, the seasons and the people who lived nearby – he never went far away from Ha Simone. Survival was all that filled his sharp mind. But Fred was lucky. Boys like him hang around the streets in every town waiting for someone to take pity on them. Some become involved with street gangs. That in turn can lead to a life of decline and degradation. Street children are a huge problem here.

One morning, Fred ran into the yard looking more than a little agitated and pulled at my hand. He jumped up and down several times and then ran away towards his hut. I followed him.

"What's the matter?" I yelled, unable to keep up with his lightning feet leaping over the grass in front of me. On the doorstep of his hut, a cow was busy eating from a small sack of *mealie* lying on the ground.

"Tsoa – Tsoa! " he screamed, *"tsoa tsoa Khomo!"* (cow –get out !")

The boy was so distressed that I went to fetch Rose. Shouting a few meaningless exhortations, we both took sticks, shushing and pulling the reluctant animal away from the doorway of the hut. The sack from which it was munching was obviously the family's own supper. Fred promptly sat on his haunches in front of the hut, thin stick legs poking out from torn trousers, his little face set with firm resolve. Nobody in the whole world was going to steal *his* supper. Later his mother came to thank me for helping her son.

St John's Church nurtures an unconditional belief in the power of Holy Water. Its members accept that water represents the Holy Spirit and embodies their faith. Baptism is their way of committing themselves to the Holy Spirit, and this ceremonial rite may be sought many times during their life-time. A priest may baptise his members by immersing them seven times in water and saying the words of *The Blessing*.

Four times a year, mass services take place in the river at Teyateyaneng with hundreds of participants. The queues are long. Immersions may go on for several days with priests standing up to their knees in the river for hours at a time. Their faith is constantly renewed.

Ha Simone operates on a much smaller scale, though water is the essential part of the service. Members of Stephen's congregation go down to the river to fill their containers. At the beginning of each service, the people place their water jars on the floor near the door of the church. During prayers, the water is blessed, then sprinkled on the head of the communicant. Hymns and Psalms are sung, Communion is given. When all is said and sung, the water is taken away, carried long distances by truck or taxi or head. It can then be used to give healing to other members of the family or it may be sprinkled around a house to ward off evil spirits or to help with a difficult problem. It is widely believed that this practice helps to heal not only health related problems but also social and emotional problems. The power of prayer and water are seen as very real providers of the working of the Holy Spirit.

In Ha Simone, the church was started by the parishioners themselves. Before the present building, the people used a tiny hut where the roof leaked and the winds came through the open doorway. Then in 1984 Stephen got this bee in his bonnet.

"If we pool every penny we have, we could buy the materials to build our own church. Everyone can help - even the children. We will do it with the sweat of our own hands. One day it will be finished, not this year, not next year, but one day it will be enough. We must keep our faith. God will help us."

Everyone said it was impossible. They didn't even have enough to build the first foundations. But Stephen Makibi is not a man to be deterred; as the play unfolded, the real charisma of the man was revealed.

The first season saw the first row of bricks laid. Then the snow came and all ideas of building were abandoned. It was so cold even the river iced over. In the Spring of 1985, the second row of bricks appeared. Every family gave what they could; ten rands, twenty rands, a hundred rands –the women made fat cakes to sell across the river. Even the smallest coin was counted.

During those long years, the project gathered momentum. The congregation continued their daily worship in the small hut with the minister praising God, from his makeshift pulpit – the seat of a chair - with communicants kneeling on the mud floor. Then, they didn't even have one Bible between them. Their main objective was to pray for the future of the building in which they all took a share. With sheer dedication, the people continued to sing their chants and shout their prayers to the Almighty.

Stephen Makibi insisted it could be achieved. Rose supported his ideals. She knew Stephen when he was like this. He never gave up. The building of the new church became a fixation.

"This church is my dream," he ranted, "we must work harder. Who is responsible for erecting the next lot of timbers? We must make sure the roof is on soon. The rains will soon be here."

Every boy for miles around learned how to lay bricks. If they dared to dodge duties, the priest would seek them out. It was impossible to escape for a game of *morabaraba* on the rocks.

"Come on boy! Why are you sleeping? There is another hour of daylight left!"

The building slowly took shape. Resourcefulness was a novelty at first. People toiled from morning until night and Sunday services were conducted out in the open in sight of the new church.

"Look at our beautiful church!" he would shout to the congregation "Joseph was a carpenter. Jesus himself learned how to do this task. Think about the wall of Jerusalem! The people worked together in those days, the same as we are doing." His words were relentless.

The ladies did much of the fetching and carrying, some of them young mothers with babies, The work was hard. A zillion tasks were demanded. Water was constantly needed and in the good months it was fairly easy to fetch supplies from the river. In the winters when it snowed, the people couldn't get across from one village to another and labour temporarily came to a standstill. The following Spring members again converged on Ha Simone. Building work was tackled with renewed energy.

It was time to put on the roof. Ladders were made and large pieces of corrugated tin brought to the village by teams of men. Strong wooden beams had to fetched. These were erected to make a sloping roof, but without an interior ceiling. It would resemble an English tithe barn with a high roof space. There was no church tower, simply a roof.

The builders needed feeding and this was another problem. The women shared out the small amount of food. Money as well as materials were in short supply. Tempers grew worse. Arguments flourished. Some threw down their tools and went. Stephen could not sleep with the worry of it all. He prayed fervently for answers.

Eventually the building was finished. The windows had been glazed and the doors hung and painted. It was agreed that their labours had not been wasted. Gladness filled their hearts.

Stephen's dream had taken seven long years to come to pass. He went alone in the evening to the river; to sit in the darkness and go over in his mind the final stages of his journey. It was enough to be alone and quiet, away from the sounds of drills and hammers. His beloved church was complete. His community had built a symbol of their faith which would last for years and years; a place to which the people of St John's could feel they belonged; in which they would always have pride.

The stars were out and the heavens shone clear and luminous like a deep lake. Stephen could just make out the silver shapes of the mountains beyond the Caledon River. There was an eerie glow in the sky. A storm was coming. His mind focused for a moment on everything that had happened and tears sprang to his eyes. In his heart there was joy, yet a deep sadness swept over him. The night was very still. The damp scent of the kraal was in his nostrils. Somewhere amongst the rocks behind him he heard a voice call out.

"Dad, its me….. Walter."

A shadowy figure came towards him out of the darkness. His eldest son had come to share his quiet thoughts. Walter took his father's outstretched hand and clasped it. Stephen spoke as though his heart was filled with heaviness.

"My son....it is done. Our church is built. Yet, I feel sadness ..... and the reason is our work together has ended. We shall no more be one family, united in our trials and tribulations. Everyone will go home and in a few years the children will not remember what their parents did." His voice shook with choking tears.

"They *will* remember Dad. I am young and I will tell them. A part of every person is in those walls. *Your* sadness is that the work has finished"

He took his father by the shoulder and looked into his tired face. " Now you must celebrate. We will *all* celebrate. You almost drove us too far – but now all the people will come. Our church will grow and grow. God will know that we did our best for Him."

Walter drew his arm round his father and they walked together back up to the house. Their mission was complete. The new roof of the St John's Church stood out against the sky. Somewhere from the direction of Butha-Buthe the sound of thunder rumbled and a flash of lightning lit the ground far away.

"It will rain tonight," said Walter, "tomorrow we will know if our roof has leaked!"

Chapter 7

A tank and a hijack

I hate farewells. Liliane was leaving to go back to France. Our adventures together were legendary. My journeys out to the mountains would never be the same. She would leave a gap in the social life of the camp. In addition everyone at Ha Simone adored her. Walter and Liliane had become good friends.

"Why are you leaving us? I'd like you to teach me some French," Walter said as we walked down the steps to the river one last time. "We do not want to lose you."

"You see Walter, my two youngest children must go to school in France," Liliane began. "I am needed there now. They both must start their new schools. Butha-Buthe school is not stretching them enough. They need competition and tougher challenges." She took Walter's hand and held it.

"*Au revoir* Walter, look after my friend here."

"You can be sure about that," he replied. "We'll take Nettie to the festival at Teyateyaneng in August when we pray for the rain. I wish that you and your husband could come. I will pray for your journey to France. It must be a good country if everyone is like you."

That evening, Ali drove his wife and two children to Johannesburg to board the flight to Paris. Barrie and I decided to go to the entertainment at Butha-Buthe Camp, where there was to be a display of Basotho dancing for the engineers. I was distraught and in no mood for a party. The electricity had gone off again and we could not see to dress. The night was so black. As we drove out on to Mandela Road and down past the Caltex garage, thoughts of hijacks once more crossed our minds. We usually drove in convoy with Ali and Liliane. Tonight we would be returning late by ourselves.

As we reached the entertainment hall, lights and music were blaring. Everywhere was buzzing with life. Performers rushed past in their costumes. The action had started. We could hear the sound of loud drumming. Engineers from LHDA (Lesotho Highlands Development Authority) made up a large part of the audience. For Barrie it was an important social event and as a new wife, I was expected to support him. LHDA was the body who supervised the overall project making sure the engineering work was carried out to perfection. They were directly responsible to their client, the Lesotho Government.

For the dam to be successfully commissioned, all elements in a long line of structures must be complete within the original programme scheduled. The priority for all concerned was to avoid being late with deadlines because this would incur heavy penalties. Time is money on a job this size and when things go wrong or get held up, engineers, tunnellers, administrative staff have to pull together. The stresses of the job can be smoothed out to mutual benefit if both parties come together at musical events such as this and get to know each other. Someone placed a large glass of wine in my hand. House lights went down.

Dancing is an important part of Basotho tradition. Tonight we were in for a feast. No one bothered about sound systems or amplification. The men were going to dance the *mohobelo*, which is a seriously vigorous movement. It involves much swinging of the body and rhythmic stamping of the feet. This dance is used as part of a traditional 'rain ceremony'.

A torrent of ladies dressed in pink and blue traditional dresses with voluminous skirts, crashed onto the stage. Large ladies with large skirts look – well, large. They received wild greetings from their many friends in the audience. Several performers were the wives of the local Basotho men employed on the site. This concert was a truly international affair.

"Shh…. the *mokhibo* has started," announced the Master of Ceremonies.

From a kneeling position, whistles in mouths, using movements of the hands and rhythmic jerking of the body, the dancers shook themselves. They were able to twist the top half of their bodies into amazing shapes, while the bottom half was still. The engineers loved it. Men were shouting (in French mostly) or clapping and the *molilietsane* (high pitched yells) from the women, heightened the temperature inside the hall. The fun had started.

One of the men in the audience broke away from his seat and leapt into the air, making high kicks and yelling loudly. He landed on the stage via some very fancy footwork, while mimicking hand–to-hand combat, his eyes rolling wildly to the ceiling. This had to be some kind of warrior dance. Others joined in.

"This is the *mokorotlo* dance. It means - in praise of the ancestors," shouted a voice on a microphone.

A dozen women were still on their knees. Gyrating arms, shoulders and bosoms pounded to the beat of the drums. The audience shouted for more. *Ululations* grew louder. Bodies shook with excitement. The sound was deafening. Africa's free expression filled the room.

Barrie nudged me and nodded towards the door. We slipped unnoticed out of the hall back to the car.

"It's a shame but we mustn't be late," he said firmly, in answer to my protests to stay longer at the party. "Need to make it back to Leribe in one piece - we're on our own tonight." I put down my empty glass.

We drove swiftly past the camp guards and out onto the main road. Moonlight shone through the dark silhouettes of trees and buildings. A bunch of horses tied to a post outside a store – as in western cowboy film – snorted the night air, waiting for their riders. Abandoned polythene stalls in the market place rustled ghostly in the wind. The heavens rippled with moon clouds and the sky moved silently in a counterpane of light. There were silver trails on the mountain tops.

We drove fast along the empty road towards Koenaneng. The African rhythm had got into my brain and I wished we were staying to the party. My husband was being dutiful, but I was disappointed.

"Barrie, stop the car – I want to look at the stars."

"Nettie we can't stop here."

"Why not – it's such a wonderful moonlit night. I feel like dancing."

Two glasses of fizzy wine and a cigarette to deflect the mosquitos (I don't normally smoke) had gone to my head . The party mood had spilled over into the car and I giggled. We pulled over to the verge and I got out of the car and started walking down the deserted road, my heels clicking loudly on the hard surface. Barrie pulled my arm, "Look honey, we could be in danger, we don't know this place at night. This isn't the moment to dance."

"Okay – you win – only let's walk a bit, the sky is so beautiful. Just look at that moon! And we had to miss half the party."

We linked arms for a few minutes and walked on together, gazing up at the sky. It was a perfect night. On either side of us, the black mountains showed no sign of life. The air felt deliciously cool

"I love you Mr Glenn and I'm so glad you brought me to Africa."

"You mean, you followed me to Africa – come on honey, back in the car," he protested laughingly. I knew he was only thinking of our safety. "We really do have to go."

Not for the first time, he put his foot hard on the accelerator and drove the next ten kilometres at Totoyta Corolla high speed. I wished he wouldn't. On the outskirts of Leribe, a bridge was being repaired. Barrie pulled back where the road narrowed. A pile of rocks left on the tarmac was a sure sign of work in progress, but it didn't take a genius to work out that not much was being made. It had been like that for several months. The road was only wide enough for one car.

The mountainsides were inky black. Few homes had electricity so that the only sign of life would be where a fire glowed out on the hillside. To anyone lurking in the darkness underneath the bridge, the headlights of one car would be seen from a long distance. I glanced at Barrie.

"Hold your breath honey, here we go."

We were both thinking exactly the same thoughts. In a few seconds we were across the bridge and the car picked up speed. There was a little distance before we reached the entrance to our road to the camp. Audible sighs of relief were on both our lips.

Piri, the guard who was on duty all night, shouted, "Goodnight Mr Glenn," as he locked the barriers behind us.

"Goodnight Piri."

Our wheels hit the rough grit which led to the office block and circled the camp. We slept well that night.

The next morning there was such a commotion outside the house; vehicles coming and going, wheels sounding urgent on the gravel car park. And it was Saturday. I wondered if it could have been some urgency about the job. Something felt different. There was a feeling of disquiet in the air; voices raised, movement of *bakkies* in and out of the gate.

Not long afterwards we heard that one of the engineers had been travelling alone back from the party in Butha-Buthe, when his car was stopped at gunpoint somewhere on the road - the same route as we had taken. He was a young Frenchman who had recently arrived at the site. The thieves had stolen his keys, driven him to a remote spot up in the hills, then let him go. It had taken him several hours to walk home. He had arrived in the early hours, extremely shaken and scared, but unharmed.

Everyone was shocked. Especially me.

"If we had stayed late at the party Nettie, it might have been us," said Barrie firmly.

"I know…. I'm sorry, you were right to make me get back in the car…..that poor young man. I would have died on the spot."

"No you wouldn't, they wouldn't have harmed us. It was the car they were after. Remember how poor the Basotho people are. They see all these powerful vehicles going up and down their country every day. It would be a marvel if there weren't any robberies. It happens on any job, in any country…. but it is frightening, especially when they wave guns around. They may not have been loaded."

"I feel awful…. I was wrong to get out and walk – I'm sorry."

All day I felt really low and the fact that Liliane had left for France was hard to bear. Suddenly the incident of the death of one of our drivers some months before, struck home, reminding us yet again, of strange and serious happenings in our part of the world.

On an ordinary work day, Sam, one of the regular taxi drivers. had been instructed to drop off a member of staff to the airport, and return to Leribe Camp. But he didn't arrive home. His wife called in after six hours, worried about his long absence. No one seemed to know where he was. The police were called. After a search along his well known route, the company's vehicle was found parked by the road a few miles outside Johannesburg, neatly turned, facing the main highway. Sam was dead at the wheel. He was not off his route and his key was still in the ignition. None of his possessions had been tampered with. Nothing was missing. No violence had been used either on driver or vehicle.

Sam was always polite and charming. He would often put in more hours than his duty required. His loyalty to the company was unquestionable. He had been employed by LHPC from the beginning of the project. One of his duties was to meet visiting senior management from overseas at Johannesburg Airport, and transport them to a construction site on any part of the job, which could involve many long driving hours. On Fridays we ladies often had the benefit of Sam's company on our trips into Bethlehem. He and Kenneth took turns to drive the *kombi* and bring us back safely.

The whole camp was shocked. Utterly reliable, punctual and professional, Sam had gone out one morning to complete his normal duties – and died at the wheel of his vehicle. No light could be shed on the circumstances surrounding his death. He was forty two. His death brought no answers – only more questions. Not only had the company lost an employee, but families on camp had lost a caring colleague. His reputation in every quarter was one of friendliness, dedication and popularity.

Rumours circulated widely and there was a family funeral. Official sources said that he had died from natural causes. The medical report stated that Sam had an old scar on his lungs from a childhood illness and it was suggested that a slight cough could have instigated a spasm, which he could not withstand. After the funeral Thabo, Petros and Kenneth appeared on duty with shaved heads. It was tradition for those who wanted to pay their respects to a dead comrade. Compensation was later offered to his family from his employers. It was the least they could do. Deaths of this nature always attracted bizarre speculation. We would probably never know the real truth.

LHPC decided on a policy of painting registration numbers on the roof of every vehicle in black letters so that in the event of a hijack, helicopters could spot contraband from the air. Everyone knew this wasn't foolproof. Barrie's car had to be done and we felt very conspicuous.

Everyone dreaded hijacks. Relationships between the company and the Basotho were excellent. At Muela, almost a thousand men were employed. Many were foremen and held positions of authority. Jobs and security brought good hospitality in the local villages. In the three camps, hundreds of local women held jobs and their excellent contribution to ex-pat families meant far more than just having a maid or a gardener. In the schools, canteens or the offices, the rapport between different nationalities was legendary. The concert which had been put on for our benefit that week generated so much good will. And yet it cast a shadow over our lives.

Fear affected us for several weeks. Gossip about the hijack was daily talk at both Leribe and Butha-Buthe Wives were advised not to go out alone and if a journey was essential, only during the day. At night every vehicle had to travel in convoy. New anti-theft devices were introduced into the bosses' cars as they had many business meetings to attend, but even they were told to make their journeys in pairs. A single driver was deemed to be much more vulnerable.

*   *   *   *

My own daytime agenda was different from most of the other wives on the camp. I was no good at playing 'Bridge', hopeless at tea parties and had no interest in cooking if it wasn't for Barrie. I wasn't one to spend time on ladies coffee mornings or bar talk. The other wives must have found me quite dull. Engrossed in reading or painting, I was much happier writing letters to England or planning and marking work for my pupils. Afternoons spent at Ha Simone with Rose and the family were also part of my week. Walter and I drove many distances in the Silver Fox to see his friends in other villages and Emily and I spent hours discussing English literature, often on a walk to the spring to fetch water. She declared her wish to succeed to a better grade at school. Bernice desperately wanted to learn to speak English too and I was astonished how quickly she improved after a few sessions. Sometimes, when it was too hot to work, we used to switch on the car radio parked in the yard, turn it to full volume and dance….then run to the river to cool down. Often Walter and Petros would carry cans of water up the hillside to wash my car, as it seemed forever caked in dust. I counted these times as happy days and feared when they might end.

My life was beginning to develop in two rather opposite directions….and I became aware that some of my camp neighbours were disapproving of my friendship with a local family….it was implied by a few people that perhaps I should find more time for in-camp leisure pursuits. Stretch marks were beginning to appear between Afrikaner and English.

Clothes washing days at Ha Simone were fascinating. The more I watched Rose and her daughters carrying water up the hillside, the more I wanted to help them. For quite a time I had been trying to fathom how I could obtain one of the huge green water tanks, which littered the main scrap yard at Butha-Buthe.

"How can I get hold of one of those big tanks in your yard," I asked half jokingly to Barrie.

"You're not on the staff, Nettie," Barrie had said firmly, "you just can't do that. They belong to the contract."

"But they're just lying around! I've seen dozens of them – nobody wants them."

Barrie wasn't keen on asking favours, that was all. He was not impressed when I admitted to ringing Mr Plu, one of the most senior bosses at Ha Lejone, to voice my request. Wives didn't usually phone the big chiefs. My husband was not best pleased.

"*Bonjour Monsieur,* my husband is employed at Leribe Camp. Is it possible that I could steal one of the empty plastic tanks at your yard in Butha-Buthe – the ones which are thrown away?"

"Of course – why do you need one ?"

"There is a Basotho family I know, who live in Ha Simone. I would like to have one for them to collect rainwater….it would be so useful to them."

" *Mais oui* Madame. Okay by me. Please take a tank if that is what you require. Ask one of the drivers to collect it."

The request was granted with no fuss. I was thrilled.

"*Merci beaucoup Monsieur,*" I said "I won't take up any more of your time."

Hurrying down to the dumping site, where the refuse containers were emptied, I found Henry, who last week had driven me to my hospital appointment in Bethlehem. He was cleaning one of the company vehicles and turned in surprise.

"*Lumela,* Henry. Beautiful day isn't it. Please will you do a job for me?"

His teeth shone white as he smiled. There was nothing Henry loved more than earning a few maloti.

"Next time you have some space on your lorry, would you go to the yard in Butha-Buthe and find me a tank – an empty one? Mr Plu has given his permission."

"Okay *'M'e.*" he said inquisitively.

"Would you be able to take it to Reverend Makibi's place? Just ask for him by name. He will tell you where you must off load it." I slipped a twenty rand note into his pocket, "and come for a cup of tea this afternoon if you have time."

Sometimes Henry and I used to stand in the garden and chat, after he had collected the bins and rummaged through them. He loved politics and used to take any old newspapers away and read them. He was also a family man. His dearest wish was to increase his offspring. He had worked in the mines in South Africa for twenty four years for the equivalent of three pounds for a thirty day shift. He left to become a priest, because of the things he witnessed in the mines, but took a job as a lorry driver instead.

"We have four daughters," he had told me, "and they are such good daughters, but it is my wish to have a son. My wife does not like me to come home – she says I am upsetting her."

He beamed mischievously at me from under his cap. *"Kea Leboha 'M'e.* I will go to the yard today. My truck will pick up a tank and take it to Reverend Makibi. Then I go home to see my wife."

He laughed uproariously.

"Henry you are wicked."

The next day I called in at Ha Simone. One bright green plastic tank, the size of a small Cessna aircraft , was standing in front of the house. With no apparent way of fitting it under the roof, it was questionable whether it would be any use at all. My effort was probably a useless exercise.

"Stephen, you have no drainpipes," I said in alarm after first noticing their deficient drainage system. "How will you catch the water?"

"Don't worry Ma'am, that is a job that my sons will do - when God sends the rain, we will tell him to put it in here." He patted the side of the tank affectionately. "Nettie, you're an angel!
Please thank your boss man for us. It is a beautiful present."

Rose had gone to see her mother in Johannesburg for a few days. I hoped she would be pleased. Walter appeared in the yard laughing hysterically, pointing at the tank.

"We thought it was going to be big – but not this big Nettie…what do they use them for?"

"I don't know - all I do know is that it would find a use here. I couldn't bear to see them lying around in the yard. Do you like it?"

"Yes, but there is no bung in the hole at the bottom."

"Well, you'll have to invent one, it shouldn't be too difficult."

Emily came up from the church path at that moment, carrying a large container of water on her head. She looked tired and her forehead was glowing with perspiration under her scarf.

"Hi Nettie. Wow, the tank arrived last night, how did you make it happen?"

"Emily, don't ask! Rose says it will hold the rainwater for washing the clothes. It should save you a few trips to the river. Boys, you must find a bung, and Walter – none of your fancy plumbing - just a bung."

Emily walked into the house and I heard her pour the water into the big container by the door. "Em, do you want to hop into town? I'm going past there. They've got offal at the butchers. I saw the queue this morning."

"Yes, Nettie – wait for me. Walter, do you want to come?"

Walter came towards me, his face seriously altered from a few moments ago.

"We heard there was a hijack the other night on the road, Nettie. Was anyone hurt?"

"No….but it was very frightening for the young French guy. He was okay. Do you know anything?"

"We are ashamed that there are still people who would do this to you. It makes my father very angry. We said prayers in church for hours last night. If a *Mosotho* kills an engineer, there will be big trouble around this place."

He sat on the *stoep* and looked up at his father. Stephen's stern expression showed what was in his heart. He put his fist in the air as he spoke.

"We here in Ha Simone are glad that you come to see us. We want you to know that we are having the strong words in our prayers. These people will be caught and punished."

"Barrie and I were on the road that night." I said quietly. "We were coming home from Butha-Buthe and once we got out of the car to look at the stars."

Guiltily, I stared at my feet.

Stephen's expression was one of complete shock. "Nettie, please don't do that again. Promise me you will stay inside your car. Don't look at the stars! Just travel with your headlights full on and your hand on the horn. That way you will frighten them away. They don't want anyone to draw attention to them. One day in the future, I will know who did that bad thing. Someone will tell. Soon the thief will have no friends – and I shall hear of it."

The following Sunday Barrie, Ali and I embarked on our usual outing to Golden Gate National Park to ride up at Bokpoort Farm, near Clarens, though without Liliane. I felt lost and didn't feel like riding. Driving for an hour across the border, the crisp winter sunshine and the mountains made me more cheerful. I loved the colours of sky and rocks merging into each other.

"Liliane will be thinking us for today, she will miss our South African Sundays," Ali commented as we got out of the car. He had read my thoughts exactly. "And the kids will miss riding too, Claire particularly." His daughter Claire was an excellent horsewoman.

The Bokpoort ponies were coming into the yard for the ride. With a schoolboy-happy grin on his face, Barrie saddled up a chestnut stallion. He was eager for this Sunday treat, despite sore Mondays. With absolutely no experience of western saddles, but enough enthusiasm to learn how to use them, he struggled to fit the tack while in conversation with the leader of the ride.

"Before joining Bokpoort, how long since you have you ridden a horse?" the guy asked.

"Fifty three years," replied my husband, mildly thwarted at having to admit his age. "I rode twice round a field in Rotherham in 1942.

He and Ali, who was an experienced rider, were accompanied by Christo, the owner of the farm and a crew of fit and able youngsters. They always had more adventures when Christo went with them. During the ride, which could be rough terrain, they might be on a collision course with scatterings of blesbok, mountain reedbuck, black wildebeeste or zebra - horses splashing through small rivers and streams. Zebra sometimes galloped alongside.

Barrie gave me a thumbs-up wave. Wearing strong sunglasses to shield my eyes, I watched them gallop off into a cloudless blue sky. They would be gone about two hours.

Liliane and I usually went exploring while the men were out riding. The spectacular ochre and purple cliffs and butter-coloured sandstone peaks eroded by time and weather, offered easy medium length walks, occasionally a rope ladder up to a higher cave or a boardwalk swinging over a drop. The views were fabulous. Sometimes we came across baboons playing on the hillside, squealing and chattering. We often passed serious hikers who would be staying out in a shepherd's hut for the night, who couldn't be bothered to stop and speak. They would have the proper gear, boots and a compass, not our style of haversack, bottles of water and running shoes. This area is a safe challenge, appreciated more for its beauty than its dangerous wildlife.

A couple of Sundays ago, we had visited the Connemara ponies at Schaaplaats Stud Farm, near Clarens, run by Christine, a qualified riding instructor. She explained how her ponies had originally come from the green hills of Ireland. We admired her beautiful old stone cottage set into a back drop of mountains. There was a big open yard, where everything seemed to be breeding. Kittens mewing round a mother cat. Chickens pecking around the yard. A pale gold Labrador bitch suckling a litter of puppies, stretched out like ripe tomatoes in the sun.

"These ponies are the most finely tuned animals in South Africa," explained Christine as we walked over to the securely fenced paddock. The farm was extremely well organised and you could sense a love of animals in every direction. We hung around, watching playful mares frisking round the field in high spirits. "Connemaras are bred most successfully here - make wonderful mounts for this kind of terrain. By the way, watch out for the black eagle on your walk – there are still plenty around."

Clambering up from the farm that day, we walked on some slippery rocks near a waterfall. On the roof of a shallow cave we came across bushman paintings. Fascinating! Fragmented drawings in the shape of buck and antelope outlined in deep red colours, which were fairly indistinct with the passage of time but they were truly representational. It was strange seeing things we had read about, with our own eyes. Evidence of those nomadic hunter gatherers who lived here thousands of years ago, are still to be found in parts of Lesotho and South Africa. Many drawings are full of symbolic messages, composed under the influence of trances and mystical experiences. There is evidence that other animals such as lion, hippo, buffalo and leopard once lived here. Now there are none.

Returning to Bokpoort Farm to watch our husbands come in from their ride, Liliane and I were always followed by this very smelly goat. The goat seriously liked Liliane. He obviously felt a considerable attraction for the French. Whenever she went, the creature would come and rub itself on her coat. We never did find out why it behaved as though it was surgically linked. It stank and we tried to avoid it, but like a veritable detective, it would seek her out .

Then we would drive to Clarens, a small town with a choice of restaurants and spend a pleasant gastronomic evening dining at the Guinea Feather. The owner, who wore a kilt and played the bagpipes was a wonderful host. His jibes were always distressingly personal but one got used to them. The goat came with us. It was a standing joke that Liliane would have to sit next to the window. Confronted with one of Eric's large gin and tonics and a chorus of 'Scotland the Brave' on the pipes, none of us minded the fusty smell rising from beneath the table.

This particular week, we ordered simply *three* glasses of wine and *three* tandoori chickens.

"And what have you done with the smelly old goat ?" said Monsieur le Patron unkindly.

"My wife's gone back to France," said Ali, looking Eric straight in the eye, "she doesn't like your cooking so she's gone home to her mother!"

Everyone laughed. Eric's guests fondly assumed it would be a quiet evening, but at the Guinea Feather things tended to escalate. Nothing was ever too much trouble to Eric and as long as you didn't object to rude stories or bagpipes, he would cook whatever you wanted. To stuff a grouse or de-bone a chicken was no problem and if one of his guests orders trout, he has been known to go to the lake and catch one. Spare ribs were described as *'spare parts'* on the menu, crocodile stew as *'jaws soup'* and porcupine pie as *'pins and needles'*. Other fascinating concoctions too numerous to mention lined the walls of his cuisine, and his Chateau Clarens was a singularly effective powder keg of red wine made from South African grapes and the hair of the mountain wolf. Eric loved pleasing his clientèle and so did his wife Anne, who made the most delicious ice-cream, served with strawberries tasting of South African sunshine.

Dough was cooked in an old-fashioned brick oven in the wall. When it was ready, a forest of spicy fruits and cooked vegetables were piled on top as high as a mountain. Sauces and herbs were added and taste buds would almost burst as diners watched Eric dishing up pizzas onto wooden platters. After one of Eric's pizzas you could sink like a stone.

The three of us gave our order. The chef disappeared into the kitchen to prepare our chosen feast. As engineering was at the core of our existence, it was at the heart of conversation in leisure time too. The two men looked very serious.

Soon Phase 1A of the Highland Water Scheme would be drawing to a close. Completion dates and deadlines were on everyone's lips. Under the terms of the original Treaty drawn up between South Africa and Lesotho, everything must be completed according to exact specifications throughout the entire project. Of all the many contracts which comprise Part 1A, Muela underground power station had had the most troubled progress. It suffered a catastrophic and complex dispute which delayed the start of the work. The impasse persisted for more than a year. Working schedules were often tight – this one was very tight.

Because the completion of Muela Dam would provide the vital link to the downstream delivery tunnel network to South Africa, the present part of the contract was at a most critical stage. This was the talk at the table tonight. Without water in the Muela reservoir, delivery of water to the Ashe River and into the Vaal Dam in South Africa, where it would serve the whole of Johannesburg's huge population, would not be possible.

"Thirty thousand maloti a day penalty, if we fail to meet the deadlines," said Ali emphatically. His expression looked deadly serious. Liliane's husband was one of the chief engineers on the job. "That's too much money."

He and Barrie went on talking. The restaurant filled up with more guests and the pungent smell of garlic and herbs wafted round the room. Our bottle of Cape red was disappearing fast.

"Do you think it'll be finished on time?"

"Who knows? If there are no more riots, or strikes or floods …. or anything else to stop progress – in this country you never know."

Often, Ali would have to dash out of bed at before daybreak to some remote corner of the site, to make sure that the projected inflow was within safety standards. Safety was prime consideration on every job and sometimes heavy rain in the mountains or freak storms would be particularly problematic. The need to carry out in-situ stress measurements was high priority and his work was very important to the success of this part of the venture.

Engineering jargon fascinated me. After a year of being an ex-pat wife, I knew what a TBM was; telescopic shutters were those things they used to hold wet concrete inside the tunnels. A muck truck is exactly what it sounds like. I knew about 'spillways' and 'adits', 'vertical stresses' and 'horizontal stresses' *and* the emotional stresses which the men suffered when pressures were high.

"What will happen to the landscape once all the construction work ceases ?"

"The sites must be returned to as natural a state as possible. All machinery and buildings will be taken away, all the equipment will be removed. By the end of this year, it will be hard to tell where the tunnels have been dug. Layers of top soil will be laid over, then seeded and everything will revert to its original landscape."

"And the lighting from the site will disappear," added Barrie, "the villages will be returned to natural daylight. They are used to their area being lit for twenty four hours a day."

"It will confuse the animals I guess," I commented – remembering what Rose told me once how all the chickens up at Katse refused to lay eggs because it was never dark.

About ten o'clock, we left our table and called out goodnight. Monsieur le Patron, red cheeked with kilt swinging, noisily played us out to '*Bluebells of Scotland*'.

"Au revoir Monsieur," said Ali, winking across at the proprietor's wife, "Could you ask him to learn '*Under the Bridges of Paris*' for my wife – she might come back to Lesotho if he could play a French song."

Making a note on her menu *Madame* smiled. "That can be arranged."

Chapter 8

A Beetle in my Leg

I was awoken by a loud knocking at the door, early one morning. There was a gentle hurricane blowing. The verandah table had overturned in the night. Débris lay on the garden and Sophie's kitchen across the way had suffered a broken window from a bit of flying tree. As I drew the curtains, the knocking continued.

"Mrs Glenn, Mrs Glenn!"

It was Betty's voice. And she wasn't due to come to work today. Quickly I went to answer it.

"Please can I speak *'M'e?*"

"Yes, come in Betty, why are you here – it's Monday and no work day. *O a phela?* " (are you alright?)

She was alone.

"Please *'M'e* I have come to tell you that de *sangoma* has seen my disease. I have been there. He saw the swelling. He says I must tell you."

"What must you tell me Betty?"

"That there is a beetle in my leg?"

"What? I can't believe that Betty! You have a swollen leg joint because you have just had a baby. It's fairly common. Let me look."

Betty pulled up her skirt to reveal a very outsized knee. She was wearing the new dress I had given her and looked very pretty. She hopped awkwardly onto a stool and I could see that walking all the way to the camp had not been easy for her.

"Betty, you must stay at home and rest that leg – all day - until the swelling goes down. Have you any medicine?"

"No *'M'e*, the *sangoma* say I must go and see him again and he will give me medicine – to kill it. The insect go up and down and we must see where it bites again. *Ke a kula.*" (I am sick)

There was no point in a shock horror conversation about the diagnosis, as she was already worried about losing her working time.

Anxiety was etched across her face.

"Betty, you're ill and that can't be helped, but we must get you well again. I'm taking you home in the car and you can rest. Give me five minutes to get ready – and where's Oliver?"

"That girl is looking after him. But she no good. I don't trust her." Betty gave a huge sigh and looked close to tears.

'That girl' was a young woman who was notoriously disreputable, but cheap to hire for a few maloti – for most jobs. It was babysitting of the worst kind.

"Did you tell the doctor that the swelling was also in your ankle last week? You remember, I asked you about it then?"

"Yes 'M'e but he say insect is in there. He cut my leg to let it come out. I must pay him money or he make bad things happen to me."

I did not argue. Helping her into the car she agreed the knee was painful. Perhaps there was an infection there? Basotho beliefs and practices are very strange to our ears. Opinions are divided on how traditional doctors use their power or skill. Betty clearly thought that the *sangoma* could help her and she wanted to carry out his instructions, which were unclear to me at the moment.

Belief in ancestor influence in daily life is common. Any illness can be attributed to the ancestors, although the Basotho also believe that ancestors can cure an ailment as well as cause it. If a person goes to see a *ngaka* (doctor) and asks for an illness to be diagnosed, it will probably be by divination that the remedy will be revealed. After a few dramatic incantations, the *ngaka* will throw his bones on the ground. Depending on their position and the angle they fall, the patient can be diagnosed. Bone throwing is an art, which is widely used in Lesotho. It is believed that bone throwing can foretell the future of a person, the health, and the positive and negative forces in their lives. Then, after his palm has been crossed with silver, the *sangoma* may recommend treatment made from herbs and natural sources.

Their time-honoured knowledge of the organic world is impressive. Beliefs have been modified and nowadays it is not so much about black magic as an intrinsic knowledge of herbal remedies. It was generally the case that the maids on camp used a. *sangoma's* advice.

Sophie who suffered from swollen feet and legs had paid her money to the traditional healer, who told her to do the most unlikely things. First she must buy a cow. Then the cow must be slaughtered. Various parts of the animal skin must be hung, drawn and quartered. She must then *wear* the cow by plaiting certain of it into a kind of garland decorated with beads, to be worn round her neck, so that everyone would know a healing was going to take place. Sophie would have to wear heavy jewellery, sing and dance herself around the area for several days, collecting money from people as she went. Then a return visit to the *sangoma*. He would pronounce her well and her ankles would be swollen no more.

In her sassy way Sophie laughed and her shoulders shook like a jelly. She always seemed to have a private supply of laughter swirling around her so that other people caught onto the moment, reminiscent of the 'Laughing Policeman' at the fair.

"You will hear me when I come into de camp 'M'e – loud and loud and more loud. I will blow de whistle and shout and I will make de big noise. Everyone will hear me. Then the bad spirit will leave me. Mrs Glenn – you will come and see me heh!"

Her eyes sparkled and her plum cheeks shone. One of Sophie's considerable attractions was that her manner was entirely without self-consciousness. She had complete faith in the *sangoma*. I dropped some money into her 'cow collection' tin. With a great shriek she danced round the chairs in the canteen, yelling praises aimed at the mountain tops.

"Sophie your feet!"

"Okay *'M'e*, I hear you but I want de Lord bless you very much."

It appeared that it was much more expensive to buy a cow in the Lowlands, than it would be from a farmer up in the Highlands. Sophie was faced with a choice of walking a cheap cow down the mountain for three days – or paying a high price to buy one locally. Her bad legs prevented her from walking anywhere.

"Don't forget – I will come to your house and you will see my cow costume. You will be *very* surprised."

"Sophie I will be ecstatic!"

Betty's house in Leribe village was through a maze of twisty lanes and horrendous troughs where the rain had left deep potholes – hardly the sort of terrain for a lady with a swollen knee. The shanty homes were not the worst I had seen. The dwellings were small, yet there was a feeling of good neighbourliness about the area where Betty lived. She paid a small rent for a one-roomed house with a tap a short distance away. As we drew up the baby-minder arrived with a plastic container of water intended for washing Oliver, who was still asleep inside the house. Betty looked enormously relieved.

".....and don't come back to work until you're better." I said, helping her inside. I looked round for a safe place to put the bottle of antiseptic. "Use this for bathing the cut on your leg - and where's that man of yours? He's the one who should be helping you."

"He no good *'M'e* – him always drunk. No good to look after children."

Heavily, she sat down on her bed, waking up little Oliver who opened his eyes, looked at me and screamed loudly. Betty roared with laughter while I pretended to be offended.

Whites going up to the village was quite a spectacle but a white lady taking home a black maid in a car was a matter for big gossip. As if from nowhere, a host of ladies and toddlers had formed a queue near Betty's fence. Dozens of pairs of brown eyes watched uncertainly as the car engine flared into life. Betty shouted goodbye. I waved. My departure had been noticed. You have to remind yourself that your skin is a different colour and they are not used to white faces.

On my journey back down the hill, apart from a battered looking vehicle and a bony man with a bony cow - I passed no one. At the bottom I ran into trouble. There was an area of ground used as a picking up point for passengers travelling either to Ficksburg, Maseru or Butha-Buthe – loosely known as the 'bus station'. All taxi queues seemed to be on the move like a circus of ants. There were no organised stopping places – just a melée of mini-buses and impatient travellers trying to get somewhere. Youths shouted against each other, touting for cheap fares – so that any passenger with a hint of indecision on his face was swept up and hurriedly pressed into a seat. Wheelbarrows used as luggage carts careered through stationary vehicles. Broken down *kombis*, held together with packing paper and string, looked destined more for the scrap heap than a trip round the Mountain Kingdom. Gas cylinders rubbed shoulders with sacks of grain or goats tethered to the wrist by a piece of string. Drivers wearing baseball caps, shorts, leather purses slung around the waist and no shoes, welcomed their passengers aboard

Musical journeys were *de rigeur.* Loud tunes blared from every exhaust. That was if indeed an exhaust pipe was still attached to the vehicle. Of the many rusted parts found lying on the ground, exhaust pipes seemed to be the most popular. Even the most resolute driver would think twice before crossing the car park. My own code of survival was to make a dash for it when I saw a space. I felt doubly lucky because it was fine and sunny. After one of Leribe's cloudbursts, your car could sink without trace in a sea of mud.

"Hello Mrs Glenn," a voice shouted from somewhere behind me. I turned and saw Augustine, one of our camp drivers.

"*Hantle haholo, Ntate,*" I replied, surprised that anyone recognised me. He jumped out and came over as I pulled to a halt.

"What are you doing here *'M'e* – are you okay? It is not usual to see one of the ladies from the camp out here."

"Yes thanks, I've been to take Betty home to the top of the village. She can't walk."

Wearing a 'Made in China' shiny purple jacket, he leaned his huge frame on the bonnet and beamed a disarming smile. This was to impress his friends. Always a sharp dresser, Augustine was a big shot around Leribe. His nickname was 'Mr Mafia' and there wasn't a smoother operator this side of the Caledon River. Born and bred in Leribe, not much about this town escaped Augustine's knowledge. This week he was running his football team lottery. There was a distinct possibility he would know who would be winning it, before they won.

"I heard you sent a tank up to St John's Church at Ha Simone."

"News travels fast here eh?"

"Oh yes *'M'e* – that kind of new travels even faster. You are a lady who think about people who are poor; we appreciate that because you are an engineer's wife." He slid off the car and straightened the creases in a pair of denim jeans with panache.

"Anyway, I will go and see Betty tomorrow and bring her to work in the car if she can't walk. Has she a problem?"

"Augustine, you also have a big heart. Yes, she has a beetle in her leg."

Without turning a hair he replied, "that's not so bad – it could have been a snake."

Chapter 9

Diamond Time

All winged creatures migrated to our kitchen at night. We got so used to insects battering against the fly screens that the odd grasshopper or misguided moth became a normal feature of our evening meal. Quite often, entombed in our wok, were the telltale lacy wings of a common- or-garden Lepidoptera and if not spotted in time, invariably ended up as an entomological stir-fry. Creepy crawlies didn't look good on chips and it used to turn my stomach to see a Christmas beetle with salt and vinegar on its back. They were blood red, similar to ladybirds but bigger. At night they used to come hurtling into the kitchen, bash themselves on the wall and die. Most of the other houses had a fly screen on the main outside door – ours didn't, so we asked Petros to find one.

"Yes Madam, I will find you de fly-screen, no trouble."

The following day Petros dismantled the fly screen off the house next door and screwed it to our door frame. We saw it and smiled to each other. Petros's abundance of goodwill was known throughout the camp. In fact we still dined out on the stories of how he got rid of the vermin in our roof, several months ago. The poison had been put down. The stench in the living room had become the nose-wrinkling sort people left home for. The Director of Infestations (Petros) had been summoned.

"You must stand and watch where de flies go in 'M'e.'"

In statuesque pose with arms folded - Petros had insisted he remain motionless at this same spot by the willow tree under any circumstance. After three days, we concluded his *modus operandum* was to keep as still as possible, for as long as possible, while on full wages. Quite soon, our down pipes were lined with dead mole rats *(Khoiti)* and Petros reigned rat-catcher supreme.

Keeping up with correspondence from home was a labour of love. Regrettably, and even though I had spent a long time with my daughter on my last visit to England, first hand news of Abigail was scarce. She had seemed well when I saw her in June, yet, I couldn't make out why there was no progress on her mobility – or rather lack of it.

"Is anyone doing anything about her legs?" I had asked Lizzie more than once when we were out shopping together.

"Mum, stop worrying. I'll write and let you know when the hospital gives me an appointment. I'm more worried about her not eating properly. She refuses more than she eats. I am sure that the school weighing machine isn't working properly. They say she's put some weight on but I don't think so. I try her with different things but some days she eats like a sparrow."

I nodded. It was true. Abigail looked too thin for her height. I wished there was something I could do. Still my question remained unanswered.

"Mum – I don't want to talk about it any more."

And that was how we left it. Lizzie was willing to be pushed so far and no further and there was no point in contradicting her. Five years into the grannie generation, one realises one has to take a back seat. I did what all distant grandparents do. I worried a lot.

The support services in Hertfordshire were excellent and so far Abigail had benefited from physiotherapy, speech therapy and periodical medical assessments at the Health Clinic. She had progressed in terms of movement - using her body to roll over in order to reach her toys on the floor. As for walking – it had just not happened.

Her disabilities inflicted a great deal of limitation on Lizzie's life. Normal daily routines can easily become stressful when there is no one to help. Abigail still has to be spoon fed and will probably never be able to feed herself. My concerns for my daughter were that she should be given emotional support now that Abigail was attending school. I felt a degree of impatience that things were just not happening quick enough and helpless that I was too far away to help.

"I've got an idea, " said Barrie quietly. "Why don't we have our Wedding Blessing in October in Datchworth Church – and have Abigail christened at the same time?"

He had noticed my mood. Another empty mail bag. Tears on the brink. He took my hand. "Come on lets go for a walk."

Together we pondered over the question of a ceremony in the church with our two families together. Combining the two services would be good; a memorable occasion for us - and a time of acceptance for Lizzie. The psychological burden of knowing she had a child with cerebral palsy had made my daughter strong, but how many years would it take for her to accept it? It had been hard for her – especially without a partner's support.

No doctor would attempt to give us a confident prognosis. None of us knew what her future would be. This little girl, who had been ours for six years, who had brought us all so much joy, would be baptised into the church at the same time as our wedding blessing. We could arrange for our favourite Reverend to officiate - and invite the nation. The Willoughbys and the Glenns would meet each other. A champagne celebration would be good for us all.

"Yes Barrie, I think you're right. We should go home in October."

"That's settled then. Now I suppose you're going to worry about what to wear."

"I shall wear shorts and show off my brown knees Come on lets take Hercule for a walk."

It was early July and getting colder by the day. There was snow on the mountain tops and my second hand computer had been delivered. With reverential care the young man who came to install it, placed it on the table in the smallest bedroom and stood back to admire this plastic box with the look of a mother hen with ten chicks.

"That's the one," he said proudly, "you'll have everything you need there."

"I expect you're dying to get started," he waxed, "let me know if you have any problems."

From the anticipation of the pleasure of owning a computer, I was actually terrified when it moved in. Plugging it into the electrics was a complicated procedure and not without its own natural hazards because we were lit by an industrial generator which frequently suffered from blackouts. At the prospect of operating the new machine – my heart sank. A possible source of help was this '*Manual for Idiots*' which came with it written in French, German and Dutch.

"My brain isn't meant for the technological age," I pleaded, almost in tears when the senior engineer came home from work. "I think I'd rather have a sewing machine."

In a couple of days I could switch the computer on, find a blank page and write my name at the top. Apparently you had to wake it up and send it to sleep. I made friends with a mouse and a disk defragmenter. Life became a series of snacks between 'cutting and pasting.' Complaints from the male half of the household were met by scrawled messages on the kitchen table saying, 'sorry about the dinner. Insufficient memory.' After a crash course from a friend, my flying fingers were busy writing. I never realised there were so many different languages Expressions like 'headers' and 'footers' with 'justified vertical alignment' became part of breakfast conversation.

After two weeks of 'crashing out' and 'booting up' I could not leave my machine alone. How had I managed to live so long without one? The benefits of a word processor not only fired up my inclination to write letters home but set me on the road to the publication of my first book. Barrie's only complaint was that I spent more time writing than cooking.

Everyone on the camp was anxiously awaiting the outcome of tenders which had been submitted for the new job up at Mohale, on the Senqunyane River, where the next phase of the project would be built. It was to be the largest of the three main contracts of Phase 1B, due to start in March 1998. Officially, we had now been told that Barrie's contract would extend beyond original plans and our release date from Leribe would probably be the spring of 1998.

"Would you like to stay here if we got the contract for Mohale?" asked Barrie as we sat by the heater writing out invitations. Glenns and Willoughbys were flying on and off the list. It was the stuff of nightmares and arguments. The guest list grew. Barrie was meditative and musing and kept putting pencil marks across my 'definites' and writing, 'who?' in red pen in the margin. Richard Syms, the vicar at All Saints, Datchworth, had kindly agreed to officiate on 11th October for our ceremony and include a baptism service for Abigail.

"I'd be thrilled if we could stay in Lesotho for another couple of years – who do you think will win the contract?"

"No idea, but it'll be very different from Leribe. Higher up for one thing. Mohale is much more remote than here. Phase lB includes the interconnecting tunnel between Mohale and the Katse reservoir. The tenders have gone in. It's up to the people at the top who decide these things. Who knows?"

Many of the environmental and social impacts of the Mohale project were well under way. Early consultations with local communities to inform and prepare them for the start of construction had taken place, as well as matters of resettlement and compensation. The project would involve hundreds of new jobs and the beginning of a whole new phase on a different construction site. Wherever possible, workers would be recruited from villages which were directly affected. This meant that large numbers of Basotho would benefit from employment. Resettlement programmes had already begun. There was a feeling of expectancy around the whole camp.

Going to England for our wedding blessing in October grew firm in our minds. In the deepest corner of my heart, I was suffering from strangulated indecision. My daughter needed help. We didn't know what Abigail's future was….but how could I refuse to stay in Africa with my husband? I began to suffer from sleepless nights. The answer was not going to be simple

We had recently discovered a new global telephone link by satellite from America. The company promised fantastic results. First you rang a number in U.S.A. and then put the phone down quickly. They rang you straight back and the connection was made – far cheaper than by any other telephone company – forty per cent cheaper, they said. It sounded too good to be true. When the bill came it was four times what we usually paid. They had omitted to tell us their system didn't work in Lesotho. Over the next two weeks, it transpired that we could make cheap calls to anywhere in the world except to their Complaints Department. It was not often that Barrie lost his cool. Distress rockets - visible in the entire southern hemisphere - went up from our home phone line. I found it a rare sight. Using words I had never heard before, Barrie eloquently put their little satellite out of orbit The company was never heard of again. We reverted to Lesotho Telecom who were once again on strike.

At last my computer had come into its own. Letters to England about our forthcoming trip could be written much quicker. My musical sister Marje was delighted by the invitation to play the organ at Datchworth for our 'do'. She was heavily into country dancing and energetic 'Eightsome Reels'.

"Can you play one of your musical interludes without breaking into a gallop during the first few bars? Don't forget Barrie suffers from gout and

I've got a bad back....?" I mailed her. "How nimble is your *Handel's Largo*, not to mention *Ave Maria* and *Queen of Sheba*-the arrival of?"

A first grandchild was expected on Barrie's side and the parents had very cleverly arranged it for mid -September; another reason for us to be home that month. Secretly, we hoped he or she would be born early and make an appearance as our youngest guest.

The invitations were finally agreed and posted. On paper, the Glenns and Willoughbys plus friends looked a tidy pile. There was nothing further to worry about once I arrived in England except to buy a new outfit, meet with the vicar, the caterers, the musicians, have urgent dental treatment, see my doctor, organise the reception, decorate the hall and choose the wine for the main reception. With reliable phones – it might just be possible. Barrie was due to fly to England a few days before our big day.

On my last visit to see Rose and Stephen, I had taken a pair of Barrie's old hiking boots and three pairs of scouts' socks for Walter.

"Thought you might like these Walter."

His face lit up. The boots were a fine fit. He put them on and grinned with pleasure.

"I've never had such a good pair of boots.... Tell Barrie I thank him. I'll give the socks to my father."

Walter had been busy helping his father to write the letter to Reverend Syms telling him about St John's Church, what it stood for and how their community endeavoured to meet the demands of increasing numbers of destitute families. I was to deliver it to Datchworth Parochial Church Council members so that they might arrive at a final decision.

St John's Church of the Apostolic Faith Mission at Ha Simone was founded in 1939 and based on the Anglican Church of Lesotho, with the same basic doctrines and principles as the Church of England. It has grown in stature and is the centre of worship for many thousands of people. The established mother church of St John's in Durban has a large and dedicated following. At their small church in Ha Simone (Stephen calls it the 'Branch line') Stephen and Rose uphold the same clarity of vision and spiritual care to the people in the lowlands of Leribe, Maputsoe and Butha-Buthe. They run it on a shoestring of goodwill and empty pockets. With single-mindedness and hard work they both carry out their duty as church leaders, at times exhausted by their duties, at other times completely worn out.

"It will all be done," Rose often said. "God will help us." She seemed to possess an extra degree of composure and serenity. There was a working brain in Rose, which was nourished by her unfaltering faith in the Lord. She believed in the power of prayer. Where Stephen sometimes went at a problem like a bull at a gate, Rose calmly set about orchestrating the finer details. Whatever the Lord called upon her to do, she tackled on a no nonsense basis.

"Petros, you will have your tooth out today," Rose said one morning, with a brisk nod towards the *stoep*. The procedure was purely a matter of number three son sitting down, opening his mouth wide, while his mother pulled with a piece of cotton. Such moments were rare but dentistry was carried out at home just like any other task. The extraction took precisely five minutes.

Rose went back to her job of winnowing, while Petros returned to the pasture. It was Rose's job to separate the kernals of maize rom the chaff in a plastic bucket standing in a head wind behind the house, until there were enough to put under the grinding stone. The grinding stone is a valuable family possession. Then the ground maize is cooked in a three legged pot until it becomes like a stiff porridge, known as *Mealiepap,* served with stewed greens or soured milk. On festive occasions, they might eat meat or chicken.

For those who have no personal experience of the rugged nature of Lesotho, it requires a little imagination to visualise the hardships and courage of mountain dwellers. Books by earlier missionaries tell of the loneliness of priests, who travelled hundreds of miles on horseback to bring Christianity to these areas Today many different kinds of churches flourish. From the times of their first King, Moshoeshoe the Great, missionaries have been welcomed. Moshoeshoe was an enlightened progressive leader, who is considered one of Africa's great statesmen. Realising the need for his people to acquire Western education to compete in the new world, he invited the Paris Evangelical Missionary society to establish a mission station in Basutoland.

In those days (early 1830s) it would have taken a journey by sea of three to four months to sail from Europe to Cape Town. In addition, a journey from the tip of South Africa to Lesotho by ox cart or horseback would have taken another few months. The courage and sacrifice shown by travellers of that time should not be underestimated. Christian churches everywhere owe a great deal to those first French pioneers, Arbousset, Casalis and Gosselin and others who came to bring the word of God and start the first schools.

The emergence of the modern Basotho nation is attributed to the integrity and compassion of Moshoeshoe, The Boers wanted to take away his territory. The king defended his tribes from attack by building a fortress near Butha-Buthe and later on at Mount Thaba Bosiu, the flat -topped mountain near Maseru, which he made into a safe retreat for his people. He wanted peace above all and believed Christianity was the key to a settled future.

In the past, a chief would be elected as the spokesman of every village. With the help and wisdom of his ancestors, he would represent social order. The chief's dwelling would be in the centre of the main homestead, his principal wife next to it and those of junior wives in rough order of seniority in a circle facing inwards. Alongside the huts would be the *kraal* where his animals were kept. If a man was polygamous each wife was allocated her own house and fields for the use of herself and her dependants. The women would be responsible for collecting water, grinding meal, cooking and raising the children. They must also understand the sociably acceptable task of brewing beer.

The system of chiefs and missionaries and the king's good judgement began a stable society. Many permanent settlements grew around the foothills of Lesotho. Moshoeshoe was regarded as the father of their nation and the people looked to him for leadership and guidance. Many of his relatives, members of the Royal household, highest chiefs and other important leaders were baptised Christian. The King himself, despite his support of the mission stations, would not convert to Christianity. He realised, wisely perhaps, that the old traditionalists would not find such a move favourable and it would probably have split the nation.

Each village was made up of several units of the extended family. There was no historic or traditional format that bound them, as they were basically a collection of different tribes. Although the various groups who have come to be known as the southern Sesotho today, had much in common linguistically and culturally, they were not united politically. *Moshoeshoe's* people came from a large number of different 'clans'. The integration of these clans grew over a period of time.

Everything in the letter to Richard Syms was written in best English and full of charming *exempli gratia* about themselves. It wasn't an easy letter to write.

"We will pray for the people in England who want to know our church, that they will be a sister and a brother to us." Stephen put down his pen. "When will we know the result of our letter?"

"I can't tell you Stephen. We must wait for some time I think." I did not want to raise their hopes too much. "One small village in Hertfordshire, England will soon be reading about you and making a decision whether to go ahead with a link. Did you tell them about this year's poor harvest?"

"No, I didn't tell them that Nettie," answered Rose. "They wouldn't understand how it is in our country....it is a matter for us to deal with ourselves, "she said proudly. "Sometimes we can eat the weeds which are called '*theepe*'. It is like wild vegetables and we like it when it is cooked."

Theepe can be eaten from September to December and even through the summer when there is no *mealie* to be had. Once more Rose had turned negative into positive. I wondered what the outcry would be in my country if weeds were the only diet for weeks on end.

The debate of whether it was better to burn off the maize fields at this time of the year was still raging. It is said that when it rains, these areas are vulnerable and the thin soil would be washed away altogether. Stephen's opinion was that it was better to leave the remaining crop for the cattle to salvage and not burn the residue. He would miss the early growth of the healthy green grass at the beginning of the season but he had to make a decision. It was a dilemma facing every farmer.

Soil erosion is still a big problem all over Lesotho. Once erosion has thinned and damaged the soil and the ground is only partially covered with vegetation, the variety of plants decreases. The small bushes disappear altogether. These are the only brushwood for lighting fires. Hence, stories of the people cutting down telegraph poles for firewood.

Erosion affects the land in a number of ways. Most of the rainwater runs off quickly and the soil cannot act as a sponge. Surface water goes into the nearest river and does not seep into the ground. This can lead to floods or droughts and the cycle is repeated until the surface of the land cracks and opens – seen in many places in Lesotho. These deep gullies are known as 'dongas'. In recent years, more and more rivers have dried up during late winter or early spring. On the higher mountains where cattle, sheep and goats are reared for grazing, the fertile soil is washed off during heavy rainstorms and deposited on the low lying areas.

The village where Rose and Stephen live has many interesting geological features. There are dinosaur footprints along the river bed just below their church. In the Upper Triassic period, three hundred million years ago creatures of many kinds existed in Lesotho, some of which were dinosaurs. At some time there had been an ancient dried up lake. Along the banks of the Subeng River which runs through Ha Simone about four hundred metres from the road bridge, two different kinds of fossil footprints can be seen. There are several well-defined claw shapes of a three-toed almost bird-like footprints made by fleet footed dinosaurs who probably ran mostly on their hind legs, the *Prototrisauropus rectilineus.* Then the heavier ponderous five-toed crescent shaped footprints, repeated along the river bank at intervals. Somewhere it is written that this creature took ten steps.

It was Walter who first showed us these impressive remains of antiquity. I remembered clearly that day in early February when Walter, lean and tall and dressed in his best suit for the occasion, waited by the Ha Simone bus-stop for Liliane and I to arrive. He had invited us to come and meet his parents a few days after I had been stranded in his village on the main road between Leribe and Butha-Buthe in my car.

"There are some dinosaur footprints in our river," he had told us.

"Dinosaur footprints!" Liliane and I had stared at each other in amazement.

From that day our remarkable friendship with the Makibi family began. In the hot drowsiness of that memorable afternoon, we walked down to the river and saw with our own eyes the evidence of giant creatures who existed millions of years ago. Walter led the way.

"Unbelievable!" Liliane and I had exclaimed. "What a thrill! How old are they Walter?"

"Rains have fallen on these rocks for centuries. Storms have blown. The sun has baked the ground. These creatures left footprints in the mud of the great lake, which have hardened. and turned into stone. Many people come to see the rocks," said Walter earnestly, "we see cars stop on the road and then people start walking towards our church. We know they have come to see the dinosaur prints."

He shielded his eyes from the sun and gave a dazzling smile. "We know they are important in the history of mankind. Somewhere there is a book which tells about them."

"At that time Africa was not isolated from the rest of the world was it?" I mused, trying to desperately to recall my school geography lessons. "We were all one continent."

It was a difficult concept to absorb.

Liliane nodded.. "What must it have been like for early explorers to find them? Where can we find out more information Walter?"

"Go to Morija Museum" he answered, "in the Archives there. I promise you will find out lots of things. Some famous explorers came from France."

Liliane raised her eyebrows and grinned "We go to Morija, soon, Annette."

*   *   *   *

It was now the middle of Africa's winter. Barrie and I had promised ourselves a trip to Kimberley, the Diamond City, on our next short break. It is about ninety miles west of Bloemfontein, five hours drive from Leribe, via the N8.

In 1867 the first diamond was found north of the Orange River. In the 1870s fifty thousand diamond prospectors converged on Kimberley in the hope of becoming part of the wealth which was up for grabs. A gaping 500metre wide cavity known as 'The Big Hole' now exists where thousands of diggers scratched in the earth, hoping for a lucky find.

When in 1914 De Beers closed the mine, twenty two million tonnes of earth had been excavated, entirely by pick and shovel and fourteen and a half million carats of diamonds had been recovered. It is the deepest hole ever to be mined from the surface.

The weather had turned very brisk, winter clothes came out of the trunks and we travelled with hot water bottles and blankets in the car. Langberg Farm in the Karoo had the coldest accommodation we had ever known. It was a beautiful farmhouse scattered with lemon groves and shady vines, as described in the brochure. The hospitality was wonderful.

Farm breakfasts eaten with your coat on, can taste divine. South Africans don't seem inclined to spend money on heating. Instead, they give you hot water bottles, brandy to drink and mountains of warm blankets. The dining room was so cold I actually didn't finish my spiced *bobotie,* peach flambé with fresh cream and coffee with liqueur. We took a small brandy each and fled in haste to feather beds. The pillows were decorated with chocolates and wild scented roses….and we were given a bowl of ice cold water in which to wash.

Peacocks the equivalent of English farmyard cockerels, woke us at dawn. It was one of those days when you could taste the frost on your skin the minute you put out a hand from the bed covers. We breakfasted on creamy porridge and honey, turkey eggs and ham - thick enough to sole your boots – still wearing coats. By then the yellow sun had warmed the ground and farmyard sounds drew us out of doors.

Fortified with enough body fuel to last us a week, Barrie and I set out for the 'Big Hole' to look for diamonds.

"Walk with your head down and pick up anything that glitters, honey."

"I promise I'll share it with you."

Today the town of Kimberley is a tangle of streets surviving from the days when it was a rowdy shanty town, sprawling across the *veld,* where men from all over the world pitched up to go diamond prospecting. In those days of the diamond rush greed was the main motivator. Life was tough. Most of the prospectors lived in tents although some built small houses. Living quarters were extremely basic and squalid. At first it was thought that there were diamonds just below the surface, which allowed virtually anyone with a shovel to get lucky.

On further excavation many diggers faced dangers of collapsing earth, where small areas were roped off. At one time thirty thousand men were working in a huge crater, criss-crossed with a spider web of ropes and pulleys for hauling out the earth. It resulted in chaos, when sub-division after sub-division caused squabbles and fights between the diggers.

In the late 1800s the price of diamonds fell because of over-production. This allowed greedy investors to buy cheap claims which later made them into diamond-rich barons. Dishonesty and corruption were par for the course. In 1871 Cecil Rhodes, the son of an English parson, had arrived on the scene. He bought every claim and every mine he could lay his hands on. In twenty years virtually the entire diamond industry was owned by one man. Rhodes had become the richest and most powerful man in Africa.

Rhodes was a favourite of Queen Victoria and in 1890 he was elected Prime Minister of the Cape. Not satisfied with personal wealth and power, he dreamed of extending the British Empire throughout the length and breadth of Africa., setting up resentment among South Africans. Eventually he came to grief and was forced to resign as Prime Minister, causing embarrassment for the British Government. After several more major political and financial escapades, Rhodes died in 1906, leaving a legacy of wealth which redeemed his reputation somewhat, by setting up Rhodes Scholarships for the benefit of students from around the Commonwealth to study at Oxford University.

The Mine Museum is a wonderful mish-mash of buildings representing cottages, shops, auction rooms, taverns - things to remind you of the days of prospecting. Saloon bars where many a squabble broke out looked more hospitable than they would have done in Cecil Rhodes' time when he and Barney Barnato were in charge. There's Barney Barnato's Boxing Academy, the diggers tavern, the diamond buyers' offices and De Beers' private Pulman Railway Coach full of treasured items. Exquisite silver tea services with crystal glass decanters set for a meal which one could only imagine. Starched linen and pure silk tablecloths. Curtained apartments furnished with leather writing desks, where secret letters could be written. Ivory inkwells fashioned with jade. Accoutrements and fancied treasures – the best that money could buy.

Museum shop windows displayed items of period fashion. Saloon bars flaunted a collection of frills and furbelows, ankle-length pantaloons bedecked with lace and ribbons, worn by the scantily dressed floosies who danced in the bars. Wherever there were men in numbers, one could expect a following of females. In those days of instant wealth, a man could be a bachelor in the morning, married by noon and the lady, a rich widow by midnight. The bigger the share-out, the more suitors a man could accrue.

Prospecting came to an end in the 1930s when open cast mining became too dangerous and many lives were lost. The mile round 'Big Hole' filled with water. It looks eerie and gruesome now – the derelict towers standing guard at the top, not like the kind of place that has produced 2,722 kilos of beautiful diamonds. A lake of green water - deep, irksome and foul.

Close by, a shaft was sunk to open up the Kimberley Mine, in the name of modern technology, to a depth of 1,100 metres. One could only imagine what it was like to work in a mine in those early days. Deep in the network of tunnels without light or fresh air, miners at the mercy of drilling and crushing machines in the darkness would hear sounds of blasting and falling rock and the noise of steel chains hauling up truck loads of muck. All this day after day, with a mountain of granite above. The mine closed in 1914 after producing 14.5million carats of diamonds.

To the south of Kimberley rises a skyscraper known as Harry Oppenheimer House, where all South Africa's diamonds are graded and valued. In De Beers Hall, some of the world's most exciting uncut gems are on display, including the largest in the world, the 'Eureka' diamond, discovered in 1866.

In a small theme park with an almost fairground atmosphere. We did try our hand at picking out small diamonds from a tray of gravel. One gets a real sense of the lucky gambler streak at this point.

"If you find the real gem, it could change your fortunes for ever," said the taciturn character taking the money at the gate. "There's one in every tray."

With a Tony Hancock smile, the man smirked oddly and I couldn't make up my mind whether he was tipping us the wink or merely squinting, from underneath his greasy flat cap. There wasn't a hint of humour in his expression.

With glee we remembered the thrill of the 'roll-a-penny' pinball machines in the amusement arcades of our youth. Mountainous heaps of tiny pieces of stone and carbon mixed with worthless gems of glass, danced before our eyes. The reward....one real diamond. With a vision of being able to afford himself that vintage Aston Martin sports car, Barrie dived in.

After two tons of dust had gone up my nose, I left him - still digging. Half an hour later, covered from head to toe with a fine layer of grey pebbledash, my other half stumbled up the steps to the refreshment area.

"I don't think there's anything in those trays," he said with childish disgust and a nod towards the ticket collector from East Cheam. "I bet he couldn't bloody find it."

We couldn't leave Kimberley without visiting *Magersfontein*, the battlefield made famous during the Boer War, between Boer and British. In 1899, many soldiers of the famous Scottish Highland Regiment lost their lives. It was inhospitable country to those young men. They lay in their trenches in disarray, not enough water to drink - punished by the scorching African sun.

The regiment was ordered to launch an attack on the Boer trenches. No one had checked on the position of the Boer ranks. At the onset of their charge, they were shocked to find the Afrikaners were much nearer than they thought and on level ground. The massed ranks of Scots were cut down within yards. Row after row of them. Pinned by barbed wire and hit by shells and mortar fire until all were dead. The temperature rose to 44 degrees in the shade. Hundreds of young men died, not to mention horses, laying in agony on top of one another, while marksmen picked off their comrades. No field ambulances were able to reach them.

The graveyard was headed by a lone Celtic cross, inscribed with the names of more than seven hundred Highlanders - in granite. It was a pitiful reminder of the victims of needless slaughter. Here was a real sense of savagery and death. I was struck by the utter barrenness of the soil, the ghost-ridden open ground and harsh dry grass. One could almost imagine the fever of cries from wounded and dying men.

The mania of war in any clime is a terrible thing, but this foul killing field was a sobering experience for us, having sons of our own. Almost without exception, names of the dead began with the Scots 'Mac'. I thought of young men torn from their homeland at such a young age. Through the silence of the afternoon, a haunting eerie sound of bagpipes swirled in the air, filling my ears and my mind. A final lament in this far-off field of war.

We left this unhappy place, glad that we had seen it, but not sure how we would forget.

Chapter 10

Praying for the Rain

People who lived in the *rondavels* as high up the mountain as Grandma Makibi had a big advantage over the people down in the valley. They could see everything that happened on the tarmac road which moved like a river below them. They didn't have to come down the mountain to ask if the maize was being harvested or if the cattle had moved across the valley. They were afforded panoramic views of the Malutis, could see the river and St John's Church, knew when the weeding had started by observing the coloured scarves of the women workers scattered across the landscape. They watched the taxis pick up and drop off passengers at the bus stop and although it was too far to recognise anyone. They knew the regular pattern of comings and goings along the main highway through Ha Simone. Funerals could be seen for miles as there was always a marquee erected for the mourners and by this, the folk on the mountain would get to know who had died.

The idea of all the senior citizens living together at the top, each in their own small house, seemed common sense. It was effectively a retirement home without a warden.

It was mid July when Walter, Emily, Joshua and I went up to visit 'the old lady', as Stephen called her. Joshua had been a herd boy until he was eleven years old. Now he was studying at school and trying to catch up on his education. He was a charming boy with gentle manners and a quiet disposition; one of the thousands of Basotho children whose life had been spent herding cows, both winter and summer. Attending school was all that mattered to Joshua now and his ambitions knew no bounds. As we slowly wound our way upwards he told me that he hoped to become an engineer.

The views over the mountains were cut-glass clear and every stick and boulder seemed razor sharp. I had forgotten what the word 'pollution' meant since living in Lesotho. Fresh air at 1,700 metres was never less than exhilarating. How stunning the Malutis looked today, with mimosa spreading along ridges, crevices and along the shelves of bare rock. Heavy with blossom, their cow parsley heads peppered the saffron shade. At the side of the track, stalks of picked maize poked up their headless stems like tin soldiers – just like any English harvest. But no combined harvester had done this job, only raw hands and aching shoulders.

"You see Nettie, in the old days when the marauders were coming across the plain, the old people would know they were coming and have time to prepare."

"Prepare for what?" I asked Walter. I felt the sun on my back as we climbed.

"To roll big rocks onto the enemies or to go and hide themselves. This was their only defence," he explained.

"Does Grandma know we're coming to see her today?"

"Yes, somebody will see us coming and tell her. They will all know she has a white lady visitor. I hope she's not drunk today. If the *joala* is good she might not be very sober. We'll see when we get there. But she'll be pleased to see us – she loves visitors."

Grandma Makibi, a septuagenarian, was queen of the *joala.* She supplied the whole village. Who could blame her if she wanted to indulge in the art of brewing beer in her old age. There wasn't much else to do.

"What does she put in the *joala* Emily?"

" Oh I really don't know Nettie, anything she can find – judging by the smell, it could be a pair of old boots."

"Oh no! Really?"

"Well it always smells so revolting, but the people still come and drink it." She wrinkled up her nose in mock despair. "All I know is she has a nice time in her old age. She has no money and she hates the winter. She usually comes to see us about once a week except in the cold weather. Then she hibernates. We always come up every few days to make sure she is well. Some of the old people die in the winter. It's too cold for their bones."

"What does she eat?"

"You'll see when you go inside her house."

I stopped asking questions and concentrated on where I was putting my feet. The path was rough and the potholes deep. The usual army of strangers stepped out with us. A white person in rural regions will always be followed and stared at. Today it was a gaggle of girls from the school who hid their faces when you looked in their direction.

We had almost reached an expanse of flat rocks with a few trees erupting from stony soil. As if from nowhere, Grandma Makibi appeared walking quickly towards us, holding up her stick. She wore a blue dress with a blanket tied round her waist and a white hat. Her tiny frame was all energy and fire crackers and plenty of shout.

"Oh my goodness, she looks a bit angry Nettie, she has something to say to us," Walter said quietly. He was directly in the firing line. Grandma did not mince her words. To her, Walter was still a small boy, not a confident twenty-four year old athlete. There was no question who was the boss. Admonishing him with her stick, Grandma fired her bullets while Walter hung his head. She could shout loud for such a small person. Not a word of English was spoken but I knew that Walter was apologising.

She beckoned us up the path in front of her house and led us purposefully to the door. She didn't walk – she hurried. Every now and again she turned and yelled something at Walter – lest he forgot what it was he should be reminded of. He just smiled his lovely smile and let her carry on.

In the middle of the room stood one small table covered with a plastic tablecloth with a chair beside it. The walls were painted turquoise blue. There was a chest of drawers in the corner and a picture of Christ on the wall, otherwise the room was bare, except for the linoleum floor.

We stood around the table while Grandma sat on the one and only chair. Her eyes shone with excitement. She looked so small in the faint light from the lace-curtained window. Walter and Emily translated.

"Grandma is very pleased that we've come to visit her. She's never entertained a white lady before. She apologises for not being able to speak to you in English."

"Emily, would you tell her that I am also *nkhono.*"(grandmother)

This news produced a beaming smile accompanied by a squeal of delight. She took both my hands in hers. Those high cheekbones, the thin aquiline nose...a face once beautiful. Her skin was very black – yet the features in her now wise old face did not have the negro full lips or wide nostrils; there was some other ancestry here. Tribal genealogy was not my forte, but I felt sure ancestral clans of some other part of Africa were here in this room.

"Thank you for inviting me," I replied, wondering what I should do if she offered me *joala.* I took out a photograph of Abigail and placed it in front of her - time for the two of us, though belonging to opposite ends of the world, to share a precious moment. She looked at me full in the face, picked up the photograph and uttered a torrent of words I didn't understand but their meaning was plain. I blinked back my tears.

"Nettie, you asked what Grandma eats. Come and look," said Emily.

In a second room, spotlessly clean and neatly furnished, was a single bed with a blanket laid on top and in one corner, heaped on the linoleum, the old lady's next few months' rations. Just as my Grandmother used to have coal delivered into her cellar to see her through the winter, Grandma Makibi had a store of *mealie* poured onto the floor. She would know when her stockpile was running low by just looking at it. No complicated decisions about the pantry shelf – just a pile of yellow grains in the corner of the bedroom. The only other commodities she quested after were sugar and salt.

A few yards from Grandma's house stood a small traditional *rondavel* built from mud and clay with a thatched roof and a door – no windows. We took a step inside into semi-darkness. Animal skins covered the earth floor and piles of raw sheep's wool sat in heaps around the fire in the middle of the hut. Smouldering ashes emitted a few wisps of smoke and a sour smell hung in the air. A tin bucket was thrown on the side. One could imagine the ambience of the gathered company, who would have been here to witness its brewing, waiting for the fermentation stage, holding out their plastic cups to taste the frothy beer.

Again, I asked the question. "What is in the *joala?*"

The answer, translated into English, was "barley, oats and wheat....and some other ingredients."

It began to get colder as the afternoon waned. Grandma's neighbours, all curious to know who her visitors were, came out to say goodbye, including the communal cow, who rejoiced in the name of 'Breakfast'. Walter patted her rump with affection.

"She's good for when the *joala* runs out," said Emily, grinning, "that's if she hasn't gone for a walk."

I looked down for the last time to the stunning view below. The sun was going down and the sky was turning pink. Half a dozen senior citizens waved us off. Grandma smiled and prodded her grandson one last time. It seemed this country bred the sort of characters who were needed to live in it. Her childhood had been a harsh one. As a young girl, she had been made to walk for days to gather firewood which she carried home on her head, even in the coldest weather.

Grandma Makibi was old now, her days of fetching firewood were over. She had five grown grandchildren to help her and a fine son and daughter-in-law. She was not one to sit and wait for death. She was the kind who would meet him full on, still brandishing her stick, somewhere along the mountain track.

Down in Makibi's yard preparations for a journey were under way. Stephen wore a suit and Rose was ironing church uniforms on a table in the yard with a flat iron. A suitcase lay by the door and Fred was sitting in it. Walter left us to go inside his house across the yard. Later I saw him asleep on his mattress.

"We'll see you and Barrie at Teyateyaneng on Sunday, Nettie. When you arrive at the gate just ask anyone to come and find us," said Rose. "There will be hundreds of people and you may not find us easily. Stephen will be busy at the river with baptisms for most of the day."

"Will it be a big festival?"

"It will last more than a week, people come from everywhere – as far away as the Transkei. We're pleased that you and Barrie will come. I want you to meet some important people there. Petros will look after everything here. Somebody has to see to the cows."

Rose's lined face gave away her weariness. She had been on her feet since early dawn.

"Thank you for going to visit my mother-in-law, Nettie. She needs company now, as she has been in mourning for too long." We walked slowly towards the car. "Her husband - he died last year. In our culture when a husband dies a wife must wear black for a year. It's good to see her smile again. Was she drunk?"

"No – she was fine. I think she enjoyed having visitors."

"Oh, the story of you going up there will be news for a long time. No one from the engineer's camp has been ever been there. The old folk will be celebrating tonight."

"In *joala?"*

"Of course."

The next morning, someone from Teyateyaneng came to fetch them in a truck. Justice and Emily went with their parents to help set up their tent. I wondered how they would manage. Their belongings were so few. Walter was to follow in a couple of days. He was to hold the service at Ha Simone in the absence of his father with the help of Augustinus, who was staying at school for some extra studies. Petros knew his duties well and anyway preferred to be with his beloved cows. Bernice had gone to stay with an aunt. There was no food in the house and Rose had only a few coins to leave on the kitchen table. The boys would have to manage until their mother returned.

17th July was the King of Lesotho's birthday and a national holiday. LHPC camp offices closed down for the day. Barrie and I decided to go to Bethlehem and invest in decent haircuts. Hairdressers in Lesotho were non-existent and I was fed up with chopping chunks out of my hair with kitchen scissors. We also needed some African music to play at our wedding party.

"Why don't we go to the cinema? There might be a good film on."

"That sounds like a good idea as the computer's broken down," I said with feeling, given the uninspiring option of no telephone, no bar and an empty fridge. "We could even do some food shopping. They might even have some imported stilton…you never know. I dreamed about it the other night."

We both laughed, remembering how we used to take our favourite food for granted. My recurring *Branston Pickle* dreams had lately disappeared.

On the way to the South African border we stopped off at Walter's to drop in some food to see the boys through the next few days. As our car drew up to the house, Walter appeared on the *stoep*. The usually busy courtyard was empty.

It had rained earlier and the sky was an intense violet blue as if a storm was brewing. There was a departure from the normal ambience of the house as if a shadow was hanging over it. Makibis' yard resembled a stage setting for a film. Everywhere was still and quiet. You expected actors and cameras to appear at any moment; the blue door of the house standing open, the red polished *stoep* with two half motor car tyres placed upside down in concrete….. to give the entrance a bit of character. On the opposite side a small square dwelling; the redundant ox-cart standing with its shafts pointing towards the ground. No bare footed children chased up and down. No voices sang out from the church.

"Walter," I called out, "we're on our way to Bethlehem to shop for a few things"….my voice trailed off. Unsaid words hung in the air. As if in slow motion, Barrie put the box of goodies down on the *stoep*. I felt my burden of helplessness. How we lived was nothing like the Makibis. We were about to go out and spend money on ourselves, on luxuries, food, music and entertainment - because in our lives we were utterly divorced from this reality.

"We thought we'd drop by with a few things….. a chicken for you tonight if you would like it, something for tomorrow…." The words stung my throat.

"We'll see you at TY on Sunday, Nettie. Thanks for supper. My goodness, you have no idea what this means. You are always helping us so much."

His voice sounded weak. Embarrassment and guilt engulfed us. Barrie started the engine. The dust on the yard was neat and undisturbed, just as Emily and Bernice had brushed it before they left. Our tyre tracks showed like a camel-train in the Sahara.

Walter slowly lifted his arm to say goodbye but could not raise the slightest hint of a smile. Nothing we said would make anything any better for them. This was how it was in Africa.

We were almost at Caledonspoort. Purple clouds filled the sky and the land was soaked in minutes. The steep grey rocks on both sides glistened with moisture and the road was awash with a river of slip from the pasture. Women from one of the villages were walking along the road ahead of us in slow ceremonial fashion, carrying the clothes of a deceased person on their heads. Several of the women had shaven heads, as a gesture of respect. When someone dies, all their belongings are collected together by the relatives and washed in the river. Then the ancestors are happy.

"There are days when I feel completely alien in this country," I said to Barrie, who was concentrating hard on the twists and turns of the corkscrew road. "I felt so sorry for Walter today….so helpless."

"Where are the passports honey? We'll have to stop at the border gate in a minute. Look we can only do so much, we can't change their lives. Only they can do that. One day things may improve for them. We can only hope and pray their lives will get better in the future. Meanwhile – where are we going for a meal tonight?" He gave my knee a hearty slap, "and Walter doesn't look well either does he?"

The guard on duty saw our number plates and waved us through.

"So you did notice?"

"Of course I did, but I wouldn't embarrass him by saying anything. He would hate that."

Bethlehem was buzzing. It was a typical South African town, busy with traffic and noise. First we went to the butchers to buy frozen meat after making an appointment at a hairdressers for later in the day. It was months since this luxury had been on our agenda.

At the pharmacy I had a long list of medical needs. A helpful assistant at the '*Apteek*' found us everything we wanted. With the jingle of money in his pocket, Barrie bought himself a pair of shoes and a watch he had promised me for our wedding blessing. To his disgust the bank card machine ate his credit card. Suddenly strapped for cash, we found a bank which was actually open and knew what a credit transfer was. To our absolute amazement it was quite a simple procedure and our finances were restored, but the plastic card was lost in the labyrinth of an unfathomable South African banking system.

Meanwhile, I was 'doing Woolworths' - as in Royal Visit! (Woolworths is the equivalent of *Marks and Spencer* in England). The sight of the New South Africa's winter separates in new fabrics, triggered a chain reaction to spend. I had rarely encountered so many bargains and had almost forgotten how to write a cheque.

"Kan ek u help?" said the rosy cheeked girl at the desk.

My memory returned and my pen slipped – several times. At the music shop (there was a music shop!) we spent hours browsing. Listening to tapes was our sole entertainment factor on camp. We emerged triumphant clutching our then-time favourites and looked forward to hours of good listening.

"It's time for my hair appointment. I'll see you in an hour." I left Barrie at Edgars and tripped across to a pink salon full of ladies topped with plastic hats, clouds of hairspray and toxic perm bleach and sat down in front of a mirror. My hair looked like a dog's breakfast. Months of wanton hacking showed.

"Goeie middag, Mevrou, wat is die!" (Hello Madam and what is this?)

"A Lesotho haircut," I replied.

She grinned. That was the end of niceties. From then on it was a wrestling match between the coiffeur, the scissors and me. We came to the conclusion it was better I went home with a well shaped head, rather than hair. It remained to be seen if anyone would recognise me.

Our meal at the funny little restaurant full of potted palms, where the proprietor liked hanging the entire contents of his garden shed from the ceiling, was nice. The art of making a place look interesting, without making it into a joke, hadn't quite worked. The menu was excellent. Cutlets of lamb prepared with roast vegetables and a delicate sauce with wild mushrooms, followed by peach flambé with brandy, produced a predictable and contented afterglow. At the creak of a cork and we lingered to drink a toast to the King on his birthday.

"Het julle die ete geniet?" asked our host. (have you enjoyed your meal.)

"Ja dankie," we both replied.

"Ry veilig huis toe." (safe journey)

"Goeie nag." (goodnight)

Afrikaans did not come easily to either of us, but we managed a few basic words of greeting when pressed. We shook hands amicably and promised to come again. The evening was not expensive and the hospitality warm. We told ourselves we deserved a treat occasionally, though neither of us escaped a feeling of guilt when passing Makibis' homestead on the way back to Leribe. How does one equate these opposing forces, without conducting an all-out attack on one's mental stability?

*   *   *   *

Teyateyaneng Festival was as busy as any English race meeting. By eleven o'clock the showground was seething with people. Looking towards the mountains from the tarmac road, we could see dozens of marquees with flags flying. A fence of barbed wire, possibly three hundred yards long, had been erected alongside it. Lines of wet clothes were drying in the wind.

Hundreds of people were flocking to be baptised. During this ceremony, it was tradition to be fully immersed seven times. The priests had been standing up to their knees in the river since early that morning. Stephen Makibi was one of them.

After talking for a while to a group of children playing *morabaraba* on the rocks, we drove towards the entrance. St John's festival was obviously very popular. There was an air of great excitement in the crowd. In minutes we came to a dead stop in our first ever grid lock - not of vehicles, but humans – similar to the *Kumbah* thronging towards the Ganges. From the crowd stepped a man wearing a suit and a friendly smile. He motioned us to follow. He parted the crowd with his stick and the car inched forward, almost running over people's feet. The organisers had prepared an area for cars, which were few, compared to the number of tents and caravans. With a great flourish our guide motioned us to a good parking spot.

"*Ntate, 'M'e*, we're so pleased to have you at our festival. Are you the guests of Reverend Makibi? I will take you to him. He is with the Archbishop – come with me."

He indicated to stay close to him as the crowds were heaving around us and it would be easy to lose each other. A sea of black faces surrounded us. Those carrying bundles on their heads towered above the crowd, there were small children tied on with blankets, young men carrying mattresses or blankets, old people shuffling along with sticks. A few had arrived on horseback.

Over to our right we could see acres of tents and a melée of campers, housed under anything from a single sheet tied between two posts – to a piece of plastic or an umbrella. In front of us about two hundred yards away, loomed the imposing red sandstone building of St John's mother church, stately and comforting in the fierce sunshine – boldly outlined against the backdrop of the mountains and a clear blue sky. The sound of a band came from somewhere near the church.

Out of the crowd stepped a familiar face. Walter came towards us, smiling, dressed in his white coat with a blue sash, the official St John's uniform. He thanked our good shepherd who left us to go to the main tent.

"Barrie, you have arrived, wow – Dad and Mum will be so pleased – I see you were looked after by Dad's friend. We sent him to look for you. Justice and Augustinus have a stall here. They want you to go and see them – it's right in the middle. First I'll take you to see our tent."

Walter gave me a hug and he and Barrie shook hands – our friendship had come a long way. The significance of our arrival at TY showed in the profound look both men gave each other. That we should be here at all was amazing. When I had suggested it to Barrie, he at first wasn't keen on the idea.

"Love, it will be us going into their territory," I argued, "they want to show us the best that they have. Rose and Stephen want us to be a part of their lives. They want us to celebrate with them. They believe that water is life – baptisms are all part of that."

"I'm not sure Nettie – what if they want us to be baptised?"

"Just pack a towel!" I answered frivolously.

"Okay I'll go – but I am not getting involved in any water sports."

In the clear light of day Walter's handsome face showed no trace of the strained look of a few days ago. Perhaps we had imagined it. He even had a lady with him, who looked as though she were attached to his sleeve. They were overjoyed to see us. In a crowd of two thousand Basotho – we stood out like beacons.

The stall holders were selling everything from a sheep's tail to a donkey's elbow. Petros, who was just here for the day, had made a few *maloti* by selling his drawings and poems. He was an excellent artist. His decorated cards designed with tender loving care by the light of a candle - on very ordinary notepaper were proudly displayed. Augustinus had made dozens of small badges from plastic key rings, emblazoned with the face of the Archbishop. Emily was selling some of her clothes, Justice was trading his home-made candles and joss sticks for burning in the evening – to keep the midges away. Rose's fat cakes had already gone. The combined talents of '*Makibis Inc*' moved me to buy two bottles of psychedelic bath salts, to remind me of our Basotho boot sale. I looked forward to emerging purple and blue striped from the bathroom.

Then Rose arrived, looking resplendent in her blue uniform trimmed with a white crocheted collar, suggesting that later we could see the Archbishop's water blessing ceremony. She was delighted to see us and kept on smiling and holding me by the arm. Many of her friends came to greet us including the lovely large Theresa whom we knew already. You could always tell where Theresa was by her loud infectious laughter.

"When does the blessing take place?" I asked, forced to shout at the top of my lungs in competition with the ladies' band. Smartly in time to their music, approximately fifty or sixty ladies in a blur of blue and white, with bosoms heaving, blowing hard into a multitude of wind instruments, practised their march past. If anyone from the BBC camera team wanted a front page scoop, now was the time.

"This afternoon at two thirty Nettie, would you first like to hear the singing …..it is very wonderful?"

We followed Rose through an army of people to the main door of the church. In the heat of the afternoon the upper windows had been flung wide. The sound of massed voices accompanied by trumpets and trombones reached out to the waiting crowds. Melodic tunes of their beautiful old hymns washed over the heads of the multitude. People around us were joining in, the volume similar to the crowds in Wembley Stadium on cup-final day. The outpouring of praise from people who were surrounded by such poverty really moved me. A thousand voices lifted up to heaven. African singing always has an effect on the hairs on the back of my neck and the lump at the back of my throat. I closed my eyes and held Barrie's hand tightly.

"That is where Stephen is now," said Rose, nodding towards the interior of the church, "he is translating the words of the service into other languages as the Archbishop speaks. We can go inside if you wish."

I had never been in a building this size so full of people praying and singing. On one side there were the people who spoke *Sesotho,* on the other, those who spoke *Zulu* or *Xhosa.* Stephen was a small dot at the front of the church but I immediately recognised his voice, repeating the words of the Archbishop – first in one language then in another, sometimes in English. A tide of human beings united by their suffering, were sharing and shouldering their differences and their faith. Again, the Archbishop's voice amplified loud and urgent, then Stephen broke in translating in his clear strong voice. He was fluent in so many languages.

"Rose, you must be so proud of him," I whispered.

The heat inside was so intense that we didn't stay long. Barrie and the others were still standing around outside.

"Now then Walter, have you been baptised today?" asked my other half, still fascinated by their stories of total immersions.

"I have – at eight o'clock this morning," conceded Walter.

"But you're dry," Barrie laughed.

"Yes – my wet clothes are drying on the fence over there. I can tell you it was cold. Come, I will show you something."

He led us towards a tiled swimming bath with deep water in the middle which was shallow at each side. Small children were having great fun playing in it.

"Look the priest stands in the middle and the people queue on the far side," said Walter pointing. "It's quite a thing to watch. Every person is immersed seven times. The priests stand down in the river as well. But they've finished for today because the main service starts at two thirty."

Emily was standing next to me. She whispered in my ear. "Nettie, the Royal Family have arrived, you will see them. Queen Mamohato is here."

Rose was beckoning us to follow her through the crowds, where we could stand to see the blessing. She pointed towards a concrete arena which had been roped off.

"You and Barrie will be separated," she added, "all the ladies will be here, where we are now – and the men will sit at the opposite end, over there."

We felt strange having to be segregated into gender compartments. I was reminded of a similar incident at a county cricket match many years ago when, after erecting my deckchair in the 'gentlemen's enclosure' at the start of a game between Middlesex and Hampshire, I was politely asked to leave.

The tension around us increased. Gleaming dentures look fabulous in Basotho crowds. Black faces, white smiling teeth, purple cloaks with white collars are very dashing - especially on the young. Priests in long velvet cloaks and black hats dashed around the arena, making sure everything was ready for the arrival of the Archbishop. The logistics of the operation must have been a nightmare. A silver band wearing the St John's distinctive blue and white uniforms - probably a hundred players - assembled at the rear. Barrie was suddenly whisked away by an official and plonked in the gentlemen's enclosure. We could just see each other, and being the only whites, were seen by everyone else as well.

"Emily I've only brought my straw hat – will it do?"

"Yes Nettie don't worry. You weren't to know. Everyone will appreciate the gesture. The Archbishop already knows you and Barrie are here."

A man in a purple cloak suddenly took my arm and inching me forward insisted, "Come come this way."

Before I knew it, the band had started up and I was seated on the front row almost next to the Archbishop himself who was being escorted by his entourage onto the platform. Behind him were several elegant ladies in flowery hats and a few men in suits. The band struck up appropriate Elgar-ish music and dignitaries took their seats.

"Is this the Royal Family, Emily?"

"Yes, the mother of the King, Queen Mamohato and her younger son, Prince Seeiso."

The Archbishop wore an imposing long velvet cloak over a blue robe and a mitre. He carried a tall silver staff. Emily sat on my left. On my right, an elegant lady with long fingernails and a brightly-coloured blanket draped across her shoulders smiled at me as we sat down. I switched on my pocket tape recorder as this was one occasion to remember.

Facing us was a platoon of purple clergy. A plethora of plastic bottles and containers, each tied with a label were stacked in a large arena. The mountain of plastic was about to receive its blessing. Then, it was as if contestants were called to the starting line and someone shouted 'go'. Equipped with bowls of water, a regiment of bishops and priests circled the central arena. They moved slowly round as if on silent roller blades as you could not see their feet. Murmuring prayers, they sprinkled Holy water with white gloved hands, their robes billowing in the breeze.

A very small man carrying a tea-pot, ran round filling up the empties. He would regularly run back to his big bowl of water run all the way round again to catch up with the next empty dish – and pour. It seemed as though his tea pot was bottomless. It might have been better if there were two filler-uppers, but that would have meant they might keep bumping into each other. I was betting on the old priest at the end of the line having the last sprinkle as he moved very slowly and insisted on facing backwards. With impaired vision and no sense of direction, he might have won – but then it wasn't a contest.

At last the imaginary whistle blew and the priests retreated behind the Archbishop, who had risen to his feet, staff in hand - ready to chant blessings and sprinkle even Holier water. This was the moment of glory for the filler-upper. Bending almost double in deference to his most Worshipful Head of Church and walking backwards, it was no simple matter. First he had to decide *how fast* he would be required to pour, *when* he could pour and at the same time make an educated guess as to *how much* he had left in his tea-pot. Any cricket captain would have been proud to field him in the slips. His footwork was nifty and his catching of dribbles superb. What he lacked in stature, he made up for in enthusiasm. In the wake of the last Holy sprinkle the band played appropriate Vaughan Williams-ish music to the satisfaction of the nodding priests.

By this time the crowd's sympathies were with the teapot and it was when the Archbishop retired to his position on the platform, we realised the tumultuous applause was not entirely for His Holiness.

The band was limbering up ready to start. Trumpet players were clearing their wind pipes and making elephant noises behind me. Euphoniums, tubas, whistles and flutes were also creating a small diversion. Then the first oompah ripped through the air like a thunderclap. I turned down the volume on my tape recorder. They were off.

As in First Battalion of the Royal Scots Guards at the Edinburgh Tattoo, the body of St John's Church band was on the move. They launched into a foot-stomping rhythm. As far as the eye could see, in rows of four, they marched forward. Not to be outdone, the giant-sized drums – with Herculean drummers to match, rolled into the chorus of the next hymn with great flamboyance at the rear of the parade. Percussion players carrying tambourines or cartwheel-sized cymbals stomped by, each player in full flood. My position on the front row afforded me the best view in the house. In spectacular formation, the whole shooting match let rip – in heaven's glorious name.

You have to know that Basotho people cannot march without dancing. A throbbing beat, a multitude of brass buttons and belts - some at bursting point round large girths, tight skirts, swinging hips, all doing a kind of three steps forward and two steps back routine. The mood was completely infectious. Every foot in time, every white glove waving, trumpet spit blowing in the wind right past my ear, the marchers went forward. As in any tango or mazurka, precision footwork was all important. The ground trembled beneath us. The moment brought up memories in my mind of a Yorkshire Colliery brass band in the Bentley Park of my childhood. This was one of those tunes which went on and on and just when you thought it was going to end, the drummer would lurch afresh into another verse.

Regally the Archbishop rose to his feet. He stood waiting for the band to stop. He fluttered his gloves and looked very hot in his heavy cloak. Stepping forward, he patiently took a deep breath ready to open his mouth to speak. He took off his gloves, coughed mildly and put them back on again. Meanwhile, the drummer continued banging fit to burst a blood vessel. Quite unable to see anything from behind the rim of his drum, he blindly pounded into the seventeenth verse. It didn't seem to occur to him to stop. All eyes were on His Holiness. Some thoughtful genius standing behind the drummer somehow managed to untie the strap from round the player's neck and mid-bang the instrument fell off his chest. In slow motion the drum rolled forward in front, bringing the solo performance to an abrupt end.

I glanced at Barrie and saw that he was trying not to smile. A few noticeable chuckles rippled through the ranks. With sweating brow the Archbishop finally began his address. Now the crowd greeted him in silence. My straw hat was biting into my head and the sweat ran down my neck Inside the collar of a tight uniform the heat must have been unbearable. Basotho foreheads shone with perspiration. I thought the whole assembly might expire.

Then suddenly, without warning, we were all up on our feet with both arms in the air, praying hard for something. In unison the crowd cried out to the Almighty.

"Emily, what are we praying for?"

"Oh Nettie, we are praying for God to send the rain, just follow me."

We turned to the east and shouted some more. Then 45 degrees round again, each repeated cry louder than before, until the air was full of voices pleading for the heavens to open. By the time we got to North, the sweat was pouring off me. I hoped God would act quickly. The nice lady took my hand and dragged me along with her for some yards. Barrie was some way behind next to the Sergeant Major and was also being cajoled into joining the parade. I kept going, my feet catching the rhythm nicely. I was beginning to enjoy myself. A kind of fanfare loud enough to cause brain damage pounded in my ears. My eyes were on ground level most of the time watching everyone else's feet. Looking up, I suddenly realised that I was only one step behind Queen Mamohato and the Royal party. They were heading straight for the Bishop's banquet. The fanfare was for them.

Without turning to look for Barrie I fled into the milling crowds. This was definitely not for me. I knew my place. The man with the silver stick followed me. A few steps into the crowd and I felt a hand on my arm. Appearing not to notice my protestations he guided me gently back in line. Barrie was at my side now and whispered that we ought to go with the invitation to dine at the Royal banquet, otherwise it would look quite rude. He was right of course.

The Bishop's house was swarming with honoured guests. Stewards in white coats and ladies in flowery hats, all dashed about on Royal duty. A high level of excitement filled the room. Long trestle tables groaned with food. As the queue moved slowly towards the top table, we helped ourselves to plates of lamb with rice, chicken platter with vegetables. The unhurried courtesy of my trusted friend was very flattering as we glided slowly by the Royal party, who were already tucking in. There was plenty of cold ginger beer.... no alcohol. The lady introduced herself as Amelia, and guided us gently through the formalities of Royal banquet procedure.

Reclining in easy chairs, eating as elegantly as possible (without cutlery) receiving interested nods and smiles now and then from purple-frocked priests with plates, Amelia and I chatted like old friends.. She spoke with a beautifully cultured English accent straight out of a debutantes' finishing school.

"This is a day for celebration. To have guests from England is very special...our Archbishop insisted that you were invited to eat in his house. Reverend Makibi and his family are well known to him. As their guests you're automatically his guest also." She paused. Her long fingers patted her neat dark hair. "Afterwards you'll meet one or two members of the Royal Family. Basotho people love to be hospitable to visitors from overseas."

My throat constricted and the chicken got jammed. Barrie gave me one of his stern looks. He thought I was going to do one of my Yorkshire 'eeeeks'. I managed to swallow and look unfazed. I needed to visit the bathroom. There actually was one but I dare not mention it to Amelia. My bladder was bursting. On Lesotho away-days it usually clicked itself onto 'hold'. Not today. Amelia noticed my expression and bid me follow her.

The bathroom was capacious....furnished with lavatories - in pairs. Unceremoniously, I answered nature's call, smiling inanely at the elderly person in the next seat.

Amelia Masupho was quite a lady. She was the Foreign Secretary's secretary and worked on the top floor of the Foreign Office in Maseru. We exchanged telephone numbers and I invited her to come and visit us in return for her kindness today.

"Annette, I would love to come and visit you and your husband in Leribe. Ring my office and we will arrange a date." (It was only some time later that I learned who she really was.)

Afterwards in the garden at the front of the Bishop's house we were invited to speak with Prince Seeiso, King Letsie's brother, newly returned from Birmingham University. According to popular rumour he was a most sought-after bachelor. The Prince was very keen to demonstrate his accomplished English accent.

"Did you enjoy England?" we asked him.

"Everything except the weather." he replied with a smile. "Oh, I liked your race meetings – the horses of course." His dark eyes flashed.

There was nothing supercilious about the Prince. Looking very handsome in his exquisite suit of clothes he declined to be drawn into further conversation as there were many people waiting to speak to him. Handshakes were in order though and I can honestly say I have shaken the hand of a Prince.

Outside once again and surrounded by crowds of people, we searched for our hosts. There seemed to be an exodus of Biblical proportions moving towards the setting sun. Buses were leaving for Cape Town, Durban and the Transkei, Kenya, Botswana and Pietermaritzburg. Travellers wandered around looking for their own vehicle. Hands were shaken and tears were shed. Families hugged families and children fell asleep in the arms of loving grandmothers. Long distance coaches hit the road and roared off in opposite directions. I felt sun kissed and extremely relaxed..

We squeezed as many as possible into our elastic-sided transport for the homeward journey. Walter, Emily and couple of lads with their camping gear were loaded on. Gallons of Holy water sloshed around in the boot. With the crimson sunset blazing across the heavens, we departed. The youngsters were so excited because they were going home by car. By way of a thank you they sang for us all the way to Leribe. Emily's voice would for ever be etched into my memory, singing 'One Way to Heaven' accompanied by the sonorous tones of her 'alleluia'backing group.

"Sing up you lot," cajoled my other half (who hadn't wanted to come this morning) "I can't hear you!"

Chapter 11

A Lot to Learn

On 30th July, a meeting of the Datchworth Church Council had been planned, regarding our request for an official link with Lesotho. Reverend Richard Syms would be putting forward our proposals on the other side of the world. It was more than three months since my visit to England when Richard had promised to put the idea to his committee.

During those same three months, down by the Subeng River at Ha Simone, Reverend Stephen would kneel by the square table with the lace tablecloth, take a light and hold it close to the white candle. Perhaps this year, or next, or the one after that would be the time that help would come. He would pray. The clock on the wall would show five am. Each morning Stephen went into the church a few minutes before the congregation arrived for the sunrise service. Sometimes only a few people came. He was always ready to welcome them.

It would be like a dream come true. Ha Simone was a world away from Datchworth., Hertfordshire. The minds of the Parochial Church Council would be on many village matters and how much money could be raised towards repairs to the church tower. There were always urgent matters to discuss and pressing financial needs for the church. I wished I could be a fly on the wall at this most important of gatherings. If our idea was successful it would be more than I ever hoped.

My day did not consist of a meeting of church elders. Instead a visit to Ha Simone to help Emily with her lessons. To spend time with Rose talking over the problems in their lives. Standing by the river I watched a group of village women approach and set about washing the family's clothes. The outsize packet of *Omo* washing powder looked strange sitting on the river bank.

"Which washing powder are you using?" I called out.

The women held it up for me to see when I asked what they were using. A few sheep came down to view while the energetic gang bent their backs, slapping their clothes on the rocks to get them clean. Wet clothes were then loaded into huge zinc bowls and lifted onto heads. I asked if they would allow me to feel the weight of one of the bowls but failed to even lift it off the ground. Everyone laughed and Emily said something in Sesotho which made them laugh all the more. My attempts were pathetic. All the ladies looked very slim and were physically strong underneath their thin cotton dresses and wrap-around blankets.

"Today is the day of the important meeting in England Emily. Have you remembered?" I said as we strolled back to the church.

"Yes. We said special prayers this morning that the people will accept us."

"There will be an answer soon." I said, pleased that she had remembered.

Walter came to walk with us, "Will it be the answer which means we start to know your church? Myself, I am afraid that that they will not really want to know us…" His baggy shirt hung on his body and I could see the bones in his shoulders poking out. His weight was not as it should be and lately I had caught him looking terribly unwell.

"Walter, I am sure the news will be good. Where's your faith?"

Sitting on the *stoep*, Emily and I did some language work together in preparation for her school examinations. She was a hardworking pupil and deserved to succeed. Several new phrases were added to her English comprehension homework.

"If I pass it will be down to you Nettie. You make things so clear to me."

"As long as you get a good sleep the night before the exam, you'll pass," I told her.

Across the yard Justice had been busy making a fire and the smoke billowed out of the doorway of the hut. The sky over the Caledon was streaked with changing colours and I knew it would soon be time to leave. I never stayed after dark. Emily put down her books and threw a handful of corn. into the huge pan, the size of a dustbin lid – in fact it was a dustbin lid. The kernels crackled furiously. Putting her fingers to her lips she whistled loudly for the boys to come and share. It wasn't long before Fred and the others appeared with open hands, cupped ready to receive. The roasted corn tasted good. I noticed that Walter had gone to lie down. It was unusual for him to be absent when I was leaving.

At five o'clock my Silver Fox hit the track. I bumped crazily over the potholes, where the path turned away from the river up towards the road - the kids waving and running pell mell across the field after me. They could catch up with me again by the bus stop. Pulling away onto the tarmac, the sun full in my eyes, I could just see a multitude of arms waving in my rear view mirror until the incline obscured them from view.

The following Sunday over a lazy breakfast, Barrie and I decided to visit Franshoek Farm just over the border in South Africa. It was our day off. We liked to go off camp if we could. Owned by a dynamic farmer and horse trainer, named Christian Findlay, Franshoek Farm was a sandstone mountain lodge near Rustlers Valley surrounded by hidden gorges, waterfalls and caves containing bushman paintings; the perfect recipe for unwinding, an ideal place for two ardent ramblers who like getaway weekends.

We weren't the bulging muscles and biceps types, but liked to leg it out of Lesotho sometimes to discover our neighbouring valleys. Hiking boots and backpacks breed good conversation. We needed to discuss our forthcoming trip to England and the possibility of a link between Ha Simone and a small Hertfordshire village. Barrie wasn't into the game of polo but watching the horses being groomed and prepared for their next event was interesting. The lodge itself was a thatched building tucked behind the Witteberge Mountains. One or two lean-looking bay ponies were being exercised near the stables as we passed.

About an hour's walk from the farm on the edge of a forest, several gum trees – the kind that two people couldn't touch hands around - had shed their bark. Peeling curling shapes, grotesque and gnarled like the witch-fingers of an Arthur Rackham fairy-story – hung their giant tendrils over our path. We brushed them aside and foraged deeper to look for the water source somewhere nearby. A clear stream gurgling freely over high slime-green rocks opened into a cave of trees – a perfect setting for a scene from Macbeth; an oasis of moss, pine and birdsong. Our boots crackled in some dry bracken and a flight of feathers flew upwards into the high branches. A crested bird with long tail feathers squawked noisily from a patch of undergrowth, clearly disturbed by human voices. We thought perhaps it was a loerie.

Christian the owner of the farm was away. By request, he had permitted us to freewheel his valley and enjoy the peace and tranquillity of this little corner of the Free State. We had met no one all day. Beatrice a friend of ours, who also happened to be mother of the owner, had raved about her son's place. She had told us how it was in all the seasons but she had forgotten to tell us how beautiful it was in winter. Early August was just as she promised – and more.

Without their leaves, larches hung like filigree lace and graceful river bushwillows dropped their seed pods onto a thick carpet of leaves. Their bare branches plaited intricate patterns against the sky. Small rivulets of water criss-crossed our path. The sky was a perfect blue. We took out sketchbooks and began to draw.

In this part of South Africa the soil is fertile. A farmer grows which crops he chooses. His animals have good grazing. There is rain in plenty coming down from the Malutis, and money to be made in wheat and cattle crop, known as lucerne. Franshoek boasts large numbers of sheep and angora goats which roamed everywhere.

Christian's Basotho workers lived in rondavels on the farm and were paid sufficient wages to afford to give their families a good lifestyle. The walls of their houses were attractively painted with bold colours surrounded by a woven lapa-style reed fence. The head of one family was an excellent cook and produced some of the most popular dishes for the people who came to stay. The wives worked as maids in the guest house. Some years ago a son of one of the Franshoek families took part in the European International Games and returned with a gold medal. His name was Jaapie and he will long be remembered as a talented athlete who was proud to come back to Franshoek as a champion hurdler and hero, bearing a top prize.

The thatched lodge with accommodation had been built by Christian himself. It was often filled with paying guests who came to ride and learn the skills of polo. At certain times of the year, when a match was due, rich guests stayed over and this was the healthy side of the business. Christian loved his horses, trained them himself, gave them good stabling and they rewarded him on days when the heat was on and his team were geared up to play a match. In the evenings his restaurant would be bursting with thirsty players and the inquest on the match would go on across the bar for most of the night.

Working seven days a week for many years had earned Christian's lodge a good reputation. He could do every job on the farm and expected high standards from his staff. He could afford to take a weekend off ski-ing on the new slopes at Oxbow once in a while. Before we left Barrie and I called at Reception to book ourselves a dinner date. The cellars of Franshoek Lodge had looked most inviting. After we had come back from England we may have something to celebrate.

*   *   *   *

The following week Amelia rang to say she was coming to Leribe to visit me, to assist me with research on my book. Panic set in. My diary went something like this:

Amelia Masupha coming for lunch – <u>prepare for Royal visit.</u>
Instruct Gideon to let her in at the main gate. Cut flowers and decorate verandah.
Agnes to make bread - allocate a day for finding yeast in Ficksburg.
Gold tooth to be found – lost last week in a sandwich - empty rubbish bins.
Book Buntingford Farm, Hertfordshire for three weeks in October.
Organise concrete slabs to be dropped at Ha Simone – don't forget Henry's pocket.
Pupils from Ha Mohlolo to finish their letters to England – two mornings editing.
Letter from Liliane – coming back from France. Yippee! Must fix a welcome party.
Stephen Purdy (my godson) to visit Leribe with his girlfriend. Difficult to arrange in view of no telephones – contact from Ficksburg street phone – long distance calls, new rules. Cuts you off after three minutes!
Abigail's birthday on 24th. Ring offspring to hear news and send sloppy kisses.

Embarking on the jobs with my usual brand of inconsistent logic, I decided on the last one first. From a kiosk outside Ficksburg Post Office I spent half an hour trying to speak to my children for three minutes each. New South African Telecom rules meant a two-way exchange of news in three minutes. James tended to be monosyllabic until the last few seconds of a conversation and then everything came out in a rush. He couldn't ring us so we used to call him. Recalling his latest dilemma regarding a new job, I decided not to ask. As long as he was well, solvent and Chelsea F.C. hadn't been demoted the news should be the same. It was. Pips started. End of conversation.

After speaking to my daughter, I discovered she had arranged with Reverend Syms that Abigail's christening would on the same day as our wedding blessing at All Saints Church. Things were fine (she sounded a bit vague) but yes, she would like a new dress. A social worker had been to try and help her with Abigail's feeding problems. Lizzie sounded quite stressed. No news on physiotherapy at the hospital. No news on a sight test. An appointment at a clinic for nutritional help.

"Mum, we are both absolutely fine. Dying to see you in October. Love you lots." Pips….

I was left with a sinking feeling in my stomach. In hindsight, perhaps it was better not to call home at all. The silence after I put the phone down was almost a pain. Then I called Carole Purdy in Essex, asking her to pass a message to her son Stephen and his girlfriend Catherine 'somewhere in Durban'.

"Tell Stephen to turn up at four o'clock on 3rd September at Ficksburg Post Office in the Free State and we'll be there to meet him. He can't phone to confirm, no phones on camp – this is Lesotho!"

Carole told me afterwards it was one of the strangest telephone calls she had ever received. No time to think, no contact numbers, just a voice from South Africa – then the pips. Lesotho Telecom must have felt very powerful.

After that, I shopped for yeast powder at the bakery in Ficksburg.

"It will bake a dozen loaves," said the lady assistant.

"I hope so – it doesn't look much like yeast to me. All right, I'll take it."

If I was found guilty of poisoning the Royal family, it would be curtains. In the hot afternoon sun, it was a slog to go food shopping but there would be no meals at home if I didn't. Evidently Shoprite had fresh vegetables in today. I walked through the maze of street sellers trading in dud watches, past the six hour queue of black workers camping on the pavement until their wages came in at the First National Bank – a shabby way to treat people I always thought, and into Shoprite. They were busy having a power cut and all the refrigerators were shut down.

The only thing to do was go into the Library and see if my books had come in. Marlene, the Librarian extraordinaire, who always knew where and how to get things, was on lunch break. Over in one corner of the 'travel' section I noticed one of my ex- students from Thotlisong High School. He was deep in thought when I nudged him.

"Jacob, Hello – remember me?" He looked up and a refreshing smile lit his face.

"Hi - Mrs Glenn, yes of course I remember you – how could I forget the music concert last term. That was such a wonderful event."

"What are you doing here Jacob?"

"I'm teaching myself Afrikaans, otherwise I'll never get a decent job."

"I admire your determination Jacob, so what else is new?"

Jacob lived up on the township outside Ficksburg, known as Meqheleng. He had been one of my brightest students. Aged about twenty five, this gentle giant hated the crime and violence of the area in which he lived and longed to take his brothers and sisters away to a better place. But he had no money.

"I need another language, you see, I only have two languages, Sesotho and English. To earn promotion, I have to speak Afrikaans. The good jobs are all in South Africa. It is what I must do." His big frame shook with emotion as he spoke. "I want to move my family to Bloemfontein. That is a good place. Too many bad things here 'M'e."

He wouldn't exaggerate, I saw in his eyes, those wounds of living through painful years.

"Jacob, do you know where Mr Malebo is – you know, our headmaster of Thotlisong School? I heard that they had moved up to the new premises in Meqheleng. I need to see him again. There is money from the concert fund. I want to tell him the good news."

Jacob's expression clouded. He looked at me anxiously.

"'M'e, I think you shouldn't go up to Meqheleng by yourself. There's big trouble up there. They've tried to set our school on fire… there's a dispute about who should be in the new premises. Didn't you know? There's a picket line round the school building."

"I bet they'd let me in Jacob. Why don't you take me up there. We can talk our way through the picket line. We could use my car for part of the way. I may not have the opportunity again and Mr Malebo knows us both. He'd be pleased about the money…."

Jacob rolled up his shirtsleeves and picked up his books with an expression of resignation.

"Okay 'M'e. You've convinced me. I'll take you there myself. You'll be safe with me."

As we passed the desk, Marlene grinned when she saw Jacob and his briefcase.

"There's a keen worker - spending his time down here studying, when he could be outside with his friends. He's a good man."

"Marlene, I'm going up to the new school at Meqheleng with Jacob. Will you phone and tell Barrie where I am – in case I'm late home."

Marlene was a good friend. She was also an excellent librarian, the right person for the job, often helping the local kids with their homework studies. Nothing was ever too much trouble. She knew their families and their backgrounds and had lived through some of the most difficult years in this town.

Jacob and I drove through the outskirts of Ficksburg and up the hill to Meqheleng, which spread like a rash along the border between South Africa and Lesotho. It had erupted as a place for Africans who had come in search of jobs. Ficksburg could not support them and the biggest problem was still unemployment. Many had arrived with hope in their hearts, from even worse places. On the outskirts, the new arrivals make their houses from anything they can find – pieces of tin, shells of old cars, plastic bin-liners held together with rope and sticks and somehow they fashion a home for a family to live in. Further into the centre of the village, houses made of concrete blocks stood in rows, some with fences and little gardens and here and there, people selling from pavement stalls.

We drove through the 'best streets' with a few brick single storey houses. I noticed broken windows and front gardens which yielded a glut of rubbish tips. Unfortunately the estate did nothing to mitigate the poverty of its occupants. Some families had made an attempt at tidiness, with flower beds and grass lawns. One featured a garden sculpture made from a wheelbarrow heaped with empty drink cans and sprayed bright pink. A plastic garden gnome with paint-peeled eyes, stared from between the handles.

We took a left turn onto a rutted road and parked on a piece of open land with a few other cars.

"This is where we must leave the car," said Jacob coolly. "It's no good going any nearer. You see the high wire fence. That's the new school."

There were several groups of young men hovering around the school gate but they weren't threatening and there was little, if any, action. Jacob's hefty figure and square shoulders, stood out like a landmark. It was obvious he was a respected student as they let us pass through without question. Sticking close to the heels of my companion, I smiled nervously offering my 'Lumelang' greeting as we ran the gauntlet to the gate, which was locked securely with chains. A posse of students gathered inside the fence. Someone shouted through the wire and asked who we were.

Jacob stood his ground. He glanced back over his shoulder to make sure I was okay.

"Please tell Mr Malebo, the Headmaster, I have brought Mrs Glenn to visit his school. She is our English teacher. He will let us through. Please hurry."

A rush of feet across the playground, while we waited outside the barricades. These young ruffians didn't look more than fourteen or fifteen years old. Their intrinsic respect for this white lady, who looked old enough to be their grandmother, melted their scowls and fazed them somewhat. Meqheleng was not without its informers. It would be known that I was not part of their dilemma; a possible reason for their lack of aggression. The spokesman inside the yard re-appeared, his voice a semitone lighter.

"The headmaster says you may come in."

Outsiders bristled. The padlock was opened. Jacob and I entered. The gate was locked behind us. I felt like an outsider from another dimension.

The new brick school building was immensely pleasing to the eye, and a thousand times better than the premises they had previously occupied in Ficksburg, which had been akin to a demolition site. I had been teaching there until a few weeks ago. I had loved my time working for Solomon Malebo. It was an experience I should never forget.

As we rounded the corner of the building, Solomon was running towards us with arms high in the air.

"Annette, you are here with us again!"

He threw his arms round me, picked me up off my feet and twirled me round several times to the amazement of everyone watching, including the heavies who had escorted me from the gate. Solomon was extremely tall and my feet lifted high off the ground. A huge cheer went up from all the kids including those up on the balcony of the first floor.

"My sister, my sister!" Solomon yelled in my ear, while I tried to get a word in edgeways. "You have come back to us – it's a wonderful day that you are here. Did you know the trouble we've had? My school was set on fire – the classrooms were almost destroyed." He set me down on the ground. His handsome face showed his abhorrence at the memory. Solomon was a committed Headmaster, who only ever wanted the best for his kids. His standards were high. The things he had achieved were astonishing – not least the accomplishments of his school choir in national music competitions.

"Solomon, I knew nothing about this, when did this all happen?"

"After the concert, when we moved up to Meqheleng. Another school wanted these premises – but it was our school from the very beginning. There have been terrible things happening. Come inside. I will explain. I want to show you round."

"Jacob brought me up here today, otherwise I would never have found you. Listen for a moment, there's money for your school – for musical instruments. We raised four thousand rands at the concert."

He sat down, his face wreathed in smiles.

"Ahh. That's wonderful Annette, your people did us so proud. We need so much school equipment. By the way, did your engineers enjoy our music?"

I had forgotten how deep his voice was – engaging and full of humour.

"Of course. It was the highlight of the term at Butha-Buthe school. Yes, we collected more than we ever thought possible. Thotlisong choir is legendary. The ex-pats loved it. What voices! It was worth all the hard work... now Solomon you must buy what you want for the school with the money."

"Annette, do you remember the journey across the border on the night of the concert?" He slapped his knee and grinned his huge grin. "We got all the kids across – in spite of the hold-ups and ...... and when the bus broke down......" He broke into a fit of laughter. "Oh my life, will I ever forget!" His eyes sparkled with pleasure and he threw back his head.

"And *dear* Mr Mepetuani, who had to go and find us another bus!" I giggled., remembering the nightmare journey with all the kids on board.

We swung into easy conversation, laughing hysterically at the memory of it all on that evening two months ago. Solomon and his choir of fifty kids - without passports! They had entertained our international audience at Butha-

Buthe camp with African voices and brought tears to the eyes of unsuspecting engineers. And the driver of the bus, Mr Mepetuani drove like a lunatic to get the pupils safely back home to Ficksburg only just in time…what a night it had been.

Solomon keenly showed me into his new entrance hall. From the staff room came familiar voices.

"Hi everybody," I said quietly, putting my head round the door.

In seconds I was overwhelmed by greetings and ululations of delight from the geography teacher who was rather keen on excitement, given the slightest excuse.

"Would you like a verse of 'Glory to God in de Highest' just to remind you 'M'e?"

"If you insist," I joked, "…. came to see your new desks."

"The kids are always asking after you When are you coming back to teach?"

"I'll come up next week with all the photographs – the kids will love the video of the concert. You know it broke the sound barrier!"

"Come Annette, " said Solomon dragging me away for a moment. "I will give you a tour of our beautiful building. Some kind person gave us roses today to plant in the garden - can you imagine the school having a garden…. such wonderful things we can grow next year."

Solomon's excitement about his 'new baby' was utterly infectious. He had been through nightmares to keep Thotlisong School Elizabeth, their music teacher, and I made a date to go up to Bloemfontein to spend money on school instruments. I departed about five o'clock amid cheers, laughter and promises to meet again.

Solomon saw us back across the yard and out of the gate. All was quiet and the heavy brigade had gone. They were well informed about who to leave alone and who to harass.

Jacob and I returned along the route by which we had come. I dropped him in Ficksburg and then went on through the border into Lesotho. We arranged to meet again in the library. I quite forgot to buy food.

It was an easy journey once on the Lesotho side. Trucks and taxis were scurrying along picking up tired workers Ladies were carrying containers of fresh water back to their homes. Men carried kerosene cans. A team of keep-fit addicts were doing after-hours exercise routines under the trees. Behind the Caltex Garage an old man we knew prepared his newspaper bed. and lit his fire next to the petrol storage unit, quite oblivious to the fact that he could set the whole of Leribe alight. .

I arrived home later than usual and the house lights were on. Barrie had finished work early and had already taken Hercule for his evening walk. Looking relaxed in track-suit and trainers, he came down the steps to meet me.

"Hi honey, had a good day? You'll be pleased to know Betty found your gold tooth at the bottom of the dustbin, wrapped in a paper tissue," he volunteered.

"Brilliant," I replied, "that means I've saved you four thousand rands. Now, would you like a gin and tonic?"

"Yes please - go easy on the tonic," he smiled, "thank goodness the tooth's turned up, that was a nearly expensive visit to the dentist."

My adventure with Thotlisong School in Meqheleng would have to wait. My husband was a worrier and I was quite glad that Marlene had not managed to put a call through earlier telling him where I had gone. It would have been a mistake. He was much happier thinking about not having to fork out for another gold tooth. My own worry was - how to prepare for our Royal visitor later in the week.

During the last few months, on my walks round the mountains, I had collected several children who were keen to come and learn English. The kids and I had become friends and often it could be said that they were the teachers and I the pupil. They would turn up once or twice a week and ask the guards to let them in.

Heleyne, dressed in her school uniform, was the first to peer through the fence. She danced up the steps to the back door. She had just completed her latest entry in the running competition at Mount Royal High School in Leribe, and won. Her eyes shone.

"Now I can run for my school in de contest against Botswana," she said while jigging up and down on the carpet.

The previous week, Heleyne had been chosen to represent her school, but was disqualified from the competition because she had no shoes. Liliane and I had searched until we found a pair to fit her. The girl was tall and strong and could run like a hare. Heleyne's attendance at school was only made possible because her older brother worked in a gold mine in South Africa. He sent money home every year to pay school fees, so that his sister could attend Mount Royal.

"Congratulations Heleyne, I'm sure you'll do well," I said, "now you can show me how you can write - and where's Annacleda – is she coming for her lesson?"

A few minutes went by and Annacleda arrived, looking tense and tired. She always looked like a badly wrapped parcel. In fact today she looked quite ill, and much older than her years. Annacleda's attendance at school was much more sporadic. It depended if she had to keep an eye on the younger ones, if there was any money to pay – or if she was selling fruit for her mother. School, for many children in Lesotho is not even an option.

Her twelve year old brother Kaizi and an assortment of siblings traipsed in after her. Kaizi beamed, showing his terrible teeth, (discoloured through not having the right nutritious food as a child) yet he had the loveliest eyes. The little ones sat cross-legged on the floor and looked up at me with large saucer eyes.

"Mrs Glenn, I will write de letter….. it will go to England with a stamp," said Kaizi eagerly, taking from his plastic bag, a sheet of paper and a pen - evident signs of progress.

"Well done Kaizi," I said quietly. "I think you will write well for me today."

"Can I please go to de bathroom?" asked Annacleda. "I like to see your bath."

What she really loved was to see the hot water come out of the tap in the sink and examine the contents of my toiletries cupboard. Her large dark eyes searched the collection of shampoos,

perfumes and sun block creams with childish longing. Annacleda remained grimly ignorant of the vanity needs of European ladies, while I remained grimly ignorant on the subject of a *Mosotho's* basic washing facilities. She told me her family had to walk a long way for water – but that was before they had moved to the agricultural college, where her mother had a new job in the canteen. Now, things were slightly better and they had more food in their stomachs. The chasm of differences in our respective lifestyles severed the moment.

Kaizi, dressed in torn t-shirt and shorts, stared with keen eye at the huge world map on the wall in my dining room, surrounded by the siblings. He wanted to know how big the world was. His head turned from side to side – trying to make sense of his first experience of cartography. While little brothers ate raisins from egg cups, Kaizi focused his attention on the contours of the African continent with wide eyes.

Then a question from the girls floored me.

"Would you answer a question for us *'M'e* …. is it possible for a fifteen year old girl to have a baby in your country?"

Unflinchingly, I tried to find an answer, without sounding too troubled by the contents of their request.

"It doesn't matter what country, a girl of fifteen can have a baby - yes, but it would be wiser to wait for babies until a girl is older. Why do you ask?"

Annacleda turned quickly answering swiftly, almost in defiance.

"A girl in our village wants to know if this is true."

She tossed her untidy mop of dark hair and turned to Heleyne and they both giggled the girlish laughter of children who had stumbled upon some hidden secret. Heleyne's hand settled upon her book and opened it. She was ready to work. Annacleda was in no mood to write and went into the kitchen to stare at the cooker and the washing machine, which she often did. Nothing in our house resembled her kind of life and she was totally bewildered by it. Later I found a note she had placed on my worktop. It read, *'missis glen we love you'.*

The kids ran off back to the gate of the camp, wearing their books on their heads. As they left, I wondered what they would eat tonight. They made no secret of their lack of food, yet it was pointless to think that I could feed them. They'd survive another day - another week, on *mealies* and sorghum - and be back to write more words in a few days. This was Africa.

A perfect baby donkey wobbled on stilt legs near the bus stop at Ha Simone. Its mother was nearby, having decided the middle of the tarmac road was a good place to teach her offspring to walk. The sky was cobalt blue. Herd boys gathered round the donkeys and tried to pull them to safety onto the soft grassy verge. Like a prima donna on roller blades, the animal was not keen to co-operate. It was a typical happening along any mountain road and one wished the eye could photograph the delightful scenario of small child pushing rump of donkey and older child pulling length of rope. I was on my way to visit Walter.

The tension of waiting for a result from Datchworth was bothering me, so was the uneasy conversation with my daughter. It would soon be Abigail's birthday; an important milestone and there was no mention…oh well, perhaps Lizzie would write and let me know later. No more news of when Liliane would arrive from France. On top of everything, my computer had broken down. In addition our friends Lily and Alex Sheppard and their two children had departed for Switzerland for a long holiday. I would really miss them.

During weekdays, when there was little for the children to do on the camp, four-year old Sean Sheppard had taken to coming with me to Walter's. Their river was his playground and he loved jumping across the stepping stones. Walter would let him climb up into the ox cart which was parked in the yard. Emily made him cakes. Always the centre of attraction, he was a charming addition to my days with the family.

Sean had a Swiss dad and a Mauritian mum and their home language was French, but he was picking up English quickly in the way that toddlers do. Sean's arrival at Walter's house always began with, '*Bonjour tout le monde,*' delightfully tuneful and engaging, especially for the Makibis as it was a language about which they knew very little. One particular morning in Rose's kitchen, Sean had watched and listened as Petros was explaining about the birth of a new calf to his father – in English. Several nocturnal excursions to his precious cow had kept Petros awake and he was wolfing breakfast with the air of someone who hadn't eaten for a week. Stephen was anxious that the calf was protected from prying eyes and advised a day and night watch. Unfortunately new animals are sometimes stolen after dark.

"Sean do you want to see a surprise?" asked Petros kindly, setting down his empty bowl.

The boy nodded his head.

"Come."

Petros took his hand. Together, he and Bernice guided Sean towards the *kraal,* which was some way behind the house. All three stood silently gazing down.

"Sean - look underneath the straw. Do you see anything?"

Wide eyed and innocent, a beautiful dark haired child stared down at a newly delivered calf, still wet with mucus and saliva from its mother's birth canal. She was lying beside it, attempting to lick her offspring with a long pink tongue.

"What do you see?" asked the older boy.

"A cow baby!" said the child in a whisper, holding his breath lest the vision disappeared. Still clasping Petros's hand tightly, he looked up, his black eyes sparkling. Then a smile of pure joy crossed his young face. A unique moment, almost magical - was caught in my camera's quick eye. I stood some distance away, while my heart missed a beat.. A black boy, a white boy - each smiling at the other - wasn't this how things were meant to be?

"I will sleep here tonight," said Petros quietly, "in case my calf should be ill."

The list of natural hazards was endless and the boy knew where his duty lay. He would not leave the calf until it was suckling properly. His bed would be the stable for the next few nights.

This particular morning, Elizabeth, Theresa and another lady passed me along the track. They were Rose's friends and members of St John's congregation, walking in the opposite direction. They usually helped to run the services on Thursdays which were for ladies only. Noticing the empty passenger seat, they called out.

"No Sean today, why is he not with you?"

"He's gone to Switzerland," I answered.

These women would not know where Switzerland was, nor the kind of life into which Sean had been born. Basotho children are actually now part of a wider world – yet circumstances would always isolate them from children born to qualified engineers who travel around the world. Sadly, it is still the case that the one knows almost nothing about the other.

No ox carts rumbled along the track now, the mealie was harvested and the land dry and parched. In some areas farmers were burning off the stubble – winter fires burning out of control were not uncommon. The ditches were dry as tinder and any small breath of wind could carry sparks from one field to another. The early peach trees were just coming into bloom and the one beside Rose's house was already a mass of pink blossom. Emblazoned across the landscape in September, they would make a beautiful sight.

Walter was sitting on the *stoep* with a bowl still brushing his teeth, when I drove in.

"Hi Walter – how's everybody - you look a bit fed up ? Are you sleeping late these days?"

"Well, you know what Dad's like – if we're not at the dawn service, he's not happy. I sang the hymns and went back to bed," he answered with a mouthful of toothpaste. Stephen Makibi held a five o'clock service every morning and expected his children to attend.

"I came to ask if you'd come and help me talk to Amelia tomorrow. Its not every day we entertain a Royal guest. Agnes is busy baking bread for the whole of Africa."

"I'll be there Nettie – don't worry, I'm not usually this late. What time will she arrive?"

"About lunch time. She phoned to say she is coming by taxi. I shall pick her up from the bus stop in Leribe."

"Rose, how do you think we should treat her – is she an easy person to get on with? I know very little about the Royal family. It scares me a bit."

"Nettie, she is charming" answered Rose, who was busy writing letters for the church. "She will be a wonderful guest at your house. We always meet at the TY Festivals – even though they are Roman Catholics, they always support St John's. She is an easy person to talk to. Don't worry about that."

"Is she really a member of the Royal Family?"

"Yes, she is."

I couldn't get my mind around this strange situation. Amelia had sounded delighted to be our guest, when I phoned her at the Foreign Office. The question was a delicate one – but why wasn't she being driven to Leribe in a Royal car? A further thought had occurred – would she come alone - or would she bring a bodyguard? And should I mention my important visitor to LHPC?

"I'll send Emily to help you if you want, Nettie," said Rose, shuffling her papers into a neat pile.

"No, I think that would upset Agnes. She's quietly cherishing the thought of dishing up a Royal stew."

Early the next morning Agnes arrived to start the polishing and cleaning. Five newly baked loaves stood by the side of the fridge. Pulled from the gardens around the camp, masses of foliage draped and dangled from roof to floor. Betty had scrubbed the verandah table and chairs. A modest lunch had been prepared the night before. A bottle of Barrie's best Chateau Stellenbosch had found its way into the fridge and I had lured several able-bodied young men to tidy the rondavel in the garden and carry in more chairs.

Everything was ready for the Royal visitor. At eight o'clock, Barrie walked up from his office to let me know that the phones had gone down…quite normal for us. We were more often segregated from the rest of the planet than linked to it.

Now, which of my clothes befitted an Honourable? My wardrobe was more suited to classrooms or scrambling up mountains than Royal entertainment. A total impasse was reached after three different outfits; ethnic coloured skirt and blouse seemed the most appropriate. Thabu had cleaned the car until it sparkled. I would drive down to the taxi rank around midday and wait for my guest to disembark. Buses from the city centre do not run to a timetable, and only depart when they have sufficient passengers. As we weren't able to phone each other, I would have to take pot luck. Amelia might be late - but I would wait.

The journey from Maseru should take about two hours and there were plenty of taxis. At the slightest sign of a vehicle pulling in, I strained my neck to look. Already I had aroused mistrust, as white ladies in cars were not in the habit of frequenting the local taxi rank, dressed like a posh hippy. An hour went by. I went home. Then feeling extremely guilty, I drove back to my position as watchdog and as discreetly as I could, waited some more.

Barrie came home from the office and he and Walter demolished a loaf between them, though they were forbidden to taste the Royal lunch. Walter had borrowed a suit and looked very smart. Agnes was wearing her best frock.

"Where do you think she is?" Barrie asked as the afternoon wore on. "Perhaps there's been a change of plan and she's been summoned to do a Royal duty somewhere. I imagine she'll appear soon," I suggested hopefully.

By four o'clock the whole idea of being visited by a Royal personage was quite hilarious. Gideon had saluted me so many times through the gate, he must have thought I'd gone stark raving mad and the guys at the taxi rank were beginning to interpret my loitering as none too clear.

"She's probably gone to take Royal tea with the Queen," I said to Walter and Agnes, slicing like a bayonet through the icing on a very large cake. "Come on - this calls for an overdose in chocolate sponge."

With equal abandon, Royal sandwiches spilled from plastic wrappers onto china plates and were devoured hungrily by those who had helped to make them. Hercule happily licked a plate of chicken fritters and squishy banana pudding quite clean.

On Monday morning a call came through to the office from Maseru for me. It was Amelia.

"Annette, I am so sorry about Friday. I ask your forgiveness. My father had an accident and they took him to the hospital. I was there with him all the day."

"What kind of accident?" I asked, suddenly realising that my friend has suffered a crisis.

"It was with his cow," came the quick reply. "It trod on him. My father was injured very badly. I hope I didn't put you to too much trouble."

I am sure my eyebrows rose just a little.

"No, no - not at all."

Thoughts of my own blood, sweat and tears were instantly forgotten, as she described her poor father's state of health after being run over by his favourite cow – very heavy and very large by all accounts. It was all too bizarre.

"Look - why don't you and your husband come and visit me in Maseru instead? Come any day next week – and bring Walter."

"Yes, I'd love to – what about next Saturday?"

"Perfect, and this is where to find me."

Now my heart was racing. I was thinking Royal palaces and servants. It didn't sound like the kind of address I was expecting, but then I knew very little about Maseru or the Royal Family. My exuberant imagination abandoned all attempts to be reasonable. I saw Walter and I sitting down to roast ox on a spit, at the very least. There was no mention of turrets and gardens with lawns or palatial staircases, although Amelia did mention a security screen and a wide front door. I expect her security guards had their weapons discreetly holstered underneath padded jackets. Ahead lay five days of pure anticipation.

It was a cold windy morning as my well-polished Silver Fox found its way to Ha Simone to pick up my own bodyguard the following Saturday morning. Barrie was at work. As I turned off the track towards the house, a large heap of concrete blocks loomed across the entrance to the yard and my car came to a dead stop. Fred and his dog were sitting on top, like guards at the palace gate. It looked as though my latest plan involving Henry the lorry driver, had worked. I had asked him to take some broken concrete slabs to St John's church to be used as paving. The slabs had been discarded by LHPC and were occupying valuable space on the rubbish tip at one of the main sites. One of the foremen overheard my plea for Ha Simone and asked if I would like them. After that it was only a matter of crossing Henry's palm with silver.

Walter and Rose were up and about. Petros was still asleep.

"Walter, go and call Petros, if he doesn't get the cows out this minute – I'll take a stick to him," called Rose from the house "tell him to wake up now."

The hut where Petros slept was about a hundred yards from the house down below the church. He and Augustinus and Justice loved their little haven of space. The hut had neither door nor window – it was simply a mud floor, where they rolled themselves to sleep in thick blankets, kept their school books and school uniforms and knew that they were lucky to have even a roof. The lads were as likely to spend their evenings building a fire or playing football with old tin cans, as naturally as their teenage counterparts in modern Britain soaked up television and video films. Special effects inside the hut were provided by the scratchings of a pet rat who used to come inside out of the cold. The art of keeping warm at night – according to Petros - was to keep as energetic as possible, dive under a blanket while the blood was still circulating and fall asleep looking at the stars.

Stephen's service was just ending. The sound of rapid rhythmic clapping, followed by fortissimo hallelujahs could be heard from the church. Emily had gone to the spring to fetch water. Bernice had gone to school. The cows were still tied up. It was a typical weekday morning at the Makibis.

Walter slid into the passenger seat.

"Heavens – you look terrible," I said, "are you sure you want to come with me? You look so pale. You almost look like a white boy, Walter."

He smiled weakly and fastened himself comfortably into the seat belt.

"Wouldn't miss this for the world Nettie, anyway who will look after you if it's not me? I'll be fine. Been having a bad cough that's all. By the way you look nice."

"Well I thought as it was such a special occasion….when did the concrete slabs arrive?"

"Oh, yesterday afternoon. Henry brought them in an enormous tipper lorry. Dad asked him to drop them by the church but he couldn't get the lorry down that far, so he left them here. They'll be so useful for us. We want to make a flat area where we can hold ceremonies. David's coming tomorrow. He'll help."

"Bye Rose, we'll be back this evening – not too late. I promised Barrie we'd be home by five o'clock. We'll have breakfast on the way," I yelled, pointing towards Walter's stomach.

Passing underneath the impressive avenue of peach trees, somewhere near the outskirts of Kolonyama, we breathed in the glorious blossom that hung in a veil of petals across the sky. I loved this road to Maseru. A wide sweeping landscape of fields used for agriculture, interspersed with *dongas* and ditches slicing through the *veld*. Pinpricks of cattle grazed as far as the eye could see. Higher basalt peaks on either side of us glowed softly purple in the morning light. The road wound through Lekokoaneng and the Berea Plateau, close to the Free State border town of Ladybrand.

Fascinating village names dedicated to chiefs or headmen were painted on stones or pieces of wood. Names of mission stations, started by the Paris Evangelical Missionary Societies - from which spiritual and educational centres have grown, were painted boldly on signs and nailed to a gate or a tree. I read them all, but remembered none – only marvelling at such rudimentary navigation.

"Do you know the area where Amelia lives, Walter?"

"Yes, I can take you there with no trouble, it's off the main road into Maseru and up a short hill."

I knew Walter and his ideas of short hills. They usually turned out to be little mountains.

"Can we drive up it in the car – or do we have to walk?" Since the occasion when we had carved our way up to see his Auntie at Butha-Buthe hilltop, I didn't trust Walter's motoring instructions. "If you think its too difficult, tell me and we'll hire a donkey. I'm not banking on arriving at the Royal palace with four split tyres. Besides we've got to get home tonight."

A quick dash into 'Kentucky Fried Chicken' on Kingsway for breakfast. Walter wolfed it down in one. Then we were on our way. We turned off the main road. Several impressive large brick houses with tiled roofs and big yards lined the entrance to the wide dirt-track road, pock-marked with bumps and hollows, such that the suspension on my car was truly tested. Glass in windows and drainpipes was a sign of comparative luxury. This was 'Des Res Suburbia' – complete with guard dogs and burglar bars.

In second gear we kept on climbing. Men and women dressed western style, strode purposefully past us into town. This was Maseru Kensington High Street for sure and reflected wages and salaries. You can cross time zones and cultures and still find girls wearing frayed denims with chunky belts and flip flops. My hero was a man in a black leather jacket and a fez, who was heading downhill on a home-made bicycle, pedals tied on with raffia.

A couple of *bakkie*s bounced along the ruts on the other side The track became narrower and the houses fell from 'smart' to 'economy'. Barbed wire instead of wooden fences, chickens instead of guard dogs, cabbages instead of lawns.

I was spared the disappointment of not arriving at a palace gate, when my back tyre burst and my sturdy steed sank up to its fetlocks into a large muddy hole. My appearance in a punctured car, wearing mud-soaked pale cream shoes was not quite the dignified entrance I had planned. Walter did his best at playing footman, as by now it had started to rain. He steered me across the maze of puddles towards Amelia's house. We entered through a wide doorway, safeguarded by iron burglar doors into Amelia's 'Royal apartments' to a genuinely warm welcome.

The next few moments were a landmark in my learning. Fragments of thoughts and conversations of previous weeks seared through my brain, as I tried to cope with a few simple re-adjustments. In Lesotho, members of the extended Royal Family were not granted a grand grace-and-favour apartment. Extravagant lifestyle, in Amelia's case, meant having a good job at the Foreign Office and coming home to cook the dinner. The house boasted furniture which was modest and attractive, not elegant and sumptuous. 'Special services' meant fetching water from a tap in the yard when you wanted to wash or cook - and making do with a privy in the garden.

My imagination was always light years ahead of my brain. Barrie was always telling me so. Misinterpretation did nothing to dampen my spirits as Amelia introduced me to her son Paul, a very handsome nineteen-year-old. We shook hands. Hiding behind him was his sister Rose-Mary, seven years old. She was the image of her mother .

"Annette welcome to my home. I am delighted that you and Walter have driven all this way to meet my family. I hoped that your husband would come. We have so much to talk about."

"Thank you for inviting us. I have not been to this part of Maseru before. I'm afraid that my car needs some attention and Walter has offered to go and find a garage while we talk."

"That's wonderful. I want to ask you so many questions about England and your Royal Family......your own family...come and sit down."

We spoke eagerly, realising that the circumstances of our first meeting at the TY Festival was such an unlikely encounter; sharing a meal at the Archbishop's house, eating under the same roof as the Royal Family, meeting Prince Seeiso. That Barrie and I should have been there at all was improbable in the extreme, the icing on the cake was that Amelia and I had warmed to each other, enough to want to meet again.

"Paul is one of twins," Amelia said with pride. "His brother Peter is away at the moment. Their father was killed over twenty years ago at Butha-Buthe in a war. Joseph, my eldest son is away at boarding school. The boys have never known their father. I brought them up alone…..it was hard," she paused. Her dark eyes clouded with emotion. She looked away. "He would have been so proud of them."

In the soft gentle tones of Amelia's voice, I caught the feminine side of a hurt which was still deeply painful. She had been bereaved with three baby boys to raise. In the falling light of the day, I listened as she told her story, her long elegant fingers trembling slightly. Her dead husband was the brother of the present King Letsie III, whose Coronation would soon take place.

Amelia had been one of many young people chosen to befriend the heir to the throne and they had fallen in love and married. His life was to be tragically cut short and Amelia became a widow in her twenties – and a member of the most prominent family in the land.

"Then, you would have become Queen, if your husband had lived?"

"Of course."

"And Joseph……." I faltered a little, "would have been heir to the throne….?"

Amelia, seated regally in her chair, slowly inclined her head, clasping her hands tightly in front of her. Unfolding before me was a story of enormous consequence in terms of 'if only' – yet misfortune had struck a blow to Amelia, from which painful memories still lingered. As a mere listener, a newcomer to Lesotho, I found it hard to absorb the significance of my friend's personal tragedies.

"Twelve years later after living a very solitary existence, I fell in love again…..this time I could not marry. Rose-Mary is our child of that union."

"…but you deserved happiness …..the loneliness must have destroyed you."

"Yes, Rose-Mary's father wanted to marry me, but because I am a member of the Royal Family, I can never re-marry. In our country it is not permitted. After a while he went away. He wanted a wife."

Looking closely at this tall slender woman of mature years, I glimpsed an image of a beautiful young girl, who had suffered a cruel twist of fate. I saw the lines of suffering in her face. Traditional rules of protocol in the Royal Family forbade her to be married for a second time, even though her husband had died many years before. I looked at Rose-Mary playing with her dolls; the child of a man who, though he loved her, would not be there to watch her

139

grow. Amelia had raised her family single handed, which was no easy task. She was a proud *Mosotho.*

I realised that I was shivering as the house had no heating. Amelia went to find something warm for me to put on. Both wrapped in our heavy traditional Basotho blankets, we laughed and drank *rooibos* tea together and warmed our hands round china cups, while the candles burned merrily around us.

"Thank you," I said mercifully, "now I know why you people wear these lovely garments. Amelia, would you help me with my research? You know that I am working on a book, so that one day people in my country will know about yours......but I need help to understand many things."

"Yes Annette, I would be so pleased to teach you"

And then we stumbled across a point of interest to us both. Amelia was fascinated that I had a disabled granddaughter. She wanted to learn how we, in our society, were able to provide for children with disabilities.

"We know that Abigail will never walk," I explained, "she will always be dependent on others. My daughter will receive every kind of help ....special schools and good doctors who know much about microcephaly. We say that they are children of 'special needs'. "

"Annette, would you be able to find me books so that I can read about these special children Soon I will become a Chieftainess and I need to learn about the problems with the disabled. Many people will come to me for advice about all kinds of things. In some ways I have been privileged....yet my education did not put me next to ordinary people, with ordinary lives......I need to learn a lot."

Chapter 12

Double Tragedy

Driving along a wet road with no white lines, full of twists and turns, at night, was the ultimate nightmare. Every few minutes the sky was ripped apart by a knife of white lightning. Rain sluiced the windscreen in sweeping torrents from a black sky. My eyes hurt trying to see the road when lights from oncoming cars shone directly in my eyes.

"Walter – will you watch the edge of the road for me? Shout if we get too near the edge," I almost screamed above the thunderbolts.

"Go slowly Nettie. When the lights come towards you dip your lights."

"If only people wouldn't drive with headlights blazing. They're blinding me. How do you feel Walter?"

"Lousy. Never mind it's been a fantastic day. Amelia's a hero isn't she?"

"I agree. I feel as though she's a real friend. What an interesting lady… and what a life she's had ….oh look people are still out on a night like this walking by the side of the road. They must be absolutely soaked…..shall we stop?"

Walter's coughing fit prevented any further conversation and I decided it was best if we pushed on home.

"Take these Walter."

I threw him a packet of throat lozenges from the glove compartment. He swallowed the lot in one. The convulsions racked his chest and for a time he slumped in the seat and appeared to go to sleep. I knew Barrie would be worried about me. He wasn't to know we had been delayed by a puncture but would know about the storm. We should have set off earlier. Accidents could easily happen in these weather conditions – especially with no spare wheel and an unconscious navigator.

For the best part of two hours I battled against high winds, hailstones as big as conkers, lashing rain and an unfamiliar road. Other drivers had pulled off onto the verge waiting for the storm to abate. I dare not stop in case some other emergency overtook us. On the outskirts of Leribe a cow had been run over. The roadside scene was lit by lanterns. Men with ropes were jumping off a bakkie and I knew it would be an event associated with much anger and distress.

"That is a serious thing when a cow is killed by a car," said Walter who suddenly jerked awake as I skidded to a halt in the middle of the road. There were no warning lights to inform oncoming traffic of the disaster. "People get very angry about this kind of thing – the herd boy will be in trouble. He will receive a *sjambok* for sure."

"But it might not have been his fault. The animal was probably frightened by the storm."

"The family who own the cow will not understand this reason. Someone will be blamed a lot."

We drove on in silence. After Leribe, we had another three kilometres to go. I had never driven to Ha Simone at night before. In daylight everything looked completely different. From the main highway there was nothing to indicate where the track started and I had to feel my way along the uneven sodden ground in pitch black. Though I knew it well, it was an eerie journey. My car lights probably attracted attention three villages away. Nobody drove on this mountain at night unless it was the police. Every dwelling round the church looked drenched and not one candle shone in the sleepy homestead until we reached the main house.

I tapped on the door and as I did so Justice opened it. Emily was close behind him, with a small flickering candle which threw weird shadows around.

"Hi you two. It's very late. Nettie, Barrie has been here looking for you a couple of hours ago. He's worried because you didn't come home. Are you okay?"

"Thanks Justice," I whispered, "Walter's not too well. Take care of him won't you. It's that awful cough again. Can you make him a hot drink?" It was all I could think of in the circumstances. "I think perhaps he should see a doctor."

"I'm fine, really I am....just very tired," interrupted Walter, who was close on my heels. "I'll be better when I've slept for a few hours. Nettie I'll be here for you on Wednesday to go and meet your godson in Ficksburg. Don't forget, I'm coming with you to meet him."

His voice was nothing more than a whisper and he looked all in. Emily took his arm.

"I haven't forgotten. Just try to rest. Goodnight everybody."

My stomach in knots after the drama of our journey, dazzling lights still dancing before my eyes. I ran back to the car. The family's vulnerability was beginning to overwhelm me. Medical help was not an alternative for Walter. The illness would have to take its natural course. Somehow I found my way back to the main road. My throat dry with worry. It was far from safe out on the road at night.

It was almost nine o'clock when the LHPC guard opened the gate to let me through.

"Mr Glenn took de car to look for you 'M'e, he was worried," shouted a voice from the darkness.

"Yes Piri, I know – but I'm back now. Thanks. Goodnight."

The gate clanged behind me. With relief, I parked the car under our parking lot and ran to the house, the rain running down my neck as I dodged the seeping foliage. The minute my foot reached the step, Barrie was there.

"Nettie – you're here! Where've you been? I was worried sick......I borrowed a car and went looking for you at the Makibis. Did you get caught in the storm? Did you find Amelia? Look at you. You're soaked."

"Yes to both. It was a scary journey home....Barrie, don't think about me. Walter's ill, I know he is... I think there's something the matter. He could hardly speak to me when I left."

Words tumbled out. Barrie wasn't listening. He was so relieved to see me and produced a tot of brandy, a hot bath and some warm clothes, before I could explain the full saga of our visit to Maseru.

"Look - I don't think you should have gone without me. Next time we go together."

"....but you were at work."

"Why can't you stay in the camp like all the other wives, instead of dashing off on some crazy adventure?"

"Because I'm not like other wives!" I yelled at him angrily.

Our harsh words were the result of me putting myself in danger. In our situation that was bad news.

"Nettie you must be careful. You can't go careering around at night by yourself. It's just not safe. It's a risk we can't afford to take. If anything happened. I'd never forgive myself...and my job is to build dams, not to be worried about you."

"In future I shall stay home and become a nun," I answered sullenly.

"Nettie, they wouldn't want you," answered a very quiet voice.

"Why not?"

"Because you're much too disobedient – and far too contrary. You couldn't stick to rules if you tried," the corners of his mouth erupted into a smile. "And that's why I love you..."

We both dissolved into laughter. The crisis had passed.

"Come on, drink that brandy and lets go to bed"

The following day we had been invited to lunch with some friends in Ficksburg who had asked us to go and share a *braai* and meet a few of their colleagues. It was essential that we kept our appointment – a strikingly different scenario to my adventure with Walter the day before. Barrie's position at LHPC was paramount to our future. Struggling with racial issues was not easy, especially in the light of South Africa's history from both sides of the border. At times, we felt integration weighed heavily upon our shoulders.

Our recent wedding in Ficksburg had brought us into contact with new friends, many of whom were struggling with the newness of *'reconciliation'* and the breakdown of apartheid. The inevitability of the New South Africa was a hard pill to swallow and they were still talking about the new government through gritted teeth.... 'this Mandela bloke better have something to say.' It was a difficult time for everyone. 1994 was not so far away and things had been very different then.

Ficksburg was Afrikaner territory, but it was a good town and we liked it. Lesotho was a black Kingdom, an independent country, exclusive of apartheid and yet dependent on South Africa in many ways. Black culture rubbed up against white supremacy here in this part of the Free State. Old disputes about land and borders still rumbled on. A spark thrown into that tinder box was lethal. People here had long memories. They kindly reminded us we were *uitlanders* and didn't expect us to understand the present situation. The result was that we were left sitting on a pile of razor blades.

After breakfast we phoned Borrie and Elsa to say we were on the way. I picked a few flowers from the garden for Elsa. Barrie had the foresight to take a favourite bottle of wine for the table. We drove smartly out of Leribe feeling rather subdued after the previous evening's events. The sky was a radiant blue.

Watery pasture sparkled emerald in the sun and spring was in the air. Mimosa shone yellow in the hedges and around the villages. Gangs of children were out playing football on slimy wet sports fields, where mud isn't a problem for players without boots. The traffic police didn't even bother to challenge us today. Sunday was their day for popping up from behind hedges. Even Maputsoe market place felt upbeat, the streets were litter-free and clean Road drains were running with clean water.

A weekend treat for ex-pats was to drive into Ficksburg to buy a newspaper. Standing by the till in the newsagents shop on the main street, the lady assistant, recognising our accents, enquired in a quiet tone,

"*Lumela 'M'e*. Did you know Princess Diana is dead? She died last night – in a car crash ......I think it was in Paris...."

My heart skipped a beat.

"What did you say? I don't think I heard you properly."

"It's been on radio early this morning. I think the accident happened last night I'm not sure exactly when – but....." Her words dried up as I stared at her in horror, still trying to take in what she had said. My brain was not receiving this messages. I wanted to cry.

"Did you know her?"the girl enquired.

"No - well yes, but not personally. She was a Royal Princess. In our country it is different. Tell me what you heard again please."

"Barrie did you hear? Princess Diana has died in a car accident. Let's drive to Elsa's quickly They're sure to have some news. I can't believe it."

"What?" He looked up from reading the football headlines and stared hard at me as though I had suddenly grown two heads. "Are you *sure*?"

Our day was spent listening to news bulletin after news bulletin from London. All radio stations and TV channels were broadcasting the same horrific tale. Repeatedly the story went on, coloured by opinions of different broadcasters so that we heard most of the main facts. Our South African friends were as shocked as we were. They were as sad as we were. Diana, Princess of Wales, was loved here as much as she was in England.

The *braai* in the garden was lit, but no one wanted to cook. Conversations fell apart as people tried to voice their thoughts. Drinks were poured out and left. Our lunch party was collectively in shock. Judging by the television reports, so was the rest of the world No one wanted to believe it. Every hour snippets of information were announced.

The grief went on all week. At roadside stalls. On the camp. In the local shops. People came up to me and put their hands on my arm and looked into my face.

"We are sorry, we love Princess Diana. Please tell her family we know her."

Barely able to string two words of English together, a man wearing an old jacket with holes in the sleeves, selling vegetables in Leribe market, tapped me on my shoulder and escorted me round the back of his stall. Still waving his cabbage stalks in the air, he muttered, "we are sad, we are sad. She very beautiful lady."

A shop window in the main street displayed a picture of Diana with the words, 'We love you' daubed across her face. I have often wondered if the Princess realised the extent of her popularity in this far flung corner of the world. These were poor people who had no newspapers or television – maybe a radio if they were lucky. How did they know her so well? One dear lady who sold second-hand clothes from a steel container on Mandela Road, asked the question,

"What will they do with her clothes?"

At the butchers Amelia looked distraught when I went to buy meat. She had recently given birth to twins. Rounding the end of the counter she came to hug me, her blood-soaked apron sticking to my clothes. Her broad shape and child-bearing hips labelled Amelia a symbol of fertility all of her own.

"The Princess is dead! *Ehh....*de children, de two boys – dey have no mother. Ehh… In Lesotho we saw she was de loving mother. To a Mosotho that is good. *Ehh..em 'M'e."*

A wave of grief was sweeping the whole country. Annacleda and Heleyne who religiously used to search my English magazines for pictures of the Princess, could not stop talking about the tragedy. Unsurprisingly they heard about the accident the very day she died via their own jungle drums.

"She is a beautiful white Princess – we love her," said Heleyne sadly. "I want her picture to make sure that I remember her. I want to be as pretty as her. Please *'M'e* can you write her name in my book?"

Perhaps it was because Lesotho was once a Protectorate of England, perhaps it was that our countries were linked in the historical sense. Perhaps it was the persona of Princess Diana herself, but the depth of their shock and grief touched me deeply. Everywhere I went people felt moved to tell me about their own sadness.

Later that week Amelia rang to see if Walter and I had arrived home safely. She had been very concerned about us setting off back to Leribe in a storm.

"Annette we were deeply sorry about the death of your young Princess Diana. Everyone here in Maseru is talking about it. The Royal family from England will be represented at the Coronation of King Letsie in November. Perhaps the Princess was even coming here. It's terrible news...we are so shocked."

"Thank you Amelia, yes it's terrible...we're all stunned."

"The next time you come to Maseru, please come up to my office in town. We must talk again sometime Annette. It is good that we've become friends. I enjoyed your visit very much."

Wild rumours of events leading up to Diana's death circulated between colleagues and the pool-room bar until it wasn't easy to detect fact from fiction. We stopped listening. It was too dreadful. Fourteen days to go before my trip to England. Perhaps I might find out more about what actually happened.

At four o' clock in the afternoon of the 3rd September, Walter and I were outside Ficksburg Post Office, hoping that my godson, Stephen Purdy and his girlfriend Catherine would arrive. The rendezvous, based on a single phone call to Stephen's mother in England many weeks ago, was all I had to go on. No communication had taken place between us since then. Many times in the past weeks I had wondered if it was all a figment of my imagination.

Stephen had recently been on holiday with his girlfriend in Durban. He had been to South Africa on a couple of rugby tours in 1993 and 1994 and that's when he fell in love with the
country. His ambition on this trip wasn't so much that he wanted to take home the winning shield for the Moseley Rugby Club, but to take home quite a different prize.

Shoppers meandered along the main street beside us. Busy feet tramped up and down the new Post Office steps. It had been a hot day. Walter and I parked nearby and hung around like spare parts, expecting a white man with splints and a broken collar bone to pitch up any minute. In the very unlikely event that Stephen would arrive, we waited.

Walter had insisted on coming with me to the meeting place, one because he couldn't believe that he was going to meet an English rugby player and two, because he would get a ride in a big car; the latter would be the biggest thrill of all. When I mentioned that we would like to show my friends more of Lesotho later that week, Walter agreed to accompany us. He would make the perfect guide and we would have our own interpreter.

"I'll take you and your friends to see Thaba Bosiu, Nettie, where King Moshoeshoe I is buried. It is where our nation began. You will see how beautiful our country really is," he enthused.

He wouldn't admit that he was sick and refused to even discuss Saturday night. Rose had taken me to one side and told me that Lesotho medicine would make him well and I was not to worry. I didn't know what she meant, but in their culture there was so much unknown to me that I believed her. Walter looked handsome today in smart trousers and cream linen shirt. He was wearing my husband's best boots – well polished, and a turquoise silk tie, late of Bromley Marks and Spencers and more recently, Barrie's wardrobe.

He wanted to make a good impression. Metro-Goldwyn Mayer had no studio in town. If they had, I would have pushed Walter through the door. Somewhere in his ancestry there must have been a trace of movie star gene – he always seemed to have his own remarkable and perfectly natural brand of charm.

Suddenly Stephen was there. Laughing and smiling, all six feet something of a relaxed rugby player, holding the hand of his lovely English girl, both clearly happy to be on their way to a Lesotho adventure. A glimpse of the pair of them together told me all I needed to know. This was love.

"Quite a journey – we made it from the Drakensberg in four hours. Hi Walter – good to meet you. This is Catherine…"

Walter's face was a picture. He had plainly reckoned on the tough-guy image of a fit sportsman but he had never clapped eyes on a blond blue-eyed fair-skinned beauty like Catherine before. I think the word 'dazzled' would be appropriate.

"Come on let's get you two through the border, Barrie will be home from work and he's dying to meet you. We've still got a few miles to go. Passports ?"

"Okay Annette, we're parked across the road." He turned to Walter. "Walter would you like to drive through with me? Catherine can travel with Annette?"

The smile on Walter's face as he got into the passenger seat of Stephen's new white Toyota Corolla was something I shall never forget. If there was ever a moment in Walter's life which encompassed pure joy with pure luck – it was this. His smile as they drew away from the kerb would have won a Hollywood Oscar.

After a slight hold-up at the border with clearance papers, we drove in convoy through the centre of Maputsoe and, just as my eyes had been opened on my first visit, so were Catherine's. She saw for herself the bustling crowds of an African border town which were a challenge to one's senses. Lodged in a traffic jam of horse drawn carts, taxis, touts and a noisy verbal sort-out, we manoeuvred our way onto the home straight. Many of the stallholders were clearing up after the day's business, knee deep in cabbage stalks and empty boxes. Carcasses of meat were being trundled out of container lorries by lads doing balancing acts with wonky wheelbarrows. We passed a metal hut surrounded by gargantuan heaps of old car tyres. A tangled heap of wrecked cars littered the ground nearby. This was the local garage. Customers used to drive their front wheels up a rusty metal ramp for inspection and park over a deep hole. The scene looked like a disaster waiting to happen.

Scores of workers were making their way home on foot in the late afternoon sun. My passenger had lapsed into silence. As we drove towards Leribe, the crimson sky had melted into shades of strawberry pink. The air turned soft. Fireflies lit the grass.

Barrie was waiting to welcome us. He said to me afterwards that he thought Stephen would never stop expanding outwards and upwards as he unfolded himself from his vehicle. The intervening years had changed the youth into the man. The same mop of dark curly hair and brown eyes as I remembered but the scale of the physique had altered beyond recognition. Catherine looked so tiny beside him. He and Barrie shook hands warmly.

It was a treat to meet someone from the old country. Carole and I had been friends for thirty years and our families knew one another well. Stephen had learned to throw a ball as soon as he could walk. His rise to fame on the field was hardly unexpected with his father's stoic support. Stan had played Rugby for England against Scotland in the sixties. There was no doubting either Stephen's ability or his talent as he grew up. His University soon discovered his skill as a player and he was made captain of their seven-a-side team during his student years.

"Hello Barrie, thanks for the invite. We've been looking forward to seeing you both out here. What a trip from the border. A bit different to South Africa eh!"

"Yes, you could say that," answered Barrie, "anyway welcome to our humble abode. We hope you'll see a bit of the country in the next few days – and meet a few more Basotho people. If I know Nettie, she'll take you to meet Walter's family in Ha Simone. Just don't expect them to know anything about Rugby Union......!"

Formalities over with, we settled down to a cracking good meal with a glass or two of full-bodied wine from the Eastern Cape, while Stephen gave us a potted version of his goal-scoring past. Barrie had also played rugby in his youth so the stories became more animated with every glass. I could quite see that opposition teams wouldn't stand much chance against Stephen's erg-powered biceps or his size twelve boots.

"I got to know the pitches in SA pretty well on my tours in '93 and '94" said Stephen, " in fact I got a job in Durban for a year. I almost decided to take up permanent residency."

"And if you had, you wouldn't have met Catherine."

"That's right. I did go home and worked hard for a couple of years, and often wondered if I

had made the right decision. But to be honest, it was worth it." He looked a little sheepish. "I proposed to Catherine yesterday in the Drakensburg....and she said yes."

The following morning we were up early. A violet dawn glowed over our mountains

"Where do you plan to take them Nettie?"

"To Roma first, then up to Thaba Bosiu to see Moshoshoe's grave. Walter says he'll show us the way."

While we prepared breakfast in the garden, armies of tiny ghekos swarmed between cracks in the stone stairway, already basking in the warm spring sunshine. Tall irises shone blue around our doorway and the faces of my pansies danced in the rockery like approving parents at a child's birthday party. Hercule paced lion-like, up and down the fence between us and our neighbours. He watched our every move. Plates of bacon and eggs simmering only a few feet away were enough to make his eyes water. He began to emit discreet whining noises, politely at first but soon turning to long pathetic howls. Betty came to remove him and tied him up near the back gate where he proceeded to bark ferociously at all callers to the guard hut – especially if they were black. Hercule was an out and out racist.

It was refreshing to hear news from Stephen and Catherine. During breakfast Stephen recalled his meeting with President Mandela on the beach in Durban during his previous visit in 1994, an event quite inconsequential, yet memorable. He and a friend had been playing off-duty cricket on the sands. A group of men walking along the beach suddenly started to take an interest in their game.

"We realised almost straight away it was Mandela," Stephen said. "There had been lots of speculation about the forthcoming inauguration, so much coverage on TV. There were about thirty or forty people accompanied by a Channel 4 camera crew from UK. Dave and I were the only people on the beach. I was holding the bat. Mandela was strolling along within a few yards of us, obviously enjoying some leisure time. I couldn't think what to say so I offered him the bat and asked him, 'would you like to take a swing, Sir?' Immediately he walked towards me, took the bat and walked over to the crease. He smiled, then said, 'I've never played cricket in my life.'

"Did he hit the ball?" we both asked.

"No. I bowled a couple and he missed them both. Everyone took it in good part. Mandela laughed and handed me the bat. I suddenly realised I was engaged in a knock-about with the new President of South Africa. He thanked us for inviting him to join in. He was charming. It was the voice – when he spoke I knew it so well."

"Did you ever see the footage?" asked Barrie.

"No such luck. I phoned the family in England and had everyone watching Channel 4 News for weeks. It might not have been used. I don't know – but it was my claim to fame."

He caught hold of Catherine's hand and pulled her up from her seat.

"Come on let's go and see Walter."

Later that morning, we drove up to Ha Simone in Stephen's car to investigate the dinosaur footprints along the river bed. They were both relaxed about meeting a Basotho family.

"We would not have have had the opportunity to do this, had we been hitched to a glossy holiday brochure...shame Barrie has to go to the office," said Stephen as we went along the track.

Driving towards the Subeng River, they noticed the treeless landscape and rocky terrain, scarred by deep dongas. Even thorn bushes were in short supply near Ha Simone.

"They burn every stick for firewood. No electricity at Walter's place," I explained. "And they have to carry water from the spring. Look at the quality of the soil here. Lesotho is in deep ecological trouble....over-farming, over-grazing. Torrential rains wash away the top soil until it gets so thin nothing grows.

A gaggle of children pulling a donkey stared at the car as we passed Albert's tin toilet factory
near the road. They were used to seeing the Silver Fox driving in the direction of St John's Church but puzzled by my appearance as a passenger in Stephen's large people-carrier. We drove slowly across the new bit of road which the boys had made for me, on past the church and across the yard. Rose and Emily came out to greet us. I read their expressions. Something was dreadfully wrong.

As we got out of the car into the hot sun, I clutched Stephen's arm.

"Look at Walter – oh my God."

On the stoep, Walter was hanging onto the shoulders of David at one side, Petros at the other. They were supporting his weight because he couldn't stand up. He was coughing up blood onto the ground and Petros held a towel up to his face. All three of them looked terrified. They could do nothing but stand there while he spluttered and coughed, his head hung low over his chest and his feet buckling under his own weight. His strength had forsaken him. He was wearing an old anorak and some awful old trousers. As he tried to stand up, I saw how thin he really was. The horrible inevitability suddenly confronted me.

"Rose – what's happened? When did Walter become as ill as this?" She didn't reply."He came to Ficksburg with me only yesterday. By the way this is Stephen, my godson from England – and Catherine, his girlfriend." Momentarily, I had forgotten that this was why we had come to visit. "Walter even offered to drive us out to Roma, he wanted to show us Roma..."

I stared horrified as the boys moved Walter gently inside the house.

"Nettie he's been hiding it from you. He didn't want you to know how ill he has been. These bouts of coughing have been getting worse. And last night... he was so sick .We bathed him with water. He had a raging fever. He has slept a little, but his cough wakes him."

"Has he seen a doctor?"

"No, Nettie – there is no doctor for Walter, we have no money to go to the hospital."

I looked across at Stephen. He just nodded his head in silent agreement There was only one thing to do. Catherine was the only one with a voice.

"We can't go out sightseeing today. It's impossible. Annette, let us help to get Walter to a doctor or a hospital. Where should he go ?"

"But you're only here for a couple of days ….it seems such a shame to forfeit your holiday."

"There's nothing else to be done," agreed Stephen, "come on, get Walter into the car."

Stephen drove very fast. Butha-Buthe General Hospital was a place I had never seen. It was hidden behind the main street and I had never noticed it before. My hand held Walter's shaking fingers. He could not speak.

At the gate of the hospital a guard was leaning nonchalantly against the post. Hardly a symbol of confidence for new arrivals, he sauntered over to open the boom. When we asked where to take new admissions, he waved his arm vaguely in the direction of the reception block without speaking a word. We parked the car outside *'Accident and Emergency.'* There were no other cars in sight. Patients came by foot – not wheels.

Walter managed to walk holding onto Stephen. Once inside the entrance we saw it – a three day queue. No wonder the guard was in no hurry to let people through. We looked at each other helplessly. I felt numb. Catherine with her long blond hair, wearing trendy shorts and t-shirt, with sun-tanned legs looked completely incongruous amongst the crowd of Basotho women wrapped in blankets. People were sitting and standing along both walls; mothers with children, men leaning against each other for support, others laying on the ground….. just waiting. Those who had made it onto the few wooden benches at the front of the queue might just be seen by the doctor today. By no stretch of the imagination would we make it to a stethoscope this morning. The atmosphere was full of tension.

A white person in the crowd was of course a spectacle. Stephen stood six inches above the tallest Mosotho. Catherine and I tried to make our way along to the front to take a look at the situation. My Sesotho was not very good, but a few words here and there helped enormously. We knew Walter needed treatment urgently, but it was awful seeing all these people waiting for medical help.

A lady in the crowd who looked like someone with authority spotted us and came over to speak to Catherine and I. We were being pushed by the crowd and had to move some distance up the corridor before we could find room to talk.

"Why are you here?"

"Lumela *'M'e*. We have a very sick young man with us….we are trying to get him to a
doctor. Is there someone who could help us?"

"Not before tomorrow - or the next day. You can see for yourself."

"Is there somewhere we can take him - if we have money?" I asked, not having the faintest idea of their treatment systems. There was no hope in this hospital and Walter might be dying. I turned my head to look for Stephen but he was swallowed up in the crowd.

"Look here," she answered, "you could take him to a private doctor if you can pay. I will tell you how you must go. It isn't far away from here in Butha-Buthe. I think he will be able to see you today if you go now."

I had already decided that if this was the only way we would get treatment for Walter, then it was what we must do. The woman started to explain where to go – in Sesotho. I didn't understand and asked her to explain, in English. Suddenly she offered her own help.

"I will take you there myself. I know Dr Sekhesa. He is a good doctor."

"We'd be very happy if you'd come with us – can we go straight away?"

Once outside reception the lady took one look at Stephen's car – the only vehicle in the whole hospital compound – and beamed. She carried a slight odour of antiseptic and sensible soap and I was beginning to like her. Shooting Walter one glance, she agreed that we needed help urgently. He was shaking uncontrollably and Stephen had put his own sweater around his shoulders. We could hardly get near the car. Other patients were giving it a mighty close inspection and some were trying to peer through the windows. Catherine and I had to battle to open the rear door. We had the feeling if we let it swing open, we would have ten extra passengers.

Our guide yelled loudly and at her words they fell away from the sides of the car. Rarely had I felt more grateful for the help of a Basotho guide.

"My name is Estelle," she said, "we need to hurry if we are to catch Dr Sekhesa before he leaves his surgery. Take the road towards Oxbow and turn right behind the bottle store."

Stephen followed her instructions. Outside the gates of the hospital, the coffin lady was setting up her stall. A row of coffins leaned up against the shop front, advertised by a placard which read, '*Makese Coffins, Steel or Wood, Come in and Look.*' As we passed she waved to us giving us a bright smile.

Walter sat hunched in the back of the car with Catherine and myself.

"Try not to worry Walter. We'll get you to a doctor. He'll be able to tell you what's wrong. We can't let you go on like this."

Beneath his skin a there was a pallor I had not seen before. Beads of sweat stood out on his forehead.

"Nettie I am so cold …your two friends are so kind to drive me to the hospital. I'm sorry to cause so much trouble." His voice was nothing more than a hoarse whisper.

"Try not to talk Walter….save your energy," broke in Catherine.

Dr Sekhesa's premises were somewhere between a brick factory and a bottle store. Stephen manoeuvred the wheels between moulds and wooden shuttering on the one side and piles of sand on the other. Every hod carrier in sight was suddenly glued to his ladder. The arrival of our car in the middle of their building site did little to conceal the confidential nature of our visit. Patients on foot wouldn't have raised so much as an eyebrow. Finally we found Dr Sekhesa's clinic. Looking terribly ill, Walter staggered to his feet.

There was a small waiting room with benches to sit on and a dispensary. Walter sat down heavily and started to cough. As he spewed into a towel, I saw the red stain once more and closed my eyes.

Dr Sekhesa asked me to go into the treatment room and I went willingly. Someone had to fill in the blanks - Walter's family background, how long the symptoms had been occurring...I did my best with what little I knew. The doctor was kindness itself. Walter sat beside me, staring into space. He probably heard nothing of our conversation. He was concentrating so hard on not letting another racking cough escape.

"I will pay for my friend's treatment. He is the son of Reverend Stephen Makibi. My husband and I know the family well. Please forgive my lack of Sesotho. I want you to treat him as one of your patients. He is my responsibility."

"Walter has pneumonia. That is all I can say at the moment. There may be complications as he is already very weak. His lungs may be damaged – but I can't tell until I see his X-rays. Can you get him to the hospital in Leribe tomorrow?"

"Yes, of course."

"Take this letter to the X-ray department and tell them I want it done immediately. I will ring them tomorrow night for the result. Then you must bring the negatives here to my surgery. I will give him something to ease the cough and let him sleep. He stood up and shook my hand firmly. "My dispensary is outside. The medication will be ready in a few minutes."

"Thank you Dr Sekhesa."

"I want to see him in two days time. Thank you 'M'e for taking care of this boy. I will see that he gets good treatment."

Within five minutes the nurse called us. Neither the tablets nor the bottle were labelled. Barely had I paid the bill of seventy five rands, when Walter almost collapsed. The waiting room buzzed with more flies than patients. The air was hot and muggy. We laid him on one of the benches. Estelle had gone home and left my friends waiting by the car.

"Come on Walter, swallow these." I heard Stephen's voice. He held a bottle of water to Walter's lips. "You may as well start your treatment now old chap."

Watching him swallow the pills was heartbreaking.

Back at the house in Ha Simone, I cannot begin to describe the emotional scene with Rose and the family. My godson had proved to be the hero of the hour. Catherine too. We all felt terribly tired and I suddenly realised we had been away from home since breakfast time and hadn't eaten. The pair of them had not only missed out on a trek to the most famous national monument but on meeting the Makibi family under happier circumstances.

Stephen went in to say goodbye, looking huge beside Justice and Petros. He looked so fit and healthy, if a little awkward in their small kitchen. He didn't quite know whether to stand up or sit down. Catherine was shaking hands with Emily – and smiling They would have liked longer to get acquainted.

"Cheers Walter. It's been an unforgettable day," said Stephen. "We're glad we could help you find a doctor. We're leaving Lesotho in the morning. Catherine and I wish you well. Sorry our visit has been so short, but we have to leave Johannesburg tomorrow night."

Shaking, Walter took the outstretched hand. A flicker of a smile crossed his face. He was trying to brighten a little for the sake of the visitors.

"Thanks for everything Stephen - especially the car ride," then with an admiring last look at Catherine, he mouthed in a croaky voice, "the boys think your girlfriend looks like Princess Diana."

The following morning, on their way out of Leribe and unknown to us, our English friends called at the Makibis for another farewell. They gave the entire contents of their suitcases to Walter, to share among his brothers and sisters – and two hundred rands for Rose to buy a kitchen table. We had told them Rose had never had a table in her kitchen. Stephen and Catherine travelled back to England in the only set of clothes they still owned.

The queue in the X-ray department at Leribe Hospital was not quite as long as the one in Butha-Buthe. At least people were seated in some kind of orderly fashion. I was holding Walter by the arm and he was still very weak, but at least not coughing. His grey and navy anorak made him look even more grey and he was stooping slightly.

At that moment we were called into the X-ray room by name and one of patients who had been seated, stood up and began shouting in anger. Intuitively I recognised the tone of her voice. The words bit through the silence for all to hear.

"A few years ago, you - a white lady - would be seen before a black. But not now. I have waited longer than you!"

There was no doubting her resentment. She did not spare my blushes. My face stung with embarrassment. How could I reply? Walter tried to apologise.

"It's okay Walter, it must seem insulting to her. You are a private patient. That's all."

The radiographer put his head round the door, calling 'Makibi' even louder.

"Come through 'M'e, I want to see you first." Dr Sekhesa's letter was in his hand.

There was only one X-ray machine. It looked very basic but it photographed the insides of peoples' bodies and that was all that mattered.

The pile of X-rays on the radiographer's desk looked as though they had been accumulating for days. Negatives of rib-cages, broken femurs and cracked elbow joints littered the floor. Unidentified body parts were slithering in all directions The harassed radiographer, while taking urgent telephone calls, still attended to a line of stripped male torsos – all waiting for the machine to spew out their negatives. When eventually we did see Walter's X-rays appearing, I'm afraid to say I grabbed the pen from the desk and quickly wrote his name on the top. Goodness knows how many patients had reached the operating table, only to be prepared for theatre using someone else's x-ray plates.

In the days which followed there was another visit to Butha-Buthe, another meeting with Dr Sekhesa, a handing over of the X-ray plates in a sealed envelope. Walter's crisis was just beginning.

"I want Walter to have two more tests please *'M'e."* Now I was being addressed as the responsible parent. "Go to the Public Health Department in Butha-Buthe. He needs a sputum test and a Mantoux test. He may have Tuberculosis. The tests will confirm the disease without a doubt."

Walter's state of health had deteriorated so fast, yet the news was still shoocking. Although he had taken the prescribed medication, the tablets were only keeping the true symptoms at bay. Walter didn't seem to hear Dr Sekhesa's comments. A dark mood had descended on him. I had never known him like this. Our days of happy carefree laughter had ended. Our journeys through Lesotho in the Silver Fox were over. From now on my days with his family were to be clouded with unhappiness and worry.

We drove back to Ha Simone in deep gloom. Walter's head was low on his chest and his breathing was laboured and shallow. He seemed disorientated. Like a mole, he buried himself inside his blanket. As I dropped him off at home, Rose came to help get him out of the car and took him gently into the house.

"Rose, will you be alright?" I felt my emotions being torn apart. Walter's suffering was horrendous to watch. "We shall be away this weekend, but I'll be here for you next Tuesday when Walter has to go for tests at the Public Health Clinic. I'll drive him there so don't worry. Just keep up his medication."

Rose may not have wanted to know Dr Sekhesa's opinion, so I didn't tell her – she would know soon enough.

"I have made up his bed in the little house over the other side of the yard. He must be kept quiet and the others won't be so upset seeing him so ill like this. Petros is terrible. He cannot speak to him."

"That's a good idea Rose, in case he's infectious. Keep him quiet and let him sleep as much as possible."

"May the Lord bless you Nettie. You and Barrie have been so kind to our family. We will pray for you......and for Walter. Stephen has had to go away to Johannesburg with the Archbishop for a week. The whole church is praying for him."

At home an assortment of pressing jobs had been neglected. To arrange a wedding blessing ceremony in another country with dodgy phone services was not easy. Barrie was working long hours. We had both agreed that we must give Walter our full support. Once again, we were caught up in our professional commitments and our connections to life in a Lesotho village.

"It's just a shame you have to take Walter to the hospital without me. Do you think you can manage?"

"Yes I'm taking him for blood tests on Tuesday to the Public Health Department in Butha-Buthe. He can't do these journeys alone. He's too ill now. I am worried that nothing will be done in time. Barrie will he die?"

"Of course not. He's got us. Think what he would have to do if you weren't here to get him to the hospital. It would be public transport or nothing. It's the least we can do. We wouldn't forgive ourselves if we let him down."

He took my hand and led me over to the calendar on the wall. "Now, have you forgotten we're going away at the weekend? And have you forgotten about Sarah?"

"Oh, Sarah's baby's due isn't it and we're off to climb in Clarens for two days. Barrie – your first grandchild - it's exciting heh...."

"Secretly I'm hoping it's a boy....but then a girl would be wonderful. I don't mind really. Shall we ring and talk to them tonight?"

*　　　*　　　*　　　*

The Maluti Lodge in Clarens had a television set. Every minute of commentary Diana's funeral in Westminster Abbey completely absorbed us. Sitting in our Hotel room we wept liquid waves of tears. Seeing tributes pouring in from every country in the world and thousands of Londoners lining the route to the Abbey, we were overcome by homesickness. I wanted to be among the crowds of mourners. The silence across London was unreal and so dreadfully sad.

But we hadn't come to Clarens to weep. On the Sunday there was talk of eland-stalking. We were up early, determined to shake off our melancholy. A friendly eland lived high in the cliffs of Golden Gate Reserve and its recent appearances on the lower slopes had the locals a-flutter .

"Come on," said Barrie gruffly, "let's go find him."

A three-hour hike produced no eland, only thorn bushes and a dam set about with willow trees. Marvelling at the colours in the sandstone cliffs, ochre, red and purply black, we slipped and slithered our way through rock crevices and splashed in streams dappled in sunlight. Eventually, after a hot climb, we came across something we had hoped for. Cave paintings.

In the shadows beneath an overhang of rock we recognised the drawings of the early san bushmen - perfectly drawn figures of buffalo, zebra and yes - the stately eland. How thrilled we were to have found them.

It was our last day's vacation together before I left for England. South Africa is often prone to rapid weather changes and that evening a heavy snowstorm loomed. The journey was a seething mass of flakes running against the car lights, with visibility only a few yards. Road signs were wiped out. On reaching Leribe camp we found the power had failed. The LHPC generator, a device known for plunging the entire camp into darkness in thirty eight seconds, was out for the count. Engineers are known to sleep very soundly. We spent a freezing cold night huddled on the sofa, wrapped in blankets and drinking cold tea from a vacuum flask.

At six thirty the phone rang. I leapt across to answer it. The room was stone cold. Nobody ever rang at this hour of the morning. Barrie was still asleep.

"Hello, who's speaking?" I whispered, hardly daring to listen in case it was Rose or Stephen with bad news.

"Hello 'M'e, sorry to wake you so early - it's Theresa.." She was a nurse friend of Makibis. "I am telling you to go with Walter very soon to the Public Health Office in Butha-Buthe. They close at nine thirty so you must be there by nine o'clock.. It is critical you go today. He is very ill. The Public Health Officers have to close the clinic and go up to the remote farms in the Highlands. I only know because I work there. It is urgent I am telling you."

"Thank you for letting me know Theresa, I shall be there in an hour. Don't worry I'll get him there on time."

There was a dimension of fear around Walter now, that had not been present before. I left the house immediately.

Rose and I helped the patient into the car. He could not speak. I saw the mask of fear on Rose's face. The yard was deathly quiet and none of the family were awake.

I put my foot down hard on the accelerator and hoped there were no stray animals wandering along the Butha-Buthe road at this hour of the morning. Walter sat hunched in his blanket in the passenger seat, his face as grey as slate.

"Sit tight Walter, I'm putting my engine through its paces."

Just before Levis Nek, my worst nightmare happened. A Police road block.

"Oh God Walter, look – we'll be held up for sure."

My car screeched to a halt. I stopped inches away from the feet of the Highway Officer on duty. They were stopping all vehicles and searching everything. A queue of trucks was pulled up on the verge. The place was crawling with uniforms.

Chapter 13

Valley of Darkness

For reasons which at the time were unclear to me, the policeman beckoned me to get out of the car. I thought he was pulling me over for speeding.

"Sorry," I began, "I am taking a very sick boy to hospital in Butha-Buthe. I must get him to a doctor straight away...."

He looked hard at Walter, then at me.

"Please pass *'M'e*" he answered swiftly, his eyebrows showing surprise at seeing us together. "Go now, take him there, no search – just move on please."

I could have kissed him. On his belt dangled a pair of handcuffs. His duties were not yet accomplished. It was not a white woman with a Mosotho, for whom they were searching. This was the last thing I expected.

"*Kea leboha, Ntate.*" I answered swiftly, S*ala hantle.*"

As we drove into the car park of the Public Health Department in Butha-Buthe, the doctor was locking the outside door and preparing to leave the building. It was nine o'clock exactly. A powerful motorbike stood beside him with engine running. Goggles and crash helmet were placed at the ready. I left Walter and ran.

"Please... would you see a patient, doctor? He needs a Mantoux test. He's very ill. Could you see him before you go ...please ...Dr Sekhesa sent me." I burst out, pausing to look for Walter as he came slowly towards us from the car. He couldn't fail to sense the note of panic in my voice. He followed my gaze.

"A Mosotho?"

The Doctor's expression was one of surprise.He looked from one to the other, then took off his gloves, placed them on the seat of his motorbike and unlocked the surgery door. There was an air of refinement in his manner which surprised me and his attitude was not unsympathetic.

"Yes, he is the son of my adopted family. I would like all the tests for TB to be done today."

The doctor looked me straight in the eye for a long moment, then produced a chair for me to sit down. I did not have to spell it out. He knew what to do.

"Wait please *'M'e*, we will attend to him."

Walter was given a sputum test, a blood test and a *Mantoux* test, which the doctor said would react in two hours – but the reading must be done in seventy two hours. We were to be back at the clinic on Thursday. He insisted that we must not fail to return for the result of the Mantoux test. I felt confidence in his manner. The way he held himself and spoke reminded me of an actor whose name I couldn't quite remember.

"Thank you Doctor."

"It's a pleasure Ma'am. English eh….I don't often see whites in my clinic. Please give Walter lots of water to drink, let him rest as much as possible and take these. They're sleeping tablets." Then, out of earshot to Walter, "He is a very sick boy, but you are strong. You will not catch the infection. Tell the family to be sterile with bedding, towels and clothes. They must wash everything."

"They have already isolated him from the rest of the family."

"That's good."

We shook hands. The fee was agreed. Walter winked at me and gave me very knowing look. He gathered all his strength in an effort to say something. In a croaky voice he rasped, "She is my new mother, don't take any notice of the colour of her skin….she is the same colour as we are on the inside."

"Come on, let's get you home Walter, Barrie wants to see something of me today, he's taken the afternoon off so that we can do some planning. He's got to write a wedding speech before next Friday. And he's going to book a car to get me to Jo'burg. Have you remembered that I'm going to England soon?" I reminded him gently. He didn't reply.

As we approached a familiar bend on the homeward stretch the same traffic-control policeman was still standing on the same bit of melting tarmac. He pulled me over, not because he wanted to give me a speeding fine but to ask how the patient was.

"Is the boy okay – will he live?" I saw his shirt was soaked in perspiration. Several khaki uniforms hung on the barbed wire fence a few feet away. Vehicles were standing behind and in front. This morning there had been an intensive search to find a vehicle containing drugs, which perhaps had once more slipped through the net.

"He will live – don't make a mistake about that," said a voice from inside the blanket.

The officer looked straight at me. His hat was tipped back from his forehead. I reckoned he was about the same age as my patient.

"If you carry this sick passenger to hospital 'M'e, tell the duty officer and he will let you pass through,"

"I appreciate that. Thanks very much."

The next seventy two hours were the longest I ever remember. I was aware that Walter's illness was taking its toll on the family. His fate weighed heavily upon the minds of his parents, brothers and sisters. Their laughter had flown out of the window. Except for the singing in the church, the atmosphere at the Makibi household was tense and silent. Walter had always been the strongest, the leader, the one who knew what to do in times of crisis. As the eldest son, he took responsibility for the direction of his family. It was as though they were looking into an abyss. His father was beside himself with worry.

Rose's constant presence was unswerving. She bathed him down when he was hot with fever. His dreams were nightmares of sweating and unrelenting fear, wakeful moments were racked with chest pains. He was now too weak to walk by himself. His medication did nothing to stem the flow of the bleeding from his lungs.

We counted the hours until three days had passed. I continued with my writing, but within nudging distance of the phone, in case any member of the family should ring up with news. The only light moment was a message from Amelia telling us that the King Letsie's Coronation would take place on 31st October and that we were invited.

"Amelia, we won't be returning from England until 28th October, but we hope to make the Coronation. Thank you for the invitation. We will make contact when we arrive back in Leribe."

"May God Bless you Annette and your husband - and in all your hopes for the link between our country and yours. I intend to visit the Makibi family while you are away. Poor Walter, we are all praying for him."

It was strange being on the verge of our second wedding celebration in one year. It would be very different from our first one in April, when Barrie and I had made our vows to each other in a South African garden, with neither of our families present. We were now going back to England as ambassadors for our new country. This visit was to be a golden opportunity for a formal link to be set up. The longed-for letter from Richard Syms and the Parochial Church Council in Datchworth had finally arrived. The idea of a link with Ha Simone had not fallen on stony ground. The P.C.C. had listened to our request. Reverend Syms had invited me to meet the congregation on a date in September, in readiness for the launch of our ambitious scheme with Africa. Barrie's work in Lesotho had carved out a path for me; one which I knew I should take. But first, we had to pray that Walter would be well again.

Now was a precious moment. After months of waiting, the news could be broken to the Makibi Family.

"Morning Petros, where is your father?"

"He's still in TY. Mum's at home – she's with Walter across the yard. I'm just going out with the cows – do you want to come? Walter is too sick to come today." He spoke in a plain manner, not affected by emotion, but he was downcast.

It was a glorious day and the challenge of a new climb, exhilarating. We parked opposite the house, crossed a shallow ford and went up the bank on the other side. Petros guided us along a steep rocky incline, some distance from the river. We walked in silence for some time, then Petros became talkative. He needed to talk. His favourite chat line was animals. Looking behind us in the distance, we could see St John's Church and the houses round it, as small as matchboxes. A herd of cows met us on the brow of a hill, accompanied by a boy who gave a wave to Petros. They obviously knew each other.

"We look out for each other, especially when someone attends school. I have a friend who looks after my cows when I go to school, and I will do the same for him."

"Do your cows recognise you Petros?" asked Barrie playfully.

"Yes, they know me. They will come running when they see me or if I whistle, even from a long way off."

"In England the farmers use dogs to help with animals. The dog can be trained to fetch a herd in or take it to another pasture."

"I would like to see one of those dogs, is there a picture in a book?"

"Petros, I will bring you a picture of a sheep dog when we go to England," I said. At this, he stopped dead in his tracks and stared at us, unbelieving.

"Why are you going to England Nettie?" There was a note of panic in his voice. "Are you going for good?"

"No, no we're going for our wedding blessing and to see our families, then we'll come back," I said quietly. Barrie put a hand on his shoulder.

"Petros, we may have some good news to celebrate……we are hoping to set up a link between your church and an English church."

It wasn't the way we had planned, but it was the way it happened. Forgetting his sadness for a moment, Petros began running and yelling at the top of his voice, aiming his message to the sky and the rocks and his beloved cows.

"An English Church will love us. The people will love us." His voice carried far and he started to run back towards home to spread the glad news, arms whooping the air.

Very early the next morning, before daylight, I was awake. Padding silently over to the window I could just make out the volcanic mountain, Qoqolosing through the misty light. The sky was streaked with a pale mist and no stars showed. Barrie was still sound asleep. He would wake at six when the alarm went off.

Shrouded in heavy dew, the garden reminded me of November mornings in England, when bramble hedges ripple with old man's beard and leaves are stained purple with over-ripe blackberries. It was cold. Sleep had deserted me. I shivered and pulled on a dressing gown.

All night, thoughts of my trip to England had tumbled around in my mind. My maternal impulses were mixed up with thoughts of Walter. I was never more sad than this moment. Who would be there for him? Would he die before I came back? I straddled two cultures, divided and confused.

I prayed that this unplanned hour of quietness and solitude would clarify my decisions, as I sat on the verandah steps, a mug of steaming tea resting in my hands. I watched the silver sky change with the dawn. Even the gravel in the car park, where the men came in early for work was as quiet as the grave. From his cave underneath the house Hercule growled a yawn in recognition of my presence. This was the day I had dreaded.

At nine o'clock Walter and I were back at the Public Health Department in Butha-Buthe. Justice and Petros had almost lifted him into the car. He was now unable to walk unaided. He spat constantly into the bowl on his lap, holding his mouth with a clean white towel that Rose had given him. The forty minute journey seemed endless. No police road block.

The same doctor we had seen three days ago was preparing to leave the compound. Another man was with him. Two motorbikes stood nearby They were doctors of mercy alright.

"*N'tate* - would you read a Mantoux test result before you leave?" I shouted through the car window, desperate that we should be seen today and not have to wait any longer for a diagnosis.

The first doctor recognised me and smiled. He took a ruler out of his pocket and measured the length of the scar on Walter's outstretched arm.

"10 mm reactive. You have tuberculosis Walter." He looked directly at me. "*'M'e*, you must get him into a hospital. Go to Leribe, if that is where you live. Go now. See Dr Sekhesa first and tell him that is what you must do. Walter is very sick. He needs treatment – otherwise he may die."

I can't remember driving back home. My head was reeling with the news. Even though I knew really. The shock was unbearable. Rose was in floods of tears when we reached the house. Emily had gone to the spring and arrived back a few moments later. She brought water for Walter while he sat in the car, but he could only shake his head and lean back onto the seat, with eyes rolling. Facially, his cheekbones protruded and it was obvious he had lost a huge amount of weight. This lovely twenty four year old boy was fading away before our eyes.

"Rose, we must get him to hospital. There's no time to lose. Walter must have treatment. I will go and do what I have to do. We must try and reverse the tide of this sickness. I will do my best."

Rose did not reply. She and Emily supported each other as I turned and left the yard.

Leribe Hospital is a huge sprawling building. The Infectious Diseases Unit was at the far end of the complex. I didn't know where to begin. In one of the outpatient clinics, a helpful nurse directed us to the TB Ward, which it seemed was the furthest outpost. Walter was finding it hard to walk holding my arm and he was spitting the whole time into his plastic bowl. There was a wooden bench under a tree in the grounds. I left him sitting in the shade.

"Wait here Walter, I am going to find someone of authority."

There wasn't a wheelchair in sight. Shaking with tension from the task I knew I must do, I walked over to the reception point in the 'Infectious Diseases' area, where a lady wearing a uniform was presiding over a work station.

"Is it possible to see the Divisional Medical Officer – I would like to speak urgently with him?" I asked politely.

Her expression registered a nil response. Plainly it meant, 'get lost'.

"Madam," she began loudly, "we would all like to be speaking to the DMO. There will be no doctor here until tomorrow. Today I cannot help you." Her heavy bosom heaved with sarcasm as she turned back to the paperwork.

"Do you know which is Matron's Office?" I asked, hoping she wouldn't demand my reasons for wanting to see Matron. Sarcastically, she nodded in the direction I had come, without managing to look up.

I went back to find Walter under the tree. He still sitting upright and for a few minutes the coughing had ceased. He raised a limp hand and a ghost of a smile played around his dry lips.

"Nettie, thank you…," he started to say.

"Be quiet and listen," I said, almost in tears, "we're going to pay Matron a royal visit. No more words from you my lad."

It was the first time he managed to find his voice. I felt so tense, I would have cried rather than hear him thank me. I was doing this because I cared what happened to him.

"Try and hold out Walter, I'm going to get you a bed in this hospital, if it's the last thing I do."

I left him, bowl in hand, sitting on a bench, while I found my way into the sprawling innards of the hospital. My instinct told me to go to the top of the establishment. It was now or never.

After a long search through endless corridors, I discovered a door with 'Assistant Matron' written on the outside. I knocked boldly. From inside the room I heard, 'Come' and went forward, my heart in my boots. A meeting was in progress. Several senior members of staff were sitting round a desk. From behind a row of clipboards, wide eyes glared in my direction. There was a pregnant pause, then a rustling of papers. I expected a severe reprimand – but those inside were so taken aback by a white woman barging into their inner sanctum that no one spoke.

"Please may I speak to you about a patient." I asked nervously.

Walter wasn't yet a patient, but I had every intention that he was going to be. Then a voice said bracingly, "Wait – I will call you."

Whether a miracle happened or whether I was in luck at that particular moment, I don't remember. Apart from not knowing who I was, the Senior Matron did not usually deal with individuals, certainly not individuals who invited themselves into her office in the middle of meetings. The wait was not a long one.

"Now, can you explain what this is all about?" said the large uniformed lady when I was seated opposite her. Her expression was brisk but not unfriendly. I decided I was in with a chance.

"I need a bed for a very sick young man who has TB. It is urgent. The disease has progressed and he is extremely ill. Only your treatment will save his life. Dr Sekhesa sent us."

Her face was kind and her dark eyes flashed as we continued our dialogue. She picked up a telephone and spoke to someone. After a few minutes, she started to write something on her notepad and after scribbling furiously, handed me the letter.

"Go and see this man. He knows you are coming. Give him this paper."

I couldn't believe my good fortune. This lady had a talent for efficiency. In a few moments I was guiding Walter from the tree in the grounds over to the 'Injection Room' past a double row of waiting patients, straight up to a door marked 'Duty Doctor' where we sat together on a wooden bench. A moment later an attack of coughing sent Walter flying over to the sink in the corner, where he spewed up volumes of bright red blood. Alarmed at the fiasco taking place in his lungs, he threw me a look of total horror. Then from somewhere outside, a group of relatives and a small girl were brought into the room, the relatives taking turns to howl and cry out with raw grief. The child didn't move and looked as though she were transfixed with some dreadful trauma. Her pretty dress was torn and her dark hair fell around her shoulders. There were no tears – just a terrified gaze and her arms hung limp by her sides.

"She's been raped, Nettie," whispered Walter, when he had recovered his composure. "Her father and mother want to kill the man who attacked her."

" My God Walter, do they want us to go outside?"

"No, let's wait. We have the letter."

Another loud wail came from the mother, which brought forth a nurse, carrying a large plastic sheet. She took the girl gently by the hand and led her away to another room, followed by the weeping wailing entourage.

Once in front of the duty doctor, I felt for the first time we were making progress with Walter's case. Matron's letter was the key. Her bold actions. had got us through this far. I held my breath. The doctor gave me a hard stare.

"I want you to have another set of X-rays done Walter and then you must go to the TB Ward for another blood test. You will be admitted immediately. I think we can help you if the disease is not full blown. You are suffering from malnutrition. That does not help recovery, so we must feed you."

I could have hugged him. Walter and I exchanged glances – it was the best moment so far. If the treatment started immediately, he was in with a chance. The choking started up again, at the sheer movement of his chest. He bent over and spat on the floor. Dear God, if only there was a trolley to put him on, some sterile bowls... anything .... I held onto his arm and guided him towards the door.

The young doctor looked at me quizzically. "You white lady.... you are helping this man. Why?"

"Because we know his family well. They are good people."

"I have not known this before...but you are English - yes?"

"Yes, my husband works with LHPC on the Highland Water Scheme."

"Ahh....now I understand...it is good. We are glad you come to our country." He nodded towards Walter. "Good luck."

At last we were inside Ward 6, this time with the magic letter to wave at the establishment. There was no medical staff in sight. The orderly spared us no favours. She growled roughly and it was obvious from the first that she could not (or would not) speakie de English.

"We have no beds!" was her only greeting.

164

"The doctor has given me a bed on Ward 6," said Walter breathlessly. I stood behind him and drew myself up to full height – all of five foot two. The orderly wasn't impressed.

"Fill in this form," she snapped without a hint of sympathy.

She threw us a white sheet of paper bearing enough questions to keep a patient busy for a week. I looked round. There was one chair and nowhere to write.

"My God Nettie I don't know the answers to half these questions,"said Walter as he cast his eye down the list. He could hardly stand and his hand was shaking so badly it was impossible for him to write.

"Could we have a bowl please?" I asked, looking her straight in the eye. Her mouth was set firm. There was no answer – just a long glare. She pretended she hadn't heard.

I turned to Walter struggling with his sheet of questions. He had written his name at the top but feeling so utterly exhausted had given up. I took the sheet from him and threw it back on the desk under the nose of the lady.

"Where is Walter's bed?"

"In room four. He will have to wait for the bed to be changed. A man died there this morning."

"Right Walter. I'm going to find somebody. Sit down on the chair. I'll be back.."

I felt a surge of outrage coming on. From the long corridor I could see into the wards. Most were full to overflowing. At least the beds looked clean and there were some toilets. There just didn't seem to be any staff. One office I passed was empty and another room, full of mops and buckets, looked decidedly organised and neat with things labelled and hung on hooks. There was no ringing of telephones and I gathered this ward didn't have any. Telephone links within the hospital were limited to senior members only. Many sick people were sitting on the ground outside the wards obviously waiting for beds.

My search was futile so I returned to Ward 6 where I was greeted by a different nurse (in uniform) who had just come on duty. The dragon had gone.

"Please would you come into the office. Walter's admission has been explained. I have Matron's letter." She waved it with an air of professionalism. "I have his X-rays here. His bed will soon be ready. I know he is Dr Sekhesa's patient. He has advised the treatment and it will start straight away."

Whether it was the name of Dr Sekhesa, the note from Matron or my white skin that altered the attitude of the Sister-in-charge, I had no idea. But whatever the magic ingredient was, it had worked. She was now a central figure to Walter's recovery and had assured me that he would receive the best treatment. It was too good to be true.

I braved the inside of the men's room and helped to sponge Walter's face and neck. His skin was a ghastly colour, somewhere between dark brown and misty grey. When I left he was lying in clean sheets, in a four bedded ward containing six patients. There was an eyesore of a sink where empty sputum cups had been discarded. No towels or tablets of soap. No lockers between patients. The space between the beds was no more than ten inches. No nurse arrived to tell him what to do or what to expect.

The old man next to him was more corpse than alive and I dare not even look in his direction. From the other side of the room someone coughed a terrible cough. Other patients were spitting into bowls. These people were extremely sick. I wondered if they all had TB or something worse.

Like a chameleon I kept my eye on Walter's face until he fell asleep. Turning to walk away, I gave him one last look. He was spark out. Now all I could do was to say my prayers and leave my young friend in the lap of the gods.

When Barrie came home from work I was still sitting in the bath with soap bubbles up to my chin. I felt as though I would never be clean again.

"Honey you've done well to get Walter admitted to hospital. It's the best thing you could have done."

"Oh Barrie, it was so awful....seeing all those sick people in there. I wanted to wave a magic wand and change it all.....I know it's the same in our country but somehow it was more depressing. Standards of hygiene were terrible, poor staffing - I suppose through lack of funding....but that Matron was fantastic! It was she who got him admitted. I know I shouldn't have broken the rules but I had to do something to get Walter the right treatment."

"Nettie - you didn't break the rules again," he teased, " I'll have to have a word with God about you."

"Yes, tell him I'll make up my own rules and if he doesn't like it – that's tough."

I liked to get in a dig at Barrie sometimes, when he threw his principles at me. He was a far deeper thinker than me and I liked to knock him off his pedestal sometimes. I was more of a hands-on person and usually got where I wanted, though not through the same channels. My husband still carried a touch of guilt with him from the dogma of his religious upbringing. Cutting corners was not his scene. He was an engineer who designed everything on squared paper, then carefully built things which didn't fall down. He has a saying which goes: 'if it can go wrong it will go wrong' and plans his life accordingly. I have always lived by the seat of my pants.

"Well, come on - what have you said in your wedding speech about me, I want to know now, before I walk down the aisle with you on 11th October."

"I've said you're only worth ten cows and a donkey ...and no more. Ouch...!!" he ducked as I splashed bath water over his suit. "Into the kitchen woman, where you belong."

He got up and went towards the dining room.

"Heh Barrie - did you realise there's only five days to go until I'm on the aeroplane…..let's open that bottle of champagne and drink Walter's health. I'm not leaving it for you to sozzle when I'm gone."

"There you go breaking the rules again…..yes, why not?"

Chapter 14

Have Faith

Barrie and I visited Ward 6 that evening. The man in the bed next to Walter had regressed to the point of no return during the afternoon and passed away. Several of the other patients looked in the same pitiable state. A row of sad faces gaped as we entered the room. We were pleased to see our patient was connected to an intravenous drip. Nursing staff were not in evidence, but someone had found him a locker so that he was now further away from the dead man, whose body had been covered over with a sheet, but not removed. There were no screens.

Walter was dozing when we arrived. Barrie was shocked at the state of him, as he hadn't seen him for about ten days. There were no other visitors in the room.

"Hello Walter, thought you'd like to know we've told the family where you are and they'll be along to visit tomorrow. How do you feel?"

He opened his eyes and smiled weakly. His voice was almost inaudible.

"Glad to be in hospital and not at home. Did you know Barrie, Nettie got me an emergency bed. The doctor was really kind …he…says I have a chance of recovery if I get some nutrition." He started to cough and jerked the drip in his arm violently. We waited until he could speak. He was gripping my hand so tightly.

"They've started the injections and they're terrible….their needles are like pokers. I yelled so loud I'm surprised you didn't hear me across the road."

"Don't talk Walter, we've just called to see if you are okay, we'll leave in a minute. They've started your drip – that's good news, it means the vitamins are going in." said Barrie, sounding more positive than he felt.

Checking round the emphysemic water system, I discovered the tap in the sink didn't work and the abandoned waste in the sink hadn't been cleared for several days. In fact it was useless as an aid to recovery. In the face of galloping germs a bottle of TCP was the only answer. As we left the ward, a drugs trolley came into sight, commandeered by an elderly lady without a uniform.

Early the next day, I presented myself at the hospital security post. The guard viewed me with suspicion. It was seven o'clock and a beautiful sunny morning. He asked me where I was going. I smiled breezily and managed to convince him I had a patient to look after. I think he thought I was a member of staff.

There was no one around. Despite the night shift, no one had so much as looked at the communal receptacle in the corner of Ward 6. Armed with a bottle of disinfectant in my handbag, my task included the eradication of everything remotely unsavoury from within twenty yards of my patient. I cleaned the offending sink – twice, washed the tiles underneath, spruced up Walter's bedside locker and threw out half a dozen sputum cups which were rolling around inside from the last patient, among a clatter of enamel mugs and plates. I found a mop and washed the floor under the beds of four sleeping patients, throwing as much Dettol around as I dare. The gospel according to my mother was 'soap never hurt anybody' and if pulmonary diseases thrived on micro organisms, then they weren't getting any today. Walter was still asleep. I left a bottle of Aqualibra on his locker and departed.

*   *   *   *

The kids at Thotlisong School were on good form as I drove in to see Solomon Malebo. Thankfully, the picket line in Meqheleng had given up the ghost and anyone visiting the school was able to enter normally through the big gates.

The journey through the township was uneventful, apart from a boy pushing a wheelbarrow landing in a heap in front of my car as I turned into the road to the school. A wise precaution in the face of a runaway wheelbarrow is to place foot hard on brakes and wait for crash. Out of a cloud of dust rose a skinny lad of about eight or nine wearing a sorry smile. His hair was shorn and as he bent over, the familiar ringworm fissures showed on his head. I didn't get out of the car but spoke to him through the window.

"Are you okay?"

"Yes *'M'e.*" He looked at me sideways and rubbed his elbow. "You a teacher 'M'e? I know your car. You come to the Shoprite for food – I see you."

I can't say I recognised him, but yes, I had met a number of the kids who frequented the supermarket car park in the centre of Ficksburg, where they gathered in swarms to earn a few coins by pushing trolleys for customers.

"Well then, I will look for you next time. *Lebitso la hau u mang?*"

"I am Moses."

"Okay Moses I will hire you – and you'd better be good."

I shoved some sweets into his hand and he touched his stomach and bowed before picking up the heap of iron and wheeling it away. Other kids followed, making pleading gestures for a share of the goodies. They ran in a crowd after my wheels and I carried on, not wanting to attract attention in this volatile area.

The creation of a new spirit since the repeal of the apartheid laws has meant that areas such as Meqheleng should be free from trouble and unrest but as the living conditions had hardly changed at all since 1994, the same old problems still exist. I hadn't seen one white face during my journey to Thotlisong which came as no surprise. Ficksburgians did not want to come face-to-face with the shabby streets of Meqheleng too often and the same old questions were still on everyone's lips. Will Mandela's government change things? Will stability come to white towns while hundreds of shanty villages like Meqheleng still exist? Will there ever be better homes for Africans?

"Annette, good morning - I am pleased to see you. Where is Walter?" exclaimed Solomon when he saw me enter his large new office at the school. The figure of the headmaster dressed in a blue suit and tie looked very much in charge and there was an air of pride in the place. Selina, Solomon's secretary, came through to greet me. A working 'hush' permeated the building.

"Solomon, he's very ill in hospital and he needs your prayers. Please tell the students – a lot of them know him. I've come to say goodbye – for six weeks. I can't come up to teach for a while. I'm going to England so thought you might like to see photos of the concert."

"You are coming back to Ficksburg? We need your help with the careers class. Will you come and do some teaching when you come back?"

"Yes I will – as long as your choir keeps on singing for me."

He gave me a broad smile.

"Did you know we came first in the Johannesburg Music Festival? That's all due to the music staff – Elizabeth and Miriam. They've worked really hard. I'm so proud of my choir. They deserved the prize – after the concert at L.H.P.C. their confidence really improved."

As he spoke, a contingency of kids from the old 10A class knocked on his door. They had recognised my car. It was the first time I had seen them all since they had sung in Butha-Buthe for our engineers a few months ago. We greeted each other fondly. They grew boisterous. Solomon didn't object. He knew the score. He worked them very hard most of the time. They were allowed a few moments release from class.

"Lumelang bana secola," I said. (Hello kids)

"Mrs Glenn, are you coming to teach us? Will you still come – we can sing for you? We won the competition in Jo'burg.......we won first prize." Arms flung themselves in the air as they whooped at the recollection of their day of glory.

"Yes, I heard. Congratulations! When I come back from England you must learn to sing English songs for me. I would like to hear Christmas carols...." Turning to the girls I asked, "Would you like to see the photos of the concert?"

Like bees in a honey pot they clustered round. I was pleased to see their smiling faces and cheesy grins. A flutter of giggling erupted across the corridor at the pictures of uniformed sopranos with their mouths wide open. Most African children never see themselves on film and they think it's very amusing to see themselves through the eyes of a camera. I don't suppose many of them even had a mirror at home.

Solomon walked me to the car.

"Annette, I hope your English wedding is happy and give my best wishes to Barrie. Please come back and see us. There's always a place for you in our school and you can be sure we will pray for Walter. The kids will probably go and visit him when he's recovered."

"*Au revoir* Solomon – that's kisses from Liliane! She's coming back from France soon. I'll bring her up to see your new school."

He stood and waved me off. The memory of our big adventure together a couple of months ago - crossing the border with fifty kids on a battered old bus - without passports, would always bond us together. In truth, we had crossed many borders that day.

Post pulmonary tuberculosis occurs mainly in young adults but can occur at any age. Walter had showed all of the symptoms during the last few weeks but as I had never met the disease before, I did not recognise how ill he was. Lack of energy, weight loss, persistent cough, the chest pains, the night sweats. Then the dense shadow on the edge of his lungs, seen on his X-ray, brought the whole disease into focus.

In hindsight, his job had come to an end a year ago, with disastrous consequences. He had become stressed, anxious and worried. The family ate maize most of the time, but there wasn't really enough. Walter said he often went hungry. He had always been thin. He tried to keep fit when he had no job, by running across the mountains. On an empty stomach, this perhaps wasn't such a good idea. In the winter the family found it hard to keep warm. Bitter cold spells had meant that they shivered for days inside the house. They all had shoes, as for socks….I knew they had none because Liliane and I had taken several pairs over and they loved the feeling of something warm on their feet. Petros kissed me when I gave him socks. Sometimes when they had cracks in their skin with the ice and snow, they would rub animal fat into their sores. Rose hated the winter. She said it made the whole family depressed.

Rest, good food and nursing care had arrived just in time. The hospital had put him on doses of Streptomycin, which we hoped would eradicate the tubercle bacillus from his body and help him to recover. We had no idea how long this treatment would continue. And I would have to remind him tomorrow that I was going away in a few days.

During that night Walter's condition worsened. He couldn't breathe and the pains in his chest were so bad that he thought he was going to die. He struggled to call for help – but there was no one to call. His strength was deserting him hour by hour. Walter was no fool. He knew that in this ward patients were left to die. He tried everything to attract attention but was too weak to move from his bed. Duty staff were not available during the night.

Reverend Makibi arrived during the early hours of daylight and found his son in a semi-comatose state. The drip container feeding into Walter's arm was empty. It was the first time Stephen had visited and he was in no state to cope with his eldest son's condition. He tore into the main hospital like a mad bull. He shouted at Matron. He exploded with a torrent of abuse at the night sister. He shouted at everybody. By seven o'clock he was on the phone to me saying that he wanted to take Walter out of there and put him in a hospital in Johannesburg. Today he was going to make sure Walter would be moved.

Poor Stephen – the outburst was because he cared so much. Bewildered by his feelings of anxiety, he could do nothing else but induce panic into the entire place.

"Stephen, if I offer my phone number to the hospital staff to use in an emergency, would that help?"

"No, because there are no phones on the ward. Nettie it makes me so mad – they are dying these people......and the government, they don't care. I shall take my son away to South Africa."

The next injections were to be at eleven o'clock that morning. I arrived a few minutes before eleven, just as Sister came in with her long needle for the inter-muscular jabs.

The routine treatment was halted by the arrival of a small deputation of women, who stood between me and Walter's bed. Word had gone round that there was a white lady who came every day to see a patient in Ward Six. I was suddenly surrounded. One of them wearing a white headscarf and faded cotton frock stepped forward and addressed me in English, pulling my arm. She seemed to be the spokesperson. The others all watched her intently. She moved a step closer.

"You are kind lady… can you help me to send my daughter to school? I have no money. If you help this man, you must help me."

I was so surprised by the forthright request, I couldn't answer. Walter raised himself on one elbow, looked across at me, then shook his head

"That will not be possible, I am here in Lesotho on business. I cannot help you." I answered.

"Why do you come to the bedside of this man? We need money to send our children to school. You white lady have money….give me some."

It was the first time since coming to Lesotho that I was confronted with such head-on cheek. A feeling rather like revulsion washed over me and I wanted to run away. The woman's demand had transgressed the sensitive rules of the game.

"Right young man …. roll over. Let's get it over with," announced the nurse with the needle. That was my cue to walk over and take Walter's hand. The little group melted away. As the plunger withdrew, he shut his eyes. Tension, pain, fear, paralysed his face muscles. Through clenched teeth, he smiled – then after a long minute slowly relaxed his grip.

"Thanks Nettie. You came just in time. Not so bad this time. Where is my father? He has upset the whole staff. He can't do this to me"

"He wants to get you transferred to Johannesburg to another hospital, he's phoning round today. Look Walter, he feels frightened and he wants the very best for you"

"I know, but I wish he wouldn't. Last night was very bad, but I want to stay here. The boys came to see me last night. My mother sent me a pair of pyjamas, Nettie they're awful." He wrinkled up his nose and it made me smile, remembering how my own son had been appalled at the thought of wearing a hospital gown when he was a patient in an English hospital.

"Walter, your Mum means well. You must wear them when she is here."

"She made them on her sewing machine Nettie. I know she did this for me, but I can't wear them…. and everybody has heard about my Dad."

"Yes I heard it from the girls in the laundry. They asked me who he was because they know me now. Apparently he could be heard all over the hospital. But he is very frightened Walter, he loves you."

"Well I wish he would say that. He upset everybody."

"Look I've brought fruit for you today and fresh cold water in a flask."

Food was not provided for the patients. Relatives, if there were any, were expected to feed the sick person. If a patient was well enough to walk, he could leave his bed and fetch himself food from outside the hospital. There was no supervision. Patients plus germs, could easily slip outside and return without anyone knowing.

"Nettie I know you will be leaving Leribe tomorrow. I want to write to James. I want to tell him certain things. Will you write down my words on a letter because I have no energy."

"All right. Barrie and I will come in tonight after work. We'll do it then."

"Can you come to hold my hand for the big needle at six o'clock? It helps me so much to know you're there."

He still looked a dreadful grey colour. His eyes looked too large in his face and his cheeks were hollow. His condition was still critical.

"Walter, I want to see you looking better when I come back from England…."

Suddenly, my voice would not say the words. My hands shook. The drip, drip of a tap somewhere sounded too loud and the room was swimming. A sob rose in my throat, but didn't come. What if he died when we were in England? We wouldn't even know.

As I walked back through the hospital laundry, the girls waved. They knew my daily routine and although nothing was ever spoken, they knew my mission was with a Mosotho. The girls sang as they draped the whole yard with bed sheets. Like butterflies, they lifted with the warm breeze and dried there, colours of lilac and pale yellow fluttering on the grass. The girls were mostly young and I guessed loved their jobs - loved the fact that they had a job. I was so pre-occupied and almost bumped into a lady crossing the compound. She was wearing a pale blue uniform and smiled at me. I don't know what it was that made me stop.

"I'm sorry 'M'e, excuse me I wasn't looking where I was going."

"Good morning. You are the lady who comes here every day to see a boy on the TB Ward?"

"That's right - how do you know me?"

"Everyone knows you *'M'e*. My name is Isnett. I am a physiotherapist in the hospital. My home is near Leribe. I have seen you many times with your husband walking with your dog. When a white person comes into our hospital, we are curious. Is he a friend, this boy?"

"Yes, I have been visiting him every day," then, on impulse, "but tomorrow I leave for England. I am worried because he is so ill ....Isnette, would you do something for me? Would you keep an eye on him... go and visit sometimes when you are in the hospital. He needs friends. When I come back I will come and find you to get the latest news of Walter."

"It will be my pleasure *'M'e*, if I can help in this situation, yes I will do it. Come, let me show you where my office is."

We walked together across to the Physiotherapy Unit. Isnette knew far more about the situation than I realised. I liked her instantly. We shook hands.

"Tomorrow I am coming to see Walter for the last time. In the morning. Then my husband will visit for two more weeks before he comes to England to join me. After that we will need your help.... I am so grateful....he has a good family. His mother and father are both priests in Ha Simone. *Kea leboha 'M'e"*

"I will take care of Walter. Please have a safe journey and come back to Leribe. I would like very much if you will be my friend."

Driving up to Ha Simone later that day, I tried to reason with myself. If only Walter's treatment worked. It struck me that I should ring my own Doctor Nettleton to ask if I myself should take any precautionary measures against TB. I would be in England for the best part of six weeks. In that time, there would be no news of Walter or anyone else in Lesotho. I wondered why he wanted to write to my son. Tonight I would take him a diary, so that he could record his progress and mark off the days.

The few small communities along the Butha-Buthe road looked sleepy in the afternoon sun; time for tail-switching cattle to doze and drowsy herd boys to lay out on the rocks with closed eyelids. Three abandoned cars on the outskirts of Leribe, swarmed over by a gaggle of children, stuck out of a donga like rusty teeth, providing the neighbourhood with its own adventure playground. Abandoned vehicles were a gift from God as far as the youngsters were concerned. Metal carcasses were hung with trophies, braided with ribbon and grasses from the fields and the hero of the game could stand on the roof and shout his conquest to passing sheep. I waved to the children. Let them play their games I thought. In no time at all their wild imaginations will be encumbered by the harsh world of reality.

Houses made of breeze-blocks, others made of clay and thatch, straddled the hillsides. Occupants worked on their mealie patch with hoe and spade. Yellow rock roses grew by the roadside in large clumps and willows hung prettily, making boundaries around the homesteads. In the sky, birds flew higher and higher as larks do in England on a spring day. September spring in Lesotho - and I was leaving for an English autumn.

Emily and her friend Selina were washing blankets in the big tub up on the bank when I arrived. Somehow I had missed Rose because she had gone on foot to the hospital. Joshua, David and Augustinus were busy painting pictures for me to take home to show Datchworth children, a lovely gesture. Drawings of African huts with animals in the foreground were placed on the stoep ready for my arrival. David presented me with them quite officially. He spoke like a shortened version of the prayer book because his English was limited to the words he said in church.

"Mrs Annette – *Re leballe ditlolo tsa rona* (Forgive us our trespasses) *Modimo o lerato* (God is love) *Ke bala Bebele* (I am reading the Bible) – please teach me the language of English people. I am in a hurry to learn. Heaven will bless you."

Then he bowed and I took the paintings from him. David was a hefty lad of about twenty, who laboured for Stephen whenever he was asked. He was regarded as part of the family. His mother lived nearby and had no money to send him to school. I knew his love for Walter as a brother went very deep. This terrible time had been too much for him to bear. David's sadness gave me a knot in my throat. Suddenly all the boys took my hands and held them. On this spot every day, the boys prayed together for Walter to get well and come home. His illness had ripped the heart out of the family. The four of us stood close together outside the little house – now empty - letting go of our tears.

"Nettie, we love you and Barrie," sniffed Augustinus," God will bring you back to us. We want you to bring Hercule here and walk over the mountains. We will be happy to see you again. Please will you bring me a book on architecture from England, it is what I want to be when I leave school. My teacher says I am a good artist."

"Only if you do one thing for me. All of you. Go and get yourselves tested for TB. I would hate to think any one of you may have caught the infection from Walter. Please promise me you will do it."

"Yes – we will do it. And we will tell Petros and Justice. And there is something else I must tell you Nettie. A man who Stephen knows has sent for me, he is a builder. He will employ me and pay me money..... only temporarily, but it will be my first job until I take up my studies."

Augustinus was very clever. Everyone said so. His ambition to become an architect would be within his reach, if he could only gain entry onto a university course and if he could find a financial grant to support him while he studied. In Lesotho there was only one option. The Manpower Services Commission. The only educational body who could make it possible. If Augustinus was lucky enough to get through all the legal requirements, he might qualify for a place at Maseru University funded by the MSC.

"Good luck with the new job Augustinus....I'll see you in October. We are hoping to be back in time for the King's Coronation.....Goodbye Em," I shouted, "see you in six weeks."

She looked up just as I clicked the camera. The girls were still bending over the tub. White headscarves and aprons contrasted prettily against blue dresses. Behind them the blankets draped soaking wet on the barbed wire fence.

"Oh Nettie, we'll be having our bottoms up in the air on the camera.," they shrieked.

The result of mountain poverty is that mountain children are among the toughest, yet friendliest on the planet. Their way of life is notoriously hard, yet they will make you as a visitor with a car and a bank account – feel humble.

It was duly recognised that Walter would not be transferred to Johannesburg. After his initial outburst, Stephen was satisfied that Leribe Hospital was doing all it could for Walter and went in to apologise. The staff were doing their best with very limited resources.

"They've told me I'm going to another ward tomorrow where they have only patients with TB. And Mum has been with some new clothes," grinned the patient, sitting up in bed proudly flaunting a white polo necked sweater with 'Rugby Tour' written across his chest. "Your godson Stephen gave it to me.... do you like it?"

"Well it makes a change from home-made pyjamas Walter." I smiled, "it seems to have made an improvement."

"He and Catherine left us their clothes that day when they flew back to England. Oh God here comes my injection again! Promise you'll stay for a while."

Barrie held one hand and I held the other. The lad drew in breath and we all shut our eyes.

"Now, young Walter Makibi," said Sister playfully as she withdrew the instrument of torture. "I shan't have the pleasure of pushing needles into you any longer. From now on it's tablets only. You'll be going out tomorrow to the main TB ward with all the other men. Pity...you were my favourite patient," she said, "your medication will be reduced to once a day now."

"And I'll be there to make sure you do as you are told," laughed Barrie. We were both surprised that he seemed to have turned a corner since this morning. It must have been the designer sweater.

Dr Nettleton assured me that there was no need to take any precautions against TB. He said there was no danger of Barrie and I being infected. Our general health and levels of nutrition were such that we would not be in danger of contracting the disease, providing we kept up the hygienic precautions outside the hospital.

The cases were packed for my journey. The truck was to arrive at two o'clock and a driver would take us. We had been listening to local radio and heard that ambitious preparations were being made in Maseru for King Letsie's Coronation. It was rumoured that Prince Charles was to be there. It was to be his first tour since the death of Princess Diana. Festivities were to be held in the National Stadium, which would contain 40,000 people. A thousand Basotho horsemen, riding in from many remote villages were expected to come and pay their respects to their new king.

"We might be there ourselves Barrie if all goes well with our flights from London. Let's hope Amelia can send us invitations."

Walter and I said our sad farewells. Pleased at the prospect of no more injections and being moved out of the 'death ward' as he called it, he promised to give Barrie all the news so that I should know the latest events. Petros, Justice, Augustinus and Emily had visited him in between their school lessons, as well as his best friend Michael, who had taken things very badly. To give him something to do in hospital, we had taken him a jigsaw puzzle. Barrie dismantled one of our cupboard doors and took it across, so that he was able to place the pieces on it. Walter had never seen such a thing – and wasn't very thrilled at the prospect of fixing dozens of silly shaped pieces of cardboard together. It wasn't the success we hoped it would be. It didn't help that I was leaving.

"On the day of your wedding blessing, I shall light a candle, even if it is in this hospital. You will be with me in my thoughts. And when you speak to the congregation of Datchworth Church, please tell them we at St John's want to be their friends."

"Walter," I said quietly, "we will try and build a few bridges. Let us do the hard work. You must concentrate on getting better."

"My spirits will be lifted only when you come back. Now you must allow me to be sad. It is as if someone has cut off my hands."

"Walter," I said, trying to buck him up. "You're depressed because of your illness, now you must look forward. By the end of October we'll be back. Come on, its not like you to be downhearted. Think of what we have achieved already…..think positive. There will be a new and better time."

He would not look at me again, but tried to hide his face in the sheets. I left the hospital with a heavy heart. In my pocket was a letter he had written to my son in England

Walking home that afternoon I noticed a man sitting in the doorway of his shack by the road side. He was making shoes. He also sold all kinds of footwear. On a board was written: 'Shoes of the dead people. Cheap prices! Only a few maloti.'

The enterprise struck me as significant as I walked up Mandela Road to the camp. Why not sell shoes of the dead people? He was a craftsman and could make new shoes. Poor people might be able to afford the lower priced ones. He had probably done a deal with the man who worked in the hospital crematorium. Here was an entrepreneur. And a reflection of the determination of the Basotho people to survive. Poverty creates its own dimensions.

Overall one has to maintain a sense of balance in a third world country. People's livelihood depend on the weather machine, tradition and culture – not on the stock market, inflation and the price of bread. Resourcefulness is the key to survival The shoe man had opened a small window for himself in the market economy. He had just blown a hole in the country's home affairs policy. Unless one takes the initiative, survival is not even on the agenda. My hopes for obtaining real help for Walter's village was extremely limited, but blind faith and optimism went a long way. Like the man selling shoes, my project could easily fail. But it might *just* succeed..

Chapter 15

The Other Side of the Coin

My re-entry into the Willoughby family fold. was to move in with my sister in Baldock, Hertfordshire for two weeks. Marje knows a thing or two about organisation – whereas I know a lot about chaos. Her cupboards are always tidy. My suitcase is always a mess. My arrival in her small neat home, her pretty bathroom, her well organised kitchen, must have been devastating for her. It was generous of her to let me share her space for two weeks before the big day. We soon became experts at rolling away beds and inventing impromptu meals.

This was October in England – not April in South Africa. My list of requirements was vast. The outfits I managed to track down for my middle-prime wedding blessing were either too expensive, too passé or too 'mutton-dressed-as-lamb'. Disputes concerning what I should wear had already been thrashed out before I left Lesotho. Barrie had gone to the trouble of buying me pearls, so whatever I bought had to go with the pearls. Tailored suits were out, hairy tweed jackets were out and anything from Marks and Spencer was disqualified, on the grounds that somebody else was bound to turn up in it.

The hyacinth-blue wool jacket was actually not hard to find. A visit to Laura Ashley in St Albans found me the dress. The trouble was the hat.

"We've nothing in that colour blue Madam," said every hat shop in the region.

That clinched it. Confident that I had not lost my touch for millinery refinements, I paid a visit to several charity shops and a sewing stall in Hitchin Market. My purchases included a faded straw bonnet with a hole in the crown, yards of nylon fishing line, enough blue tulle to costume an entire corps-de-ballet, a black lace undergarment and most precious of all – a handkerchief-sized piece of precious nun's veiling - the sort of stuff my mother used to wear on her hats in sepia photos of the thirties.

Hats were my passion. Inventing one for a wedding, quite an adventure. Start with a crown base and simply add a few things. A bit of blue, some black lace here and there, torn fish-net tights, more blue net. The needle becomes busier, the froth wider. I hadn't spent hours sitting in the wings of 'My Fair Lady' matinées for nothing. The art of invisible stitching and gathering a flounce of pretty lace into a diamanté fastening was fairly basic. Therapeutic benefits are absolutely wonderful. Bank manager worries get wiped out, all at the speed of a long needle. The trick is to know when to stop.

Marje was out. The floor of her living room was knee deep in bits. Just a touch more blue and a few more feathers should finish it. That and a sophisticated sweep of veiling to cover the eyes. A pearled hatpin would skewer the lot.

To a gentleman, the art of kissing a lady in a large hat is to stop when you get to the brim. Mine had no brim. It sort of 'perched' on my head like a birdcage. A pale blue ostrich feather curved down the side of the cheek and almost went under the chin. Très chic.

It was at that point I realised with alarm that I wouldn't be able to wear my glasses. You can't see through nun's veiling. Then the key turned in the lock. My sister put her head round the door, wondering what other minor invasion had occurred in her absence.

"What do you think Marje?"

"Good God Nettie – its fabulous!"

"Do you think Barrie will like it?"

"It'll knock him flat."

We spent the next hour clearing away and hiding things under cushions. It was these sisterly moments which made my homecoming so special – we could almost imagine we were still in our parents' home as youngsters, sharing everything and trying to please my mother by keeping our rooms tidy.

"Listen Marje, I can't see a thing through the veil and I won't be able to read the hymns."

"Don't you dare put your specs on," she said firmly in her do-not-argue-with-me voice. "You'll just have to learn the words."

Plans for our Wedding Blessing and Abigail's christening slotted easily into place. It was so different from Lesotho. Phones actually worked, people answered queries, letters arrived on time and caretakers of buildings were not only helpful but efficient. Datchworth Village Hall, where we were to hold our reception, could not have been a better proposition. The girl who took our booking was eager to make it a success and volunteered to decorate the hall before our arrival, lay the tables and see to a display of welcome flowers.

Waitresses in frilly aprons were to serve the meal and pour the wine, which we bought ourselves and secured safely out of sight of my brother Mark who regarded the whole affair as an excuse for an evening dedicated to mass intoxication. Friends I hadn't seen for months volunteered to decorate the church, using greenery from hedgerows and autumn flowers from an obliging Knebworth florist. The carved oak altar rails, the pews, the porch and the high windowsills would be draped with foliage. Our talented organist (Marje again) tiptoed up the aisle two days before the occasion, to practice her musical interludes on the church organ. The Datchworth organist was quite a tall man. Marje is five foot and half an inch. We had to bank her up with a few cushions as her feet didn't quite reach the pedals. After that, she fair thrashed the keyboard and her fingers flew with perfect rhythm through her repertoire; 'Lord of the Dance' 'Jesu Joy of Man's Desiring', Intermezzo from 'Cavalleria Rusticana' and 'Twinkle, Twinkle Little Star', to be played at the moment of Abigail's baptism.

My daughter had chosen a long, floaty, orange dress to wear. She was a creature of some complexity when it came to dress. We all held our breath. In recent years, she would not have appeared dead in a frock. Anything resembling a skirt with feminine appeal would have been thrown in the dustbin. A deal was struck. As long as she could wear a pair of her favourite 'Doc Martins' underneath, she would conform. I half expected that on the day she would change her mind and appear in a camouflage jacket with her arms branded in tattoos. Although Lizzie had been a rebel in her teenage years, she had grown into an attractive young woman. Gutsy and strong with a dire sense of humour which could easily turn the stomach of a weak-minded social worker. But few people of her age could care single-handed for a paraplegic little girl with cerebral palsy and remain unaffected.

Abigail would be a beautiful princess in a fairy-tale carriage. She would thrive on being the centre of attention. Lizzie planned to decorate her wheelchair with flowers and ribbons. James and Claire were to be her Godparents.

Barrie's two sons, Mark and John, were coming and Louise his daughter number two, with her partner David. The only person missing would be daughter Sarah, husband Adam and the new baby - whose birth was expected at any moment. In fact, at the same time that Barrie was waiting for his flight from Johannesburg, baby Joshua was born, weighing in at a hefty 8lbs 2ozs. Barrie received the news from his son-in-law just before he boarded the flight to London marking a wonderful home-coming after his journey of six thousand miles. There is something terribly special about the arrival of a first grandchild.

"How's Walter?" was my first question when we met in the airport lounge and had finished hugging one another. My curiosity could wait no longer. Life in a Lesotho village seemed as far away from London as life on another planet.

"They transferred him to another ward and he likes it because the other men are good company. They're not dying like flies around his bed. His medication was reduced drastically and he had withdrawal symptoms and felt disorientated for a week. But now he's making big progress….he sends his love to you."

This was wonderful news. A sign that things could only get better.

"Barrie, Richard Syms has invited us to talk to the congregation at Datchworth on Sunday. I'm so nervous….and we've got to go to Beckenham to fetch your suit. You've nothing to wear for church."

"Blimey, I hadn't given it a thought. My suit is locked in the flat, of course…but first I need to sleep."

Another wave of grandfathermania came over him so we stopped at the nearest Heathrow watering hole and ordered two stiff coffees to celebrate. It was 7.00am.

"Sarah and Adam have decided to call the baby Joshua Samuel… after my father, who was always called Sam for short. It would have pleased him."

"It's okay love, silly smiles are allowed when you become a grandfather for the first time."

"I know – I can't help it," then very quietly into my ear, "I've missed you Nettie. It wasn't the same after you left. I had to put up with Betty cooking supper……she can't cook an egg without burning it."

"You're spoilt Barrie Glenn," I teased….. "come on, you look shattered."

"Wait 'til you hear what I've got to say in my wedding speech. Have you booked the farm cottage for us to stay in by the way – the one at Buntingford?"

"That's where we're going now. The car's waiting. We'll be there in an hour."

*   *   *   *

The church in Datchworth is the very heart of the village. Canon Julian Tross, an ordained priest of sixty years, Rector of Datchworth for twenty years, earned respect and loyalty from the villagers in the seventies and eighties. His concern for every member of his flock is legendary. He was a man of true compassion and dedication. Richard Syms is the present Priest-in-Charge of Datchworth and his work in the village carries on in the same committed way which it was in Julian's day. The difference is Richard makes you think more about the way you believe. He's always posing new questions or putting forward new interpretations and not for a minute does he let you sit on your laurels and take life easy. For Richard, life is about working at it. Whenever I see one of those 'Action Man' dolls, I am reminded of him He's always changing his hat to suit the job. He can be priest, teacher, committee member, detective, comforter or just plain socialite. He protests for the things he believes in, moderates when there is an impasse at rowdy village meetings and is the indomitable helper of nervous brides and bridegrooms on those very special days.…in his spare time he appears on our television screens as an accomplished actor.

Richard is happy to regard the church in this village as a family, where people can be themselves and also live together. His words in the parish journal make one realise he is very keen on different communities getting on. 'Remaining an individual - pleasing only ourselves is not the answer. Our link as a church and school and village with the community on a hillside at Ha Simone in Lesotho is not a charitable exercise, it is a linking of communities, a sharing of resources and ideas, an acknowledgement that we are all in this together..' unquote.

As I got to my feet in the Datchworth morning service, my nerves left me. With a clear picture in my mind of St John's Ha Simone, the village we knew so well – my words came easily. In my mind's eye I heard Reverend Stephen

Makibi speaking to his people with love and laughter in his voice. He used to say 'what is a minister if he can't make his people laugh now and again. What is a minister if he can't make them smile'. Stephen was a man who had found his place in life. He was happy in his own skin. He could shout sometimes. He was not afraid to tell people what he thought. He was not always popular. But being a minister was the work he loved.

The tall candle on the altar table flickered. Richard gave me a look of encouragement as I got to my feet.

"The mountain villages in Lesotho are highly impoverished. One special mountain village is Ha Simone, a name I hope you will become familiar with. ……One afternoon, after we had known the Makibis for quite some time, Reverend Stephen and I sat on the wall near his house and talked for a long time. In my mind was the seed of an idea. We spoke about St John's of the Apostolic Faith Mission, how long the church had been there and just how he was expected to cope with his 'branch-line' as he called it. Then, I asked him a simple question: 'Stephen – if I am able to involve a church in my country and if we can enlist financial help – which may take a long time – what does your community need?' His answer came back straight. "We need a borehole for water, we need light and we need toilets – in that order."

Richard has assured me that All Saints is prepared to commit help to St John's. I know the people of Lesotho will honour the friendship which started here. Children in this village will grow up knowing the gift of compassion. A Lesotho Committee will be set up. The link has already begun."

I returned to my seat. The last hymn died away. The congregation filed out through the porch and into the churchyard and the warm autumn sunshine.

"Whew! I'm glad that's over. Thanks Richard. The Basotho people would say to you '*Re a le dumedisa'* (we are greeting you) Datchworth."

"Have a safe journey back to Lesotho, Annette. Now, it is in God's hands, we must pray for the good things to come."

*   *   *   *

A visit to Datchworth Primary School was my next project. In the few days that were left, the idea of a link with Ha Simone was introduced to the headmistress. I was invited to meet with teachers and children at morning assembly, to introduce them to Leribe Primary School. Plenty of photographs and illustrations were displayed in the long school corridor and like children all over the world, they were curious to learn more.

'Did the children in Lesotho have television? Why didn't all children go to school? Why did they have to fetch water in a bucket every day from the spring? How much money was it to buy a cow? Where did the cows sleep? Why were all the children black?'

Endlessly I tried to fill in the blanks. There was no benchmark. The teachers would try and work on the concept of life in Africa so that perhaps the older children could evaluate this important connection with their village. It was a challenging task. We were charting unknown waters. Mary Willett, the Headmistress, gave it her full support. Before long the letters would be written. I would deliver them to the school in in Ha Simone.

By the time Barrie and I were ready to take the flight to South Africa, Mary phoned to tell me the letters were ready. Dozens of treasured pieces of paper, written in 'best hand-writing' by year five and year six pupils, who had taken the trouble to pen their most important messages to the children of Lesotho, were stowed inside my suitcase. Dozens of pupils were excited about a link with a schools six thousand miles away in Africa. On the large brown envelope that Mary handed me were written the important words: '*To delivered By Hand*'.

*   *   *   *

The scale of our wedding blessing was intended to be small and low key. This was the second time for both of us and was a merging of two new families, rather taken by surprise.

My mobile phone rang as we were decorating the church with flowers for the following day. "Hi Nettie, it's Priscilla. Can you find me a seat at your 'do'. I'm in Knebworth?"

"What!! Priscilla when did you arrive? Don't tell me now – just get in a taxi." I yelled. "My God, I didn't know you were coming."

Priscilla, my friend who had been my witness at our wedding ceremony in April, had decided to fly from Johannesburg to be with us. She loved giving surprises.Quite how she had got to Knebworth was not yet clear. Looking as if she had just blown in from somewhere exotic, bush hat on her wild hair, she came running into the church porch waving a pink ostrich feather, just as the girls were finishing the flowers. The scale of excitement was alarmingly high. Melody was up a ladder putting the finishing touches to carnations on the arch windowsill, Nora was de-heading the pews and filling sacks with tons of unused greenery and my friend Anne was chatting up the bridegroom and his brother, who had turned up in tracksuit and trainers after walking from the village pub – at least a quarter of a mile away. They said they had been for a long walk, which had brought on a great thirst and they had to call in at 'The Plough' to regain their strength for tomorrow. Marje was gaily running through a few arpeggios, nervously testing the organ stops, perched on a stack of Ancient and Moderns.

An unusual trio, Barrie, Priscilla and myself stayed in our Buntingford farm cottage overnight. Beyond the fence, several pure-white silken calves drooled at us with dewy brown eyes. Priscilla, who was crazy about any animal, drooled back..Geese honked from the barn and a couple of tractors trundled past our driveway, clearing up stuff from harvest. It was a fine morning.We hastily leapt into our wedding clothes. As Barrie drove the three of us to Datchworth at eleven thirty, the heavens opened. I was still plaiting blue cornflowers and white silk ribbons into a bouquet as we splashed along the wet lanes. In true Glenn style, we arrived at Datchworth Church and disembarked in heavy cloud and cold October rain.

Dripping guests ran from their cars into the church porch, high-heeled shoes splashed in puddles, damp hair frizzled and cameras clicked. Wrapped in a plastic sheet, Abigail was wheeled in her chair, pretty and smiling in her white dress which touched her ankles. Her long hair was tied with a ribbon and she carried a favourite toy. A small voice saying, 'mum-mum' could be heard throughout the service, as her fingers stroked the material of Lizzie's orange tulle dress. James, my son, always the perfect host, had the aunts and uncles slotted into pews, waved service sheets around and made sure everyone was comfortable. Claude the cameraman positioned himself as high up at the back of the church as he could without falling from his pillar and Barrie's nephew Felix tuned his guitar ready for the guest appearance.

Standing in the porch, listening for the opening bars of Bach's Chorale and Richard's official nod from the choir stalls, we waited. On my head the blue plumage - slightly damp, with raindrops sparkling over the veil. Barrie whispered in my ear.

"Just love the hat Nettie, is it one of your creations? Looks a million dollars."

"Thought you'd like it." I smiled.

As we walked through the studded oak door, we could smell the eucalyptus. It wafted from every windowsill. The scented leaves trailed across the font like seaweed under the pier after the tide has gone out. Add to that the scent of roses and carnations and the smell was almost African. We were remembering a garden in early April, six thousand miles away, full of bright sunshine….and our other marriage ceremony, presided over by a lady magistrate who sang gospel music in Afrikaans. Life had been kind to us.

Today, a blessing and a baptism in typical English weather. Countless times you go through the scenario in your mind. Our promises and our prayers were said once more, our responses reaffirmed in front of 'the home crowd'. The reading from Kahlil Gibran. The soft notes of a classical guitar. The words of a blessing. The singing of our favourite hymns. Then '*Twinkle, Twinkle Little Star*' played on the organ. Abigail's smile of recognition. Her calm expression when the Holy water fell on her forehead, the light in her eyes when ten-year-old Daniella held the candle close to her face. Abigail's voice came again in the quiet church, "Mum-mum," she repeated. Every eye was moist.

Glenns met with Willoughbys for the first time. Brothers John and Mark and sister Susan from Chester. Barrie's children, Mark, Lousie and John. Aunties are so important when it comes to weddings. They throw their arms round everyone and shower them with lily-of-the valley scent and leave lipstick marks on every cheek. Little children usually disappear when it's their turn to be kissed. One very special Aunt who had been like a second mother to me, supported me through all the years, had travelled over from Northampton. Both Aunt and Uncle shook Barrie by the hand and said they hoped we would be very happy.....and said that he mustn't expect life to become sedentary from now on. Re-unions with friends and relatives was a party in itself.

"Sedentary – isn't a word I would remotely associate with Nettie," answered Barrie.

During his speech at the reception, my husband said that although we had travelled a long way for our ceremony, it was great to be with our families again. He did admit publicly that I was only worth ten cows and a donkey. And that we were learning to love Lesotho despite the terrible poverty. He spoke of his work on the dam and said the company were extending the job until spring of next year. King Letsie's Coronation would take place a couple of days after we got back, Prince Charles and Prince Harry would be there.....our invitations by the King's sister-in-law had been promised and goodness knows who would be sitting next to us at the Coronation dinner....!!

Uncle Ivan proposed a toast to Abigail and I found myself weeping at the thought of leaving her. Barrie proposed a toast to his new grandson Joshua Samuel Glenn and was overcome with tears. The afternoon passed in a blur of eating, dancing and kissing. The Glenn family are a bit 'von Trapp' when it comes to music. Teenagers danced and showed us oldies how to jive! Things went downhill slightly during Barrie's rendition of 'The Spaniard that Blighted my Life' sung with Kevin (late of the Caterham 5th Scouts) My bridegroom and I introduced a dance known as the 'Shosholosa', straight from the gold mines of South Africa., which we had performed at our first wedding ceremony. The rhythms flowed.

Later that evening guests adjourned to The Horns Country Pub in Burnham Green for the final onslaught. Greene King Ale plus exhaustion was a fairly powerful concoction. After a couple of hours of serious drinking, and even more serious singing, the landlord cashed up and wished we would all go home - or back to Africa. The cat on the windowsill was snoring gently.

The moment had arrived for final goodbyes. In the Willoughby family, they always go on for a fortnight. By the time everybody has said goodbye to everybody, somebody else has bought another round of drinks and sat down again. You could play another hand at double rummy by the time every hand has been shaken and every cheek has been kissed.

The last days flew by. Visits to relatives and friends become all the more precious when you are leaving to live on another continent. Unmissable was the day we were able to visit baby Joshua All new parents have that kind of haggard look. After a week of no sleep Sarah looked pale and drawn, Adam, just pale. Crates of nappies were everywhere and somehow the red wine had slipped into the bottle warmer. A proud grandparent is unbelievably slushy. It was hard to drag Barrie away from peering into the face of his new grandchild, whose head when stroked, felt like down on the breast of a dove.

The time for our visitations was over, air tickets checked and taxis arranged. There was barely time to squeeze in a trip to St Albans Abbey and a rapid shopping trip to the Antiques Arcade in George Street for Priscilla to buy presents to take home. It was like handing lollipops to a baby. She fell in love with antique jewellery, antique glassware and antique photographs, simply not to be found in the African bush. Quite soon her credit card reached its limit and her bags were stuffed with booty. Triumphant with her newly acquired possessions, we drove like the wind to Cockfosters Station to catch the connection to Heathrow, in time for the evening flight to Johannesburg.

Sadly, smoking cigarettes was Priscilla's worst habit and she knew she couldn't inhale from now until Heathrow, then there would barely be time for a quick drag before the main abstention of eleven hours. The train came in as she drew on her last puff of nicotine. With two suitcases on wheels both bursting at the seams – seemingly driving in opposite directions, Barrie assisted her into a seat, in a state of confusion.

"I don't know if I'm coming or going," she breezed, "I'll probably die of withdrawal symptoms before I get there….anyway, see you in Africa! Have a safe flight tomorrow."

"Yes, it's a pity we can't travel back altogether," we muttered, (our flight was the following day).

The train drew out of the station. What we didn't realise was that three out of four trains go direct to Heathrow. Every fourth train goes to Hounslow. Apparently, the events which took place shortly afterwards, in Priscilla's compartment, were unprecedented. London Transport passengers were treated to a rare Priscilla panic – in loud American. In an effort to correct her mistake other passengers agreed she must get off the train at once. She must change to another line. It says something about British stiff upper lips when the entire compartment rose as one voice, saw her and her cases off at the next station - and waved - in unison, as she departed along the platform. The saga of Virgin Flight 266 holding up the evening flight to Johannesburg for one Menthol-tipped passenger wearing a bush hat was a story we dined out on for years.

Had her arrival been three minutes later, she would have been sitting in the Departure Lounge at Heathrow waiting to greet us the next day, quite likely surrounded by ash trays and a half empty bottle of gin.

Chapter 16

Give and Receive

"Rose desperately needs a sewing machine," I exclaimed as we shot round Welwyn Garden City stores, looking for summer clothes to take back with us. October isn't exactly the best time to search for cool cotton blouses. "Let's see if we can find her one of those old fashioned hand machines. People give them away these days."

"And how do you propose we get it to Lesotho?" enquired Barrie.

"Carry it of course."

We headed for the Macmillan Hospice charity shop on the main street, which we were certain would have one. In ten minutes we had found exactly what we were looking for. A hand-operated Singer sewing machine, circa 1940 complete with attachments. The sepia 'Handbook of Instructions' was filled with bits of thread caught in between the pages and slivers of newspaper cuttings of war time - the kind of memorabilia which collects in the bottom of old drawers. All the bobbins and spools were still intact. And it worked. We looked at each other, pleased that we had found what we were looking for, with so little time to spare.

"Rose will love it," I said, "do you think we can carry it on the aeroplane? Will they let us on board. What do you think Barrie?"

The ladies in the shop were fluttering around, hoping to hear where this object would finally end up. They were as excited as we were to think it would reach a tiny mountain village in Africa.

"Lesotho? Where's that?"

From Welwyn Garden City, we drove to a small village outside Hertford to say a last goodbye to Abigail and Lizzie. We hugged and promised we would write.

"This time I really will write Mum."

"I shall look forward to your letters love, take good care of yourself and Abigail and let me know how her weight improves."

Lizzie was trying out a new regime of feeding, as our girl did not seem keen to eat all the time. Some days she would eat so little and nothing my daughter could do would tempt her. Everyone wanted to see her gaining a few kilos as she was underweight for her age, yet so tall. She seemed to have all the energy she needed but the possibility of Abigail standing by herself looked more remote than ever.

The village where my daughter lived was small. There wasn't exactly a booming social life and I knew she longed to be 'in town' with people of her own age. She was permanently short of funds. However, a constant stream of friends called by and her life appeared busy and happy enough.....but there was something under the surface that didn't add up…. purely intuitive on my part.

I lifted Abigail once more, put her in the chair and fastened the harness.

"Does the school try her in the standing frame every day?" I asked, knowing how much Abigail enjoyed standing in an upright position. It enabled her to join in with other children and have eye contact. She loved playing with the water and sand, making sloshing noises in the tray and generally making a mess. Her smiles told us far more than any therapist could.

"Yes, I think she goes in it every day – she loves all that messy stuff. Comes home covered in paint." said Lizzie, looking pleased. Anyone who has a handicapped child knows how important it is to value such minor events. To feel your child is doing some of the things a normal child does is such a boost. There was a moment when I thought Lizzie was going to say something else – then changed her mind. I didn't press her.

It was not an easy farewell. Abigail was busy tearing up crackly paper, her favourite game. This child with her beautiful smile…she was so loved.

"Come on you two. You'll miss your flight if you don't hurry." Lizzie sounded strong. Abigail blew more kisses. I blew my nose.

We were booked to leave from Heathrow the same evening. We drove back to the cottage to clean up, collect our suitcases and bale out. The afternoon was waning, the familiar oaks and beeches turning gold and yellow along the lanes and a light mist curling on the meadow below the windmill along the Cottered Road. Autumn in Hertfordshire was lovely and a pang of homesickness obscured my vision of Africa for a fleeting moment. Barrie put his hand over mine and we talked about partings and how we both hated them. I found it hard to think of leaving them for such a long period.

"James will be at the airport," I said quietly, "he wants to come and see us off. He's bringing a letter for Walter and a parcel."

"I hope it doesn't weigh as much as a sewing machine," said a quiet voice.

Only minutes away from our departure time James arrived, bearing the small brown parcel. A pair of First XI blue and white Chelsea FC. shorts. It was enough to bring a lump to my throat, even though I was not a football fan

I could imagine Walter's face when he opened it. He followed the UK soccer league tables on Radio Lesotho. There were hundreds of fans in the mountain villages. Team results circulated like wildfire.

"Terrific James. Walter will be over the moon. Nobody in Lesotho will have a Chelsea strip."

"He says you saved his life Mum….."

He gave me a hug, then, shyly held up the letter which I had last seen in Walter's hand as I left Leribe Hospital. He added, "tell him they're going to win the League this season."

A hand tugged at my elbow, "Come on honey they're calling our flight."

We took off with the lights of London below us and I suddenly felt very weary. Strong emotions and an increase in adrenalin had caused a build-up of tension so a free drinks trolley on its way from the galley had a welcome ring to it. A small brandy and good night's sleep should be easy to arrange. The straight-jacket seat had been designed to provide comfort for any shape or form.

I wriggled and shifted for hours but could not find the snooze mode. Although my body wanted sleep, my brain wanted to solve puzzles. Central to my way of life was a bed – not a sitting-up-machine pretending to be one. Languishing in the locker above my head was a sewing machine, which in my imagination was tumbling on top of us. Leering at me from the small grey and white flashing television screen bobbed Mr Bean's face. I must have dozed in two-minute snatches for the whole flight. If there's anything worse than watching a film you don't like, its watching a film you've seen ten times already, with the sound turned down. Barrie was fast asleep beside me and other passengers were snoring. The stewardess passed by and asked if I there was something I would like.

"Yes, some knock-out drops please," I answered wearily.

She brought me a cup of warm milky coffee several minutes later. After that, Johannesburg came far too quickly. I had slept through sunrise and breakfast.

"Well, how was England Mr Glenn?" I heard Kenneth our driver ask Barrie as the truck left the airport terminal. "I hear everyone say how bad the weather is in UK. People tell me about the grey skies."

Good heavens I thought, Kenneth's caught the disease of talking about the weather. In Africa people never mention it. As one of the LHPC drivers, it was part of his job to pick up staff from airports and he must have discovered how weather-bound we British are.

"Your Prince Charles is arriving soon in our country to be present at the Coronation. Everyone is talking about it. The King of Swaziland will be there and President Mandela – a lot of people will come from all over the world…and we are having a holiday. Everyone in Lesotho will have a holiday."

"Yes, England is good Kenneth. But our weather is nothing like yours."

The freeway was deserted. Familiar glitzy hoardings of prosperous Johannesburg tailed us out of the big city, then we followed the N3 towards Heidelberg. There was so little traffic along the stretch to Villiers, where views of the distant mountains welcomed us back to a new morning in the Free State.

"We're pleased to get back to the African sunshine and by the way, how is that little girl of yours?" I asked.

The face in the mirror beamed. Kenneth loved talking about his daughter who was his pride and joy. She was four years old. Her name was Hlafelo.

"I will bring her to see you, she likes coming to your house… and the strawberries are ready in your garden now. She loves the strawberries."

"Good, then I can plant my beetroot," said Barrie who was ever optimistic about his vegetable patch. He hadn't yet found anything seriously successful apart from spinach. The dry baked clay soil was difficult to cultivate, besides the rains were very powerful at this time of the year and drowned everything out.

"We could grow mealie Barrie," I said, at which Kenneth burst out laughing.

"You are becoming more like a Mosotho every day 'M'e," he replied.

After a four hour drive, we reached home. Our neighbours came to greet us and Hercule almost ate us. The thought of extra food and long walks inspired him with enough energy to break his chain and leap the fence. At the bar in the evening we caught up with Muela Dam and Butha-Buthe camp news, then discovered that most of the engineers were either planning to attend the King's coronation in Maseru or drive to Sun City in Johannesburg, for a few days break.

Betty had kept the house clean and tidy for our return and we had brought her clothes for Oliver, which I knew would please her. We had to be careful over being too generous. Betty hated to appear favoured in any way. Sometimes people were unkind to her when she walked through the area where she lived, because she had a job. We had heard stories of working women being attacked on their way home and their wages stolen. In fact we were in for a shock the following day.

Betty arrived at the usual time of eight o'clock, carrying Oliver and wearing a bandage on her arm. She looked very pleased to see us and I thanked her for looking after Barrie while I was in England.

"De rats are all dead 'M'e," she said, with a great deal of satisfaction.

"That's good news Betty – and what about this big baby Oliver? He is almost too heavy for you to carry these days...and what have you done to your arm?" I asked, taking Oliver off her back and giving him a hug.

"I have been in a fight 'M'e. With the man who stole my shoes. No, he stole your shoes."

"What do you mean?" I said, knowing Betty wasn't the kind of person to get into fights "Come and eat your breakfast and tell me."

She was looking a lot better since her leg had mended and her blue dress looked ironed and pretty with her blue scarf tied on her hair. The bandage on her arm looked grubby and about to fall off. She sat down on a kitchen stool. Barrie handed her a clean bandage.

"Take off that one Betty, let's see your arm – then we know if it's infected."

"'M'e I want you to come to de police with me. Do you remember de shoes you gave me – de white ones. A man stole them from my house and I have seen him wearing those shoes. I can prove they belong to me 'M'e if you come and tell de Police. He said they were his shoes – and I hit him. Then he pushed me on a rock."

The fact that the footwear - a pair of my worn-out trainers - were at least a year old, seemed irrelevant. I had given them to Betty three or four months ago to walk to work in because she needed some shoes. Betty knew this man. He was a close neighbour. He had gone into her house during the day and stolen the shoes. I could see her anger had got the better of her.

"Look, I cannot come to the police with you Betty but I will write you a letter to take and give the officer. Then he will believe you."

I knew it could take a whole day and I had neither the time nor the inclination to wait around the police station yard for a pair of scruffy trainers. But Betty had other ideas.

"If Mr Glenn come, it would be okay," she persisted. "Then de officer listen to a man."

"Betty, please take the letter. If the police don't listen to you, then I will come," said Barrie generously. The idea that LHPC would give him time off to go and sort out the theft of a pair of old trainers was ludicrous, but I could see this apparently trivial matter was of great importance to my maid. It was brave of her to face the thief alone.

As we dressed her arm she asked determinedly, "'M'e please will you write what size are your feet – then the man cannot succeed with this crime."

"Yes, I will say it in the letter Betty, now let me go and look where Oliver is."

Betty took charge of my vacuum cleaner like a battleship in full sail. She thought the more bangs she made with it, the better I would like it. Her attempts to clean the bathroom carpet sounded like a demolition job. To Betty, carpet cleaning must have seemed like a job for a plough and a span of oxen. A cup of tea was the only way to stop her, so I put the kettle on. (She no more understood why we drank cups of tea, especially in this hot weather., when everyone else drank cold squash).

Our strawberry patch was red with fruit which almost ripenned while you watched. They were as big as plums. Barrie's freshly dug trenches, ready to take the courgettes and beetroot, might have made the pages of 'Guide to African Gardening' as they looked so neat. Thabo had done lots of watering while we had been away and the soil was diggable. He arrived on the doorstep to welcome us back.

"Hello, Mrs Glenn, I am greeting you. And I am comin' with the water and I am comin' in England when the fruit is growing and the money it is in my pocket."

Barrie paid him willingly and he went away smiling. Later in the day, one of the other gardeners came to say much the same thing, so we told them if they did the job together then they must share the money. This kind of happening was a form of respectable cheating. Of course they tried to swindle us, but we were always fair with them when it came to tipping. Barrie often gave Thabo shirts or shoes and we used to send books for his boys occasionally. For this Thabo upgraded himself to Barrie's chief car-washer and when one of the other gardeners offered to wash his vehicle, sharp words were spoken.

Driving to St John's church on Wednesday afternoon, I was surprised to find Stephen half way down the track, gathering the fruit of his labours in a quarter acre field of peas, together with Emily and Bernice. They were picking the ripe pods ready for supper. The girls came running towards the car, tying up their aprons as they ran.

"Hi Nettie – how was England? We have lots to tell you ….Walter is home…. he is much better now…will you come in?"

"Yes, just let me park the car now." Hercule was panting with anticipation, spreading drops of saliva onto the back seat.

"Will you take him for a walk? He is going crazy to run up your mountain," I yelled through the window. I drove on towards the house.

Unforgettable, was the sight of Walter, walking out of the door of his house, the minute he heard the car pull in. He came towards me with arms outstretched and greeted me with the biggest ever hug. We were both teary with joy. The others danced round the yard with Hercule whipping up the dust and barking madly until everyone for miles around must have wondered what on earth was happening. I took a step backwards, taking in his new appearance and his widest ever smile.

"Walter – you are well again Let me look at you. How wonderful is that? We will have to celebrate …come on, tell me what happened after Barrie left. When did you come home?"

"They let me out after three weeks Nettie, but I must go in to the hospital every week to be weighed."

"Well you do look a bit too thin. We must build you up now. And what about your medication?"

His cheeks were not quite so sunken and his skin colour was coming back, but he still didn't look like the old Walter. Yet rarely had I seen him look so happy. There was still a long recuperation process to get through.

"Now, I will let you into a secret. Where is Rose? I have a present for her. Emily where is she?"

I knew the moment of the sewing machine would be very special and I must do it when Rose was present.

"I'll go and fetch her," offered Bernice, "she's in the church"

We went inside Walter's house so that he could show me all the welcome-home presents the boys had made him. "Now I am going to live in this house for good. Mum and Emily cleaned it for me and painted the walls. It is mine now. They prepared everything while I was in hospital."

A few pieces of furniture had miraculously arrived - begged and borrowed from generous donors. Conspicuously absent was a proper bed. His thin mattress which took up one half of the room, was lying on the floor.

"Walter, are you still sleeping in the floor?"

"Yes Nettie, it's the only spare bed we have. It's fine though. At least I have my own house now."

He was more concerned with making places to put hooks for his clothes, than his bed. You can't drill into walls made of clay. Cardboard shelves attached themselves to the walls with Blu-tac. Pictures of Princess Diana were pasted around. A few books were actually displayed in a very antique bookcase without any glass and an old leather chair with hollow arms and real horsehair stuffing - once somebody's treasured possession - sat by the entrance. There was no door.

"And look what the boys found me. A portable tape recorder. Somebody threw it away because the spring on the door doesn't work....but if you hold it with one finger, it plays tapes!"

"But how will it work....you don't have electricity."

"Batteries.....and cross your fingers. It plays Nettie, I'm telling you."

Behind my back I carried the small parcel James had given me and dropped it on the corner of his chair. He would find it after I had gone.

Rose was a talented needlewoman. She could design and make garments by hand. Clothes for the women and school uniforms for the kids were done with the same dedication and skill of busy fingers. Rose was seldom without her needle and scissors in her hand. She spent hours after the sun went down, working by the light of a candle. Recently her old hand sewing machine had died. She entered the room, dressed in a dark green sweater with a white scarf wound tightly round her hair.

"Hi Rose!" In my excitement, I gave her a hug, turning her so that she couldn't see the present. "It's lovely to be back in Ha Simone...and Walter is well again....I can't believe it."

"Yes Nettie, he is home now. It is wonderful. Oh, we have missed you and Barrie. Tell us about England. It seems so long since we saw you."

Rose turned round as one of the boys lifted the heavy square box onto the table in the living room and took off the lid. She stared in disbelief. With hand clasped over mouth, she drew in a sharp breath and did not speak for several seconds. Then the tears spilled through her fingers and splashed onto the table top. Behind me, Stephen started chanting a prayer. He fell on his knees. In terms of a surprise, it was everything. Rose tried to say words but couldn't. Knowing how precious the moment was, Stephen reached for Rose's hand and together they said the prayer, Rose still with her eyes brimming with tears.

I pointed to the drawer at the side of the machine which contained the Instruction Leaflet, written in 1940. Trembling with anticipation, she took it out and read out loud the clear simple sentences. 'First fill the spool with strong thread.......'

"Nettie, how did this come from England?"

"We carried it onto the aeroplane. Well, Barrie did most of the lifting. It's heavy...we weren't sure if they would let us bring it.....but we wanted you to be able to sew again."

Her eyes shone. Now she couldn't stop smiling. I stole the moment with my camera.

"I shall be here all through the night. This sewing machine won't ever stop working. The church members will have their uniforms. The children will have school clothes......and the ladies will help. When I sleep, they will sew. This machine will never be idle."

She and Emily danced round the room and out into the yard.

Silk ties for Stephen and the boys came next, another teddy bear for Bernice, tights and socks for Emily, a 'Complete Works of Shakespeare' for Walter. It was what he wanted.

"Nettie, this is wonderful for us. My wife is very happy. You can see her happiness.... and in return you must take these from our field. These are for you and Barrie for the meals." Stephen placed a large container of peas onto my lap....about three weeks supply. "And any time you want more, you will come and pick them fresh in the field. What is ours is yours also."

This was a far-reaching gesture of thanks. When the African has plenty, he wants to share. His actions speak louder than his words. It was fortuitous that the Makibi crops were ready for harvesting. It allowed them to give as well as receive. The gift on my lap was as valuable as a pot of gold. To refuse would have been unthinkable. Stephen and Rose were repaying us in peas.

"Stephen, I have to tell you there is one more present from England."

He looked at me with almost a comical expression. Rose could hardly take her eyes off the sewing machine.

"I spoke to the congregation at Datchworth Church at one of the services. The link is official. Your prayers have been answered."

Stephen closed his eyes and a torrent of praises fell out of him out as though he had not the power to stop them. Walter's eyes were streaming with tears. We joined hands round the table. Stephen, Rose, Walter, Emily, Justice, Petros and Bernice. I did not know what they were saying, but the prayer was eager with hope and it was long. With the sun streaming through the window and the St Albans angel sparkling with light, it seemed possible that our two families were joined together. In eight months we had come this far.

"Nettie, before you came into our lives - you and Barrie, we were weary. Now we are so happy."

"Soon a committee will get to work," I said soberly. "The church families will send letters to your congregation, family to family. The children in the school will find out where Lesotho is on their map of the world. With the help of their teachers they will soon learn. Because Lesotho is not known widely in England, these children have no knowledge of what life is like here... but we are going to change all that."

The family were united in their joy. They were delirious with excitement Many questions followed. I tried to explain to them what kind of a village Datchworth was but there was far too much for one afternoon. Knowing that somewhere on the other side of the world, people were talking about them, made them all keenly interested. The time flew.

In all the excitement, we had forgotten about Hercule. Fed up of waiting around the yard, he had gone off along the river on a sheep hunt.

"Nettie come on, we'll go and look for Hercule. He usually only goes along the first field," Walter said, remembering the paths we used to take before his illness. It seemed a good idea.

"Yes okay, but our wolfhound has become much more adventurous. He'll be miles away by now. I hope he hasn't done any damage."

By the time we arrived at the top of the ridge on the other side of the river there was no sign of him. Walter whistled loudly.

"Oh dear, not a hope."

"Look Nettie, I am not fit enough to go any further. I'm feeling weak. Do you mind if we go back. I'm sure that Hercule will come. You know, today has been a very special day. Mum was so thrilled with the sewing machine. She'll soon have all the women in the village working on it. They will be sewing twenty four hours a day. Maybe she will sell a few things. You must tell Barrie how great he was for carrying it here."

"The fact that you are out of hospital and feeling better Walter is the best news we could have......you had such a terrible time. You know, we were all so scared. And that morning your Dad went in and shouted at everyone. He was so worried about you."

"I know. It was so embarrassing. It's funny to think about it now. He scared the nurses half to death. And the pyjamas.........!" We both laughed hysterically as we walked down to the river where the flat stones were. "But I met some wonderful people while I was in hospital... that lady who was a physiotherapist – Isnette her name was. Nettie I didn't know you had asked her to visit me. I wondered why she kept coming in to see me."

"She came every day?"

"Every single day. Until I was discharged. She went out and bought food for me when I was hungry again. She didn't say a word about knowing you.....I just thought she was an angel of mercy....until the very last day."

"Look Walter....there's Hercule. He's seen us," I said as a black streak came hurtling towards us from the ridge higher up. As we reached the stepping stones, Hercule came bounding up and thrashed around in the water, sending filthy mud everywhere. Walter called him off as two young village children were playing by the river, making clay animals and standing them carefully on the flat rocks. There was a little girl of about three and a boy about four years old, both wearing raggy clothes and wellington boots. We stopped to witness a small miracle. The animals were so life-like. They would win a prize in any pottery class in England. I don't suppose these kids had ever had a lesson in their lives – animals were part of their extended family. As naturally as a child in our country would create a house made from clay, a

Mosotho child was skilled enough to sculpt a horse or a cow or a donkey with a few strokes of his fingers.

The children were not in the least frightened by Hercule and Walter slipped the lead through his collar. The boy held up one of the miniature cows for me to see. It was exactly like the one standing on the bank – complete with udders. The children stared at me and smiled.

"It's a thing every child in Africa knows, Nettie. All our family used to come down here when we were growing up. Justice and I used to have competitions to see who was the best sculptor. We used to spend hours by this river. The girls used to come and make clay pots and bake them in the sun. This was our playground."

Slowly we made our way back up the stony track It was true his body was still weak. Walter had essentially beaten tuberculosis and he would get strong again. By putting it in the past tense, he had come to terms with life. A full life. His faith had never been firmer.

"Nettie, I thought I might never have the chance to say these words because I thought I would die before you came back to Lesotho." He stopped to catch his breath and rest for a moment. He looked at me straight. "I know now that God has given you to us. When you and Barrie came to Ha Simone, I thought you would pass through our lives, like a wind. But it seems our friendship has become stronger. A link with England was a dream. Now it is a reality."

"It is only through the church back home. They have made it possible."

"Nettie, I will always thank God that you were here for me when I had TB, I would never have made all those journeys to the hospital."

"I told you, I was in the right place at the right time.I would have done the same for any member of your family."

"Nettie, you *are* my family. From now on I am your son. And you will be my new mother. Tell Barrie he is my father and James is my brother. In our culture this is possible."

The dialogue going on in my head was about feeling uncomfortable with this responsibility which Walter had placed upon me.The very idea that God was involved seemed to weigh heavily upon my shoulders.

"Walter, it helped me to see you through your terrible illness. If you had died I would have failed utterly as a human being. I would have hated myself. Your recovery has……" I searched for the right words, "sealed our friendship. Given me a feeling of fulfilment that I had not known before."

He lowered his voice to almost a whisper. "In the eyes of God, we are all one family. So you see it is God's will that you came here."

"No." I argued, "it's Barrie's fault really. Walter, if he hadn't been sent to work here, I would never have broken down in your village. Have you not heard of coincidence or fate?"

"It is God's way of saying he loves us," he insisted, "I used to have dreams about going to other countries. Well, there was no way I could go out of Lesotho, so he sent you and Barrie."

He was becoming short of breath and I knew he should be lying on his mattress, not out in the hot sun. Hercule pulled on his collar and it almost began to look as if he was helping Walter up the slope. I looked churchwards and saw Petros coming down to the river with his cows. Hercule barked and strained even more on his lead. You couldn't keep exciting smells away from this hound-dog. He was pulling towards them with a vengeance. It was both ironic and comical that the patient should be dragged home by canine power.

"Walter, I think we should celebrate with a party," I suggested, when we got back to the yard. "What do you think – a party for you *and* the link with England *and* to mark the Coronation?"

"Yes, and it's Bernice's birthday soon," he shouted through the car window.

Stephen came running from the house carrying the box of peas. In my haste I was forgetting. He thrust it through the window onto the front seat. "Here! don't let Hercule eat them."

"And it's Barrie's birthday....we don't need any more reasons do we...?" I called as I pulled away. "See you all next week. I think we're going to Maseru on Friday to cheer the king."

Chapter 17

Royal Connections, King and Country

Barrie was waiting for me at home, dressed in swimming shorts and a towel. "Come on honey, we're all going for a swim."

"Who's all?"

"The staff of LHPC. We're on 'Coronation leave' from now. First day of the swimming calendar. The water's lovely and warm." (It had been thirty five degrees today).

In the camp pool, two Thai ladies had bandaged themselves into colourful silk saris, which filled with water and made them float like barrage balloons. There was a mild display of panic as one of them went under and then re-emerged, squealing and full of air, in a bubble of bright pink. Being a powerful swimmer mattered far less than the social aspect of this sport. Squealing went on in several languages, as three or four young men emerged from the offices and jumped in to join the ladies. Riotous behaviour is a necessary result of engineers being chained to their desks for a hard week's work; their next stop was the bar.

Four year old Sean was also splashing around in the pool, his last play before he left for Mauritius in the morning. For his parents, Lily and Alex, saying goodbye was a huge wrench. They had lived in Lesotho for ten years and both their children had been born here. Sean and his little sister Shaoline had known nothing else but life on a camp in the mountains. After a spell in Mauritius, they would be moving to Berlin. The parents were worried because the two children spoke French and were learning English. Now they would have to learn German. We would all miss this special little family, none more than their nursemaid Evodia, who had looked after both Sean and Shaoline for the last four years.

Evodia, whose home was in Leribe, had been crying for a week. She could not visualise life without them. She had looked after both children, carried them on her back, watched them grow, as if they were her own. Lily had a good job working as a secretary in the offices at LHPC. The Basotho ladies were excellent nannies and Evodia was a very important part of their lives. Her job would come to an end and her only income would cease. Everyone we knew in this situation, paid their maids about six months wages before leaving, as a gesture of appreciation – but then sadly unemployment would claim them. Evodia requested to be taken with them when they left, even at the prospect of leaving her own country – but after much soul searching, the family thought it best to avoid this difficult set of circumstances.

This was a typical evening on camp; a lazy swim in the pool before supper and a round-up of the latest news. Indeed the mood was high because of the three-day public holiday. Tonight the canteen was closing down with a Royal Coronation Supper for the staff, cooked by Sophie and her team of ladies. We had been all been invited. Good meals were the highlight of an engineer's day. Sophie's menu was 'Coronation Chicken and Queen of Puddings' and already customers were filling up the tables.

Barrie and I went back to the house to change for dinner. From now on we would use the pool most evenings as the weather was getting warmer and the days longer. The camp staff didn't know what we saw in this game of swimming. The Basotho don't swim. They sincerely believed we were two pence short of a shilling.

"Did you hear the results of the tenders for Mohale Dam?" said Barrie quietly, as we dressed.

"Oh - tell me quick. Did we win the contract?" My tone was urgent.

He gave me a searching look, knowing that his reply could change the course of our lives – and our marriage. "I'm afraid the news is disappointing honey. We'll be going back to England next year….. just in time for an English summer." He came and sat beside me. "Are you sorry?"

Unexpectedly, tears started to fall down my cheeks. His fingers were helping me to click the difficult clasp on my necklace.

"When Africa gets hold of you it does not let you go," I whispered, leaning against him. closing my eyes for a moment.

In this unique Mountain Kingdom with its plundered economy, its cruel poverty; its crazy laws and ancient culture …..why did I not want leave?. Well - it had been decided. We would be leaving

"Are you disappointed?" I asked, not daring to look at his face.

"A bit – yes I am, it would have been a challenge to work on Mohale Dam. Our tender obviously wasn't low enough. Never mind – we'll enjoy our last few months here. Don't forget we've promised ourselves a trip to the Cape at Christmas."

"But we've been so happy here Barrie…and there's Walter….and the others."my lips wouldn't say the words.

"Come on – let's go and eat, there'll be nothing left if we don't get a move on."

Looking like a pair of extras from 'South Pacific', me in strappy dress with floaty scarf and Barrie wearing Hawaiian shirt and a pair of open-toed *takkies*, we walked across to the bar holding hands

"…and something else I heard today – Liliane and Ali are moving to Butha-Buthe."

The night sky was pricked with bright stars, the cicadas shrieked louder than ever, laughter floated through the open windows of the canteen and on the *braai* next to the pool, the red coals were blazing. This was such a happy time in our lives. Why did it have to come to an end? No Mohale contract after all. Tonight I would push it to the back of my mind and think about next week when Liliane would arrive back from France, bearing her usual umpteen kilos of Roquefort cheese.

Early the following morning, Heleyne arrived at the gate and was escorted over by one of the guards. We had just finished breakfast in the garden and were discussing whether we should go to Maseru to watch the Coronation, when she called out to us. It was a beautiful day and the coffee smelled good outside.

"Mrs Annette, Annacleda is very sick – I come to tell you she will not be coming for her lessons." Heleyne hopped from one foot to the other and then burst into tears. Her uniform looked as though it needed a good clean and her hair was dishevelled, "And my parents have left my house and gone to another house far away. I am not allowed to go to school. There is no more money for my school fees. Do you have a job for me on your camp?"

"Come here Heleyne and eat breakfast and tell me slowly what's happened."

Barrie left the table and disappeared to take Hercule for a walk. "I'll go and see Ali. He might like to come with us to Maseru on Friday, I'll see what he thinks about travelling in one car. Bye Heleyne – please sit down."

"Annacleda has given birth to a baby boy 'M'e. He is born two weeks ago when you were in England….." she said in a matter-of-fact voice.

The cup fell out of my hand and bounced on the tablecloth. "I didn't know she was pregnant…..she never said a word, but then I haven't seen her for a couple of months. Is she all right?"

"Yes, the child is healthy. She will bring him to see you. A man raped her in a forest near her house and he is not a good man. He is living far away…..her mother is going to tell the police, but…..that's why she did not come to your house. She was sick when the baby was coming, but I am her friend all the time."

"And what's this about your family moving away?"

She put her head down and the tears spilled over. She sniffed into her sleeve. "A bad thing happened in my family. I have been sent to live with my grandmother, but it is terrible. I am not allowed to come out. I have to stay inside the house. I cannot go to school. Please 'M'e will you have a job for me? I would like to come and work for you and Mr Glenn, not stay with my Grandmother."

This was all most difficult to take in and I admit to being confused by the turn of events. I had never met Heleyne's parents. All I knew was that her brother worked away in the mines and sent money home periodically for her to attend Mount Royal – until now it seemed. She was such a clever girl and was doing very well with her studies.

After a plate of toast and a drink, Heleyne was composed and asked if she could do some writing in a book, as usual. I left her with a pen and some paper at the big table in the garden, while I washed up and tried to think what to do. Perhaps Betty might want a nursemaid for Oliver.....but I didn't know all the circumstances of Heleyne's recent change of address. At this point, I realised I could not become involved. These were problems far out of my reach. I decided to withdraw.

"Heleyne, I will see you and Annacleda and Kaizi for your lessons in the afternoons next week if you still want to come, but I will not be able to solve your family problems. You must do what Grandmother tells you. And I will ask Betty if she wants to employ someone on a temporary basis – but no promises."

She seemed satisfied with this explanation. There were a host of reasons for not getting involved. Her expression was still very sad and at the gate she smiled wearily and hitched up her untidy dress, straightened herself until the badge on the pullover was at least facing the right way. I gave her a note telling Grandmother where she could find me if she wanted to discuss Heleyne's education at home. It might help to smooth the waters. The girl was obviously bitterly disappointed about not going to school. She had recently been chosen to represent Mount Royal High School in Botswana, to compete in an athletics race and was looking forward to it. I watched her walk slowly down the drive towards the camp gate - head down and feet dragging the dust.

No communication had arrived from Amelia about the Coronation and we had been listening to Radio Lesotho with a keen ear, to find out arrangements for the Royal festivities. We had been warned that the crowds would be pouring into Maseru and transport by car might prove difficult. Kings and Prime Ministers and representatives of other countries would be attending and there would be a strong police presence around the capital plus a thousand Basotho horsemen, who were to ride through the stadium in procession to salute King Letsie. Visitors to Maseru had been advised to leave their cars at home and come in by bus, specially provided for the occasion.

The night before the Coronation, there was to be a banquet for the hundreds of wedding guests. We marvelled at the fortitude of President Mandela, who earlier this week, had attended the biennial Commonwealth Conference in Edinburgh as a guest of the Queen, the first in Britain for over twenty years. Representing New South Africa, he looked perfectly at ease in the pictures we had seen of him in England with all the other Commonwealth delegates, now he was back in Lesotho, on another official duty supporting King Letsie. We were thrilled that we might catch a glimpse of him at the celebrations.

A call from friends on the camp later that evening, made our minds up about travelling to Maseru. They suggested that we might borrow a television and watch the celebrations at home as we might not see much of the ceremony at all, if seats were not allotted for good viewing.

"There's always the danger that you might get stuck in a large crowd and not see anything. For a start you would have to make it by bus and the journey will be risky. The cameras will have the best view of the dancing girls and the whole pageant. You'll see much more this way."

"We're rather relieved actually, I think that's a good proposition," agreed Barrie, "it'll be very hot and we might be standing all day without shade. I suppose there's a chance we may not even make it into the stadium."

It was agreed. In England people were still coming to terms with the death of Princess Diana. Prince Charles, determined to try and put aside his personal feelings and the traumatic weeks of bereavement, had promised Prince Harry an unusual mid-term break. Together, they were to fly to Southern Africa, where son would enjoy his first safari with a school chum and father would be visiting Swaziland and Lesotho. Prince Charles was scheduled to fly into Maseru International Airport from Swaziland today as a guest of Queen Mamohato, in readiness for the wedding banquet this evening, under the stars.

The tables were laid, the ice cream prepared and the beer, cooling. The LHPC lads who were going to Sun City had left, the ladies in the canteen had hung up their aprons and Thabo was leisurely dredging the pool ready for the next water-sports day. Apart from planting out our beetroot and booking our Christmas holiday, Barrie and I were reasonably free.

"Two weeks at the Cape Peninsula at Christmas," said my other half, after spending several hours sorting out reservations. He had just strolled in from the garden and I noticed how pale he looked beside the guys who worked outside. Baked in an office with air conditioning all day wasn't the best way to increase the tan. He had been fully occupied with completion dates and had been working at full stretch. We ladies had to take a back seat when the pressure was on.

"This place, Bloubergstrand which you mentioned Barrie, what's it like?" I said, turning the pages of a 'Getaway' magazine.

"It's a beach which has a magnificent view of Table Mountain, and you wake up within the sound of the sea. Popular for windsurfing and paddle skiing. The hotel serves local wines at the dinner table - fresh seafood...etc etc," he said, reading from the brochure, "not expensive either. I've booked the room."

The acquired television set had been rigged up since early morning. I was preparing cakes, papayas, and strawberry fool - adding a few tablespoons of brandy here and there. Agnes had made fresh bread. Everything should be ready to serve by two o'clock, when the Coronation commentary would be well under way. I was under oath to run and fetch all the male spectators when the dancing girls came on.

Dancing has always been the national pastime of the Basotho – dating back to the bushman scenes painted in the caves, which depict hunting, fishing and dancing in their everyday lives. And when you see them dressed up with their national costumes, it can be a considerable attraction. Watching two hundred bare-breasted maidens dancing in traditional dresses with drum accompaniment, should be a truly magnificent spectacle.

The crowds in Maseru's main highway were thronging their way to the city stadium. There is nothing the Basotho loves more than a celebration at national level. Riders of Basotho ponies, dressed in traditional blankets and conical hats, had transformed Kingsway into a tapestry of colour. Brass bands were playing, people were marching and waving; women ululating against the cacophony of the street. Children bearing streamers and flags and troupes of lithe young dancers filled every walkway. Chiefs dressed in ceremonial garb and beaded costumes, surrounded by dignitaries, bowed to the camera. It was a gala of enormous proportions. Bishops and priests sported flowing robes and tricorn hats, for once walked along devoid of their bibles.

Wheelbarrows and pedestrians spilled into the road. Every taxi and truck was overloaded with passengers waving and shouting, clinging to the side or sitting on top of a moving vehicle. Banners rippled and whistles blew. A glimpse of Moshoeshoe I International Airport some twenty kilometres away showed convoys of delegates and diplomats, Royal princes and heads of state – each with their entourage of staff, being escorted to the palace. Suddenly gold seemed to be the most popular colour. Breast pockets were fully flagged with medals by the mile.

Limousines glided alongside uniformed marching bands. Fanfares of trumpets waited to greet each Royal party outside the airport. I was so captivated by the spectacle that I almost blotted my copybook and forgot to tell everyone the dancing girls were on. Every chair in our sitting room was sudenly filled.

From what we gleaned, Prince Charles had suffered an unfortunate incident when his suitcases had temporarily gone missing on his arrival at the airport. Then a multitude of livestock on four legs surrounded the royal motorcade at some point en route to the palace, an event hardly comparable to London's pomp and circumstance. However, the Prince looked dashing in his naval dress uniform, if a little hot, as he took his seat on the podium beside King Mswati lll of Swaziland., who, it had been rumoured, was to bring all of his six wives. Gossip had been circulating wildly all week.

The British-educated King Letsie has reigned not once, but twice. His father King Moshoeshoe ll was deposed in 1990 and his son Letsie took the throne for five years, but abdicated when his father was reinstated. In January 1995, King Moshoeshoe died when his official car plunged off a mountain road in bad weather, which is the reason his son inherits the crown for a second time.

Schooled at the Benedictine Ampleforth Public School in North Yorkshire, the young King enjoyed the pleasures and pursuits of English country life before returning to the Paramount Chieftancy of Lesotho. Now he was the most desirable batchelor in the land. Letsie made no secret of the fact that at thirty four, he wished to find himself a wife. Indeed Queen Mamohato had focused her attentions on finding her son a suitable wife. She would like to see him settled and of course was worried about the next generation of the royal lineage. It seemed Letsie was rather shy - a good enough reason for a man to seek solitude. Queen Mamohato however, was not to be deterred. She was busy organising parties and official functions so that he would meet as many single ladies as possible.

The weather had turned extremely hot and we felt sorry for the people in the stadium without shade. It was the turn of the girls' choir from Emily's school to perform their songs for the Royal guests, led by a famous conductor/composer of many glorious pieces of music. Their voices reached out to the mountains like a powerful river of sound. The Basotho are born singing. No gathering or celebration ever takes place without a display of voices. They sing from the heart; no need of baton or microphone. No teacher can teach these people more about harmony. Whether male or female – whether child, adult or sage, a Mosotho reaches for his voice into the depths of his being, and like the rarity of the bouquet from a ruby-rich claret, it comes to the ear of the listener in a wave of uplifting joy.

King Letsie appeared on the podium. Tall and broad, he was an imposing figure, wearing a splendid cloak of leopard and lion skins and a beaded headband decorated with a single feather, which denoted his status. He carried an ebony and stone knobkerrie, the equivalent of a Royal sceptre. Looking seriously nervous and dignified, he stood to the cheers of a packed stadium and the crashing music of Lesotho's own military bandsmen, while the distinguished guests melted in the heat. His speech, delivered in Sesotho through a bubbling microphone, was a long one.

Flanked on either side by the elders of the Royal household, an impressive array of visitors waited to be presented. Nelson Mandela of South Africa, Ketumile Masire of Botswana, Benjamin Mkapa of Tanzania, Frederick Chiluba of Zambia, Joachim Chissano of Mozambique and Sam Nujoma of Namibia.

Malawi sent their Minister of State, Bakili Muluzi, Angola their National Assembly President Robert de Almeida. Prince Charles was representing Queen Elizabeth. Zimbabwe's representative was Vice President Muzenda.

The roll call had presented organisers of the Coronation with a huge protocol headache because invitations also included ex-leaders; Kenneth Kaunda of Zambia, John Tembo of Malawi and Terror Lekota, former premier of the Free State. One could only imagine the dilemma of the head-of-state chef who had to arrange a strategic seating plan condusive to international harmony.

On Leribe camp, tonsils were becoming well oiled and appetites well satisfied. We were just beginning to attune to President Mandela's clear handsome tones – speaking in English, when suddenly the television set went off. Knobs were twiddled, then Ali gave it his most senior engineer bash at the side. Nothing we could do would persuade it to come back on.

The Head of the Basotho nation obviously had no control over Lesotho Telecom. Stripped of power, the television transmitters had gone on strike. A long-term grievance must have gone unresolved for the equipment to be shut down in the middle of the King's Coronation. Whoever was responsible for Lesotho's communications system was at loggerheads with Royal protocol. An extraordinary piece of incompetence - or it may have been a wipe-out of electricity volts but something had taken control of the network.

Deprived of the speeches of other Heads of State, we missed Prince Charles' message of congratulation from our Queen. After all the build-up, we felt bereft at missing the march-past by a thousand horsemen who stirred up a dust storm as they thundered round the stadium, leaving the stewards to clear up mountainous tons of healthy steaming manure. The temperature in the stadium soared. The whole ceremony seemingly took six and a half hours, by which time poor Prince Charles was hardly able to keep his eyes open. Newspapers the following day, circulated the story of our own King-in-waiting, in full dress naval uniform, nodding off on the Royal platform.

When H.R.H. eventually departed from Maseru, he left Moshoeshoe Airport en route to Johannesburg, where he was to pay his first visit to South Africa, to meet with President Mandela. After that the famous Spice Girls. .A reunion with his youngest son Harry - post safari - was probably the most important part of his itinerary.

The next morning after hose-piping my garden and helping Barrie to plant his beetroot, we took to the road in a very hot car and drove to Bethlehem. I had been experiencing pain in both my wrists and arms over a period of time and Dr Nettleton had arranged an appointment for me to see a specialist in Bethlehem. The condition had bothered me for months.

We set off. Here and there, we passed many villages where small teams of oxen and horses were ploughing and planting. Hand ploughs are still used in Lesotho and it is a back-breaking job for farmers and their families. Development programmes operated in these parts to try to help people who have not the means to plant their own crops, who own neither ox nor tractor. Sharecropping systems are used to ensure that the land stays productive. An agreement is drawn up between two parties when a farmer helps to plant another man's field in return for a share in the crops. This often works, but when there is no written agreement, the system can break down and arguments break out between families or villages. A village chief often has to sort out the dilemma by ordering the two parties to negotiate or by making a decision, which is sometimes unpopular.

Stock thieving goes on everywhere. It can affect the livelihood of an entire family, if a farmer loses his cattle overnight. Stories, embroidered many times over, were put about regarding cattle thieving and we had no doubt that some of these were related to the sharecropping schemes. There was no government benefit scheme to pay money to poor households and it was inevitable that some of them ended up begging by the roadside. Many villages still do not have basic services such as water supplies, health centres, schools, roads, bridges, communications, and many families live in destitution with barely enough cash income to satisfy basic food needs. Destitution is not uncommon.

Living in a country where poverty is so widespread, it is hard to maintain a balanced view. One can only listen and learn and try to be kind to those who are suffering. The faces of hungry children sitting by the roadside eats into your heart and it isn't easy to pass them by. One wonders if there will ever be a voice which is able to articulate the aspirations of the oppressed majority, to a government who will listen and be able to turn the economy round.

Bethlehem, one of the largest towns in the Free State, was the mecca of shopping and had a certain kind of 'buzz' along its busy parades. Employment was high. Food shops always had supplies of fresh fruit and vegetables and there was no shortage of basic commodities. Restaurants and Diners were attractive places to eat on a day off camp and we sat out on the balcony of one eating-house, discussing the cosmopolitan clientèle and rather good menu.

The aim of our day was to attend the Health Centre so that I could have an X-ray of my neck and to buy a bed for Walter. It was meant to be a surprise. There had been a windfall. Barrie's sister, who lived in California, had written to say she was so moved by our letters about Walter who was still sleeping on an extremely thin mattress on the floor of his hut, that she had wanted to buy him 'a proper bed'.

We found a good furniture store and spent a long time choosing the right mattress. The cost was reasonable. But on no account would the shop deliver the items into Lesotho, to a village church which was off the main tarmac road. The manager looked at us as though we had lost our marbles.

"We don't deliver into Lesotho." The turned-down mouth and tight lips shrank into a thin line. "Do you have a customer reference number?" Hair grey-to-sandy, hands knocked about with sores and scars from loading too many tables into too many trucks, the manager glared.

"No, we don't," I replied as curtly as we had been addressed. "Neither do we have any transport. But we do have cash."

"Sorry lady, we never allow any of our delivery trucks to go through the border."

"Why not? Don't you have customers in Lesotho?"

The man's unrelenting eyes never wavered from mine. With checked trousers, striped shirt with buttondown collar, he was every inch a furniture salesman. His prominent window display of *'Special Credit Terms you cannot afford to miss – Take it Home Today'* did not mention that blacks were exempt from opening a credit contract. And on no account could a bed be delivered to a black family in Lesotho. Even if it was paid for by a white. His silence spoke volumes.

"If we wanted the bed to be delivered to LHPC in Leribe – would you be able to do it?"

I tested him angrily, thinking that I could ask Henry to deliver it to Walter's house in his lorry.

"Sorry lady," he eyed me with a steely glare, feeling our disapproval, "none of our delivery trucks are allowed to cross the border."

As some of our friends had warned us, apartheid was over, but double standards still lingered. Nothing prepares you for these kind of incidents and one is left with the feeling of a stinging slap across the face and smarting self esteem. We gave it the thumbs down sign and hurriedly left the premises.

Barrie wanted to buy a decent pair of binoculars and I wanted birthday and baby presents. You can find the most amazing leather goods in Bethlehem at the camping safari shop, baby clothes at Woolworths and binocs just about everywhere. It would be our last chance to bargain-hunt before leaving for the Cape Peninsula and I needed shoes and a new suitcase. There was a good film on at the cinema in the Pick 'n Pay Arcade and joy of joys, this afternoon we could book a seat. It was strange that we didn't really miss seeing a good film until we had the chance to see one and then couldn't wait to be swept up into that all-enveloping world of fantasy and entertainment. Tonight we could see Madonna transform herself into Eva Peron and blub along with her people in 'Don't Cry for me Argentina', the song which has been carved into my heart for years. We savoured every moment of the Evita story and Madonna's glorious and ravishing costumes were well worth the price of the cinema seat, even if the film had been lousy – which it wasn't.

The problem of the bed was resolved the following Monday morning in Leribe town centre. There was one furniture shop. The manager, with a Charlie Chaplin walk and an eye patch, was a bit abrupt, but he sold beds with mattresses. The request was easily achieved. The item was chosen, paid for and loaded onto a lorry – all within the hour. I drove ahead into Ha Simone to warn the family a bed was to be delivered which was to go into Walter's hut. Californian Auntie Josie would have loved to witness the scene at the Makibi family home that day.

Walter had just finished taking his medication. Dressed only in a pair of blue and white shorts, he was doing excercises in the yard when the Silver Fox rolled into its usual parking spot. He was so busy practising his fancy footwork that he didn't hear me at first. Then after skipping round the ox-cart, he turned and saw me.

"Nettie" he yelled, "I opened the present from James - did you know he sent me the Chelsea shorts. Look! He couldn't have known how much I wanted this ......you knew didn't you? It was as if I was dreaming when I opened the parcel.... Justice and Petros want to wear them......they are so jealous...!!"

Those legs of his looked a might stringy in the blue shorts with white trim but he was looking more and more like the old Walter. I parked in the sun drenched yard, watching a few more drop-kicks and headers through imaginary Stanford Bridge goalposts.

"Really, James must have a heart of gold. No one will believe these shorts have come from a premier league in England. It's a miracle."

"Walter, stand still for a minute. There's something else. Soon a lorry will arrive from Leribe with a new bed. It comes from Auntie Josie in America, in California. She wants you to sleep in a proper bed. We told her about you sleeping on the floor. She is Barrie's sister and she sent some money – out of the blue. We've just been to buy one."

Walter's face was a picture. He stopped running.

"A bed ….for me? How on earth," he stuttered, "but I have never slept in a proper bed….. How will I thank her? Wow!" His foot kicked the ball which zoomed into the back of the imaginary net. "Nettie, please thank her….tell her I will write a letter soon." He sat down on the ground, repeating the news over and over again.

I started to laugh. It was too much. The sight of Walter in a pair of Chelsea soccer shorts awaiting his new bed, seemed so ridiculous. Rose came into the yard with Bernice, carrying a bucket of peas, fresh picked from the field. Rose took one look at Walter and started laughing.

"Walter, what are you wearing?"

"Mum don't you know anything!"

"Hello Rose, I came to tell you there will be a new bed for Walter - it's coming on a truck from Leribe. Also, I want to ask Bernice if she will take me up to her Primary School next week. I want to meet the headmistress."

Bernice looked up at the sound of her name. "What Nettie, you want to come to my school?"

"Yes. Could you ask the head if I can visit? I would like to meet the children, then I can see your classroom too and find out how hard you are working," I teased her.

She giggled and then went on giggling, pointing at Walter's legs. He looked ridiculously happy. This was good news day.

"Bernice stop laughing at my thin legs – I like my legs."

"They look like the spider,"said the ten year old, successfully embarrassing her elder brother.

Inside the living room of Rose's house, piles of unfinished uniforms draped the furniture. Layers of cotton and calico, paper patterns and pins sat on every step and stair. It was obvious the sewing brigade hade been busy.

"Sorry Nettie, I am in a big mess. We are finishing the garments with the sewing machine. My ladies come to use it all hours of the day and night."

"Please don't apologise Rose, I won't stay. Barrie and I have been invited to a party. That reminds me – did Walter mention that we would like to give a party to celebrate his recovery, and the new link with the Datchworth Church? We wondered if you and Stephen would like to decide on a date."

"You mean here, at our house?"

"Yes, in your yard. A real party. A celebration….. .!"

Her eyes widened. She put down her needle. "We would like it very much. There is so much to thank the Lord for. He has sent you and Barrie to us. We will have a special service of thanksgiving." Softly, she added, "Walter's illness can never be forgotten – and our eldest son is alive. Stephen and I will not forget what you did for us then."

"Rose, Walter's illness is too awful to think about. I only did what any normal human being would do. I believe in this world we are all given jobs to do. I was only able to do this job because of having a car, because Barrie supports my actions and we have an income. Rose - your family has given me so much kindness – and anyway, Walter is a fighter."

Suddenly, Emily emerged from the bedroom, pinned into a half finished cotton blouse and flared skirt in pale lilac, with swatches of cotton hanging from the hem. She came to show Rose.

"Look Mum, it fits me. Can you finish it tonight?"

Another impatient daughter.... I smiled to myself, thinking of my own daughter who wanted everything to happen straight away, if not sooner.

They came out to wave me off. Dropping pins everywhere, Emily looked good in her new skirt. It flattered her slim hips and shapely ankles.

"Bye ladies - see you soon, enjoy your dressmaking."

On my way back to Leribe, a Nissan open bakkie, with a cargo of look-alike Slumberland mattresses passed me going the other way, trundling merrily over the potholes. A group of free-riding passengers bounced together in the back of the truck.

I had become addicted to writing on my computer Pleasure of pleasures, I could now mail letters to my friends in England, without using my pen. Crossed wires weren't so prevalent these days. Me and my software were coming to grips with each other. Fewer muddles and fewer sheets of paper for the waste bin. I noticed that Henry used to go through my bin and try to straighten out the not-too-crumpled pages and recycle them. Paper for a Mosotho is not easily affordable and to see us throw it away must have seemed to him, a great waste.

"*Lumela Ntate* Henry," I shouted on collection day, as Henry backed his lorry up to our kitchen door. "How is your family?"

"Hello Mrs Glenn, my daughters are becoming good girls, they are working hard in the school. One of them is taking Matric soon. But my wife is not happy to get more children. I am not good news for her. Every day, she is telling me to go away."

His eyes twinkled. He broke into a cheeky grin. "You must take me to England. I think Mr Barrie will be the Prime Minister and he will take me with him."

"Okay Henry," I joked, " would you be a good driver?"

He jumped down from his cab and lifted my dustbin off the garden path. His peaked cap sat jauntily on his mop of curly black hair. "Yes'*M'e* I will drive Mr Barrie's big car – like on television. With a fine uniform."

"Henry you are a born optimist! You don't realise what traffic is like in England ...and there's no sunshine," and so it went on, until all the plastic bags, old newspapers, polythene bags, empty bottles and balls of screwed up typing paper had been extracted and put into a black plastic bag. The job of refuse collecting meant one thing to Henry – perks.

The manuscript of my book was beginning to take shape. Gradually, I was rationalising my first impressions of Africa since 1996, having arrived from a secure lifestyle in the UK with tunnel vision, the words 'safe and predictable' pressed through the middle of my rib-cage like a stick of rock. There was so much to know about in Lesotho, *so* much to learn. Few people in England would understand how the people here survived, about the contradictions of climate, the poverty, historical grievances and the fresh hope that a new King's reign would bring. My writing time was sacrosanct. Barrie was happy to support my new interest.

I took to carrying a notebook to fuel my scribblings. Amelia and I were trying to find a day to see each other and were both so busy that we never seemed to manage it. She wanted to introduce me to Mamohato, the Queen Mother, so that I could inform her about the link with St John's Church. She promised to arrange an interview for me in Maseru so that we could speak together. Amelia's target was finding a space in the Royal calendar.

Liliane was due to arrive from France the following week. Ali and I had elected to hold a small welcome party. In my life, Liliane represented fun and companionship. She was gifted and articulate. Once again I would have an ally to drive with me out into the mountains - exchange money for plaited grass hats and baskets, laugh with the old women in the markets, go climbing and walking in the Golden Gate Reserve. Despair over our children. We would encourage one another to write, swap summer fruit recipes, tell of new books or paintings we had discovered, worry about the state of the world and give dinner parties to visiting engineers. She would once again be my neighbour, but within a week or two she and Ali would be moving to Butha-Buthe. Their garden on Leribe camp which Ali had slaved over, would be left to the slugs and the starlings. Liliane said I could pick the ripe courgettes, pumpkins and beans for our own cookpot. I would miss her dreadfully when she moved off camp....but I could reach them in thirty five minutes by car.

It was to be our first Christmas away from England – ever. No Christmas turkey, no carol singing and no cold weather. We looked forward to seeing Table Mountain via the new cable car, visiting the wine farms at Stellenbosch and the beautiful Botanical Gardens. We would also be missing out on our kids. I was still worried over the non-contact with my daughter, which left me with a most uneasy feeling. Now it seemed she didn't have a phone and neither did we – the communication system here was something you grew to live with. Letters were the only solution and if someone doesn't write, then you have problems.

It was Saurday. Mail from America had arrived and we had received another cheque from Josie in California. It was part two of Walter's bed.

There was a knock at the door, which was unusual for a weekend when the camp was quiet.

"Hello '*M'e*, how are you and Mr Barrie?"

"Betty, why are you here – it is not a working day for you.?"

Her happy smile and excited manner was unusual. She almost sprang up the back steps and landed on the lino of the kitchen floor with a soft thud. She stood looking down at her feet.

"Look '*M'e*, my new feet!" Her mood was infectious. " '*M'e* it is de shoes! The thief of my house. He is arrested. He has gone to prison for four years. The policeman he gave me back my shoes."

I was embarrassed to see the familiar pair of old trainers I had given her, washed and springy clean, neatly retrieved from the feet of a size eight criminal. "Betty, I am so pleased for you. So you didn't need Mr Glenn's evidence after all?"

"No, I gave your letter to the policeman and he measured de foot of de man. De foot of de thief was too big!" She puffed out her chest with pride. "The man say he stole those shoes. He went to prison this morning '*M'e*. He brought other things from my house which he is stolen."

It took Barrie and I a little while to appreciate the seriousness of this man's offence and equate it with a four year prison sentence. The broad masterly gestures from Betty left me in no doubt that she thought he got what he deserved.

"I came to tell you '*M'e* on my day off, because I not want you think I am dishonest. You think I sell your shoes."

We suddenly realized there was another principle involved here. Betty was afraid we might think she had sold the shoes (it is very common) and that our generosity might be dented in the future.

"The thief say he would pay me in three goats, but I did not want his goats. He must go inside prison. Some men, they say they have done these things because they want to be in de cells."

"Why would someone do that Betty, it doesn't seem sensible?"

"Because they get food at the prison and they have no food themselves. It is what some men do '*M'e*."

We could only gulp and tell Betty we were pleased with the outcome. I set her a place on the stoep for breakfast. After eating, she set about sweeping One of her favourite jobs was to tidy the verandah and arrange the chairs. This morning, feeling incredibly energised, she went all out to crash chairs for Lesotho and left us in singing mode; we could hear her all the way to the gate.

Barrie had earlier taken Hercule out for a route march round the camp. Our neighbours were away and we were looking after him. During the day we let him sit on the lino tiles just inside the back door until his tail-thumping grew so irritating, that we put him outside and gave him the run of the garden on a long rope. Anyway, I wasn't sure how far he could jump and my kitchen worktops were busy with food, in preparation for the party on camp that evening. Hercule's appetite was legendary.

Mr Darcy's cat sat licking herself on the roof of my car, which didn't help. The odd deep throated growl came from the garden as she pruned and purred just out of his reach. I was finishing my Christmas cards to England - making allowances for the erratic courier post - while at the same time, trying to bake for the party tonight, which was in honour of a visiting Senior Engineer from France. It was customary to serve a *braai* and offer a selection of desserts. All the fridges on camp carried extra supplies of wine and Castle beer. Experience had taught us it would be a late night and there was no point in trying to go to bed, as the noise from the bar would be sure to keep us awake.

The sudden appearance of Walter and David threw Hercule into a state of high excitement. The thought of ripping the pants off two young men whom he didn't recognise was enough to upset his doggie chemistry.

"Walter, what are you doing here? Come in."

"I have just been to the hospital," he called, "I had an appointment to be weighed – by Isnette. She is very pleased with me. My weight is almost back to normal. Sixty four kilos! I've brought David to see where you and Barrie live."

The two boys walked across the garden and into the house. Hercule went frantic. Barrie tied him to the tree round the back of the house as he was creating such a din.

"You've saved me a journey Walter. Barrie and I are going to the Cherry Festival in Ficksburg tomorrow. We can't come to Ha Simone….and I have had a letter from Richard Syms about the link."

Of late, I was beginning to realise that the two halves of our lives were beginning to clash. It was becoming more difficult to separate them. None of our ex-pat friends were involved socially with Basotho families. The professional lives of the engineers, the stresses of the project, in-house politics, the programme dates of the dams were the all-important topics of conversation. No one on camp had any interest in a village called Ha Simone, where the son of the village priest had been suffering from tuberculosis and where the arrival of a new bed was big news. Engineers' wives weren't supposed to get involved with local village life. How could I explain the fact that my son had sent Chelsea shorts to a young man in the next village!

The fact that Walter and David had dropped in to see us was *almost* an embarrassment. The boys asked if they could wash my car (Walter viewed that as a priviledge) I had to admit that the job had already been done by Thabo, who had distinguished himself in that role already.

"Walter, tell your father we have heard from England. The Datchworth Committee has been set up. Parcels and letters will start arriving. I have given the people in England your postal address in Leribe." David was listening intently to my words. He knew very little English and desperately wanted to understand the language. "David, say after me, 'people of Datchworth send their best wishes to St John's in Ha Simone."

"Okay Mrs Annette. I say the words."

In his less-than-perfect pronounciation, David made a brave attempt. We all laughed. Walter teased him kindly …. David threw back his head and grinned. Then Walter's expression changed and a look of sorrow filled his eyes.

"Nettie, I have to tell you that Augustinus has come home from his job as a builder. You know he went to work for that man, that friend of my father's. He has worked two months without a rest. Well - he is broken. They made him carry the stones and the bricks for long hours every day until it was dark. His hands are bleeding. He cannot work any more. He is thin. You should see him."

"Walter, I am horrified. Why did that happen?"

"My father thought the builder was a good man – but he was wrong. The man exploited the goodwill of my brother. Augustinus came back last night and he is a terrible sight. He cries in pain. He cannot use his hands." Walter's face creased and anger showed in his eyes. This was the real reason he had come to see me. "Augustinus is devoted to my father. He would not like to let him down. But it was too much to bear and he asked those people to let him come home. Now he feels totally ashamed….please come and see him Nettie. He is not talking to anyone and I am afraid for him."

Those eyes as black as midnight looked at me. Walter's appearance was now much improved. His skin colour had returned to a healthy black and he was gaining weight. His confidence was slowly returning And David was once more proud to be his right hand man.

It was complicated enough that tomorrow we were going with our friends to the Cherry Festival in Ficksburg and that during the coming week I had appointments to see a surgeon and a neurologist in Blomfontein about the 'carpel tunnel syndrome' in both my wrists. Private medical treatment was something which Walter and his family knew nothing about.

"Next Tuesday I will come Walter. I would like to visit Bernice's school to meet the headmistress. Will you come with me?"

"Yes, okay Nettie. That used to be my school as well. The Headmistress is called Charlotte. She knows me. I would like to take you there."

"I want to introduce her to Datchworth Primary School. Letters from the English children have to be delivered by hand. But first I will come to see Augustinus."

A celebration for the end of the contract was planned. A senior French engineer had arrived from Paris It was time for the men to be thanked officially; a kind of professional thankyou for the work they had done. It was a fine night and the wine flowed. In the queue for the food, a relaxed atmosphere took hold. Monsieur Gasket welcomed everyone in

French....naturally. Guests arrived from Butha-Buthe and Ha Lejone. It was great to see old friends and be introduced to new ones. Conversation with wives from the other camps brought fresh news. In-house gossip boomed. Unmissable stories of so-and-so, a touch of lavatorial humour, alarming jokes which one wouldn't usually find funny....

As a Frenchman was to be the guest of tonight's evening, dinner-party French was the only acceptable form of conversation. Barrie and I struggled to keep up. After three or four glasses of Cape red, Barrie's accent seemed to improve. It wasn't so much the right words which came out, but the gestures became more Frenchified. He waved his arms extravagantly. He was very good at mimicking accents. His three French verbs leant at St Joseph's College, Blackpool were put to good use. If we lingered another few hours, I should have to go and find him a beret and a string of onions.

The stereo system oozed piano accordians and romantic voices. Chevalier sang '*Under the Bridges of Paris with You*'. Someone quipped, "not if it's been built by LHPC". Laughter all round. It got worse after that. Hercule chewed himself out of the fence and streaked past us out of the gate and up the nearest mountain. There was no point in sending out a search party. He usually came back by himself after he had visited all the cow pats in the vicinity and rounded up a few sheep. With the smell of supper wafting across the gardens, his patience had reached zero tolerance.

The charcoal steaks were good, the *fraises a la crème* was perfect. My Madeleine biscuits were simply delicious. It was a good time to improve international relations and sing a few French songs. A Basotho guitarist, known to us all as 'Augustine's brother'arrived and joined in. No one knew his real name. Shortly after midnight, we heard splashes over by the swimming pool. It was inevitable that some guests would end up wet.

We couldn't leave the party until Monsieur Gasket retired to bed and the bottle of cognac was empty. The dying embers of the fire was the signal for those still awake to move into the bar for coffee. Several guests were staying over at the visitors' house and wanted to carry on talking. We decided to turn in. Arm-in-arm, we strolled the few yards back to our house, still humming familiar French tunes. Sleepily, we stumbled up the verandah steps, gazing up at the pale stars. The sound of the gate swinging over by the guard hut cut into the silence.

"Perfect evening," sighed Barrie, leaning his back against the wooden stairs. He lit a cigar and the butt end glowed in the darkness. The temperature was heavenly. A few moths played in silver circles near the house light. He blew the tobacco smoke through the dark strands of honeysuckle and reached for my hand. "Have you ever wished time would stand still honey? Then, with a twinge of disappointment in his voice, "We should have tried harder for that Mohale job..."

"Africa has got to us all tonight I think ....come on its late."

As we turned the house lights out, doves sitting on our telegraph wires softly started their early dawn cooing and Hercule's tired bark sounded from next door, telling us he was home.

Chapter 18

Special Birthday

The classroom floor was made of mud. A sea of eager faces filled the large room. The teacher sitting in the middle, turned to address first one half, then the other. There was a blackboard at one end with the words written in white chalk: '*Welcome to the English lady*'.

Bernice had been as good as her promise. She had asked her Headmistress if I could visit. This was my first experience of being inside a Lesotho Primary School. Walter and I had walked about half a mile from the main road, from where a wide dusty track led to the classrooms of Leribe Primary School, housing eight hundred children.

"Charlotte Mkhobo, welcome to our school," she had said, holding out her hand. "I will show you our classrooms. Bernice Makibi told me you would come. This was a surprise. Where do you come from – why do you live in our country?"

Her words were inquisitive, her manner warm. "Come and meet the staff."

It was obvious she was very fond of Walter and did not mind him acting as the interpreter. The staff were friendly, the children very excited. I was nervous.

The maths and science equipment was tragic; a few pairs of compasses, plastic measuring devices, some ancient rusty weighing scales, one or two wooden t-squares, mechanical clocks with no hands, abacus bead counting frames, a badly knocked about walking-wheel. There was a world globe, the print so faded that the African continent was hardly visible.

We passed through to the first classroom where forty pupils were beginning a lesson. The desks at which the children sat were quite new and although the walls of the classroom had not been plastered, the room was light and airy, with big windows looking out onto trees. A gang of children came in late having just finished their duties of yard sweeping. They sat down noisily and stared hard at me. There didn't seem to be many books around.

"We are studying the different methods of planting crops," explained the teacher who was pleased to show off her pupils. Amongst the multitude of serious faces, I detected a little uncertainty. The softness of the eyes, the nervous lips remained fixed upon me. I felt I had to say something. Walter came to my rescue. He must have struck the right note. Suddenly relaxed smiles appeared and loud chattering broke out. Charlotte shushed them quiet.

"The lady visitor has come with messages from children in England. They would like to be your friends."

Charlotte spoke gently to the children in Sesotho. Black curly top-knots turned to listen and a few hand-covered giggles of curiosity rippled through the class.

"Mrs Glenn has brought very important news for you. Do you wish to hear the news?"

"Yes, we do."

"You must sit quietly and your teacher will tell you. In English"

A hush fell as the children concentrated hard. Charlotte motioned us to leave. The teacher rose to her feet and thanked us. We walked outside to the older part of the school where the classrooms still had mud floors and tin roofs. The pretty young teacher smilded broadly and stood to welcome us. The seats were long wooden benches, all squashed together. There were no cupboards, no shelves and no books. Two long sweeping brooms stood by the door.

"What happens if it rains and you can't hear your teacher speak?" I asked the kids.

"We sleep until the rain has stopped. Sometimes if it is a big storm, we run home, because there are no more lessons."

I took a piece of chalk and wrote on the blackboard: 'Hello from England, I am glad to see you.' and the already excited children started to run round the classroom like a train. A lady visitor shown around the school by the headmistress, smiling teachers..... a reason to lift feet off ground and jump wildly! It was then that I realised what an impact a connection with Datchworth School would have.

Justine, the class teacher, offered me a seat at her desk which was placed between the two halves of the classroom.

"How many children altogether?" I asked.

"One hundred and ten when they all attend, sometimes more," she said, grinning at my obvious amazement.

"Gosh – how do you manage?"

"Oh, it's okay.....they all learn the same thing at the same time. They have to pick it up if they fall behind. They have good memories. No books you see. We use slates. They repeat and repeat many times." Her obvious delight at my interest in her position pleased her enormously and she and I warmed to each other. "All the Makibis have attended our school, we know them well. Bernice is a pupil just now. She told me you were coming."

Charlotte insisted Walter and I go to her house after lessons ended. Suddenly, from high in the branches of a tree which grew on the perimeter of the school, a bell rang out. A boy standing underneath pulled on a long rope as the sound clanged again and again. Within minutes, a surge of blue uniforms streamed out of lessons, the children's bare feet flying, carrying their singing and laughter out to the mountain.

"You hear that bell Nettie," said Walter tugging my arm, "that was here when I was a pupil It rings every morning to call the kids to school. Everyone used to sit under the tree before lessons. We used to fight for a place near the trunk, so we could lean our backs against it."

The marking of class registers, standing underneath the branches of a giant eucalyptus in the lea of the mountains entirely transformed junior school assemblies. Notices were read out, important issues discussed, exam results celebrated. The school had no central place where all the pupils could meet, except by the ancient tree, which had witnessed many passing years of growing children.

Charlotte and her husband occupied a large brick bungalow further down the hill near the road. She was a big lady with a heart to match. Her smile, without too many teeth, was radiant and she spoke English like a mezzo soprano – deep and rich. Nothing was too much trouble if it involved her pupils. On entering her large kitchen, we met the cowman who had just finished eating his lunch. His battered Worzel Gummidge hat was lying on the table. Albert looked after all the cows owned by Charlotte and was about to go and see to his animals.

The headmistresses's voice boomed out.

"Albert, show Mrs Glenn our prize animal. She is interested in our school and she is from England. Bring it to the house. Now please."

The cowman, reaching for his stick, ran outside. Unexpectedly, Blossom turned out to be a huge bull with large curly horns. Dark brown coat, white face and rings around the eyes. Albert beamed with pride and with a good poke of his stick, turned the bull round for me to admire a view of the rump. The whole of the backside seemed to be in motion. In situations like this one wonders what one is supposed to say.

In a state of mild panic, being close to the rear end of such a large creature, my words dried up in my mouth. There was a fair bit of snorting and stamping going on. As for Albert, I was full of admiration. The bull raised its huge neck. Two small boys who had popped up from nowhere, stood next to its head. Another prod from Albert and the bull wandered out of Charlotte's garden, followed by a posse of small children who had absolutely no fear whatsoever at the proximity of such a large piece of sirloin with horns. The cowman looked amazed at my explanation that bulls did not roam the streets freely in England and children would not dream of playing close to them.

"He is part of the family," said Albert proudly, "in Lesotho we love our cattle and the children are used to being near them, even animals bigger than this. In winter when it snows, children sleep with the cows because they are warm."

After much handshaking between Charlotte, the cowman and myself, a day was set for the following week. My mission - to establish a meeting point between children of different lands.

*   *   *   *

I had never before seen hands like the hands of Augustinus. The skin was unutterably sore and bleeding. He couldn't hold even a spoon. The skin so badly chaffed, the knuckles a mass of scabs and swellings where sores had bled and become infected. He sat on a short stool outside his hut and tried to get up when he saw me. His legs were obviously stiff and painful.

"Augustinus, why have they done this to you?"

"I don't know Nettie. I tried to please them.....I really tried to work hard and do a good job. But they gave me no protection on my hands and I was all the day lifting and fetching concrete blocks and bricks and heavy rocks." He looked down at the ground and tears came easily. "They didn't let me have any resting time.....only a few minutes. No one brought me a drink. I was hungry and thirsty...and at night they did not allow me to sleep." His voice was almost a whisper. "It was the worst experience of my whole life. I tried to be friendly with them, but they were always harsh and said unkind words. I felt as though I would die in those two months......."

"Augustinus, you did right to ask to leave. No one should put up with those things.......your poor hands. I will fetch antiseptics.....try to prevent infection. You must know that Walter and all your brothers missed you and wanted you home. We all missed you....what age were these people......young, old...?"

"They were young like myself, but they hated me."

I looked into his eyes and saw the sorrow and the pain. Augustinus, at nineteen years old was the gentlest, the kindest Mosotho. Walter, his brother in all except name, fetched him a drink of water and held the cup to his lips. I could remember no time when I felt so angry for such an act of utter wanton hurt and pain, inflicted on a fellow worker. Augustinus's hands would heal but his memory would not. I was sure there was a hidden agenda here which I could not fathom.

Emily and Walter proposed a trip in my car up to Qoqolosing to celebrate my birthday. I had received an invitation to visit Lithabaneng, a village near Ha Setsomi, high above Levis Nek, by a member of St John's Church, who asked me to go and meet her family. She had offered to prepare us a traditional meal. We accepted.

The three of us set off mid morning, the sun still low on the slopes. Walter knew the way - he said. The track was narrow and bumpy. It was obvious after half an hour or so, that not many cars/carts/ tractors or ponies had used this path for a long time. I didn't like driving this kind of teeth-rattling terrain.

"Keep going Nettie, it doesn't matter if we go slowly – we've got all day."

'It will probably take all day', I thought to myself. The collection of grasses and roots hanging from the front bumper, a major source of the thrashing sound which came from underneath the car, was bothering me and I felt we might seize up.

"Look Walter, why don't you drive? You're used to these kind of tracks."

He was delighted to be asked. Emily and I sat in the rear seats and offered suggestions.

"Okay ladies, don't worry, we'll make it before two o'clock."

When Walter says 'don't worry' it is a bad sign.

"Walter this track is going to run right out. Look there's only one house. It's got to stop here."

"No, it's fine, we'll make it." He rolled his eyes at me in the mirror, happy to be the driver of the 'Silver Fox' which he loved. The ground was boggy and the tyres were building up thick layers of mud. We continued until the track ended - precisely where Emily and I said it might.

The practice of ignoring the passage of time is an intrinsic part of Basotho life. Emily and I exchanged glances. The journey became bumpier, the track narrower. A donkey would have managed it easier. Then Walter let me into the secret.

"You see Nettie, we usually walk up. We don't usually come by car. We come up by Levis Nek and it's very quick. This is the long way round."

The scenery was changing. Fields of almost fully grown maize grew on every hillside. The dark green leaves looked glossy and healthy in the sun and the soil looked richer in texture than in the valley bottom. There were one or two scattered homesteads and plenty of sheep grazing on lush green pasture, a sign that there had been good rain during October and November. I somehow expected to see the occasional tractor. Instead there were one or two oxen and boys following ploughs. Sunflower groves spread in yellow patches and the mimosa was still in blossom. Patches of red hot pokers shone like fire in the grasses by the streams.

After two hours we passed a *setibeng* (village spring) where a few families were gathering to fill their water jars. They observed us closely. You could read their body language. They thought we were mad to be driving up here.

We had reached a point where the car would go no further. Gullies of rocks and dry river beds stretched upwards and there was absolutely no hope of progress on four wheels.

A pack of young children suddenly appeared on the horizon, obviously the search party sent to find us. Urging us forward with their cries of encouragement, Walter, Emily and I finally reached the top – on all fours. The last fifty yards meant clambering over rocks and boulders, which had rolled down a short slipway. I was quite exhausted. It had taken us more than two and a half hours.

Angelina's house nestled in the shelter of an overhang and faced a large field of moist brown earth, which looked ready for planting. Views across the mountains were heavenly.

"*Lumelang,*" came the cries from inside and there was the lady of the house in apron and scarf, coming out to welcome us, followed by many small children - wide eyed and curious. We stepped inside. "*Re a le lumedisa.*" (we are greeting you) they sang. There was no husband around and my guess was that Angelina's was a miner working in South Africa.

" 'M'e, would you like water? We have it. Come and sit down."

An empty plastic bottle was produced, handed to the eldest girl, who quickly left the hut. My knees were still wobbly from the hard climb and I felt breathless, probably from the altitude. I began to focus on faces round the room; faces of children, old people, men, women of all ages, crushed inside the house to take a good look at this white stranger who had driven from Ha Simone in a car. On the big table in the middle of the room was a hand-operated sewing machine.

The old grandmother addressed me first in simple Sesotho, which I was able to answer. Angelina beamed and kept on shaking my hand. I was given a seat at the table as food was being prepared in the small kitchen at the side. The bright blue metal cupboards in the kitchen reminded me of mass-produced utility furniture which people in England had just after the war. The doors never managed to stay shut for more than a few minutes, especially when standing on uneven floors. I began to wonder how anyone would carry a large piece of furniture up the mountain. There was no running water or electricity in the house and food was cooked over an open fire, or indoors on a primus stove.

The girl arrived back with water for Walter, Emily and myself. She was a skinny teenager in a torn was-white dress with one shoulder missing, her frizzy hair long and uncut - a challenge to any comb. She smiled at me shyly. Some of the spectators were beginning to melt away. Grandmother sat by the open door of the house, plaiting and weaving her grasses. She was wearing a cotton dress, colour unrecognisable, with a shawl around her thin body. Toothlessly, she smiled up at me and offered to show me how she made sweeping brushes. On her lap were a few strips of rubber, cut from a car inner tube, which she used to bind the grasses together into a handle. Then, as I stooped down to watch her nimble fingers, she offered up the finished item, closed an arthritic old hand over mine and nodded vigorously. She was asking me to accept the broom as a gift.

"Kea Leboha nkhono," I said, "I will take it to my home and use it."

I handed it to Emily as a way of showing I was pleased. Emily spoke words of appreciation to Grandmother, who looked truly delighted. For an instant her small dark eyes shone and she made the sign of the cross on herself, demonstrating her own simple faith.

Suddenly there was a loud commotion outside the house, which included sounds of heavy hooves clattering into the yard. Angelina pulled my sleeve.

"Come, come 'M'e, de boys are ready. I told them to bring..." she didn't finish her sentence before several kids burst into the room, dancing up and down on bare toes, holding hands across mouths in sheer excitement.

Standing right outside the back door was an enormous ox with its engine on full revs. The ground vibrated and the air was busy with flies. A tank of an animal, the square head leaned down towards the feet of two small boys the size of Irish leprechauns. They were dressed in tattered blankets pinned round their shoulders. Both held onto the end of a short rope.

" Do you want to watch the ploughing Nettie?" asked Walter, "This is their own beast. They want to show you how it is done. These kids are proud of their skills."

"Yes, but I would rather he was a bit further back. You know I'm not very keen."

Slowly the animal turned itself around to the prodding of sticks and a torrent of urgent commands, its leathery haunches rippling and glistening with sweat. We were forced to move away from the tail end as it swished at the flies and filled the air with cow dung confetti, not to mention a healthy country smell. I have always had a sneaking sympathy for the ox. These great beasts of burden work every day of their lives and when you really look at their eyes, they seem so sad. Urged on by sticks or whips upon their backs, they devote their lives to cart or plough, plodding resolutely through any kind of weather. And they don't bite. They might tread on you, but they don't bite.

This undisputed old-timer, linked onto a yoke with a second ox, hitched up by leather ropes to a hand plough, urged on by a ten-year-old with bare feet, reached a steady lumbering motion. Together they depicted a cameo of life in Africa. The boy-in-charge knew exactly how and where the furrows must be cut and holding onto the wooden handle, guided the blade, slicing through the soil with the skill and precision of his father before him – all the time looking backwards to see if we were still watching. He was proud to be able to demonstrate this important family tradition. Behind him the soil fell into furrows, like sticky dough falling into bread tins. The ox-engine turned towards the sun and we watched them disappear over the ridge with no manufacturer's handbook or emergency telephone number in case of breakdown.

Later on I was allowed to feel the weight of the plough while the beasts were standing still. My hands stroked the old wooden handle, worn smooth by generations of plough boys. Lesotho winters and summers had polished and shaped this object into a horn of velvet. Who knows how many more years this blade would continue to walk behind these iron beasts, planting seed and reaping harvest.

"How old is this plough, do you have any idea Angelina?"

"Oh yes *'M'e*," she succeeded in saying, "by my calculations, almost a hundred years. My grandfather was the man who made this plough. He was the first in our family to use it. These boys are his great-great-grandchildren….."

There was no pretentiousness in her voice. Only satisfaction and pride. The remote areas of Lesotho are by far the poorest in the country. An inevitable result of mountain poverty, combined with the high level of ownership of livestock, is that mountain children are less likely to attend school. More than twenty per cent of boys of school age are shepherds, while in the lowlands, less than ten per cent of boys herd animals instead of going to school. Most schools in the lowlands have piped water and latrines, whereas the mountain schools lack these facilities. The task of collecting fuel and water falls on the women and children, preventing them from learning more productive activities or going to school.

But poverty is not just about lack of money. This family had a sturdy house, fields, livestock and sons and daughters who were capable of work. This level of farming is non-profit making, yet it is still a way of life for the rural poor; the difference between maintaining some quality of life and total collapse.

One major asset in Lesotho is the sense of family and community. Every family above the subsistance line is helping another family and I suspect that Stephen and Rose were helping Angelina's family in some small way. In return Angelina was loyal to the Makibis and was always willing to lend a hand when they needed someone. She was one of Rose's regular sewing ladies who happily turned out dresses and uniforms from the piles of cloth which seemed to accumulate in Rose's living room.

The family meal was ready. We must have numbered nine or ten. It was Emily's turn to let me know the names of the different dishes. There was home-made *bohobe* (bread) and porridge made from sorghum beans and mealie pap. Angelina had made *makoenya* which I had eaten before, and which I loved. They were like doughnuts covered in sweet syrup. Fresh peaches, bottled from last year's crop were brought onto the table for dessert.

The boys picked up their dishes and drank the porridge. Walter really tucked in. There was another traditional Basotho dish, but which I could not name and a drink passed round the table in a metal jug. I think it was milk straight from the cow.

"Do you wish *metsi* (water) to drink instead 'M'e?"

"Yes please......."

I apologised for my lack of appetite. Actually I didn't fancy the porridge. The babble of voices in the room was loud and energetic. Arms and elbows thrusting across the table meant everyone was hungry. Angelina's family were well catered for when it came to nourishment. They were healthy, despite their lack of all the things we take for granted. Judging by their energy and motivation and their acceptance of life as it was, they could still be here in another hundred years, even working the same crops with the very same plough. But how did they survive the cold winters? I did not dare to ask the question.

Walter and Emily gave my thanks in Sesotho and said it was time we were starting back.

"Thank you 'M'e for your generous hospitality, I shall always remember my journey up the mountain on my 57th birthday. I enjoyed the ploughing lesson!"

I loved Angelina's smiley face and her quick movements. She really appreciated our visit and I felt privileged once again, to have an insight into the Basotho lifestyle. We shook hands firmly. Grandma and I had a hug before leaving. Her rheumy old eyes were full of tears.

The afternoon was cooler as we waved goodbye to Angelina and the children. The older ones ran beside us until we found the place where we had left our motor. As always, one or two extra passengers came down the mountain with us. They never can resist a car ride. Half way down we stopped to let them off and a row of smiles stood across the track waving until we were out of sight.

"Will I ever forget my birthday?" I said to Emily who sat beside me with her lap full of vegetables, sent as a present from Angelina to Rose. "This has been a very special day for me. Barrie is still at work and I will want to tell him everything this evening. He will probably throw his hands up in horror when I tell him where we went."

"Say that it was our present for your birthday," she said laughingly in time to the bumps.

"Walter, next year on this very week, I would like you and Emily to come up here as an anniversary. I shall be back in England by then…..and will be thinking of this day…..and just look at that sun going down. How wonderful is that!"

The red ball was sinking fast below us and flamenco colours made slashes across the sky. The light was fading and the bats would soon start their skilful sky-diving and cicadas would start to throb in the grass. I was beginning to wonder how I would cope in next year's grey November back in England..

"Right Walter, we'll collect you on Saturday for our trip to Muela Dam."

"I'm sorry I can't come Nettie, Bernice and I have to go to Jo'burg. We're staying with Grandma Violet in Soweto.We won't be back for a few weeks because we're looking after my cousin's baby. It's Bernice's first time to go away from home."

"Come back home in time for the December party Em, we can't have it without you."

As I drove home, a flicker of lightning danced on the far horizon. I reached the camp gates just as the thunder was booming across the valley. Another electric storm was on its way.

*   *   *   *

In addition to shopping in Ficksburg the following day, I had made an arrangement to see Marlene at the library to collect books on Basotho culture. I needed to complete my research.

"Everything is out at the moment Annette, all the schools are doing projects on Lesotho, there's nothing much left, for sure we're almost empty."

Marlene always had her finger on the button where her library stock was concerned. On the main reception desk, I happened to see a very large book opened on a page where peoples' names had been written and a purple ribbon hanging between the pages.

"A remembrance book for Princess Diana," whispered Marlene, noting my interest. "I started it a few weeks ago and it's been so popular. Look, I've had hundreds of names. People keep coming here saying they want to write something." She flicked through the pages to show me what had gone before. "This is the second book, I filled the first one in a few days. Honestly, she was so loved in this town – by both blacks and whites. Isn't it strange? There are no barriers when it comes to Diana."

I felt immensely glad that I had seen it and was able to add my own name. The child's entry before mine was: *'Diana, the hole world will miss you.'*

"There has never been anything which has brought the people of Ficksburg together like this – and I still cry when I think of it." she added, "and while you're here Annette, come and look at our painting exhibition."

"Whose paintings?"

"Beatrice Findlay. Christian's mother – you know - Franshoek Farm. She's so talented, come and see. She started painting at the age of seventy and there's no holding her."

"Dear Beatrice…" I said, admiring her style. "She certainly knows how to handle African colours, never seen anything quite like these." The leading painting was called *'The Dassie Eater'* and the cork frame was cut from the cork tree on Franshoek farm. "I guess you've had a lot of interest."

"…and a lot of sales."

Janet Barrett, my old friend from Kindi Nursery School stepped into the library at that moment and we greeted each other warmly.

"Annette - we've not seen you and Barrie up at Boschfontein Farm for ages, you must come. Peace would love to see you. I shall tell her you were in town. Look, ring me at the weekend and we'll arrange something. You don't have to wait for another gooseplucking day – just come anyway." We laughed as we remembered plucking feathers from the geese, the day they made eiderdowns on the farm.

"How's everybody at Kindi? I can't believe it's a year since I helped with Nativity, and you're practising for the next one already! Barrie's contract is finishing in the spring Janet – we have to go back to England. We're not going to live up at Mahale after all……I'm distraught. Anyway we're going to the Cape for Christmas, then we'll go see a bit more of Africa before we leave."

"Then you must come and see our photographs of Zimbabwe. We've just been for a holiday - it's a fantastic country. You and Barrie would absolutely love it Let's talk about it over dinner."

Returning to the camp that afternoon loaded with surprises for Liliane's welcome home party, my mind was on the imminent phone call to my daughter, which Barrie had planned for me as a birthday treat. A friend in

England was going to drive my daughter to a phone and we would wait for the line to ring in Barrie's office, sometime during the evening (there was a two hour time difference). Our house phones had been down for weeks and the office arrangement was a big favour by a senior member of staff. My daughter would not realize what a difficult set of circumstances this was. We would have to go down to Barrie's office in the dark to sit and wait.

We waited. The phone did not ring. An hour went by. There was no ring. I was terribly disappointed. There was nothing we could do to get in touch after tonight. I felt a nagging sense of insecurity, envisaging the worst, especially with regard to Abigail. Reflecting on the situation after a long discussion with Barrie, I was convinced that no news was good news. I was just being excessively neurotic. Six thousand miles feels a long way apart and there wasn't a flight to Heathrow tonight.

It was lovely to see Liliane and Ali together again. My good friend had returned from France and there was a small celebration in the bar to welcome her back. My French deserted me when I wanted to say something clever and greetings came out as Yorkshire as ever. A small band of well-wishers spent the evening planting a lot of kisses on a lot of cheeks and drank too many bottles of Muscadet light Liliane's return to camp meant another round of delicious Roquefort cheese.

"These olives are good Liliane," said Barrie, with a mouthful of cheese.

"I give you a thousand kisses Barrie, I have meeeesed you! What have you done to Ali – he is so fat!!"

"It's Sophie's cooking," answered her husband, purring like the cat who had had the cream. "I promise to stop eating in the canteen and come home for lunch….." Ali's smile was back.

"How do you feel about coming to see Muela Dam on Saturday ? We're taking Walter now that he is so much better. They're dying to see you at the Makibis….Liliane you've missed such a lot. There's so much to tell…. and Thabo is looking for you… he's been watering your beans…."

Everything came tumbling out at once.

"*Eh bien*…. the Lesotho tip. Okay, we will rendevous tomorrow. I look forward to seeing him again."

Saturday dawned with another glorious morning. Shiny satin clouds raced each other high overhead. After breakfasting in the garden, Barrie and I drove to Ha Simone to pick up Walter and a friend called Rose who wanted to come with us. Walter's reason for going to Muela was that he used to work there as a shutter-hand in 1995 until the strike in 1996, long before we had come to live in Leribe. He had lived in Lesotho as a boy, before the Highland Water Scheme had arrived to carve up the hillsides, causing locals to tremble at the provoking rumours which were put around. Engineering sites were not words which they were familiar with in those days. Muela is situated near Butha-Buthe at the northern end of Lesotho.

Today the valve would be open twenty per cent from the by-pass tunnel. This would enable the water from Katse to by-pass the powerhouse - the part in which Barrie had been involved. We would see water coming through the dissipation structure and down into the stilling basin; a sure test on the valve. It would be the last chance to see the valley as it was before the dam was built. Nothing else had been talked about for months on the camp. The Muela hydro-electric scheme forms a significant part of the first phase of the Lesotho Highlands Water Project. When it is fully commissioned, it will meet almost the entire electricity needs of Lesotho and will end current dependence on importation of power from South Africa.

This morning the road was full of people walking, waiting for transport, sitting or lying horizontal by the edges of the road in close proximity to passing cars. It was quite normal to see people lying down or sleeping on any horizontal surface, tilted on any gradient, or purely squatting asleep at any time of day. At one of the village kraals young boys flicked their whips on the rumps of the donkeys, women held out bunches of asparagus asking for a few maloti; young children ran in a dare-devil way, along the roadside, thrusting vegetables through open windows of moving cars.

Walter and Rose were ready waiting, eager for a car ride, Walter in smart shirt and trousers, looking the picture of health once more. For Barrie it meant a day's holiday from the office. By now, we had acquired the rhythm of Lesotho Saturdays and there was always that special ambience, a sort of shambling pace at half the Wednesday speed. No one seemed to be going anywhere fast. No engineers' cars pasting the tarmac and many more children about. Young men were out chatting up the girls, especially near the water taps - a good spot for flirting. We could hardly have asked for a more perfect day.

Butha-Buthe's bleating goats were tied to wooden fences, waiting for slaughter. Farmers brought sheep and chickens into town at the weekends and stood around, bidding and bartering. A huge lorry bringing in goods from South Africa became obstructed by animals going to market. The driver got out and sat down on the verge to cogitate. Should any chicken be thinking of crossing the road, now was its chance.

Once out into the open fields, there were patches of peas and carrots, new wheat coming on and ladies hoeing and weeding. A long queue of people was waiting by the roadside at one point and we guessed it was 'offal day'. A system of buying supplies of fresh offal at cheap prices was popular, even though it meant queuing. No electricity meant meat had to be eaten the same day.

We drove on through the red earth, which grew redder at every turn in the road. The terra- cotta colours contrasted against the blue of the sky as though an artist had drawn bold lines along the mountains.Through Qalo, then

Khukhune, where the landscape changed into a windswept but wider, gentler Lesotho, the mountains falling away, then rising again, until we could not tell whether we were going up or down the contours.

"Beautiful countryside Walter….such green pastures and lovely valleys."

"It's very traditional here. People survive without transport, shops, services. Everyone relies on family support. I love this part of Lesotho."

"It reminds me of Scotland….. those hills….and the open *veld* and the colours…. except there's no loch in the distance."

"What's a loch?"

Some of the villages looked prosperous. Elegant horsemen, wearing bright blankets rode bare-back on ponies in groups of three or four, as though en route for a grand parade. Many houses were highly decorated with patterns on outside walls and fancy stonework. Women prepared meals outside in traditional three-legged pots. The little baptist church stood squarely on the ridge above Ha Salomo, as if it knew that the people would continue to come to pray on Sundays and worship within its walls. Even after the coming of the dam, they would talk of it and tell their children about it and remember when the first lorries passed their doors - long after the construction teams had gone. We hoped they wouldn't hate us.

"It looks more African here somehow, what must it have been like for these villages when cranes and concrete pipes got mixed up with the rondavels. Can you imagine steel office buildings coming up here, on those huge carriers and then the muck lorries," commented Barrie.

"Can we stop a minute love, I want to take photographs….by that tree."

By the roadside we drew in to a spot where a single tree grew - alone in the red dust - a tall landmark in the sky. It was an old eucalyptus with a strong trunk. No leaves grew until the very top. The bark was smooth, the colour of maple wood. Through its leaves, the white clouds flew and the purple hills rolled away as far as the eye could see. I could imagine it in the winter, exposed to the harsh winds or silhouetted against the eye of a storm. It stood - dignified, challenging…. .defiant.

Swept up in a sudden surge of emotion, I *loved* that tree…..*and* this day, *and* the fact that we could share in this beautiful landscape. We wandered on a little further. Barrie put his arm round my shoulders. Walter and Rose stood by the car.

"What's the matter honey?"

"I think its because we've got to say goodbye to this place Barrie…soon we won't see all this. Just look at that tree how it stands all alone. It's so beautiful….and strong."

Tears rolled down my cheeks. Barrie turned me round to face him. I knew that he understood perfectly. We had grown to be part of this land. I felt a pain deep down inside.

"Yes - we will come back…. and we'll come and see if the tree is still here. The valley will be gone by then. It'll be a lake…..it'll be changed."

"What will the people do?" I asked, my eyes still on his face.

"They'll have new homes, new farms and they'll have jobs...." He waited for me to dry my tears. " Come on honey, Walter and Rose are waiting. Let's go."

Back on the road, we drove up behind a large heavily laden vehicle.We were enveloped in dense gritty dust which choked us and filled our eyes and ears with the smell and taste of the site. White – coated grass lay flat beside the tarmac, where heavy wheels had passed.

The many roads circling the whole area of the dam, fed various parts of the construction. Built at the very beginning of the project, they had seen hundreds of muck lorries, great concrete carriers and heavy plant through months and months of preparation. Lifelong traditions of the Basotho had been swept away, but the enterprise would provide electricity, employment and one hoped tourism. I wondered how many people understood the meaning of the project or appreciated the possible benefits that they and their children would gain.

Barrie drove in the main gate and our car was searched. His pass enabled us to drive into the site and park. We could now see in the distance, the crest of the dam itself, with the water up to Intake Sill level. Underneath us, hidden from view, was the tunnel portal leading to the powerhouse cavern which would house all the turbo generators, the nerve centre of the whole hydro-power scheme.

The drill and blast excavation of the underground power station started in June 1995. Removal of the rock was completed by July 1996. By August 1996 the maze of complex tunnels was ready to be lined with reinforced concrete and steel fibre. The water from Katse will pass into the 45km long transfer tunnel, upstream of the dam near Ha Lejone. At Muela the water will pass through the underground power station into the reservoir and from there it will go into the 36km delivery tunnel into the Axle River in South Africa.

The electrical and mechanical equipment, the turbines, generators, transformers and other heavy plant ready for the completion of the transmission to Lesotho's existing grid, were now in place. The first of the station's three turbines would be commissioned in March 1998, the last one in September 1998.

That afternoon, we were allowed to drive to the top of the surge shaft which was still under construction at 2,000 metres high. In top gear, climbing the hairpin tracks of grit, got us almost to the working platform and then we had to walk. The car was coated in a thick layer of white dust. Our eyes and mouths were soon filled with it. What must it be like for the workers, sweating and toiling in the hot sun.

A ring of galleried iron-girders pointing skywards like dragon's teeth, rose in front of us. They supported the structure of the surge chamber, formed within the shaft itself, which is only used when the pressure of water rises in the tunnels and it then acts as a relief valve.

The metal sculptures, cranes and construction plant which surrounded the throat of the shaft, were awesome; the scene resembled a great metal creature emerging from the bowels of the earth. One can only stand and gasp at the enormity of a programme such as this, which has brought together expatriates from all over the world. In addition to personnel from most countries in Western Europe, Eastern Europe, Canada, USA, South America, Australia, New Zealand, Asia and other African Countries, the contribution by large numbers of local Basotho and South Africans has been substantial. That does not even account for administration, canteen staff, drivers and security staff who keep the whole project running smoothly and efficiently. On each of the construction sites have come teachers, doctors, medical teams and financiers. It goes without saying that tunnelling teams labouring below ground have been quite the mainstay of the work force. Without them and their team efforts, the pioneers of this century would not have achieved the successful excavation of eight two kilometres of tunnels, through the mountains of Lesotho. A Frenchmen once described it as the Paris Metro without ticket machines.

The scheme has taken years of planning and negotiation by international contracting companies, each experts in their own field. World Bank provided the money. The Highland Water Scheme has had a colossal impact on this tiny kingdom, simply because the first visionaries had to consider the crucial problem of the shortage of water. The demand for water in the six provinces of South Africa supplied by the Vaal River, is relentless. In early 1998, the supplies (with this scheme in place) will only just be keeping ahead of predicted demands.

The sun was hot and my bare arms were burning. Rose and I looked around for some shade. On the ground were pieces of light wooden shuttering, which we lifted above our heads to keep cool. Walter's expression was a joy to see. As a young man, he was gifted and articulate, given to being interested in things of ecological and historical importance and his nationalistic pride was evident in his reaction to the enormity of this project. He and Barrie spent most of the afternoon deep in conversation, pointing first this way and that.

"I'm glad I lived to see this day," exclaimed Walter, as we sat down on the searing hot seats of the car for our downward ride. "The lads of my own age who've worked on the dam have contributed to the history of my country. I'm proud to have been part of it. When I'm an old man, I'll tell my children about everything that used to be here."

It was a strange feeling standing high above the plateau and looking down into the mouth of the enormous grid-creature. On the other side of the valley, the outline of village huts could still be seen, balancing on the ledges high above the dam. Those who stayed must be feeling like strangers in their own back yard; carrying on their simple lives of planting crops and harvesting, while being lit by round-the-clock arc lamps. At Muela day and night no longer existed.

Back at Ha Simone later in the afternoon, a new English ritual was taking place. Rose was preparing to brew tea. She knew how often Barrie and I drank cups of tea and was determined to learn the art of this most important English tradition. She was planning to have it ready for when our party arrived home. The intricacies involved have to be explained.

First go to the spring and fetch water. Heat primus stove indoors and boil water. Find a teapot and fetch cups (they possessed two) and enamel mugs for extra visitors. Make sure milk from cow had been boiled three times. Buy a packet of tea and sugar. Bearing in mind that Rose couldn't afford to buy tea or sugar, this was indeed a great compliment and cost a return journey into town.

We bumped slowly along the track to the church, full of Muela news to tell, quite exhausted by the heat and the long drive; the sort of afternoon when you would kill for a cup of Five Roses tea. Emily and Bernice had left for Jo'burg. The boys had gone down to the river to fetch water, so that they could wash the car when we returned. Stephen was in the church. David was on look-out duty. Strung across the yard, a wave of white shirts was sunshine drying and Fred was sitting in the tub of used water, to have himself a bath.

Some sort of celebration was definitely in order as, the previous afternoon, the first letters had arrived from Datchworth. Stephen had taken a truck ride to Leribe Post Office that morning, to find letters in St John's Church postbag - posted in England three weeks before. He came up the steps from the church to meet us, holding out both arms, hardly able to contain his excitement.

"Barrie, Nettie, we have some correspondence from your village, I shall not want to believe it in case these letters fly away and they are only in my imagination."

It was a sign that things were going smoothly in England. Anne Charles, one of the organisers of the Lesotho Committee, had initiated the proceedings by writing on behalf of the congregation at All Saints Church Datchworth. It was the very first letter to St John's. Members of the congregation had been invited to write 'family to family' to introduce themselves to one another. More correspondence was to follow.

"Okay Rose, let's have the tea now," said Stephen, "look at our visitors – they are very tired. They need a drink.....and I will propose a toast."

His smiles were most infectious. The humour was always at bubbling-over point when Stephen was around. He loved making his congregation laugh out loud – he loved it when he was the ringmaster and his audience joined in the joke. Keeping up with Stephen required an endurance test in physical and mental energy. In this family, you weren't allowed to sit still or sulk. His expectations were high – and so were his standards; no lame ducks and no skiving.

"Barrie, come - have the first cup of tea, that is the way of the Basotho – the head of the family has the first sip.... let's drink to the future of the link with England.....we don't drink alcohol, but we like Five Roses tea."

It was exciting seeing letters with English postmarks lying on their table. We were invited to share in the contents and the excitement. The tea was like nectar from the gods.

"First we must prove ourselves," said Rose calmly, "that means we owe loyalty. We will hold a special service tomorrow in our church to tell the people – they must know loyalty in their hearts. It will surprise some of our members who do not know of this association with England. Some of our people cannot speak in English – we must encourage them to learn it. Stephen will explain to them first in Sesotho."

"Barrie and I will bring you a map, so that your friends can see where Hertfordshire is."

"Would you like a board – a notice board?" asked my other half, firmly. "There are sure to be photographs and pictures from the village to show….. I'll send a piece of board next week and Walter can hang it on the wall…..I'll send it with screws and everything."

"And we'll start a St John's Diary," I said, "everything that happens should be written down. Everyone can write in it and you'll be surprised how much will happen in a year. I'll find a thick book with many blank pages."

The idea appealed to them both. The diary would be kept in a safe place in the house and everyone would have access to it.

"Yes - a good idea , it will encourage my children to write in English," agreed Stephen.

"Rose, thanks for the tea, it was the best thing you could have given us, we drink it all the time at home."

Stephen interrupted, "Nettie….this *is* your home. You and Barrie are welcome here whenever you wish…..please feel free to visit whenever you want. We want you to think of us as your own family. Walter has told me that he appointed you two his parents….well we endorse it, my wife and me - we feel you are like parents to the whole family."

It was time to leave. The yard outside was full of young men with wet cloths cleaning the bonnet, the wheels and the roof of the car. No longer was it caked with the white dust of Muela. The bodywork shone and sparkled….and under the windscreen wipers was stuck a large piece of paper. Removing it, I unfolded the card and read the words, 'Happy Birthday Nettie, may the joy of Jesus be with you. From Petros'.

Chapter 19

A Horse, a Baby and the Dancing Girls

Bokpoort Farm, best known for its wonderful horses, once more filled our weekends. In late November a large party of LHPC ex-pats and their families had booked in for a day's riding. The yard hands were busy saddling up everyone into the comfortable cowboy-style saddles. There's always the chance of seeing wild zebra or antelope along the trail, which adds to the excitement of the Eastern Highlands. Barrie was always happy when he was booked to go on the ride.

"When age is against you, its debatable whether you'll have many more goes," he joked..

This particular day he was late arriving at the stables and the ride had gone ahead. Liliane and I left him struggling to saddle Mexico, an excitable chestnut mount who was champing at the bit.

"See you later – have a good ride," we both called out as we left.

The two of us in walking boots and track-suits set off at a good pace along the topmost ridge of the trail which led away from the farm into baboon country. The sun was blazing and we wore plenty of protection cream and had our water bottles full. Liliane couldn't wait to get back into our South African Sundays after five months away. Soon we were high above the farm on a well worn trail.The grasses were long and we were keeping a watchful eye out for snakes.

"I really missed this when I was in France. There is nowhere near our home that has this feeling of space and sky. Up here – it's almost like flying,"she admitted..

"Yes - when we all leave this place next year, I know Barrie and I will miss South Africa terribly. People are already leaving to take new jobs in the four corners of the earth; the Phillipines, Indonesia, Australia, America, Berlin. Where will you and Ali go?"

"We don't know, wherever the job takes us. It is a worrying time until we are resettled in another place. The children have to go to school in France, no matter where we are. Thank goodness for my mother. She takes over when I am away. I am worrying about her all the time, but I know she would phone if there was any problem."

"Did you know Lily and Alex went to Berlin? Lily cried buckets when they left – seven years is a long time in one place. Maybe we'll meet again one day. Poor Evodia was heartbroken."

"Being an engineer's wife is not easy," Liliane continued, "I felt terrible when we left Denmark after six years – and now I am the same in Lesotho. Sometimes I don't know where I belong. France is where I spend most of my life, but I have followed my husband to so many different countries. The children love South Africa more than anywhere else though – Claire wants to come back and work with the horses when she is older….she might. She's a good horsewoman."

We walked along in silence for a while, gazing across the horizons which stretched as far as Lesotho.

"Look – over there, what do you see, down on the lower slopes?"

"I can't see anything," I said, craning my neck.

"Baboons, I'm sure. Let's see if we can miss them. I know they aren't really dangerous, but I don't like being too close."

A rope ladder stopped us in our tracks. It went straight up the rocks to a high cave, which was shaped like a pear drop with a hole right through the middle.

"Come on Annette, we can get up there."

"Yes, okay. You go first…..I'll follow."

Spread out before us was the vista of the Golden Gate Park. Ancient sandstone bastions jutted out from the topmost ridges, falling away to grassy slopes tinged with pink. The Rooiberg mountains glowed pink. The sky was pink. Hidden in the cracks and crevices were mountain reedbuck, large herds of black wildebeeste, perhaps eland and certainly small harems of zebra. From our cave nothing stirred except for the sweeping feathers of a long-tailed widow bird fanning and flapping its graceful tail far below.

"It's so peaceful up here,"said Liliane. "I have missed these views."

We rested and drank ice-cold water. Butterflies in kaleidescope colours, alighted on the rocks. They hovered like semiquavers almost touching the strings of a violin.The afternoon breeze caught our faces bringing a sudden change in the air. It could turn quickly to bucketing rain or a rapid wind storm. Suddenly the sky was filled with birds dipping and swooping. Somehing had changed in the direction of the breeze.From our high rock we could see the plains rippling far below us. They were golden and crested with light, gently moving like waves in an ocean swell.

"Shall we go?" I suggested. "It might rain."

We slithered down the rope ladder and made our way beyond the caves to the rocky hollows which led down to the farm.

Meanwhile, on the lowlands below the escarpment, Barrie had been urging on his horse trying to catch up with the rest of the party. He had made good time and cantering at a steady pace, caught up with them standing in a group by the river. Horses and zebras were nuzzling each other. The zebra is an inquisitive animal and seems to enjoy the close company of horses without any fear. A little earlier the group had seen a herd of black wildebeeste who veered away, running frantically in every direction, like startled sheep.

Leaving the zebra behind, the whole ride set off and were soon into a fast gallop then turned off left, splashing across the shallows of the river.

Unfortunately Mexico had other ideas. He had only one thought in his mind. Supper time. (Who says a horse can't tell the time?) Nothing that Barrie could do would stop his sudden flight and they battled for dominance for a short while, until the animal embarked on a campaign of non-cooperation and decided he would rather go home alone. Unceremoniously, he flung my husband off his back. Barrie rolled over in the dust and sat nursing his bruises, completely dazed at the shock of reaching the ground so fast. His horse bolted out of sight.

Had it not been for the head of the ride, who thankfully looked back and noticed the absence of his most senior rider, Barrie might never have been found. Sandwiched between a rock and a hard place, he continued to nurse his injured parts and tried not to worry about being abandoned in the middle of a game reserve full of wild animals which might cross his path at any moment. After quite some time the ranger returned, hauling the runaway horse back to his crumpled rider.

Back in the paddock, Liliane and I watched as the group cantered home. The horses knew only too well that it was supper time and the sooner their riders dismounted, the sooner they would be fed, so there was a lot of impatient snorting and stamping going on. Saddles were unhitched and girths unbuckled, like elderly ladies being released from their corsets. Still suffering from the shock of being thrown to the ground, my husband – his lips rather blue and his lumbar regions very stiff, smiled bravely as he slid from Mexico's saddle and was heard to mutter, "Fantastic ride, it was worth it - Nettie drive me to the nearest gin and tonic."

We left the farm and set off in great haste. Barrie in defiant mood, (yes, he had enjoyed himself, despite his fall) found a semi-bearable sideways position on the front seat of the car and tried not to laugh. He recalled his proximity to potential disaster. Yes, he had wondered if anyone would find him splayed out in the grass, bruised and ant-nibbled, before the herd of manic wildebeeste trod on him.

The Guinea Feather in Clarens was a great meeting place. It had atmosphere, it had fabulous food and it had Eric. Now accompanied by considerable swelling and bruising, Barrie's injuries were very painful, especially near the shoulder blade. As he limped bravely into the Guinea Feather bar, Eric, who had his own unorthodox but well-meaning style of greeting, slapped Barrie heartily on the back and laughed uproariously when he winced – as you do with a bruise the size of a dinner plate on the shoulder. Generosity was another of Eric's specialities and as he called the waiter over, a couple of beers arrived at our table and a pretty waitress hovered over us waiting for the order. There were sixteen of us. Not a problem.

"Good evening Madame," said our host to Liliane, "are you the silly old goat who used to come to my restaurant?"

She laughed and answered him in rude French. She knew he was referring to the incident with a certain animal from the farm, which had a penchant for French ladies.

By nine o'clock we were all well stuffed with large portions of tandori chicken cooked in a clay pot and sprinkled with herbs. Barrie and Ali were past the point of no return. They were sharing a bottle of red wine, which had somehow slipped itself onto our table via the pretty waitress. Then Eric's wife gave us a tour of the dessert menu. How to choose between apple pie, orange soufflé, lemon meringue or Annie's home made ice-cream.. At the end of the meal we all agreed we were so full that we must refuse to listen to any of Eric's songs. He was prone to reach for his bagpipes after dinner which conveniently hung on the wall over the piano. Of course it was all part of the game.

"We'll just pay the bill and go, Eric really – I am in such pain, I ought to go home….." said the fallen rider, who was having difficulty deciding which feet were his. Some degree of movement was necessary and he wasn't sure if his brain was still connected to his inflamed kneecaps.

"Ouch!….Nettie, can you bring the car to the front door?"

"Red wine is a good anaesthetic," said Ali, with the authority of one who knows.

There was no escape. While we tried to get the invalid back on his feet, Eric, with cheeks bulging, blew his pipes with faultless breath and squeeze. He roared up and down the gangway with his own Caledonian version of 'Donald where's yer troosers'…. until the timbers of the tavern vibrated in agony.

"Goodnight Eric, we'll remember how terrible your food is, we won't come again."

"Goodnight everyone," spoke the soft voice of his wife from behind the bar, "see you all next week."

Our Christmas courier collection was imminent and I was frantically trying to finish the endless list of letters and greetings cards, so they would reach our families at home in time. The verandah table was my office work-space and things were going well until the sky went black and a wind blew up from nowhere, like a French 'mistral'. I had been hoping to post them to both son and daughter, including one enclosure to James from Walter, written in bold handwriting, thanking him for the exceptional present of the now-famous Chelsea football shorts.

A series of loud barks suddenly sounded from Hercule. The wind had upset him and he was pacing up and down like a panther, snapping at every moving twig. His garden was closer to the guard hut than ours and any small sound was enough to spook him into a rampant threatening dog patrol all of his own.

From across the gardens, I heard the guard shout something and then went inside, scooping up Christmas mail as I went. A few minutes later, the reason for Hercule's agitation was explained. A deputation of about a dozen women were walking towards the house, spearheaded by Sophie. She was wearing a strange-looking headress and brandishing a cow's tail which she waved about. The sound of piercing whistles and wailing, more painful than a dozen tom cats reached my ears.

"What on earth ....?" I began.

Then I remembered that Sophie had told me about her healing ceremony promised by her *sangoma*, which would take place once she had bought - and sacrificed a cow. Round her neck were long strings of beads and her hair was decorated with more beading and plaiting. Her skirt was made from pieces of cowhide and slung across her ample hips was a belt with horns which jangled as she walked. Other pieces of unrecognisable animal paraphernalia swung as she moved. The ladies with her carried bunches of dry grasses which they used to sway above their heads while singing and chanting, some dressed in colourful outfits trailing with tails and beads. One carried a drum under her arm.

"Hello Mrs Glenn – I have come to bless you with the good spirit. Look at me! I am filled with the good spirit. All my sickness will soon be gone."

Some of the women were quite old and they howled toothlessly, waving their branches and blowing whistles, shouting in Sesotho with grimaces and solemn faces. I did not recognise any of them. Perhaps they were part of the *sangoma's* conscription party.

"Hello Sophie – I am honoured that you came to show me your costume.......wow! I have not seen anything like this before. You look very happy – will the ladies sing for me?"

I reached inside the house for a few rands, which the chief lady accepted gracefully. The gathered company started to hum – deep throated and pitched low, as in basso profundo. Their voices swirled around the garden - full bodied, growing louder, then bursting forth into a crescendo whilst enveloping Sophie with their branches, harmonising until a sweet-sounding repetitive chorus emerged; a kind of African plain chant.

It was easy to see how the trance-like music of traditional healing ceremonies induced the listener into a submissive state – it was beginning to have an effect on me; the ebb and flow, like a heartbeat, repeating and pulling. Suddenly the drum beat changed into a lively celebratory rhythm and the ladies started to gyrate sideways and backwards across the garden, between the strands of the willow tree, heads were thrown back and the ululating came again. Thabo had arrived with his wheelbarrow and just carried on with his work as though nothing unusual was taking place. I waved to them from the kitchen doorway. Sophie puffed out her chest to show off her cow costume, waved her arms like a windmill and let out one of her raucous cackles of laughter. It sliced through the air of the empty Saturday camp. The office staff were off duty. The wind carried their voices away as they retreated, to return from whence they came.

Personally, I saw the incident as harmless, but it remained to be seen whether Sophie's high blood pressure would return to normal. I wondered what she would do when her ankles swelled up again on Monday morning and her savings were reduced to nil.

"Barrie, shall we arrange the date for the party at Makibis?" I yelled from the depths of my steaming hot bathtub, the following morning. "It's time we gave them a date…"

"Why are we having a party?" he questioned, like men do when they have conveniently not heard you the first time.

"Listen sweetie, I will say this only once. The reasons are: celebrating the link with Datchworth, Walter's recovery, King Letsie's Coronation, your birthday, Bernice's birthday which is on 14th December, Leribe and Datchworth School link-up, and last but not least, our English wedding. We're celebrating them all in one go. Have you got all that?!!"

"That's only seven reasons. Can't you think of another one, just to make it even numbers?"

"Oh I forgot – the birth of baby Gilbert!"

"And who is baby Gilbert?"

"Annacleda's baby of course. She's bringing him to meet us tomorrow – but you'll be at work. I can't wait to see him. Kaizi told me."

The smell of bacon slipped under the bathroom door and curled itself around my nostrils. "Breakfast smells good," I yelled, wrapping my wet hair in a towel and going to turn on our Sunday music. We always played our favourite tunes on Sunday mornings. '*Lady in Red*'. was the one with the magic ingredient for us both.

"What do you think we should cook for the Makibis?" he asked.

"What if we dish up fillet steak and onions, sausages, baked potatoes and salad……and I'll think of a dessert later."

"Yes that sounds okay, we'll cook everything, put it in the car and drive it down to their house by say …. five o'clock, just before it gets dark."

"Rose says we can have a fire in the kraal in the yard and cook whatever we like. I wonder what we'll do for light after the sun goes down. Walter will have to fix up a light somewhere, though I don't know how…..and who do we invite?"

As we set about inventing a guest list, Chris de Burgh sang to himself in the other room, followed by Elton John's '*Candle in the Wind*'– which I played endlessly these days. Wonder of wonders, the music store in Bethlehem had managed to get it for me. We finished breakfast then after a Sunday waltz round the lounge, I answered an unexpected knock at the back door. It was Kaizi.

"Hello young Kaizi, what are you doing here on a Sunday?"

" '*M'e*, I want to see de map in your house. ..I want to see where is de world …my teacher she say…. tell me where is Africa."

239

The worn jacket he had on was almost armless and his toes were poking through his trainers, but he looked clean enough. He had never been here before without his sister and I was pleased that he had enough confidence to come up to the camp by himself. I wondered if Annacleda had sent him with a message.

"Kaizi, you are very inquisitive.....okay, you know where the map is. Go and look while we clear away the dishes."

He sat for a good half an hour on his haunches, staring at the map with huge saucer eyes and a look of gravity on his face. Barrie stopped to point out the continent of Africa and he knew the names of most of the other countries.

"You are learning a lot at school Kaizi."

"*Ntate*, I like to learn. I will come to England....take me to your country."

The children often spoke in short statements when it was a meant as a question. Kaizi hugged his knees and let out the next thought to come into his head, "then I have de shoes for my feet." He looked longingly at Barrie's open-toed sandals.

"Okay Kaizi, we'll find you some shoes, but we can't take you to England....you better stay here and look after your family. Your mother needs you."

Another thought was coming. "In afternoon, my sister come with baby."

"Nettie, you take over," said Barrie firmly, "you know more about this than me...."

The following afternoon at the usual time for our lessons, Annacleda arrived, looking plump and pretty in a pink cotton dress, to introduce me to the new member of her family. Heleyne was with her. After our greetings they both came in and sat down at the table where we did our work. Annacleda drew a soft blanket round her in which slept her tiny six-week-old child.

With a peep inside the top of the blanket I asked, "and *who* is this?"

"My baby 'M'e. Do you want me to show?"

The proud look of a new mother. Annacleda's eyes shone. I reached inside the blanket and there in my arms was the tiny child, sucking one very small thumb. Annacleda looked quite relaxed. A new lightness played across her face.

"Oh my goodness...and what is his name?" I asked, even though Kaizi had already told me.

"I call him Gilbert 'M'e. It is English name."

Awkward questions were not appropriate; only words of congratulations. The important issue was the bonding between the girl and her infant, born after months of depressing loneliness and rejection. No medical consultant had seen her. She was too scared to go and find a doctor to ask for help. Annacleda's utter lack of knowledge pre-natal was difficult for anyone to believe. She thought her belly was growing but had no idea what was happening inside her body. Her mother, when she realised, was angry and locked her away for a while, then went to the police to tell them about the rape. Nothing came of it. There was no money to go to a hospital. We could not begin to understand how it was for Annacleda; how utterly abandoned she felt.

She had tried to tell *me*…..but I wasn't listening. I had been so full of my own life. There was that note she left …… '*dear miss glen, I am not coming at my lesson, I am sick we have no food…..*' which I had ignored because we were preparing to fly to England for our wedding.

"Annacleda, I am sorry I did not write to you before we went to England. Heleyn gave me the note but I did not reply…..I didn't know you were pregnant. Please forgive me…now I see you have a son. He is beautiful…..you are a good mother. I can see that you know how to look after him well."

I felt the soft skin of the child's face on my hand. The tiny features, the silken fingers, the dark liquid eyes……knowing only that milk comes from a warm place, where voices are singing softly; for that is what African mothers do. I cuddled Gilbert for a few minutes not wanting to put him down. I would find him some baby clothes.

"Thank you for bringing him to see me Annacleda. He will come for his lessons every week heh?"

"He is a miracle *'M'e*. My brother and my sisters - they love him," she whispered fondling his tiny hands. Although she had spent an agonizing pregnancy, suckling her baby came naturally. Oblivious of the difficulties she would face in raising him herself, Annacleda's love knew no bounds.

"*Mohlolo,*" I said, remembering a word which Betty had taught me. "I know that word – it means 'miracle'."

She smiled widely and I saw maturity in her eyes. In a few months she had grown older, wiser. Her pains had gone by and she was a woman.

Heleyne had some news too. Her grandmother had allowed her to come out of her house. Things were better now. Her mother and father had come home to their village and the girl would soon be allowed to go home.

"And are you going back to Mount Royal?" I asked, anxious to know if she would continue with her education.

"Not this term – but next term. If it is de will of God."

"Annacleda is lucky that she has you for a friend," I said, "she needed you and you were there for her. You two girls will always be friends."

Annacleda's only emotional refuge had been Heleyne. They smiled at each other and giggled. Heleyne reached inside her bag and took out a sheaf of paper.

"I would like you to look at my papers Mrs Glenn. I am still going to write in English so that I can keep up my work if I go back to school. You will be my teacher."

It doesn't get any better than this, I thought to myself. It had seemed reckless that she should be withdrawn from her classes. With a little tuition

241

and some homework, perhaps she would survive the course. I took it from her hand.

My appointment to see a surgeon and a neurologist in Bloemfontein had arrived and my nearest and dearest promised to take me. It would be a two hour journey. In addition to visiting the hospital, we planned to go shopping and both find a hairdresser. Before leaving the camp we went to the office to collect our mail. Always the treat of the week. On top of the pile were letters from both my children and one from my friend Anne who had promised to come out to Lesotho for a holiday in February. I was delighted. The other memo of importance was a job offer for Barrie from Indonesia. Now we really would have to think about our future plans.

We left the borders of Lesotho behind and were soon on the way to Clocolan, which is a small farming town dominated by grain silos. The famous Lethoteng Weavers have a place here. You can visit the weaving sheds where two hundred women work. They use angora rabbit hair, mohair from a pedigree herd of angora goats and wool. Angora rabbit farming is a recent addition into the small stock farming industry in the Free State. The trademark of the high quality goods made by the Lethoteng Weavers means that they export to overseas markets and their beautiful African designs are now much in demand in Europe.

Ladybrand lies on the main route to Bloemfontein. We stopped for a coffee break. Occasionally the engineers went there of an evening. Excellent shopping, restaurants offering Italian, Chinese and American food were a welcome change. An overnight stay at the delightful Cranberry Cottage for one of their mighty breakfasts was very popular. It was a good place for weekend hiking, horse riding or kite flying (can be very windy up on the hills) which families also enjoyed. Ladybrand compared favourably to the further reaches of outdoor South Africa. The trade in this little dorp had been considerably increased by visitors from the Highlands Water Project and the rock art was fantastic.

We arrived in Bloemfontein about midday and easily found the flagship of our visit, where I had to try and understand Afrikaans at the Rosepark Hospital reception desk. It never failed to amaze me how the city girls like to dress for work. It's as though the mannequin parade is about to begin and the catwalk is where they go for coffee. Long laquered nails are *de rigueur*. Voices are the equivalent of English plum, but squeaky, with clipped consonants at the end so you feel it might be appropriate to salute. Nobody smiles.

Piecing together the information from Dr Nettleton, the neurologist gave me a series of small electric shock treatments on both my wrists. His grip was like steel. I told him both my arms hurt and felt hot, with pins and needles at night which prevented me from sleeping. I felt as though someone had tied a piece of cotton around my wrists and pulled tight. He diagnosed carpel tunnel syndrome and advised surgery. A small operation which would put my hand out of action for three weeks.

"Three weeks!"

"It is very common in ladies of your age," he said in a flat tone.

That put me in my place.. Obviously no life beyond fifty. I felt a sudden urge to dribble.

"And is there a cure?"

"Yes. No lifting, no handwork and no drinking."

Well that cuts out housework, computer work, driving the car and cooking. No letter writing, no sewing and no glass of wine after dinner. No going to Judy's on a Friday night, no swimming and no taking Hercule for a walk. And no weight training exercises in the garden for my keep fit routine. I might as well be dead.

"*Dankie*," I muttered. "When will the operation be?"

"January 14th - at this hospital."

For those who worship at the altar of easy options, the remedy would have been fine. I was mortified.

"Lord, I shall die if I can't do anything. It's not true is it Barrie?" I glanced sideways.. "That means you'll have to do all the driving when we go to the Cape."

"Come on, we've yet to see the surgeon."

We climbed a lot of stairs and walked a maze of corridors. The specialist looked at my neck x-rays with a gleam in his eye."I would go a little further than that Mrs Glenn. I would suggest splints."

"Splints?!"

"Yes, to be worn at night when you are in bed. They will stop you from bending your arms and causing the nerves to react.There is a narrowing of the nerve endings, so the blood is squeezed through, which in turn gives you pins and needles and causes pain."

"Oh no."

By now I had visions of sleeping in chain mail and clunking Barrie over the head with my splint every time I turned over. I shot a desperate look in his direction.

"Don't worry honey – you won't be able to do the ironing from now on!"

Later that afternoon we drifted into a trendy tea shop in Mimosa Mall both sporting scalped hair cuts. Bloemfontein hairdressers can be easily identified by their very sharp scissors. When we told them that we couldn't get into town very often, they went into snip-overdrive. Unsuccessful attempts to restrain them were obvious by the sight of Barrie's pink ears and my new hat.

"Thought I'd treat myself," I said, pouring tea from one of those aluminium tea pots that drip the minute you start to pour. "All the best people wear a hat." The usual puddle on the tablecloth caused our waitress to return with another tea-pot, which also dripped.."Especially if one has no hair *and* carpel tunnel syndrome."

Barrie suddenly burst out laughing."Nettie, if you could have seen your face when the doctor said splints!"

*　　*　　*　　*

Central to our plan of campaign for December was the Datchworth link to St John's Church and co-ordinating the letters from Datchworth Primary School with Leribe Primary School. A heavy responsibility rested on my shoulders. Alarm bells were already ringing. We were planning on spending our last Christmas at the Cape, soon after this we were leaving Africa altogether.

In January there were the preparations for a high profile official opening of Muela Dam - an international event, involving construction companies and kings; a day when thousands of people would be celebrating to the theme of 'Water is Life'. Our camp grapevine had revealed in recent days that amongst other royals and dignitaries, President Mandela had been invited. That left only February to set up a St John's Committee before we started to re-open our cabin trunks in readiness for the final journey back to England.

As for my family letters, it had pleased me that both my kids had written and the reason for the lost birthday phone call was already forgotten. James had a new job and my granddaughter was saying more new words in her limited language. Lizzie said that Abigail could understand much more than she first thought, even though her speech was slow in coming. She was happy at school and doing well, but her weight was still a worry and she was not interested in eating. Of course they would miss us over Christmas.....one glimpse of a Christmas tree and I would be in tears.

What comfort a few words in familiar handwriting can bring. Yet human nature being what it is, the mind leaps on to the next pressing worry.... has our little girl got some other problem that we don't know about. Why doesn't she want to eat? Does my daughter realise that she can get nutritional help from the nurse at school, after all it is for Special Needs.....would she even ask? Every conceivable syndrome was examined in my mind. A kind of emotional struggle began, which will be familiar to anyone who has had to balance personal happiness with family commitment.

My next appointment to go and see the children at Leribe Primary School loomed. There were the letters from the children of Datchworth School to be delivered, assuming that Charlotte could fit me into her busy timetable. I would pick up Walter first as we had arranged to go up to the school by car. Petros was sitting on a box in the yard when I arrived, seriously busy with some craft or other involving a knife and some string and bits of car inner tube, scattered in pieces on the ground.

"Hi Petros, is it a good day today?"

"Yes Nettie, I am making Walter a pair of sandals. He needs some...I've nearly finished."

"Thank you for my birthday card Petros. Your drawings are very good. You should study art at school."

His face burst into a smile showing the gap in his teeth and was pleased his sketches had been noticed. He didn't reply but held out the footwear for me to see. The straps across the foot were cut from pieces of black rubber and attached to the sole, which had been taken from an old shoe.

"You're amazing Petros, Walter will be pleased heh! He'll have something to wear for the party."

"A party?"

"Yes. We want to have a party at your house, with singing and dancing. Barrie and I will arrange a date with Mum and Dad. Will you come?"

Words were not Petros's strong point – but a party! Now that was different.

"Yes I'll come. I will make more shoes and sell them, then I can earn money to buy a shirt."

I parked the car and went to call my driver.

"Good morning Nettie," called Stephen from the kitchen door. He was off duty for a change and casually dressed. He looked pleased with life.

"Is Walter ready yet? We're going to school today. We have an appointment with eight hundred children."

"Rose told me that you and Barrie want to hold a party for Walter's recovery."

"Hi Stephen – well that's the main reason. He's the living proof that miracles can happen. And we must make a big occasion for the start of the link with England. It is a piece of history you know. Don't worry about the food, we'll bring that. You can teach us how to dance the *Shoshalosa* – wow!"

His face lit up. He was instantly in party mood. He put his hands together and gave one of his squeals of delight. Stephen had a charm as agreeable as warm muffins at breakfast.

"We thought King Letsie would also like us to hold a party for his Coronation…anyway Stephen we have eight reasons for a grand celebration…..wondered if you and Rose could organise the guests."

"You know Nettie, there has never been such an occasion at Ha Simone." He lowered his voice and gave me a solemn look. "Never has white people hosted a party for blacks. It has never been heard of in this village. Something very excellent has happened here….and all because you broke down in our village. You don't realise……"

"So you agree with it? Do you agree with 14th December?"

"Fine, fine, fine – we will make the music for you. All the people will come. This will be an evening to remember."

Walter and I drove along a narrow bouncy track up the mountain as far as Leribe Primary School. No sooner had I turned off the engine than dozens of children came flying towards us, yelling at the tops of their voices. I recognised a minor riot when I saw one. They surrounded us in no time; a plethora of cheesy grins on springs.

"Nettie, they are so excited. Look at them. How are you going to control them?"

"I think we'd better stay in the car…look here's Charlotte, she'll tell them to go back."

"They have never seen a white lady up at their school in a car before."

A wise precaution in the face of an unruly mob of ten year olds is to sit tight and wait for the energy to subside. Once in the staffroom, peace triumphed over bedlam and I was able to hand over the packets of letters, so carefully carried from a little corner of middle England. Handing out the letters to each class, I tried to explain some of the differences in the lives of the children from whom the letters came. This school had latrines and piped water. It didn't have electricity. It didn't have a telephone line and the assembly hall was the old eucalyptus tree. They didn't have many books, but they had slates. The number of children was double the number of desks. School lunches, as we know them, were non existent.

"Oh my life….a letter from an English child," said one member of staff eagerly, "it is written in English…oh my life…..this is wonderful."

Turning the pieces of paper over and over, the teachers found the letters irresistible. With good humour, they were amused at the descriptions of 'my pet rabbit' by a Datchworth nine-year-old and a 'this is my mum picture' with purple hair, holding baby with purple hair and dog on a lead – with purple spots. At the sight of Datchworth Church – there was a unified silence.

"This is our church. It is eight hundred years old," I said quietly. Everyone came to look.

"Oh……dis church is eight hundred years old," they repeated. Expressions of disbelief followed by more 'oohs' and 'aahs'. They were fascinated.

"Who built dis church 'M'e? Was it built for a king?"

One lady staff member called Veronica, bearing the alarming characteristic of examining all my jewellery before addressing me which was slightly disconcerting, observed, "I am looking at the wonderful jewels you are wearing."

I had a very flimsy gold chain around my neck and some gold hooped earrings which were very plain, my wedding ring and a watch on leather strap. She gazed at them intently.

"Do you have many jewels?"

"Well, I don't call them jewels really. They are what I wear mostly every day…."

"I would feel very beautiful if I was wearing those things….are you rich?"

"No I'm not rich. In England most people wear these things ….and some people wear things that are fashionable."

I knew I had said the wrong thing.

"What is fashionable meaning?"

Charlotte swept into the room with the air of someone about to announce the Queen. She was a motherly sort who would be a fabulous challenge to designer Zandra Rhodes on the catwalk. With a bottle of champagne in her hand, Charlotte was the type to launch a ship. (Shades of Patricia Routledge in television comedy.)

"*'M'e*, please would you sit down, we have a surprise for you. Staff please sit."

Behind her followed a group of girls approximately twelve or thirteen years old, naked except for short white raffia skirts, tied at the waist and decorated with bottle-tops on strings. When each girl walked she made a soft shushing sound. Perfectly poised and respectfully silent, the pupils made ready to perform a traditional dance – just for me. It was their way of welcoming a stranger. Altogether delightful.

In Lesotho they place great store by singing and dancing – it's on the curriculum. Other children beat a clever rhythm on drums, some were humming and clapping. Bernice smiled shyly at me from the front row. The dances began. Moving in time with the beat, the girls gyrated in unison, proud to be demonstrating their repertoire of skills. Every dance was meaningful or signified some aspect of life in Lesotho; a good harvest, a prayer for rain, fertility, loyalty, or good health. Irresistable, charming and quite moving, the dance came to an end.

Drawn into the whole fascinating sequence, I didn't notice that outside the classroom window, a crowd of excited youngsters had climbed on one another's shoulders and were peering gleefully at the girls – peering at their nakedness and small budding breasts. Soon other lads joined in, making a circus pyramid of climbers standing on the knees of other boys. The attraction of opposite genders is the same in Lesotho as anywhere else in the world.

"Boys get down!" yelled Charlotte, "get down this minute!"

She picked up a broom, opened the window and swept them down from their high perch, like insects off a leaf. The boys could hardly protest, but fell in a wriggling heap, squealing and laughing, taking to their heels across the yard, each knowing he would be in trouble if he was recognised.

"Has your dance got a name?" I asked.

"Yes Maam. We call it the *Litolobonya.* Queen Mamohato gave it to the women of Lesotho. The girls must learn it. Next time you come, our choir will sing some traditional songs. The music teacher here trains them well. She is an excellent teacher and she will prepare a programme for you."

Here in this classroom was the next generation of teachers, leaders, perhaps administrators - the fabric of the nation. Without money or books or computers, teachers were handing down skills known to them for generations, preparing children for adulthood in a simple caring way. Every child had a knowledge of his nation, his monarchy and his traditions. Every child had two languages, English and Sesotho. Every child must obey his parents and was not allowed to be disrespectful to his elders. The wisdom of elderly grandparents was sacrosanct and spirits of their dead ancestors were accepted as a part of everyday life. Jesus Christ was their Saviour.

"Now, one of the boys has something to demonstrate 'M'e,"said Veronica.

A tall boy about twelve or thirteen years old approached shyly. He wanted to show me a special musical instrument which he had made himself. He brought it over to let me examine it. There was an old petrol can. There were pieces of wood shaped like a bow and there were pieces of wire. Somehow, the boy had attached strings to the inside of the petrol can, stretched these to a stick, so that it was played - like a bow. After a long and tortuous scrape across the opening of the petrol can the boy stopped and smiled. I remembered my son's early notes on the recorder at about the same age. I praised him.

"It is called a *mamokhorong 'M'e* and it will be played by the herdboy who stays in the mountains looking after his goats. It is a popular musical instrument," explained the teacher.

It was the primitive equivalent of a guitar. Did the boy even know what a guitar looked like?

I came away full of hope that one day I could tell the children of Datchworth that their letters were a symbol of unity between our two countries. The formalities over, I was addressed as 'Mrs Annette, important visitor to the school and lady with jewels'. Every child would write to an English child.....in English. The letters would be ready for me in a couple of weeks. Charlotte's charismatic figure, hair covered by a bright pink scarf, ample bosom held in tight by a red blanket, the soul and spirit of her fine establishment.....saw me off the premises. We shook hands and I promised to go back the following week. Her action-packed day equated with that of Mary Willett without Olga....and Albert had specifically asked if I would go again to admire more his prize bull.

Amelia Masupha and Rose-Mary at her house in Maseru

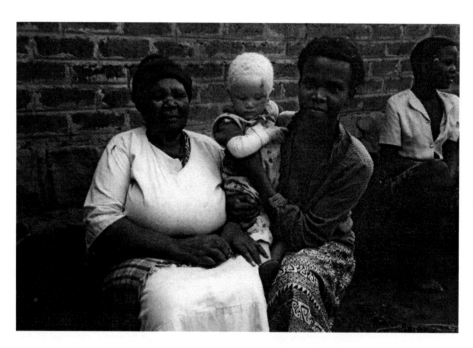

Albino child between Grandmother and Mother

Priscilla exploring her new farm

Anne Dungey, Liliane Pazuki and Beatrice Findlay

The author at the Owl House, Nia Bethesda in the Karoo

*Preparing for a truck ride near Graaf Reinet
with Gerry and Sheila Rose-Innes at their farm*

Myself and Walter planting the Tree of Friendship

Anne and Thabo in my garden at Leribe

A religious ceremony at the Great Zimbabwe Ruins

Anne Dungey, myself and Charles Zendera in Masvingo, Zimbabwe

Flags of the countries involved in the
Highland Water Scheme at the Headquarters of LHPC Leribe

Washing clothes day in Ha Simone with the local ladies

Buying rugs at Bohali Weavers in Teyateyaneng

Saying goodbye to Solomon,
Headmaster of Thotlisong High school, with Secretary Selina

Chapter 20

Strong Ties

Augustinus was making progress. The wounds on his hands were healing. I had managed to find him several books on architecture and this was part of the reason I wanted to go to Ha Simone. It was early December. Most students had taken their exams and were waiting to hear their results. Friends of Augustinus knew that he was one of the cleverest students in the school and expected him to qualify for a University place. His dream was to become an architect. The fact that he had retired hurt from his house-building experience meant that he would not have been be paid, even though he had worked for almost two months. At present he was existing on prayers and empty pockets. The books would cheer him up.

The Makibi family had been struck by the spring cleaning bug. The stoep was full of furniture turned out of the house and Fred was curled up in an armchair with his dog, watching all the goings-on. Rose was standing on a petrol drum with a large brush in her hand, white-washing the kitchen ceiling. The drips of white showed up against her skin. A large metal can containing a mixture which Rose made herself from clay and limestone, was placed by the door.

"Hello Nettie, don't look at me, I am in a mess."

She laughed and carried on painting. Curtains had already been washed and hung out to dry. The piece of wood which my husband had ear-marked for the new St John's notice board had been commandeered as a kitchen shelf. Walter knew that Barrie hadn't realised the lunacy of putting screws into a clay wall, so the item fell into the category of 'change of use', something the Makibis were good at. A church notice board would have to be re-invented.

Spring cleaning takes different forms in every part of the world. Here, not only the house must be cleaned, the cows have to be also mucked out and Petros was in charge of the animals. With reassuring gentleness, he talked to his three cows like a mother to her babies. He stroked their necks and one could imagine they were purring like kittens. No wonder they came when he called.

David, who spent most of his time helping about the place, had started his English lessons and was reading from a book within shouting distance of Petros, who was trying to help him. Although Petros was only seventeen, his English was far superior to David's who was much older. David had not been to school. I had given him some simple Junior English books and he was trying to learn.

"Sontaha, Sunday….*Mantaha,* Monday…..*Labobedi,* Tuesday….*Laboraro,* Wednesday….. I must remember…." he chanted to himself loudly from the top of the stone steps.

"Hello David, so how are you?"

"Hello Mrs Annette, very good very good …..I am okay okay okay…..I learn the English words. My book has the words. Thank you, very very thank you."

His bright eager face shone in the sun and his hair had been cut very short. Shaved heads and short haircuts were a sign that a dearly beloved has recently died. I didn't enquire.

"You must teach me some Sesotho Petros," I called, "it sounds so easy when you speak to each other….but my memory is hopeless."

"Okay Nettie – I will teach you some words," answered Petros from somewhere underneath a pile of straw and a cow's belly…….*Ke nako mang* means what time is it?"

These were the kind of days I loved. Just being here was a privilege. Conscious of the limited time we had left, I was alarmed by the speed with which the weeks seemed to be disappearing. According to LHPC, we would be going home in March and this fact alone turned me into jelly when I thought about it. The affection I felt for the family had grown very strong. They were so generous with their hospitality. To be accepted into their lives was more than just a learning curve. Barrie and I were part of their family in a very real sense.

Suddenly a loud noise distracted us. A cumbersome contraption which had seen better days, clanked past the house. With a high-pitched whine, it slewed to a halt in the yard. In the driver's seat sat Walter and next to him, a lanky young man wearing a white shirt open at the collar. Michael and Walter had been friends since birth and local gossip had it that whenever they were together, there was trouble. By any stretch of the imagination, Michael's Dad's tractor was well past its sell-by date. The lads had been instructed to go and have it repaired .

Walter jumped down and introduced us.

"Meet my Mum!"

Michael and I shook hands. His deep set eyes sparkled. Tall and easy, with a ready smile, he looked every mother's idea of perfect son-in-law. Courteously, he took my hand and held it.

"Hi Michael, your reputation goes before you. I understand you are the one who leads Walter astray!"

They both grinned and punched each other in a male-friendly way. Their mutual affection was obvious. At twenty four years old, Michael had been extremely concerned about Walter's illness and was still deeply affected by what had happened. He steadily returned my gaze.

"The trouble is I can't hit him like I used to – he was so sick in the hospital – I know one day he will be strong enough to hit me back. Then we can have stick-fights again."

Walter grinned , though slightly embarrassed by his friends show of affection. Stick-fighting was something all Lesotho men prided themselves on. It symbolised the warrior preparing for battle in ancient times and was regarded as a show of agility and strength. To perform it requires much skill.

"I know what you did for Walter when he was ill – and I would like to thank you for the life of my friend. You are welcome to visit my home – we live in the next village." He pointed over the ridge towards South Africa. "You can just see my house from here. My mother would like to meet you. She has seen you from a distance crossing the river."

"Thank you Michael, I would be pleased to meet your family, but its conditional upon you driving me there – and not Walter. He drives too fast. He thinks every machine is a Ferrari."

They drove off, disappearing in a cloud of diesel fumes – Walter once more practising his Formula One racing skills, straining the life out of the remaining nuts and bolts.

Augustinus had gone away to visit his family who lived in a distant part of Lesotho. The others said he had been depressed after the terrible injuries he had sustained at the building site. Nevertheless, the same employer had offered a job to Justice, Walter's next younger brother, who was nineteen years old. This didn't really make any sense to me. Justice had accepted the work to help with family budget in the hope that he would fare better than his brother. He would leave tomorrow.

I walked down to the little white-washed stone house where Augustinus lived, the one nearest the river, to find a place to leave my books. There was no door so I couldn't knock. Neither was there a window. Inside the one room there was an old wooden wardrobe stuffed with school uniforms, and clothes which hadn't quite made the hooks. Blankets draped heap over heap on the floor. There were a few enamel mugs and open books spread around on top of mattresses. A candle sat in a small tin tray.

Justice, Petros and Augustinus slept here in all seasons and I had to wonder how they kept warm in the winter or dry in the storms. The rain-softened ground around the entrance told of yesterday's heavy downpour and a plastic barrel rolled balefully across the doorway.

This hut was where Augustinus wrote his poetry. Powerful thoughts transcended his world. On pieces of paper - any that he could lay his hands on, he penned screeds of words which he kept locked in a tin. Augustinus was a passionate crusader of peace – and nothing riled him more than references to the humiliation of the black people in the years of segregation. He was both humanist and philosopher. Older than his years, he cared deeply for his people.

"One day my poems will be published," he had said as he read them to me one day. His voice was deep and resonant and one could imagine his success if he were a drama student in London, born into a different place under another star. But Africa needs people like Augustinus.

Justice and Petros shared his living space and were glad of it. Here the three boys slept, argued, shared school uniforms so that they could attend school on alternate days. Homework was done in candlelight after the sun went down. Together, they spoke of their hopes and dreams, sang songs, teased and laughed with each other. .... birds would come and sit on the rocks nearby and Petros knew their names. Occasionally a lizard or a snake would sun itself amongst the scrub. Only a few species of snakes in Lesotho are venomous in fact they play a useful role in controlling rodents and insects.

The river was their playground. They used it to wash their clothes *and* themselves - a dire business in icy weather. Rose made sure they had enough food – one good meal a day, two if they counted breakfast. They did as their parents asked them, attending church services every day of their lives. In Lesotho tradition, a son must obey his parents' wishes until he is married. There was no such thing as coming-of-age or key-of-the-door celebrations; no bonanza sports-car present at eighteen and twenty one, no lager parties or nightclubs. They represented a family workforce and reward for them was their father's praise.

"That's definite then Rose, 14th December for the party," I called out as I prepared to leave. "We'll make a plan nearer the time. Good luck with the painting....and here are a few things for your cupboard." A box containing bread, biscuits and bananas was put on the new kitchen shelf, "and there's a packet of popcorn. Emily knows how to make it.....oh I almost forgot, she's away at Grandma's."

"I'll make it Nettie," offered Justice in his good natured way. "I can use the big frying pan in the yard..... let's start a fire."

"Good luck for tomorrow Justice, I hope your job works out for the best."

Things had a way of working well for Justice. He was well prepared, organised and fair-minded. He belonged to one of life's non-confrontational personnel, paced himself well and exercised his rights with the air of one who knows he will get where he wants to, easily and without obstruction. He would make an admirable Minister of Justice – as his name implied. If there was a problem in the yard, Justice could be relied upon to solve it.

As always, Walter came with me to the road. Those few minutes were always our very own quality time together. He sat beside me, his eager fingers pressing the tape recorder in the dashboard, wanting to hear my music as I drove towards the bus stop where he would get out. They had no stereo equipment at home, not even a radio.

"Walter, I couldn't learn all that I have learned today if it hadn't been for your family. There are no newspapers or books where I could find this experience. There is no company in the world who can market this product. I feel a pain of sadness when I think of leaving you all."

"I cannot think what our lives will be like without you and Barrie."

A wistful look came over his face. The music died. It was the ending to a song, instead it felt like the ending to a dream. We sat for a moment in silence.

"People in England don't know what real poverty is. Your way of life is so simple. No water, no electricity...... material things don't matter. Justice doesn't care that he doesn't have a bed, your Mum never complains about fetching water from the spring......and sewing in the dark. She praises God no matter how difficult your lives are. I hate the waste and the greed of my own people. More and more I feel depressed." My throat began to hurt as I held back the tears.

"Walter, I shall find it hard to go back."

"We believe everything is planned by God.....and look Nettie, he brought you to us.... and me a new bed!"

"Look at the sky, the rain's coming – you'd better dash. I must go home and make supper for Barrie. I shall write words in my book tonight."

The first battery of hailstones hit my windscreen.

"Hurry!"

I watched him slowly walking away. He would be soaked in minutes. I knew by his hunched shoulders he was thinking of Christmas and afterwards, when our time would run out....how would we say farewell when the moment arrived. Suddenly, I knew that I had a very different agenda from the other ex-pats who were going home.

*   *   *   *

Our friends the Ripas had recently bought a farm north of Johannesburg near Cullinan in a designated agricultural area, which was shortly to be changed into a nature reserve, to be re-named Leeuwkloof Valley. A total of sixteen properties will eventually come under one umbrella. The entire valley is intended to be developed as a conservation area and every property on the estate will shortly have their own game animals and be boundaried by high fences. It was Priscilla's idea of heaven. She was dotty about wild animals, the wilder the better. The place may turn out to be a white elephant – they weren't sure, as it was very dilapidated and run down.

Their nearest town was Cullinan, fifty kilometres east of Pretoria - still a working mine, where the largest diamond was found, the 3106 carat Star of Africa, discovered in 1905. Tourists still pour into this small town, but at the location which our friends had chosen, you could imagine you were far from any civilisation. Priscilla and Guido had invited us to be their first visitors......if only to confirm that they were mad to buy such a place.

"Come for as long as you want. The property's huge, there are twenty-one hectares next to a chicken farm and a lake. The house is like a barn – it's thatched and has five enormous bedrooms. No electricity and no ceilings. I'm living here on my own at the moment with one dog and a cellphone. Camp beds and basic cooking on a calor gas stove....with tequila for afters!!" laughed Priscilla down the phone.

"Pass."

"How d'ya feel about snakes?"

"Pass."

"Bring flippers and waterproofs," she invited, in her usual American drawl, "Barrie - bring tackle. You can fish in the living room. We've got leaks all over the place, the shower doesn't work and there's a wild dog out in the barn. It's okay - he won't hurt you - just throw him a bone, he's been abandoned by the previous owner and has turned wild. Nettie, bring your umbrella, you'll be scorching hot when we go out in the bush. Bring your paints – this place is guaranteed to make you want to paint. Frangipani outside the back door. It's heaven. Don't bring lemons we grow them, just bring yourselves," then as an after-thought, "bring sleeping bags and hotties – you'll be sleeping next door for one night. We'll turn out the scorpions before you get into bed!"

She rang off. I felt exhausted already. It promised to be a weekend of riotous insanity generously doused in alcohol.

Priscilla's map was a work of art. Names of towns and highways in her flowery hand, pink ink with water colours showing little hippos along the route, cadmium-yellow fluffy ostriches in one corner showing where to turn down by the ostrich breeder and a royal blue speckled chicken for where to turn off the main road by the egg farm. Everything in Priscilla's life happened in glorious Technicolor.

It was a feat of endurance to find the farm. No address, no name of house. Tracks – that's all you could call them – went on winding into the valley for miles. No signposts.

I rang the farm on my mobile phone. They could only receive incoming calls if standing on a cross painted on the kitchen floor. I prayed Priscilla was standing on it.

"It's a big house with a thatched roof – you'll see it coming up, just aim for the mountains –plot number painted on a board. You'll see a chicken farm, and a Rotweiler sanctuary – don't stop 'til you see number 47. That's our drive – it's half a mile from there. Hoot when you get to the carpark....that'll be us. You'll see the wagon in the yard."

Looking out from Priscilla's high balcony, sprouting with purple bougainvillea, we were in no doubt that our friends *had* been taken over by the martians. From a high concrete stoep, fifty metres long which ran the length of the house, we gazed across a valley covered with miles of thick bushveld reaching to a far blue horizon. Ha-di-dahs were flying in formation eastwards, calling out their raucous screeches. A crimson sun was floating through a sensational sky. Barrie was floating in sensational sundowners. The midges were the busiest things around.

"Don't go too near the edge Nettie, the spitting cobras live underneath."

"How far can they spit?"said Barrie, lighting his slim King Edward cigar and leaning back onto a reclining chair, which was more like a double bed.

"We'll find out tomorrow when we go down there," she replied, with another swig from the ice-bucket-sized cocktail in her hand.

"Now we know you're completely crackers Priscilla. I'll buy the postcard tomorrow – to tell my company not to bother to come and look for me. What's the plumbing like?"

(Why are guys always so interested in plumbing…?)

"Yeah, well you know that guy Heath Robinson – he was born here!"

Priscilla drew lavishly on her cigarette. She wasn't going to romanticise the deal.

"Cantankerous to say the least. There's so much work to do. We've got a wind pump which creaks all night and refuses to work - even in the wind. Pipes which go nowhere and taps that flush out frogspawn before aqua……but Guido and I and the boys just love it. If it takes ten years to put right it won't matter. I feel so happy when I'm here. It's bliss after Jo'burg."

"But aren't you scared here by yourself?"

"Nope, I've got the dog….. and Norman stays with me and Guido comes home weekends. Come and have a look round. By the way I've booked you a bed at the place next door – the owners are away and have let me use it for guests. No beds fixed up yet."

Priscilla's kitchen was huge. There was a long table down the middle, with enough places to seat a premier league and their minders. We followed her into a Wembley Stadium-sized lounge which looked like a setting for the grand palace ballroom scene in 'Figaro', it only lacked a few crazy mirrors. Eight floor to ceiling doors opened onto the side verandah.

"What is that?" I asked pointing to the light fitting, which resembled a disaster at sea.

"A *Voertrekkers* cart wheel – dreadful heh – would yer like it?"

You could film an episode of '*Fawlty Towers*' along the central corridor with bedrooms orff. I fully expected Basil Fawlty to rush along the corridor chasing Manuel. The shower didn't work and Norman, the lumpy green lizard could be seen behind the toilet, stuck to the wall like a rubber toy.

"You can stroke him if you want. He lives here….don't frighten him!"

My husband emerged from the bathroom, nervously twitching. He wasn't entirely sure if it could jump as far as the belt on his trousers. It was getting dark. Houselights weren't bright and I'll swear I saw a bat fly over the twilit rafters. There were no ceilings on any of the rooms and many winged creatures had emerged fluttering out of the thatch.

"In the morning we'll walk round the estate – there's a lake and I haven't even seen it yet. I need to cut down a Christmas tree – maybe we'll find one.

Have you brought a torch and some wellies – you'll need them tonight. The dam's flooded and we've got to get you over the bridge and it's raining," said our hostess with laughter in her voice, "Heh, this is Africa!"

For '*next door*' in South African, read at least two miles. For '*dam*' read giant swamp with hippos. For '*bed*' read bed without bedclothes. '*It's raining*' - it's peeing down so hard, you don't even know you've gone across the dam.

With torch, candles and much false bravado, Barrie and I let ourselves into an unfamiliar damp, cold house, where things with four legs and wet noses ran round our feet. They were newly born pups who hoped we had brought milky porridge. Difficult to find your way to a room when you don't know the house. Mid-grumble, I heard Barrie swear that he had trodden in something wet and slimy.

Trying to find bedclothes in a strange person's bedroom in a pitch black house isn't easy. With the torch we discovered a bathroom nearby with no toilet roll. We sort of slept, listening to the rain beating down on the windows and visualised the water lapping the sides of the dam.

"Did Priscilla mention sand-bags Nettie?"

"No, she did not."

Early the next morning I felt the warm sun sliding through the double-aspect curtainless windows, onto the bed. I lay for a few moments listening to the birds, which sounded like a pre-recording of Percy Edwards. Still bleary from sleep, something rather weird caught my eye. A ladder, which was propped outside our window started to move sideways, slowly persistently....then came the sound of gravel crunching. The ladder stopped. Nothing happened. Slowly it moved again ......

"Barrie – there's someone outside the window, I can't get out of bed I didn't find my pyjamas last night," I said in strangled whisper to the zombie next to me.

"Neither did I – just go back to sleep."

"I've just *heard* something..... there's someone out there."

Silent-movie style, the ladder continued to slide, until it disappeared altogether past the end of the window. I was frozen to the underside of the duvet. Strange things happen in the bush – what kind of animal moved ladders along a wall......Rigid with fear, I tried to think where my dressing gown was.

Barrie slid out of bed and crawled naked along the bedroom floor as far as the window. This type of manoeuvre wasn't in the deal. Priscilla hadn't mentioned early morning visitors.

"I think it's the builders," he whispered. "Nobody told them we were here. Looks like they're painters, there's a few cans of paint around."

"They must have rowed across the dam – looks like we needn't call the coastguard after all.....boy the rain it raineth last night."

"I've got news for you Nettie," his voice hit a worried note, "they've got a key to the back door. Quick, find the suitcases. Where are my trousers....!"

When we told Priscilla she shook her mane of black hair, and roared with laughter.

"I forgot to tell you the builders hadn't finished. They were told to feed the pups, not make tea for the guests."

"It's not very funny having a bath when you think a guy in overalls might appear at the window any minute with a paint brush in his hand," we joked later, while lapping up the glorious sunshine in the yard. It was a sea-air fresh morning, as in Scarborough. Only the sea-gulls were missing.

"Oh, Priscilla the *rain*! It was torrential last night, we were worried about the water level."

"That was only a shower......you wait. You've seen nothin' yet. Barrie have you brought that fishing rod? You can hook up some pretty big fish in that pond out there. But first it's big breakfast. By the way Guido's cooking us a *braai* tonight – he's bringing home a half a lamb.....and Michael's bringing some friends home for the weekend."

Ripa's property covered approximately twent one hectares including a lake. Their land extended steeply behind the house, mostly rough barren terrain, populated with thorn trees and spiky stuff. The side nearest the house was more like jungle with trees and flowering bushes. A huge area of lemon and orange groves extended downhill towards the bottom boundary. The property had been neglected by the previous owner and was in need of some tender loving care. A derelict building on the edge of the estate could possibly be renovated for maid or gardener. A wind pump, which brought up the water from underground, ran piped water to the house - occasionally.

We prepared ourselves for the initial boundary-to-boundary survey; strong boots, bush hats, insect repellent cream, mosquito swats, Swiss army knife, compass, tick powder, bottles of water, emergency rations and one steel panga between us - no map.

It was blazing hot. Long grass scratched our knees, the rocks uneven and difficult, but we were galvanised into action by adrenalin and excitement. Attempts to remove all snakes from the area were taken by Priscilla as she hit the ground with the panga at every step. She was terrified of them. The rest of us had sticks. For about an hour we progressed up and over the mountain, all eyes on the ground.

Within the next few months, all barbed wire inside the valley would be replaced with game fencing around the perimeter, which amounted to many miles of metal posts for keeping wild animals in and people out. The idea was to promote eco-tourism in South Africa, create more jobs and promote a balanced relationship between humans and the environment.

"I'll let you know when the zebras move in, they'll be the first big animals to breed here – then some of the big antelopes will arrive."

"When do the lions move in?"

"After the elephant and giraffe have settled down. New animals will be phased in slowly over the next ten years. They must all gradually accept one another. But the warthogs have already moved in. Saw some yesterday near the house. And I want to surprise Guido for Christmas – I'm trying to buy a mummy eland and a daddy eland. D'ya think I should wrap them together or separate?"

Bush hats tilted and laughter rippled through the ranks. We walked on as far as the northern boundary of the farm, ending at Bass Lake, which divided their property from the next. In the bush it's easy to completely lose your sense of direction and we were glad of Barrie's compass. Priscilla identified many of the aromatic flowers. My pockets were full of bits of tree bark and razor-sharp needles from the nocturnal porcupine.

At times, acacia grew thicker and we had to weave in and out of the thornier chaps, but mostly it was open bush with tinder dry leaves and spiky, unsociable scrub. Clambering over uneven ground started to affect our ankles and calf muscles. Knees were scratched raw and my socks were full of blackjacks and thistle heads. I walked in time to my blisters. Our survey had taken almost two hours and we were heading down towards the house when we found a wonderful gnarled and knotted – half-fallen tree, broken and listing to starboard. It suddenly seemed very odd to be cutting down a Christmas decoration in the blazing sun with Swiss army knife and panga.

Ridiculous drama followed: four sane and sensible adults carefully 'walking' a dead six-foot tree to bottom of mountain, getting repeatedly caught between branches, while falling down rocks and holes; the lady of the house adamant that she wants the tree inside the lounge - with fairylights. 'Destination Hearthrug' went something like this:

"Michael, go bring me a saw."

"Mother, you can't bring that thing inside the house – it's too big."

"Michael, go open french windows."

"Mother, Dad won't want that tree inside the house."

"Michael, Dad won't *know* the tree is inside the house."

"Mum – I won't be here when Dad comes home. He won't like it."

"Michael, do you want a proper farm Christmas or don't you?"

"Okay Mum, I'll go get the saw."

Barrie and I had had a nap, bathed and changed from dusty safari into casual smart. The smell of frangipani filled our room. The green lizard had vacated the toilet and had taken up residence at right angles to my reading lamp. Priscilla agreed to come and fetch him at bedtime. At least the mosquito count would be negligible.

"He sleeps on my pillow, we're real friendly – he's so beautiful."

(Priscilla thinks all God's creatures are beautiful). More guests arrive, each carrying their own bed. Jazzy music floats from dining room. Barrie notices my freckles have swarmed and it's no good trying to rub them out with make-up. Purple hibiscus blooms have appeared on our pillows and the walls of our room are pink with late afternoon sun. There doesn't seem to be any real reason to glance at a clock. England seems so far away. By now the usual Christmas hype will have begun, when everyone feels drawn to spend money and take root in the food hall at Marks and Spencer. We are both warming to the idea of baby zebras and life in Leeuwkloof Valley.

Later that evening, with the fireflies flickering, a special supper was prepared outside. On a *braai* the size of a kingsize bed, Guido roasted a rack of lamb, fillet of beef and the not-my- favourite *boerewors*. The coals were red and glowing.Young men standing on the balcony were busy bending elbows - trying to impress one another with horrors of late night bush walks or frightening each other with man-eating lion stories. A line of pretty girls sat together on Priscilla's chaise-longue combing blond hair, chatting about things girls chat about. The bar was open and the wine flowed.We were introduced as those crazy folk who lived in Lesotho.

"You mean people actually live there by choice?"

"We're on contracts, we love Lesotho…... .."

"Do you have security where you live?"

"Yes - we live on an international construction site, with our own security…"

Puzzled looks and no more questions. We were obviously bonkers.

No social gathering is complete without stories of mugging, robbery and acts of violence committed on whites, making the post-apartheid era even more difficult to come to terms with. It usually happens after a little alcohol has been consumed. The speakers on this occasion were mostly South African, white and educated. They seemed to be talking of blacks in general rather than blacks in particular, as most families in the valley employed maids or gardeners and thought highly of their staff. It was the way of things in South Africa. Every 'madam' has a 'girl' and every 'boss' a garden boy - or several As far as I could make out, the New South Africa is seeking a hazardous passage through the ranks of this mostly white community around Pretoria and racial violence is still on everyone's lips. Newspapers hold unpleasant stories and during gatherings like this one, people talk. Fear levels are startling and loud. Everyone knows someone who has suffered burglary or mugging. Reported crimes take months to come to court. Punishments seem questionably inappropriate. Meanwhile relationships between blacks and whites deteriorate, while everyone craves for justice. Whole communities wait for the balance of power to be restored. They wait to be convinced that a black government will work.

For the final night of our stay, Priscilla had booked us into 'Pandora', a small guest house about twenty minutes away, surrounded by bushveld. After signing in at the main lodge, a tall young man showed us to our room. Our accommodation was a thatched house on stilts. We parked our car close to a termite mound in the shade of a beautiful old tree, and entered by a wide horseshoe-shaped gazebo, edged with potted palms and open to the four winds. Smooth marble tiles covered the floor underneath a high vaulted roof space, with a wooden staircase leading steeply up to the visitors' rooms. Photographs of big game adorned the walls. On the ground floor was our very own tiled bathroom, kitchen and shower block.

"You sleep in the room above," said the guy, "no animals will be able to climb the stairs. Any questions you want to ask?"

"Do the animals wander into the porch at night?" I asked with alarm. The carpet of leaves outside our house led straight into the forest.

"It has been known – but they will be frightened. If you come near they will run away."

We both gulped in disbelief. It wasn't likely to be the animals who would be frightened.

"…and the snakes, they can come inside also?"

"No, no… you see…. the animals do not like the smooth tiles, they will know it is not their own territory. Large game will not attempt to walk into your house, but you will hear beautiful bird calls. The Go-away bird will wake you," Then quickly he added, "The snakes….they do not like it either. Occasionally the small monkey jumps in here, but he is harmless. From your room in the top you can view all kinds of animals." He busied himself putting in clean towels and a crate of ice cold drinks in the fridge, to which we could help ourselves. "Goodnight - sleep well. We're linked by room telephone, ring if you need anything."

Barrie brought in our overnight luggage. Outside our bedroom on the upper deck, the torso of a stuffed kudu stared at us over the bannister. Long pointed horns, beautiful soft eyes……the smooth brown coat….he had come to grief and a taxidermist had found him.

"Barrie, do you realize if we need the toilet in the middle of the night…. we might bump into a herd of something in the dark."

"No Nettie, they won't need the toilet. You'll be okay," he grinned.

"Can we leave the light on downstairs?" I said reluctantly. "I'm not feeling very heroic."

"Come up and look at this room - never mind the elephants."

The bed was expertly counterpaned in beautiful linen and lace, the mirrors and drapes quite luxurious; a haven of peace away from the world. From the vaulted ceiling thatch a few spiders hung upside down. Generations of creepy crawlies no doubt lived there. I didn't really mind. Was this me saying I had got used to Africa at last! At least the plumbing wouldn't keep us awake.

Quite suddenly it was dark. The sounds of the forest echoed up to our cosy hideaway on stilts. Cocooned with only the wild things for company, we settled in.

"I think I'll go and have a wash," said Barrie in a low voice.

"Would you like me to come with you?"

"Why?"

"Well you never know what you'll meet on the stairs."

"Nettie I'm going for a wash not a triple immersion, I won't be more than five minutes."

Sightings of imaginary hooded cobras slid into my mind. Dark forces were at work.

"I did see flying ants downstairs."

Pandora was a defining moment in our journey to Africa. Creeping slowly down the stairs at two thirty am, my jittery nerves were comforted by the gentle breathing of the forest at night. Reflections of silver light lay across the cool floor as we tiptoed to the entrance of the lodge. Standing in the shadows, listening to the thumping of our hearts and the cracking of twigs beyond, we waited. A million stars shone down. The sky was inky black. We must have stayed there for some considerable time. Owls hooted some distance away.

"Cold heh honey? Put this on." Barrie put a coat around my shoulders.

"I wonder what's out there?" I whispered, thinking our voices might be heard. "Look how the moonlight picks out the shape of the trees.....almost lifelike...."

"You could imagine almost anything." The scent of bark and creepers filled our nosrils.

We left the night forest and climbed back up to the stairs to half a night's sleep. One stuffed kudu kept watch outside the door. It would soon be Christmas.

Chapter 21

Posh and Not Posh

With considerable liquor concealed about his person, the man in front of us at the border was asked to get out out of his vehicle and searched. It was a blazing Saturday and Barrie and I were on our way to Ficksburg with orders to bring back party food and wine for a knees-up on camp. The vehicle was driven onto the guardhouse steps and like an army of ants, officers stepped on board. The guards were jubilant. The wine confiscated.

We decided to buy food only and forego the wine. Instead, we would have to buy local brew from Leribe Hotel.

The stretch of tarmac on the Ficksburg side of the border, had abandoned its attempt to become a road and our wheels bounced off the edges of the potholes with a wracking of engines and springs.

"Wow, that was close," I exclaimed, "we'll be lucky if we have a car to drive home in....and no wine for the party tonight."

"Two hundred guests will be a lot to feed, but we should be able to get everything. Did you notice the marquee being erected by the swimming pool? I wonder who'll be on duty at the gate tonight. Somebody will have to stay sober."

Today was 'Muela Dam Day.' LHPC at Leribe had invited workers from all other sites; construction engineers, consultants and the bosses of the whole shooting match – in fact everyone from the joint venture would be celebrating. Bigwigs from overseas companies had been invited and apart from wining and dining Lesotho-style, a few business deals would be struck. This would be the last time we would all be together. Men who had worked shoulder to shoulder for more than five years, would be saying goodbye to each other – perhaps for ever.

In recent weeks, mopping-up operations at Muela had been about appointing and training a new team of professionals. The Basotho people themselves would have to operate and maintain the dam and its infrastructure. Meetings had been taking place round the clock. These negotiations were not taken lightly. It required personnel with more than just the know-how of engineering, it was crucial that they knew the ecological, historical and political aspects of the country as well. The future of the whole nation was at stake. Tonight was a chance to prove good will all round. Very soon, the men who had paved the way for this piece of history to be written, who had worked their butts off for the last five years – would be closing down the sites and going home.

Smartly Barrie and I returned from Ficksburg with enough food to sink a battleship. We had no trouble bringing it through the border. By five o'clock, it seemed the whole of our camp was on high activity alert. With flags flying, a huge white marquee had appeared, ropes tightened and a mountain of chairs stood waiting to be arranged inside. Tables of vegetables and salads had been prepared and the *braai* was already lit. Sophie was at her best when giving orders and any idleness on the part of her staff was soon nipped in the bud by her loud bellow and beating of wooden spoon on pans. In pink frilly apron, newly blancoed shoes and sleeves rolled up, she looked ready to settle the score with anyone who tried to gatecrash tonight's 'do'.

Mindful of Sophie's instructions, Thabo scuttled through the melée pushing a wheelbarrow full of rattling crockery and ice buckets. Petros, in charge of electrification, was unravelling a ton of cables and microphones tied up like spaghetti which threatened to cut him off at the knees. It looked like a heap of industrial salvage. Correct leads had to be connected to correct instruments and amplifyers. A Frenchman, whose voice I didn't recognise, shouted a warning to a waitress whose tray of wine glasses teetered on her head while she carried boxes of wine to the bar. The glasses slid to the edge of the tray and landed on the grass.

The weather had been the kind of day the terraces at Wimbledon prayed for. The sky was rich with colour as everyone went to get dressed in best bib and tucker ready for the arrival of the two hundred guests. At seven o'clock we heard the band serenading the mountains with calypso-style overtures from under the canvas awning.

Barrie and I had another reason to be jubilant. Tomorrow was the occasion of our 'other' party. The two halves of our lives were beginning to overlap. A different venue, a different eating plan – one posh, one not posh – both premier league.

"Where's my best shirt?" shouted my other half, as I tried in vain to fasten the zip on the dress I *was* going to wear. Liliane and I were still on our campaign to lose weight but had recently taught ourselves to cook Yorkshire pudding. I was considering my options. A sari or another sari.

"Barrie it's where you put it after your wedding."

Expat communities are well known for extravaganza when it comes to parties. The fact that the rand was running at a new low, did not deter the management of LHPC from celebrating in style when the time was right. It made up for all those times when pressures of tenders and deadlines ruled the day. Off-duty engineers are without exception first class hosts and have no great desire to preach sobriety.

We sauntered across to the bar to mingle with other dressed-up-to-the-nines folk and already the dancing had started. I hadn't seen so many trousers with creases in and clean-shaven men in months. Great swathes of tropical flowers hung from poles inside the marquee and the tables of food looked like the deli at Fortnum and Mason. The South African band, bedecked and beribboned in flowery shirts and bandanas went into a cha-cha-cha with fancy steps. Many couples were on the floor, gorgeous dresses swirled over the wooden decking. Conversation was high. Flirting was back in fashion.

People had travelled great distances to attend this gathering. Drinks could be ordered in any language. South Africans, New Zealanders, Germans, French, Dutch, Venuzuelan, Spanish and many other nationalities were there to share in the success of Muela. The dancing was riotous. The liquor flowed. The mood was high. For the men of LHPC, the end was in sight.

Around midnight, my dancing partner and I, having romped through the Eightsome Reel and the Gay Gordons, did one swirl too many on the dance floor, missed our footing and I let go of his hand. He toppled backwards (colliding with a large drum on the way down) then continued on his merry way, hit the canvas wall of the marquee – still travelling backwards, hit the deck and quietly disappeared. No one on the dance floor even saw him go. Once out of the heaving throng of jive and dive, I headed outside running round the guy-ropes holding up the marquee, shouting his name. About half way round, I found the waistcoat-half of my husband, flat on his back with a smile on his face, happily gazing at the stars.

"Hi honey – who moved the band?"

The following afternoon, with our car boot heavily laden with food, cutlery and crockery, we set out for a different kind of party, Ha Simone style. For weeks we had been planning this prestigious affair. Since our original intention of celebrating with the family for Walter's recovery, for which everyone for miles around was glad, a few other events had been added to the list. The King's Coronation, the new link with England, our wedding blessing, to name but three….and today was Bernice's tenth birthday. Rose and Stephen had invited the guests – and as yet, we didn't know how many.

We were a little nervous. One reason was that we had little understanding of an evening's entertainment, as in African village. Having always enjoyed the benefit of electricity, one wondered how they would cope without light and music. English parties are driven by what to wear, trendy hair styles and a good bar. There is no point to fashion if the person standing next to you can't see the pattern on your waistcoat. Designer cleavages and built-in bras don't appear in the vocabulary of young Basotho girls, who would give their eye teeth for a pair of denims. It isn't a matter of which tie a man should wear, when no one can afford a shirt. And food was something one ate to stay alive, not enjoyed as an optional extra. We were trying to bridge the time and culture gap in one evening. But what the heck!

As we came within sight of Makibi's compound, a fire out in the yard was sending a shower of sparks into the darkening light and a pale moon was already showing. Tonight would be a full moon which was good news.

"Look Barrie, there's a light up in their tree – it can't be - how on earth…?"

As we came nearer we could see it was a single bulb – on the end of a very long piece of wire which went across the yard attached to an invisible battery. A pack of children came running out to greet us. Behind them David and Walter, grinning and holding up some kind of gadget attached to a length of flex.

"Hi Nettie. Told you not to worry about anything. Look we have electric light in the yard tonight. Do you like it? And we've borrowed a tape recorder. It runs off the same battery."

The food was unloaded onto tables. Rose had prepared the kraal (which smelled vaguely of cow dung) for us to use as an outdoor kitchen. A good fire burned, with a wire grid on top. Stephen, with one hand on David's shoulder was directing operations, setting out benches and chairs round the yard. Half a dozen youngsters hovered around to see what the eating prospects were like, rubbing their stomachs in anticipation.

"How many people are we cooking for ? Do we know?"smiled Barrie.

"About thirty to forty…..or fifty. Walter says they have asked all the church members."

"I'm glad you've brought plates," called out Rose, coming across from the house smiling broadly. "I knew that I wouldn't have enough for everybody. And some cutlery. Good, I was worried about that too….and cups. Look, I've made some ginger beer. We'll serve it from the bucket on the stoep."

Guests were arriving by verbal invitation only….. no written invitations in this part of the world. Reverend Makibi had spoken to most of his near neighbours, but grape-vines tend to work fast and people further afield would have heard that there was a party at St John's tonight. The broken tape-recorder, which had miraculously survived the rubbish tip, was placed on top of the kraal wall. Tapes could only be played if someone held the door flap closed, as the spring had broken. Petros and Joshua agreed to take turns to hold it. Whoever was on duty could not move from his position.

"Walter, thanks for the illuminations," I said, pointing up into the tree. "How long did it take you?"

"Most of the afternoon. I had a bit of trouble – it stretches right across to my house. We managed to string the wires together……"

"Or you could set the tree on fire of course," joked the engineer.

The potatoes were all pre-cooked and the salads prepared. Char-grilled steaks and sausages smelled delicious in the evening air – in fact someone's dog had appeared on the scene to investigate. Fred and elder brother George from house next door were also hovering near the food. Desmond, one of the priests-in-training, arrived to help.

"Stephen, supper's almost ready," indicated Barrie. The boys had made him a chef's hat to wear, from white cardboard, and surrounded by stacks of plates, he looked the perfect cook.. "Is there any water to drink?"

Desmond put on his apron and started poking the fire.Two lads were visibly sweating as they dragged and rolled a big barrel across the yard, brought up from the spring. There would be enough water for everybody.

"Nettie, look behind us, do you see what I see?" Barrie spoke quietly in my ear. Along the yard in the darkness, a queue had formed; a very orderly queue of men, women and children, some carrying their own plates.

"Looks as if they're expecting us to serve the food. Well okay, perhaps its easier. Wait – the blessing," I said, pointing to Stephen who stood holding out his arms, his eyes closed. Everyone was silent. There was a great feeling of anticipation...then Stephen's booming voice, saying words about blacks and whites and new friendships, turning to face Barrie and myself, he announced,

"My son is only alive today because of these two people.We owe it to them to celebrate this evening, and give our thanks to God, who makes all things possible. We asked for help and our prayers were answered."

He made the sign of the cross on himself. Amens rippled round the yard. Walter, surrounded by his friends, was standing near holding a little boy in his arms. At twenty four, he was still a child himself. He looked over in my direction. Only he and I knew what really happened.

What followed was like Christmas day in a London soup kitchen. Barrie and I didn't intend it to be thus, but there was a feeling that *this* was what they expected. The meal was not lavish, though it was sufficient. As we filled one plate, so another took its place. The benches round the yard filled up. The queue kept on coming. The flames flickered as each family came near. Firelight fell on the eyes of small children. Plate after plate was offered and filled.

"*Lumelang,"* was our greeting and the people answered with smile upon smile.

"*Kea Leboha 'M'e, Ntate....*it is very good."

Eventually Stephen and Rose came to the table. Witnessing the joy on people's faces, they were both ecstatic.

"Barrie, the news of this celebration will travel up and down our country. Never has there been anything like this in Ha Simone. White people to host the black people – not ever in my lifetime......but wait, we will entertain you....."

At the point where most guests had eaten and the litter collected, we were astonished to find that pieces of fillet steak had been left untouched.Guests whose basic diet was wheat, vegetables and mealie, were not used to our sophisticated tastes. Perhaps we should have served liver. (Liver was what Betty called 'a treat'.)

It was eight thirty and the moon was risen. We turned to the sound of voices singing. The company of guests was walking towards the fire, their voices in unison, bodies moving together in the way that only Africans can move.... fluid, sensual. Through the night air came the humming, '*Round yon virgin, mother and child, Holy Infant, so tender and mild.....sleep in heavenly peace'*. Soft voices came nearer. A surge of emotion tugged at my throat as we were surrounded by a throng of village people …… *'Silent Night, Holy Night'*. The familiar words filled our ears. The circle turned. Deep-throated harmonies erupted into the night until they were absorbed into the earth where we stood. For a moment even the mountains were obliterated. Everything in our world was here in this place.

Never had the coming of Christmas been more special. The knot in my throat was in danger of bursting. The sky was flecked with bright stars. Barrie put his arm round my shoulder. Walter stood next to us, singing in full voice. Another chorus. Rose leading now, blending with the deep bass voices of her three sons; this time in their own language, backed by the whole company. Finally, *'a Partidge in a Pear Tree'*. All twelve verses. The carol I had taught them the previous week. We raised our glasses of ginger beer and toasted Christmas.

There was a pause while people chatted and drank from plastic cups. Walter made a funny speech. Petros, tall and wiry, was the first to launch into the dancing. Turning his legs into limbs of rubber, he wriggled and swayed into every possible pose. The now-obsolete tape recorder tumbled from the kraal wall. Without further shyness, the seventeen-year-old skipped across the yard like a locomotive firing on all cylinders. Other youths joined in. I couldn't say who was jumping the highest. Petros, the boy who didn't hold with words, excelling in his dancemanship.

Justice and Walter shouted, *'Shosholosa'*!

"Come on Nettie - we'll show you how to do it! Barrie! Like this…beat with your feet, turn and do it again!"

The *'Shosholosa'* is a traditional dance of the miners who laboured in the gold mines of South Africa, to signify marching feet, deep underground. A great deal of foot thumping is involved and one needs a good pair of knees. The dance had featured prominently the night before our April wedding, performed by our Basotho friends on the camp. By popular request, Walter, Emily and Kenneth our driver, danced it again at our legal ceremony the following day. Consequently, it was re-enacted at our October wedding blessing in Datchworth, much to the surprise of our English guests.

Rose and the ladies were joining in. Blankets and scarves were cast off and bare feet jumped on the ground in a kind of knees bend, heel toe, bottom wriggle action. Once the mood of dancing takes hold, shoulders and arms are shaken and wriggled with utmost pleasure, it doesn't matter if you are old, young, large or skinny, in fine clothes or just plain cut down ugly - everyone joins in. I confess my sense of rhythm was lousy, but the fun was in the doing of it. Marks and Spencer sandals aren't meant for such gyrations, so I took them off and discovered the feeling of dancing in one's bare feet. Sensational!

There are no other rules except dancing as though you were going to die tomorrow. Shoulder to shoulder, Petros and the brothers leapt and shrieked. My joints started to tell me it was time to stop.

"No more, no more!" I landed in a heap of exhaustion. "Enough, enough. Walter we must go home now, or we'll expire......"

(I needed to go to the toilet and didn't fancy the walk down the field, in the dark.)

"But the party's only just started."

Our lasting memory will be of Rose and Stephen, seated on a church bench in the middle of their yard – still eating supper, lit by the brillliance of the full moon. And still dangling from the tree, Walter's one battery-powered bulb.

The ox-cart was neatly parked to one side, on which were tied a few white paper streamers fluttering in the night wind, as if saying goodbye. It was almost midnight. Most of the older guests had gone home. A few youngsters were still dancing. The shadowy bulk of their three cows showed below the midden wall, shifting quietly in the night air. Stephen waved an arm.

"Goodnight, you two. Thanks for a wonderful party. We will never forget this night."

"Oh, let me wash the plates and dishes," called Rose, leaping to her feet, "I'll take everything down to the river – it won't take long,"

"You'll do no such thing," hastily answered my husband, "we'll take the dishes home in the boot of the car. Rose. Tonight there will be no washing up."

*   *   *   *

Refreshed after six hours sleep, we woke to the sound of the rain pelting on the roof. I lay in bed listening to the soft fall of water onto the sodden greenery below the verandah, then peered through the curtains. No sun. The garden was like a lake. Half hidden in his den below the house next door, Hercule's eyes were just visible. He hated the rain and in doggy body language it was plain he was thoroughly miserable. I would take him for a walk later.

My plans for the day were not urgent, except that I must return to Makibis to collect all our pots and pans used the night before. Barrie had a rush job on at the office and I wouldn't see him until seven o'clock.

"See you tonight honey, won't be home until late. Would you like to eat in the bar tonight? There's a meeting about the 'Grand Opening of the Dam' - we've been told Mandela's coming. There's lots to decide, it's not just a jam buttie evening." He hurried out of the house.

The road outside the camp looked as though a bomb had been dropped in the night. Huge lumps of rock were exposed and the ridges of mud and craters spelt disaster for car wheels. For a construction site road, you wouldn't give it many marks out of ten. You could sink without trace if you revved your engine too hard.

Driving and sliding carefully, it took me twenty minutes to reach the end of our track to the tarmac. The storm had been so fierce during the early hours, that a telegraph pole had come down and was lying across the middle of the road. Wires and pieces of wood were strewn everywhere, like a demented giant knitting machine.

Mid- shout, a man waved me to stop. I got out of my car and sank up to my laces in yellow mud. A horse had been tethered to the telegraph wires and people were trying to force the animal to pull. The pole did not move. Another man arrived with a bullock and harnessed the animal to the same rope as the horse, but the newcomer had a far more lucrative alternative in mind, than to simply clear the main road. Telegraph poles make good fires.

An argument ensued as to whether the pole was the property of Lesotho Telecom, the Government or the people of the village where it fell down. Heated discussions were underway. The Basotho are not reticent in conducting loud public discussion and I foresaw that things could escalate, as more people gathered. The main road would stay blocked until the problem was resolved and it could take all day. I drove onto the grass verge and managed to circumnavigate the disaster without skidding into the ditch.

Ten minutes later on arriving at Walter's house, another loud discussion was taking place. Arms in the air, purple in the face, the portly figure of Stephen was holding forth urgently to son number one.

"You must go now," he shouted to Walter. "Go today – there's no time to lose!"

Walter's chin was set. He was determined to hold out, but his father's demand looked unyielding.

Discreetly collecting my kitchenalia, I placed everything in the boot of the car. Rose looked very serious. The discussion raged. Keeping a low profile, I went inside the house to talk with Petros.

"What's happening Petros? Is something the matter?"

"Someone Walter knows has been assaulted, Nettie. It is bad news. But the good news is that he has been offered a job in Butha-Buthe, as a teacher in a secondary school."

Walter had indeed been offered a new job. Because of his excellent matriculation results, it was thought he was suitably qualified to take over the running of a school, now he was well enough. The Headmaster had sent a message via a family member and Walter had been asked to go and see him. The argument in the yard was because Walter wanted to go and find out about his friend first – but his father had other ideas. At twenty four years old, the son must do as his father bids him - before anything else. Admirably, he bit his lip.

I offered to drive Walter to the interview in my car. He accepted. Shortly afterwards we were on our way to find the headmaster of a High School, situated half way up a mountain near Butha-Buthe. Small homesteads with tin toilets were scattered over the hillside, which illustrated the kind of catchment area of the school. We passed neither pony nor donkey, only a few grubby sheep foraging in the mud at the bottom of a ditch. It was a bumpy ride. The sky had brightened to a dazzling silvery blue.

Walter's mind was with his friend who, it appeared, had been badly attacked. I asked him to drive the car to take his mind off things.

"Nettie, I hate this kind of violence. It is abhorrent to me. Why these thugs must chose someone weak who is an easy target. I will find out who did it.," he said with conviction, "and I will go and see them."

"What will you do?"

"I don't know, but I will make sure they don't come out of their village for a long time. I will shame them."

"Tell me about this school. Does it matter that you are not a qualified teacher?"

"Oh, I will be able to do the job. I have passed my grades at school and the Headmaster knows me. I will learn fast and I know how to handle young people. He wants me to teach mathematics and that was my best subject. The classes here will be easy for me."

"How much will you be paid?"

"That depends on the parents. The staff cannot be paid a salary until the parents have paid the fees for their children. Some weeks the staff cannot be paid at all. That is the way a school works."

"Does the school get money from the government?"

"Yes, but only for books and equipment. Not for salaries."

"Go on in – I'll wait for you."

Half an hour later, flushed with happiness, he strode from the building.

"Well, go on ....explain," I said impatiently, watching the smile around his eyes.

"Wow , I've got a job, Nettie – a real job." His voice was quiet and controlled.

He had been offered the job with no official contract. At the start of the new term Walter would be in employment. Next week was the start of their long summer vacation. January was the hottest month of the year and most schools would be closed.

"Now my father will hold his head up high. This will make him proud. The position here is made for me. Thanks for driving me Nettie. Can I steer you down the mountain?" The potholes didn't seem so bad on the way down."They didn't have many desks," he said quickly, "some of the rooms had nothing......and no books either. This school is very poor. There are two other new members of staff, but the headmaster wasn't there today. Nobody knew where he was."

It sounded rather bizarre to say the least. No headmaster, no contract, no salary structure, no chairs or desks and sizes of classes unknown.

"On the first day of term we will know how many pupils the school will have. There was some stationery though not much. Nettie, could you find me any waste paper in your camp dustbins?"

"It's possible yes.......Walter, I have an idea. Liliane is teaching at the French School at Butha-Buthe camp. In February when the engineers leave, it

284

will close down. Perhaps I can put in a good word for your place.....there might be a few desks and other things…"

Convinced of the value of reading and writing, he was keenly aware of his responsibilities, and his sporting abilities would be an asset. January 1998 looked a promising start.

We were nearing the bottom of the slope now and the track widened out. Several cows grazed nearby, accompanied by a herd boy with his dog. Indescribably thin, the boy clearly looked astonished to see a car coming down the mountain. It's not often you see a boy thinner than his animals and I wondered if his parents had stopped feeding him. An expression of intense sadness clouded his face like a mask. Legs like thin sticks, were poking out of his cut-down men's boots. He didn't respond with the usual wave. No life eminated from the eyes.

"Look this lad might be one of your pupils, Walter."

"Yes, that's true – you see the problems we have, I don't have to tell you Nettie. It could be his parents are so poor they cannot send him to school." Then turning to me, " Oh, I almost forgot – here is the letter for Reverend Syms." He took a white envelope from his pocket. "I have written my very first letter to Datchworth, England. Would you please post it for me." Then with real emotion in his voice, "Do you think he will reply very soon?"

Chapter 22

Cape New Year

Waking up in a beautiful hotel room in Bloubergstrand was the nearest thing to luxurious living as I had ever known. It meant waking up to the sun, the deep green sea and a classic view of the most famous mountain in the world. A promenade of white sand between our breakfast table and the Atlantic Ocean was an invitation to wander down to the rocky shore, breathe the fresh Cape breeze and gaze at the famous white cloud tablecloth. It was three days away from Christmas and I had to pinch myself to remind myself where I was. England was in the grip of ice and frost and I was searching my suitcase for a clean pair of shorts, sunglasses and my high factor sunscreen.

The easy route to the top of Table Mountain was plan number one. From its boarding station on Kloof Nek Road, the newly built Swiss cable car left every fifteen minutes – timed to reach the top in six minutes. The day was perfect; the sky aquamarine and no rain was forecast. Rapid weather changes mean visitors are sometimes disappointed of a clear view from the top, so we decided to tackle it on day one.

I had promised myself not to look down as the lift took off from the platform. Locked inside the state-of-the-art glass fishbowl, which turns a full 360 degrees on every journey, was so exciting that I did look. Being suspended over the heights is not quite so frightening from the inside as it is when you see it rise from the ground. My hands gripped the steel bar as the rock face came zooming towards us. Before I could blink, we had arrived and I was stepping off onto terra firma. The hot paved platform burned my feet through my shoes.

Table Mountain, which forms the backdrop to South Africa's mother city, dominates the northern end of the peninsula from a height of 1,087metres, flanked by Lion's head and Devil's Peak. There are many different pathways up to the top and we met people who had just done the arduous three hour climb. My knees felt glad we hadn't attempted to make our ascent that way. Statistics say that a number of hikers who do not use extreme caution, are killed every year.

The Atlantic offers mind-blowing views from every point of Table Mountain and inspires thoughts of sailors entering the Cape waters and seeing it as a great anchor in the wilderness. After their hazardous journeys at sea, no wonder it was called 'Hope'. We were astonished by the different alpines and plants growing in the crevices of soil on the flat rocky surface; a colourful carpet of pink, orange and white fynbos with patches of red hot pokers gleaming like lanterns in the bright light. Despite the hellish winds up there, over 1,500 species of plants still survive. We walked the pathways where many feet had walked before. Rock rabbits (dassies) rodent-like creatures sunbathed on the rocks. They blinked in the light like giant guinea pigs.

The north eastern views were absolutely stunning. It would take pages to describe the beauty of Table Bay and the way it curves like a horseshoe and sweeps into the land - cornflower blue sea and white sand. The City Bowl, Cape Town's great metropolis stretched far below. Robben Island was visible out at sea and the Tygerberg Hills shimmered in the far distance. Through my eyes, the panoramic views were simply awesome.

Table Mountain has provided the base for human survival, animals and rich grasslands, for more than half a million years. The rainfall has always ensured fresh water throughout the year for all its inhabitants. European explorers would not have sailed into Table Bay regularly without the provision of fresh water.

"What must you feel like up here, when the sun sinks down into the ocean!"

" Bloomin' cold!" commented my other half from behind his binoculars.

Christmas dinner in midsummer was going to be strange for us, nevertheless the restaurant had advertised two sittings, so we guessed the food must be good. We made a reservation for our three course meal on the promenade at two o'clock. Christmas morning service in a local church was a delightful experience; the singing divine, though fairy lights and tinsel don't have quite the same effect in bright sunlight.

We watched a sympathetic version of the nativity with black children and whites together, holding hands around the tree, then shook hands with the vicar, who blessed us in English and Afrikaans. A short stroll down the seafront with the wind blowing a Southeaster and we started to pretend it was Christmas Day in England. Ladies selling pin-on proteas on the street and a barrel organ playing 'Oh Come all ye Faithful' added to the feeling.....and a few posters of Santa flew merrily from lamppost tops. We had been warned to beware of pickpockets or people who approached you for money and youths with aggressive-looking dogs who hung around the bathing areas looking for empty take-away cartons. Yuletide wind surfers with second-skin rubber suits were no less in number at Big Bay than the day before, taking off into the waves like sea butterflies. Superb to watch, they performed their skill and artistry - dancing on the rollers in a spectacle of drama and colour. The atlantic is extremely cold, but is no deterrent to these sporty types who pitch up in designer swim wear every day of the year.

All this action brought on a healthy appetite and we hurried to our table. Nothing could have prepared us for the shock of facing re-constituted sliced turkey from a tin, re-heated in a micro-wave and served on cold plates. I hasten to mention that this Bloubergian chef had never heard of sprouts. You can't really spoil roast potatoes, but the sage and onion stuffing would have been better left in the packet. Both wearing reindeer hats, we pulled crackers and chewed on tinned turkey legs and plum pudding. However, we were saved from an attack of homesickness by an invitation to see Christmas night celebrations at the V & A Waterfront in Cape Town that same evening.

Buzzing with atmosphere, the Waterfront cafes and bars were full of happy people, singing Christmas carols, kissing each other and dancing round the tavern tables, like a scene from Lionel Bart's 'Oliver'. Angels in white frocks assembled in the square accompanied by an all-singing-all-dancing Father Christmas who gathered up all the children and led them like the Pied Piper to the fish and chip shop. We ate monster prawns from paper bags and supped oysters at a friendly bistro, wore flamboyant hats with other diners and got throughly sozzled with Christmas spirit. A short distance behind us fireworks rained over the bay and explosions of light fell across the water making bendy patterns around the little boats as they rocked against the harbour wall.

We drove home late and were greeted boisterously by other residents of our hotel who had gathered round a bottle of Stellenbosch in the bar for a nightcap. Feeling very sociable, we joined in. Somewhere between the first glass of vintage '94 and Boxing Day morning we put the whole world to rights and sang a song which I didn't know the name of, but which had a lot of Ya Ya's in it.

After Bloubergstrand, we moved to a tiny cottage in the garden of a house in Knysna, owned by a kind elderly lady called Mrs Nelson, who walked up the garden path every morning to bring us fresh peaches for breakfast. She apologised that there was no cleaning lady and went on to explain that on New Year's Day all the blacks go to the sea for a holiday.

"It's their tradition you know, they swim in the sea every year on the same day."

We didn't mind in the least – in fact it pleased us to do our own cleaning and clearing up. The house was surrounded by bougainvillea, protea, colombine, wisteria and a host of other blossoms...and banana trees. Daily, we gorged on fresh pineapple, mangoes and bananas, dined Mexican style at the local brasserie and Barrie discovered 'Tequilla Sunrise', served up every evening by a dusky maiden in the bar, was a perfect ending to a day's hiking.The Knysna forests are famous for their ancient yellowwood, stinkwood and milkwood trees, some of them up to eight hundred years old. You can explore a wildlife trail or do a guided walk and see a huge variety of birds, especially at this time of the year or take a lazy swim in a lagoon as a way of cooling down. Languid days of doing everything or nothing at all, filled our remaining holiday. We promised ourselves to come back one day, for more of the same.

The Outeniqua Choo-Tjoe (translated Ootiniga Choo Choo) is the last scheduled mixed goods and passenger steam train which runs between Knysna and George twice daily in the summer. On New Year's Day 1998 we bought tickets for a ride out to sea on a train. The historic journey was two and a half hours of breathtaking scenery. 'Puffing Billy' chugged along gently past lakes and forests, wild valleys of stunning mountain flowers and onto a spectacular bit of track called Kaaimans Bridge, where the track runs out to sea. At one point the track rose above the edge of the water, where hundreds of families were celebrating their New Year, waving to the passengers on the train. As far as the eye could see, colourful tents and makeshift awnings had been erected along the beach. Whole families, all fully clothed (no bathing costumes) were enjoying their annual dip in the Atlantic, even though it was freezing cold. The thousands of workers who slave the year round for white families have made this their traditional day of rest. Similar scenes were happening all round the coast of South Africa.

The leisurely pace of the steam engine, tooting and hooting under tunnels and over bridges, made one think of life fifty years ago, but in those days, there would have been more wildlife to see on a journey like this. Elephants used to live along this part of the coast and were able to survive on the vegetation. Over the years, loss of habitat and/or poachers have succeeded in eradicating the herds and now there are few elephants left. Efforts have been made to introduce new young herds, without much success.

Our two remaining days were spent sampling crayfish and oysters at local restaurants and watching fishermen at high tide in the swirling waters of The Knysna Heads, where two sea channels meet. The men stood on the rocks pulling in their catch, almost being knocked off their feet by the swell. Stories of tourists standing too close, being sucked into the sea by the force of the tide, were common knowledge and we were careful to stay within the red flags. Walking the sands at Plettenburg Bay we took a last look at the dolphins, as they swam gracefully close to the shore, diving through the rollers like dancers in a ballet – an amazing sight as the sun went down on the water. A moment of intense gratitude overcame us, as we drove north from Cape Town in the early morning of our departure day.

Our next stopover was a town called Cradock, surrounded by the Karoo and situated on the Great Fish River where the hot springs come out of the ground. It turned out to be a town full of surprises. We made a blistering five hundred kilometre journey from Plettenburg Bay to Cradock in six hours. This was helped by the blissful absence of traffic. The Karoo has a strange beauty; harsh mountainous landscape where nothing grows - no shade nor shelter under the burning sun, though ostriches and tortoises seem to like it.

May's House in Market Street, was one of several attractive frontier style houses - neat and well preserved, full of Victorian olde worlde charm with a dash of camphor in the air. We had the whole house to ourselves....it reminded me of the Bronte Parsonage.

"And there you are my dear - Cecil Rhodes's bed. Sleep in this room if you like," exclaimed Desray in her flamboyant Afrikans voice, as she waved us round the house. Shiny beads jangled across tight sweater, worn under purple silk blouse. She reminded me of a Blackpool landlady with that haughty expression meant to impress new arrivals. A huge bunch of keys tied with a crushed-strawberry scarf braided her many-ringed fingers. "Breakfast is served in the Tuishuise on the other side of Market Street."

"Gosh, did he live here?" I asked, ignoring the breakfast routine.

"No, he just slept in this bed and our guests like to sleep in it!"

Desray swept before us in a cloud of gardenia soap. It made my day, or should I say my night! The bed itself was enormous. Dominated by a mahogany canopy decorated with a carved bust of Queen Victoria, as in figurehead of any naval vessel of the era; the wood polished to perfection; the quilt, in delicate white lace, draped over.

In the parlour - a tall mahogany bookcase full of blue china, tapestries of English aristocracy, pictures of the Spanish Armada, an elegant oval dining table set with porcelain and crystal, high backed chairs and footstools made a sumptuous display of high living. The windows were hung with beautiful drapes, the walls lined with books and pictures, the kitchen with its polished pine floors and collections of war-time memorabilia was fascinating. Not quite the kind of house one expected in the middle of the desert.

Hanging in one of the bedrooms was a full length Victorian wedding dress, made of silk and lace with undergarments of plain calico, delicately threaded with ribbons and bows. Who was the bride I wondered? Perhaps the daughter of a Boer family, finally joined in wedlock to a Cradock farmer, about to embark on married life in the isolated plains of the Karoo?

"All the houses in Market Street are owned by one lady, named after her friends," chatted Desray, holding forth on tourist information for our sole benefit. "Sandra Antrobus has restored each one in a different period and style....including the Victoria Hotel. In ten years she has put Cradock on the map. She would love to meet you. Come for dinner tomorrow night and she will tell you the story of the famous bed."

We slept well after our journey, despite the ominous presence of Queen Victoria's bust. The next morning, having awakened in time to watch the sunrise, I padded round the house in bare feet, still fascinated by the story of the famous bed. As I peeped into the room where the wedding dress had been, I looked at the ceiling expecting to see it hanging there. The dress was in a heap on the floor. I looked again. It was difficult to see how it could have slipped off the hanger by itself. There were only two of us in the house.

"Barrie, have you been in this room since last night?"

"Don't be silly...." came the muffled reply from under the bedclothes.

Had the ghost of Queen Victoria been up to mischief, or the ghost of Cecil Rhodes himself - angry because we had slept in his bed. It was impossible for the dress to have slipped off by itself. The room was quite empty. The incident remained in the back of my mind all day.

The name Olive Schreiner was closely bound to Cradock. I had already come across her book 'The Story of an African Farm'. Schreiner was a far-sighted progressive, regarded by many as one of the greatest South African Writers in the English language, but limited by the feminine boundaries of her time. She endured a strict Methodist upbringing as well as harsh Victorian discipline while living in Cradock, where she wrote about her experiences of being brought up in the Karoo in the late nineteenth century. She came to England in the 1880's, and published her book in the name of Ralph Iron, knowing that her freedom to write would be curtailed if it were to be known that she was a young female, voicing issues connected with colonialism, depravity and patriarchal dogma.

Her novel caused a whiplash of controversy for it was extremely radical for its time. Since then, other well-known writers have penned their own acknowledgements of Schreiner's forward-thinking ideas, bold outlines and spiritual isolation. She has been called poet, visionary, genius and pioneer and the impact of her book changed the way people thought about women in society. Historically it was a novel far ahead of its time.

She attracted the attention of Cecil Rhodes, then an influential person in South Africa. Gossip has it that she was in love with Rhodes, which may account for the wrath she poured upon him and it is clear from her book that she lamented over his soul. Her perception of Rhodes was that his greed and ambition should not be disguised to look like the face of a conquering hero. Through her writing fame, her house in Cradock has been made into a museum. Like other visitors, we found it fascinating.

We stayed in Cradock long enough to see the church which looked like St Martins-in-the Fields in London and to meet the new owner of the bed.

"Ah the bed....well it had been kept in a damp room for years," said Mrs Antrobus, after we were introduced in the Shosholosa Bar of the Victoria Hotel, after dining well on Karoo Lamb.

"It had gone mouldy and was a wreck. I took it apart, cleaned it thoroughly, gave it a new horsehair matress. The mahogany was repolished and everything refurbished – gave it a new lace quilt. By the way, did you sleep well last night?"

I found her an inspiring lady, who had set her heart on renovating this town from small beginnings because of its proximity to the desert. She wanted to add quality to the lives of the people here, including those of Cape coloureds who live in the shanty townships nearby. She employed a lot of local people in 'The Street' and had built up tourist trade enormously, helped the Schreiner Museum to get started, so that it would have something interesting to offer visitors. In ten years a lot had happened to Cradock, because of this lady.

"What made you come to visit Cradock?" asked Sandra after we had talked a while. She had never met white people who had lived in Lesotho before and her deep searching questions about the country, were remarkable.

"I have heard it is not safe to live there."

"Don't believe everything you hear," said Barrie teasing her, "we heard there were ghosts in Cradock."

I liked her on first meeting and left our London address....had a feeling we would meet again. We drove away from Cradock, sad that we didn't have time to see the famous mountain zebra, but feeling very pleased that we had stayed at May's House in Market Street. Then Hofmeyr, Steynsberg, Burgersdorp – small towns on the long straight road which eventually joined the N6 to Aliwal North and onto the Blomfontein route. In two hours we would be home. Time to reflect. Time to think about my journey to England which I would soon be taking. Time to think about the ghost of Cecil Rhodes. It was not until I unpacked my suitcase that I realised I had left my best blue silk dress at the guest house, in Cecil Rhodes' wardrobe.

Chapter 23

Winds of Change and the Opening of Muela Dam

January in Lesotho is a most beautiful month, gourds grow fat and pumpkins ripen while you watch. The bees are heavy with pollen. We picked figs fresh from our garden. Most days we dined outside enjoying the warm sunshine. It didn't get dark until seven thirty and we often swam until midnight.

Work on the final phases of the Project was tricky and Barrie would have his nose to the grindstone from now until the end of the contract. He didn't mind me going home. I had decided to postpone the surgery on my wrist, with Dr Nettleton's approval. He advised me to wait until we were permanently back in England. A short break with the family was what I needed. Communications had been somewhat threadbare during the past few months and I had that homing instinct. We booked me a flight to London. Compared with the hot balmy weather we were having in Lesotho, England was bound to be a shock.

One evening just as pay weekend was about to start and most of the engineers were off-camp, a sense of urgency broke out, precisely the time most of the phones were shut down and the senior staff had gone off duty. Someone had discovered a sabotage attack at the Muela site. A message got through from one of the drivers that the powerhouse, which contained all the electrical instruments controlling the flow of water through the tunnels, had been flooded. Intruders had forced their way through the security fences, overpowered the guards, climbed inside the big cage and opened up two massive valves. It happened on the Friday night – obviously aimed at maximum damage, as it could have gone unnoticed until the staff returned on the Monday. As luck would have it, one of the junior engineers discovered it early enough and reported it instantly. The valves were closed immediately and the water level contained without more damage, though some parts of the machinery were ruined. It was indeed an uncomfortably worrying attack. A major incident was narrowly averted.

After this, extra guards were positioned around the main access channels and gates as a precaution against further mischief. The saboteurs were never identified, but it was suspected the men who were sacked during the strike in 1996 who may have been behind the initial stoppages, were to blame. In any high profile project, there are bound to be factions of discontent, opponents and even sworn enemies. The prophets of doom had not won this time. Even more crucial was the fact that the handover was about to take place, and high volumes of water from Katse would soon be flowing into the Muela Reservoir on full power. At this stage of the venture, it was imperative that not even the smallest nut and bolt should be missing.

Barrie and I had gone to Sandton near Johannesburg for a weekend shopping trip and knew nothing about the incident until our return on the Sunday night. Everyone on site was flabbergasted by the audacity of the intruders. Guards on all camps were put on full alert in case there was more trouble. At times like these, a brooding air of discontent hung about the camp. Bar talk was clipped and jokes forbidden. The pool table was empty. Morale declined among the engineers and new sentry posts hastily positioned on main gates. I wasn't sorry to be leaving in a few days time.

Walter would be twenty five years old on 9th January. For his birthday, Barrie and I had promised him a hundred and fifty rands to pay for his driving licence. It was his dream. He had been able to drive since he was a boy, but had never had enough money to obtain his licence. He had to take an oral exam in addition to driving on the highway. I dropped him near the test centre, nervously going over his notes. After three hours I went to meet him.

"How do you think you fared Walter?"

"I think I did well – but they don't tell you the result straight away. I'll have to wait and see. It was a hard test and the examiner was not very talkative.....but that's okay I guess."

Within a few days, we learned that Walter had failed his driving test. Furrows lined his forehead as he sat on the old horsehair chair in his room, carving deep weals into the stick he was making for Petros.

"It's because I didn't pay the bribe, you see Nettie. That's the way it is." He pursed his lips into a thin smile and tried hard to conceal his disappointment. His words lingered in the air.

"Walter, that's terrible! Is it true? Were you asked for one?"

"No – they don't tell you that, you find out the hard way."

Other people confirmed our fears. Bribe money is part of the system – Walter woukld have to take his test again – and it would cost a hundred and fifty rands plus bribe. We had wasted our money.

Before I left Lesotho it was essential to form a committee at Ha Simone made up of St John's representatives, so that I could tell Datchworth Church with whom they would be dealing, once the link started. Barrie and I, Rose and Stephen were agreed on the matter. In a country where there are neither communication systems nor transport, a simple task of sending messages to individuals who live in different villages, is a nightmare. At a considerable cost to his feet, Stephen volunteered to fetch the people to attend the meeting. A rough calculation would have been ten mountain miles, three days, plus endless sweat-soaked collars.

The day before my departure to England, I arrived at Ha Simone to meet the elected gathering of my first Basotho Committee - in Rose's kitchen.

Stephen, refreshed and eager to start, had finally gathered his members together under one roof. He smiled liberally as they were sworn in.

"This is a historic moment. The spirit of Christ is with us. It is a new beginning...."

As resident priests, both Stephen and Rose were elected. A remarkable lady, Evellyne Hlabi had been voted in. We had met many times. Evellyne was an energetic church secretary - efficient and skilled to take on the task of main correspondent. Theresa was a qualified nurse who worked for the Highland Water Scheme, a competent clinic medic and a very dedicated church member. The last person was a senior churchman and relative. All five representatives would vote on any issue involving the link with Datchworth. There was much excitement as they all signed their names in the new St John's Diary.

Some time later, Rose prepared to leave for the spring. She looked tired.

"I miss Emily and Bernice you know Nettie. They were my helpers. Now I must go for the water alone. I shall be glad when they return from Soweto. My boys are not so good at fetching water. Walter has his new job and Justice is away and Petros is away in the fields. Anyway - this is the Lord's work and I must do it."

"I shall think of you when I speak to my friends at home Rose, perhaps one day we will be able to save enough money to give you a well - here in the yard. We will put our hopes on it."

Her face looked lined and I knew the problems she had to cope with were manifold. Every day was another mountain to climb. Rose maintained her dignity and her pride without any loss of affection from everyone who knew her. There was no compromise.

"I want to borrow Stephen this afternoon for a couple of hours – would you mind? Barrie and I would like to plant a tree somewhere on your land – perhaps near to the church. I wondered......if Stephen came to the nursery garden place in Ficksburg this afternoon, we could choose something we like...."

"A tree? Oh that would be wonderful - I don't want to think of you and Barrie leaving us – we will find it hard......it feels as if you have always been here in Lesotho." She turned and took the empty bucket. "Yes, Stephen will go with you...and tomorrow we will have an official ceremony of planting – to mark the joining of our hands with England."

Slowly she walked across the yard, part of her wanting to sit down and rest, not balancing a heavy load on her head and walking two hundred yards over rocky ground.

The priest and I chose a 'mophead' tree. They lined every avenue in Ficksburg and I loved their swathes of tiny delicate leaves, which rippled like waves and made a rushing noise on a windy day. In maturity, my tree would grow to be the shape of half a moon, flat underneath and curved on top - wonderful for shade.

"I know the very place to plant it Stephen," I said, as we passed through St Monica, where graceful eucalyptus trees stood just off the roadside. The ten foot sapling we had bought was half lying in the back seat with its branches sticking out through the roof of the car. "Just outside the church on the ridge, where the ladies sit on the grass to feed their babies."

"Okay Nettie, wherever you wish it – only leave me a stick tonight in the ground and I will get the boys to come and dig a hole, ready for the planting. Can we do it tomorrow before you leave?"

The following day there would be just time to dash to Ha Simone to do the planting, then call at the school to collect letters from the children, to take to England. The car to take me to Johannesburg would leave at two'clock from the camp.

At Makibi's yard David had gone off in search of a spade. Stephen had borrowed a pick and between them they were seeing to a deep hole in the ground. Rose approved the chosen site. One has to be reminded that only peach trees grow near their house. With rain fall which is either torrential or non existent for weeks on end, the poor quality clay soil barely supports weakling bushes and scrub, otherwise it's a treeless landscape.

In her resolve to mark the occasion with a sense of history, Rose had invited another highly regarded lady priest, who came to the spot to pray with us. Stephen gave a short speech and said prayers while we looked down the hole. David stood to attention by his spade. The sapling was placed deep in the soil and I was asked to shovel earth on top. I now know how Her Majesty feels, although my appointment book was not as full as hers! Afterwards we all shook hands.

In years to come, the symbol of our friendship would look out over the Caledon river valley; it would witness the electric storms, the sunsets and the rainbows, it would be lashed by the winds and the rains. It would know the full moon at night that lights up the valley with silver. And *I* would know it was there.

The family said goodbye to me, this time only for three weeks. David accompanied me to the road in Walter's absence. It was a lovely feeling to know that I was coming back.

"Goodbye Mrs Annette. I will look after your tree."

At the edge of the road where Charlotte's house meets the track up to the school, a gaggle of local children were struggling with a giant-sized tin tub filled to the brim with wet clothes.They had been washing in the river. The girl in charge looked about sixteen and carried more than her own weight on her head. Noticing the deep mud along the track, I stopped the car and called out to them. The rain had been heavy recently.

" '*M'e*, you cannot go there in a car – you will drive in de swamp. Leribe Primary School cannot be reached except by foot," one of them shouted.

Suddenly, a shout reached my ears, "Teacher, Teacher – don't come! Wait, wait......Mrs Charlotte she is coming!"

A boy of perhaps nine or ten was standing at the top of the ridge waving madly. Next to him appeared Charlotte, wearing her red blanket and a scarf on her hair. In a moment she motioned for the child to squelch his way downwards, shouting words of Sesotho at him, giving out instructions for him to follow.

"Go.....go....take de boots to Mrs Annette!"

The lad shouted a reply, but it was lost in a torrent of instructions from the headmistress. A few minutes later, a small child with a smile as wide as the River Mersey, thrust a pair of wellies into my hands, hopping up and down, squealing with excitement,

"Put them on, put them on – I will take you there!"

Into my mind flashed the memory of the little lad in the story called '*Kes*' written by Barrie Hines, where the hero puts his bare feet into a wellington boot full of tadpoles which his friend has just collected. I held the boy's hand to balance myself, closed my eyes and tried not to think where my toes were going, somewhere damp and smelly, but what of it....the child was pulling my hand and together we were crossing the deep sticky mud, teetering through unforgiving tussocky grass, with the unmistakable stench of Albert's prize bull rising in our nostrils.

What a welcome I received. There were children as far as I could see, cheering me on. A white lady coming to their school was one thing – a white lady wearing a pair of old boots and crossing the bog was unprecedented! Charlotte greeted me with a bear hug.

"Come. Take off de boots '*M'e*.'"

I looked down at my feet. They were hidiously black and slimy.

"Welcome – we are pleased to see you this morning. I have de letters ready for you to take to Mrs Willett in your village of Datchworth. Tell her we are sending our best wishes. The staff are already waiting for news from your teachers."

The only male member of staff called Isaac came out to shake my hand. He laughed when he saw my feet.

"'*M'e* I have something to ask you. Will you come to Qwa Qwa with us on 11th March? It is the traditional Basotho village. We are arranging a school journey – *with food* - and you will be welcome. A driver will take us on a charabanc. Shall we count on you?"

"Yes Isaac – as long as I can sit next to you. Put me on your list."

*   *   *   *

Apart from suffering a bad dose of 'flu which everyone in England seemed to be suffering from, my plan of pitching in with the family worked miraculously well. My brood were fair to midling, our flat in Beckenham was still occupied by good tenants and the Lesotho Committee at Datchworth was up and running. Barrie and I managed to phone each other but the line was particularly rich in interruptions and chain saw noises. Standing on a piece of cardboard to keep my feet warm, on concrete floor of public phone box, in my daughter's village, was not my idea of fun. I retired indoors to sit on warm radiators, to cuddle Abigail and binge on banana sandwiches and television. Lizzie was out enjoying the company of her friends, a luxury she couldn't normally afford. The snow was falling against the window and more was forecast. My longings for Africa persisted and as I played at rattling paper games with Abigail, I dreamed of beautiful mountains and blazing sun.

My letter, which had been published in the January edition of All Saints Parish Magazine, placed the Makibis squarely before the congregation. Walter's letter was due to be published in the February edition. Mary Coleman, one of the Lesotho Committee members, took on board the task of sending the monthly epistle to Ha Simone so that they might read about themselves, something she has continued to this day. (One of Rose and Stephen's proudest moments was seeing themselves in print *and* in English.) Anne Charles and Linda Dent were busy collecting baby clothes ready to send off. Others ladies were packing up parcels of sewing materials for Rose.

At Datchworth School, more letters were handed over by the children and presents of writing materials had to be somehow squashed into my suitcase. The main school corridor was plastered with photographs and pictures from Ha Simone and the questions continued to arrive.

'Why don't the children wear any shoes? Do they watch television? What do they eat for lunch?' The one which blew me away was, 'Do they have brakes on their bikes?'

Questions like these were my reward. Datchworth pupils had stumbled upon knowlege which would live in their memories for ever. Lesotho to them would not be a blank space, it would be stored in their memory banks. Who knows, perhaps one day a grown Datchworthian might pay Lesotho a visit. Our precious classroom moments were thrilling.

The '*Socks for Ha Simone*' campaign was an unbridled success. In three days, there were enough socks in Mary's office to kit out the whole of the England sqad. These also must be squashed into the recesses of my suitcase. My friend Anne, who was due to fly out in February, was to carry the overspill.

"Can we give them football boots Miss?" asked a year six child, with a pair of designer '*Kickers*' dangling from laces around his neck.

"I wish you could. Sorry no boots or shoes. My suitcase is very small."

Prepared to risk being sent to Excess Baggage, I was allowed through SA Airways check-in desk with all my luggage, at no extra cost. Farewells to my family were easier this time. My daughter was happier – she had agreed to a 'Respite Care plan' which meant she would have a well deserved break occasionally and Social Services had granted Abigail a new wheelchair. My son was happy, working in the building trade in St Albans. He looked handsomely fit, which was probably more to do with the miles to and from work on foot, as the car had finally been relegated to the scrapyard – and as a member of a local health club.....looked suitably qualified to become a super-model in the current Brylcreem advert. They both looked forward to our return home in a couple of months. I departed safely from London Heathrow on my last flight to South Africa ....or so I thought.

In Lesotho, an enormous party had been planned for 22nd January, when President Mandela and King Letsie would officially welcome kings and princes of Southern Africa to the grand opening ceremony of Muela Dam. The first part of the Treaty between South Africa and Lesotho, drawn up in 1986, had been completed. More than two thousand people were expected to watch the international tributes, displays of dancing girls, traditional warriors and marching bands. Every nation which had been part of the project would be represented.

Not far from Muela, a site had been chosen. Heavy machinery had been used to level out an area big enough to hold the event. Several giant marquees were to be erected with raised seating for hundreds of spectators, with more marquees for the employees of LHPC and their families, where they would dine after the royal proceedings.The stadium would look onto the arena, with dam and mountains in the background. A podium was to be built, all wired for sound, where royals, senior political figures and government officials would sit. Speeches by King Letsie and President Mandela would be relayed to the crowds. If the weather was kind, it promised to be the largest jamboree ever, in this remote part of the country.

Three days before the big day, the winds blew and the marquees were swept down the mountain. The list of natural hazards, which could happen to the weather in Lesotho, happened. Purple skies crashed with thunder, lightning screamed with electric sparks and rain came down in stair rods. A hurricane blew the daylights out of the Muela preparations.

"Oh my God!" was the cry from the chief engineer just as his minions were installing tons of scaffolding, fencing, decking, ropes, sound systems, flags and royal seating arrangements, as well as a giant concrete olympic–looking dish in which would burn like the olympic-looking flame throughout the gathering.

"Never mind God...... he doesn't have to get these bleedin' tents up by tomorrow!" swore the men, angry at the hostile weather which had swept in from nowhere.

Panic erupted in the enterprise department. Appeals went out for all hands to rescue mangled tents from mouth of storm. Cranes and bulldozers, manned by a hurriedly-collected workforce of spare engineers were ordered to haul in, dig out, raise up, shackle and brace – use every device known to man, to get the show back on the road.

With an all out muscle-powered effort and a little assistance from the Almighty, 22nd January dawned bright and sunny, with a fresh breeze;

marquees re-erected, arena dried out and podium tied with flags and bunting fit for a king. Food was included on the invitation and local people rejoiced. The slogan '*Water is Life*', was printed on banners, t-shirts, uniforms and hats. Peaked caps were handed out at the entrance gate.

Crowds flocked to the stadium.Only ticket holders were allowed into the main arena. Those without tickets could sit and watch from a short distance away. The setting was magnificent. A programme had been organised to provide continuous entertainment for the whole day, including an air display of parachutists who would fall from the sky and land in front of the podium. Squadrons of school children in their many hundreds, lined up around the ground, ready and waiting to hear the loudspeaker call out their names. Military marching bands, soldiers in uniform and bare chested warriors mingled on the sidelines. A sea of umbrellas bobbed about in the crowd, as it was very hot. Altogether, the scene fitted perfectly into the description of a rainbow nation.

My husband was cajoled into being official LHPC photographer, though he had never used a roving camera before. With such an advantage he was able to access privileged positions near the royal box. King Letsie arrived wearing a suit, looking very hot. President Mandela arrived dressed casually, as is his style - looking most relaxed. The crowds went wild. Other countries sent their royal kings and ambassadors..... today the Basotho people generated a great sense of pride, having such a prestigious line-up to celebrate their historic moment.

Seats in the stadium were filled to overflowing. Every conceivable part of the project, from camp gardeners, guards, taxi drivers and cooks through to the top brass consultants, clients and government ministers were seated and ready to enjoy. Sound engineers succeeded in raising excitement levels to fever pitch, relaying disco music in heavy decibels so that it echoed against the mountains. A hundred or so young girls, dressed in blue body suits, carrying blue and green flags, ran into the arena, and with precision timing, performed a spectacular tribute.

Ranks of military uniforms marched past, saluting the king with a guard of honour. And then, as a symbol of peace, President Mandela was asked to release a hundred white pigeons. The crowds loved this. Glinting feathers, touched by the sun, flew upwards from caskets on the ground. Circling overhead, the flight headed away like tiny specks of light. Hope for the future flew with them. Joyful clapping filled the air. After that, more dancing girls, coloured dresses forming patterns on the grass. Then a pretend war performed by amazonian young men beating drums, carrying spears, and dressed in animal skins and feathers – showing off their fighting tactics. Gloriously loud, the Basotho mens' choir performed traditional songs, followed by school children singing the music of their childhood, haunting and lovely.

A group of talented artists had painted huge canvasses of the project from 1986 to 1998. A canvas for every year of the scheme was displayed on a moving carriage with wheels. Over the loudspeaker system, a commentator explained each year's achievements. Cleverly painted, the artist had depicted scenes of the mountains and the valleys, how the headwaters of the Orange River were dammed, then the building of bridges, roads, how the foundations of a each dam took shape… the tunnelling system and the reservoirs.

In full colour, the impressive canvasses, told their own story. Suddenly the crowds surged forward, eager and interested. The police had a difficult task trying to hold everyone back. One could imagine that these folk had never had the details of the Water Project explained to them and were intrigued to hear every word spoken by the commentators and see the images for themselves.They had not been present at board room meetings, nor read government documents; they may not have even been to see Katse dam for themselves. Bulk carriers of heavy machinery trucking the now famous mountain road, at forty minute intervals, day and night, summer and winter, must have represented an event of ficticious proportions. Collectively, they had witnessed tremendous changes to their landscape. How good it felt to be able to give them reasoning and knowledge, which would be passed on. The black man would know that white men helped to shape the history of his country.

President Mandela and King Letsie were on good form and joked together from the podium; their speeches referring to the fact that King Letsie was looking for a wife and there were plenty of lovely girls to choose from. Mandela - content as to be an old-fashioned romantic elder statesman, said jokingly, "Just looking."

Suddenly from an invisible aeroplane, the first parachutist appeared overhead, wearing an Irish flag on his heel, zooming towards the ground. A perfect landing at the feet of the royal guests.Within seconds, a second sky diver appeared, flying the flag of his country. Italy came next, followed by France - then each country which had taken part in the joint venture. One by one the sky divers came down, heels flying, parachutes landing like butterflies, at a prearranged dot on the ground. Tears ran down my cheeks as I watched them descend – each nation proud to have played its part in the Highland Water Scheme – part of the powerful vision that *water is life.* Cheers went up from the crowds as each flag touched the ground.

The spectacular displays finally ended with hundreds of miniature parachutes falling out of the sky carrying sweeties to the children, landing on the grass near their feet. A riot of hands reached out ready to clutch the descending goodies. Excitement boiled over. The hillsides became a mass of seething jelly babies. Soon, the tide of spectators flowed away from the arena, some singing, some swaying with happiness, some drunk with marshmallow fever.

For the remaining guests, it was time to eat. Inside the big marquee, waitresses in smart uniforms were galvanised into action. 'Operation Lunch' was provided by a team of professional caterers. Tables of ten had been arranged inside the tents. Everyone was happy, hungry and hot. Plenty of chatter kept the mood intact, while staff bustled in and out with plates; plates of vegetables only. The meat was missing. Despite the fact that protein was on the menu – a hitch had occurred and the waitresses were saying nothing. The meal ended with a distinctly Lesotho twist. Somewhere in the kitchens, one imagined that a few (hundred) dishes of roast beef and casseroled lamb had just somehow slipped under the flap of the marquee to a waiting hand and a row of empty stomachs. At the tables, 'Farewell Lesotho' conversations went something like this:

"Well I've enjoyed my time here – it's a great country."

"Where will you go next?"

"A contract in Indonesia – what about you?"

Engineers on the international scene lead nomadic lives; four or five years in one country, then on to the next. Children of international engineers feature prominently in boarding school statistics. The other system of education was good grannies. Soon Butha-Buthe camp would be like a ghost town. The English School and the French School would close. All that remained were the partings, the handshakes and the tears. Heavily laden taxis were already leaving for Johannesburg Airport.

Twelve years of high employment .....now life would change. Reservoirs would bring fishing and sailing – things new to the Basotho. Farmers would become fishermen, boats instead of horses to cross a valley....and the twenty four hour round-the-clock arc lights would disappear from the Muela mountain. The animals would not protest – but the villagers might; at a return to natural light and candlepower once more.

There was bound to be great sadness. I felt sympathy for the women who worked as nannies and maids at the three construction sites, who had looked after and cared for ex-pat children, in some cases for several years. They often become an integral part of the family. In our household, we would have to say goodbye to Betty and Oliver. I hadn't told my pupils, not yet......we still had three months. And then there were our goodbyes to the Makibis......That evening I lit a candle.

Chapter 24

Just the Beginning

On 15th February, Anne flew out from England to spend some time with us and see Lesotho. Barrie and I travelled up to the Holiday Inn at Johannesburg Airport to meet her flight and to show Walter the inside of his very first hotel. He had never been to such a posh place.

"Best bib and tucker," I had explained to him the week before. "No excuses - it'll be the bees knees."

There's no direct translation in Sesotho for bees knees, so he wasn't clear about that, but he looked terrific, dressed in a casual safari shirt and fawn trousers. In the glitzy lounge of the hotel, Barrie ordered afternoon tea like we were in Fortnum & Mason. It came on a silver tray....with doilies and a waiter.

Walter wasn't good with cream cakes. The shock of seeing gateaux and pastries filled with chocolate and fresh cream gave him an attack of digestive nerves. He just kept shaking his head.

"Walter try one - it's a cream éclair made with real eggs – its delicious."

"No Nettie, I feel sick."

"Look my lad, it's no time to be thinking of mealies, this is posh hotel food."

Barrie kicked my ankle and I had to shut up. I just wanted a photograph of Walter sitting in a leather armchair eating a cream cake! Instead I took photographs of the two of them in the foyer, surrounded by crystal chandeliers and illuminated cabinets containing Cartier watches and diamond rings. There was nothing on display for less than £500. Walter's eyes were on stalks.

Anne's flight arrived on time. With trolley loaded, smiling from ear to ear, arms up in the air and a cry of 'well darling I'm here' (Joanna Lumley style) – I knew it was going to be a fun time. On the way back from Johannesburg, we made one of those disastrous navigational miscalculations – took a short cut along a dirt road and added fifty four kilometres to our journey. For a first day in South Africa it was pretty daunting to our guest, fresh out from Luton, where buses are two every ten minutes into town.

She soon settled into Leribe camp daily routines and Africa time. Together, we visited Ha Simone, bearing gifts from Datchworth village people....letters, parcels, clothes, books and a few surprises. As we left the main road and drove the bumpy track to their house, Anne turned to look at the panorama of mountains, to which I, by now, had become accustomed.

"Don't they live in the most beautiful place! No hotels, no traffic..... and the view! What would you pay in England to have this outside your window."

Our reunion with the Makibis was just like a family Christmas. All the boys came into the yard to meet us. At seventeen plus, one didn't know whether to kiss them or shake hands – they all hugged me in turn. Walter, Augustinus, Petros, Justice, Joshua and David. Emily was still in Soweto with Grandma Violet.

"Petros you have grown taller since I left. I can't keep up with you."

"Nettie, your tree has some leaves on it….come and see."

"This is my friend Anne, of more than twenty years."

Excitement registered high on the Richter Scale - it wasn't every day a guest from England arrived. We carried the parcels into the house. There was the special candle which had been lit by a child at All Saints family service, the previous Sunday. The same light would be carried into St John's Church Ha Simone, as a symbol of friendship. I held it out to Rose, who took it and placed it on a small table.

Walter loved his new silk tie, given to me at the airport by my sister Marge. There were more spectacles from those relatives at home with too many optical extras. Datchworth ladies had sent a special gift to Rose. She was so nervous. Wearing a broad smile, Stephen sat in the chair opposite, and watched as his wife quickly untied it. Yards of dress and curtain material appeared from the crumpled paper. Pairs of scissors, reels of cotton, zips, buttons, needles, French chalk, paper patterns and yet more fabric- everything a seamstress could need.

"Now my wife, you are a queen!" said Stephen with gentleness in his voice.

Her fingers were busy and her eyes were crying. Inspired by thoughts of all the future garments she would cut out and stitch together on the new sewing machine - Rose was in heaven. She stroked the fabrics lovingly and stole a glance at Stephen, shaking her head in disbelief.

"Stephen these are for you."

I handed him a heavy package. This was a new beginning– the very first offerings from the other side of the world delivered by hand. It was hard to believe that we were being received so warmly in a house made of rocks with a tin roof, handing over personal gifts from an English village, whose spirit was fast establishing itself.

"For me also - what is this?"

Two copies of Ancient and Modern hymn books, inscribed with handwritten messages from All Saints …….words written in the church on that last morning before I left, were here on the table in front of me.

"The hymns are written *in English*," an eyebrow shot up…… "now my congregation must sing in your language."

"Wait a moment Stephen, this is the best surprise of all."

I handed him a copy of the February All Saints Parish Magazine, which Mary Coleman, the editor, had sent them. We all waited while Stephen opened it. From the page opposite Parish Council Notes and Planning Applications, he read –*'To the People of Datchworth……I am 25 years old and I was born in the village of Ha Simone…'*

Walter's mouth fell open. He decided against trying to speak.

Stephen read to the end… *'I believe this letter will reach your highest consideration, Yours faithfully, Walter Makibi.'*

We all felt close to tears. Walter, dressed in silk tie and no shirt, took hold of my hand. "All because you broke down in our village Nettie…..why was it *our* village?"

"Fate Walter…."

During the following days, the Datchworth Parish Magazine was circulated to the whole of St John's community – even if they could not read in English. It came back in tatters. Everyone wanted to know about this new thing called a 'Link'. Rose produced the map we had brought some time earlier, which itself proved to be the source of many lengthy discussions. Several onlookers had never seen a map. It might as well have been printed in Chinese. From one of the many conversations – a question arose of what English people did when someone died. I was explaining that the congregation knelt on church kneelers to pray.

"What is a kneeler?" came the reply.

"A cushion which you put on the floor before you kneel down."

Looks of total bewilderment on every face…. "For your knees!?"

The question of what happened to a dead body after the funeral was lost in favour of church cushions.

Having read the print off the All Saints Magazine on the subject of dog-walkers, one young man asked, "Mrs Annette, why do dogs must fall foul into bins of disposal ?"

This threw me. How does one explain the hygiene and health phobias in relation to dogs, parks and disposal bins to a community who live in wide open mountain spaces, where the word 'pet' has no meaning and mongrels of dubious ancestry roam the *veld*. There was no short cut. The 'Fouling of the Land Act 1996' article on the page of Parish Council Notes was the cause of an entire morning's investigation into rural England.

Most frequently asked questions:- 'why are dogs walked', 'where do they walk' and 'where will the cows walk'? The subject of 'chain-link collars' could have rumbled on for days.

Later that day, Anne and I called in at Leribe Primary School, where we were mobbed by the pupils and invited into classes to watch a lesson on hygiene and nutrition. The staff were overjoyed to see us. During playtime, three or four children had been instructed to sweep the floor with hand-made grass brooms for the visitors. With the energy of a gang of hysterical go-go dancers, the kids went all out to sweep for Lesotho and pounded the earth floor in a mamoth brush-up. In seconds, we were choking in clouds of dusty grit and grime.

"Thank you children – please stop that," boomed Charlotte's voice as she sailed in to join us. "The English ladies do not need to be so clean. Please go outside and sweep the yard."

This put a whole new meaning on the *'rota of classroom responsibilites'* listed on the wall. The gifts from England delighted the staff. It was decided that our bag of socks would be given to the *most* needy families......there weren't enough. A discerning teacher asked pupils to hand in their homework in order to receive a pen or pencil from the box sent by the Year 6 class. Letters describing computers, digital watches and video recorders, written by Datchworth children, indicated their innocent misconception of life without electricity. The Leribe Primary School equivalent was ownership of goats, sheep and cows. The learning had begun.

Anne's video camera caused a rush of mass hysteria. A legion of children stampeded outside the classrooms hoping to be on film. Beside themselves with excitement, rows of little black faces giggled and grinned. They had never had their photographs taken before. Basotho excitement sounds much the same as English excitement. There was a bit of pushing and shoving but not too much. Charlotte patrolled the edge of the crowd prodding them back like a friendly bulldog. Her smiles were radiant.

It was a day none of us would forget. White teeth and curly topknots on camera – fabulous! One didn't even notice jumpers with holes and shirts with no elbows. Bare feet were not today's issue. Laughter and smiles can only be measured in memories - to be stored.....taken out of that special compartment in that special drawer and looked at again and again.

"Annette, don't forget you must come with us to Qwa Qwa in March, Isaac is counting on you," called Charlotte as we left for home. "And we want to give a farewell celebration when you leave Lesotho. Anne, please send teachers from your country to help us. We need more teachers."

Before the date of the Leribe Primary School outing ......Anne and I would have been to Zimbabwe and back......to see elephants in the wild. That was our master plan.

Matriculation results are always big news in Leribe. In February each year, all the youngsters who attend school in the area, meet under the big tree outside the hospital to beat their chests or jump for joy. Soon the big day would come. We heard it from Augustinus. He was expecting his own results. It would be the day when he would find out if he had gained a University place. Anne and I arranged to pick him up in the Silver Fox and take him to Ficksburg to share the news with his girlfriend – whether it was good or bad.

That morning, the field outside the hospital was teeming with youngsters, as they converged on the huge eucalyptus, which for years had shared the sorrows and joys of graduation days. As I pulled onto the grass verge, Augustinus stepped out of the crowd and ran towards us. He wore a very serious expression and no smile.

"Hi Augustinus. Well? How were your results?" I called out, hardly daring to ask.

He opened the door of the car and climbed in. We both turned to look at him, ready to commiserate with his failures. His eyes were downcast.

"Well - are you going to tell us the worst?"

Suddenly, he grinned, threw up his arms and thumped the seat of the car – yelling at the top of his voice.

"Ladies - I did it! I have passed with highest grades. Look at the paper – it makes me a University grade ......I cannot believe it! The message has not gone to my brain yet! It means one day I will become a qualified architect!"

"Wow! I thought you had failed when I saw your face. Congratulations! We're taking you through the border this morning to see your girlfriend. I hope you've got your passport with you."

"Yes I have it Nettie. Anne, I have to tell you these are the excellent results."

He pushed the paper across to her. His eyes shone.

"Will you get a grant to be able to buy your books?"

"Yes, for the books and the tutors and the education – but I have to find my own accommodation and food."

Just before the border, there was a document check-in. Augustinus discovered that in his excitement he had picked up the wrong passport......it belonged to one of his friends. "Well, I'll just have to be this person today. I will have to show it and hope they don't recognise me."

This small mishap only added to the excitement. We dropped him in Ficksburg and made our way to the bank. He went off grinning from ear to ear. Nothing would spoil his happiness today. The town was busy and I left Anne shopping by herself – with rands in her purse, which she hadn't a clue how to count.

Walter and I had arranged to meet so that he might open a new bank account. Now that he had a job with a salary he needed this facility and had made some enquiries in Ficksburg. He was already waiting for me on the main street, looking slightly restless.

"I've been inside and spoken to the teller. They say I cannot open an account for myself. They say I need a sponsor, who holds an account at this branch."

"Let's go in," I said firmly.

Facing the teller at the counter inside the bank, we sat down. I received some very strange looks. Walter was asked to fill in his particulars. I soon realised the bank had a different agenda. The real reason why he was not allowed to open an account personally was that he was black.

"Yes Madam, we can open an account in your name, with yourself and Mr Makibi as joint holders."

A deposit was required.

"I will pay the deposit. Will Mr Makibi be able to sign cheques without my signature?"

I noticed the girl was tongue-tied and had slightly flushed cheeks.

"Yis – that is correct. He can put money in and take money out – on his own signature."

The voice could not have been sharper. I had ducked their bank policy and she didn't like it. Moreover, she knew they were in the wrong. The fact that Walter had a regular salary didn't seem to matter. It was more a question of the colour of his skin and did nothing to restore his feeling of self-worth. This was 1998 – four years after the ending of apartheid in South Africa.

We picked up Augustinus again at the border – with the wrong passport – but nobody was worrying about anything today. The guard did not even notice us. There were four of us in the car, not three. The boom went up and we were through.

"Walter – I will go to University! Look at my paper!"

He handed over his official exam results.

"Wow - these are the highest marks I have ever seen – in every subject. They are probably the best in your school."

Walter, extremely impressed and very complimentary to his half brother, gave Augustinus the highest praise, which was very touching. We learned later, that these marks were not only the highest grades in his school, not just the highest in the region, but Augustinus had come in the top ten students in the whole country. This result from a boy who had been separated from his parents as a child, who had not a penny to his name. His studies always came first. He read every book he could lay his hands on, continued studying – often by candlelight until late in the night. He shared school uniform with his new brothers and his bed was a lying-down space in a shared hut with no door. He ate when food came his way. Self motivation was the only remedy to his situation in life.

Lately, Augustinus had become editor of the students' magazine – copied and printed by an ancient ink banda machine, which he nursed throughout the night in a basement room somewhere, because he wanted his ideas to reach people. It was clear that this young man had qualities which would take him far.

Stephen admitted, "Yes, we are very proud of Augustinus. He will be a brilliant architect one day. We wish him success – but he has to get through the next two years at the University of Maseru on his own – it will be very hard."

Anne and I had a conversation about him later – how on earth would he live and eat and study, totally without support? It was a dilemma facing all students in Lesotho. To complete a University course, they must starve. She decided there and then to try and help him.

Chapter 25

A Day in the Life of....

There was the morning we had decided to have a poetry reading in Walter's hut. We were on our way to Ha Simone with Anne's camcorder, my cassette recorder and a large packet of Jungle Oats for good measure. The Makibi breakfast was part of the ritual. We were intent on recording African verse for posterity. Yet, considering our good intentions, spontaneous distractions were about to waylay us.

I had been waving to Albert for about a year. Every time my Silver Fox went past his thriving welding factory on my way to St John's there would be a greeting. The wave became a smile and a bow, then a yell to go in and talk to him – then a general invitation to drop in any time. Albert was the local lavatory maker. His outfit was on the main road, where you turn off the track to go to Walter's. It had brilliant prospects. The genius who invented metal boxes with seats and chimneys was the entrepreneur of the 20th century. Every mountain village had one – sometimes more than one. The sign of a well ordered household was a personal privy in one's own garden.

Albert was usually up a ladder when I passed, fixing the cute little pipes on the top. He would wave while leaning over rows of aluminium boxes as they gleamed in the sun.

"You have a visitor," he called out, having spotted my passenger, "bring her to see me."

I pulled to a halt in his open yard, covered with welding equipment and loo doors in the making. A row of men in wrong-way-round peaked caps, stopped work and came to investigate. At the sight of two white ladies in the yard, they leered closer, extinguishing blow-lamps as they did so.

"Hello ladies – welcome to Lesotho," called out the boss sanitary engineer, swinging a pair of giant bolt-croppers. He had the widest cheesiest grin.

"We are not your customers Albert, we are your admirers. How many toilets do you make this week?"

"Business is good 'M'e, we are expanding. Who is this lady with you?"

He shook hands with Anne, after first wiping his oily fingers on a piece of rag. The row of peaked caps leaned closer.

"She's my friend from England, she would like to come and take a photo of you."

"Well if she has come all the way from England, she must buy a Lesotho lavatory to take back , then the Lord will bless her."

Thoughts of Anne on a British Airways flight with a loo in her luggage filled us with giggles. But the wisdom of the eco-system suddenly struck a chord with her when she thought about it. A picture of herself with the eco-loo proprietor was always going to be a hit with the toileteers at English National Heritage sites. ....or even Royal garden parties. With a bit of good marketing - who knows?

Albert posed nicely for the camera. So did the row of peaked caps. Our visit ended with a conducted tour of tin huts, including the pride of Albert's lavatorial collection – a made-to-measure version, fully air-conditioned, for the fuller figure.

"Sorry Albert, we must go. We're late already."

We shook hands. He beamed and went back to his boltcroppers.

"Come and see me before you go back to England *'M'e.*" said Albert, winking at Anne. "Your friend is always welcome."

At Walter's hut, the drama was about to start. The narrator (Augustinus) had arrived with his latest poems. The executive director (Walter) in smart black jacket sitting in a proper chair in corner of hut - and a few children who were there to watch and listen. Rose was busy in the house, so we called out our greetings and settled down with the camera equipment. Anne sat on the new bed from where she could view the whole room. Sony micro-cassette was switched on.

I envisaged a short dedication to poetry at the beginning, then a kind of Roger McGough session, with a prayer at the end from Stephen. All was peaceful. Augustinus began to recite from memory.

"*Africa My Africa* by David Diop from Senegal."

Vocally, he qualified for a reconstruction of Richard Burton and Peter Ustinov on stage at London's National Theatre. The timbre of the Basotho voice always catches people somewhere at the back of the throat.

"Africa of proud warriors in the ancestral savannahs,
Africa of whom my grandmother sings
On the banks of the distant river
I have never known you.
But your blood flows in my veins,
Your beautiful black blood that irrigates the fields
The blood of your sweat
The sweat of your work,
The work of your slavery
The slavery of your children...."

After two verses we were emotionally hooked. Then the last line "*.....with the bitter taste of liberty."*

I felt an audience should be clapping. There was a pregnant silence one experiences at the end of a good play. After a short announcement by the director, Augustinus read one of his own poems, embracing the words, pouring them into the hot afternoon like a river of molten lava. Suddenly the spirit of Africa was there in that room. The voice unmelodramatic, yet full of passion. My spine tingled. The camera lady couldn't see through the lens for her tears.

"Lesotho the Home of Peace....the land of black nation.This land was not built for anguish and sorrow, it was built for liberty, freedom and joy. This is the home of peace, the home of joy, the home of friendship.........

.........Black man, white man, one creation..."

At the end, he stepped forward and announced, *"by Mosito Augustinus Moqhekoana,"* sounding the distinctive African 'click' in the middle of the last name.

Anne and I exchanged glances, feeling drawn into this moment, wishing we understood the depth of their clan culture. The tortured words, orchestrated into dialogue, spun around in the air then were carried away, rushing like the wind across the plain. We could never hope to understand the meaning of *'loss'* or *'betrayal'* or *'stolen heritage'* like the African. Whether we were Christians or not, we were part of a culture which had its roots in a totally different concept. Listening to the poet's verse, we could not fail to be aware of this dimension.

A little girl slid quietly into the hut. She was about five years old, pretty with a tatty white dress hanging uneven at the hem. I pulled the child onto my lap. She took hold of the fingers of my hand.

"Tell me de numbers," she whispered.

"One, two, buckle my shoe," I recited and the child listened intently, watching my lips as she tried to form the words. Her black eyes watched my every move, her chubby fingers curled as she tried to count on them, as I had shown her a few days ago. "Three four, knock at the door......" She looked up into my face .... huge eyes, hungry for adult attention. A second child came and perched on the arm of the chair, wanting to join in this game of English rhymes. A child's verse, remembered from my own children's childhood, was enough to bring me to the verge of tears; saying the familiar words here in this place, with children from a mountain village.... where white people did not usually come. I saw the pretty face and shabby white dress. Once again, I was the pupil - they the teachers.

Rose walked across the yard from the kitchen, jauntily – wearing the finished dress. She twirled in front of us and sat down on Walter's bed. The skirt billowed out around her.

"Oh Rose you look lovely. And the scarf to match"

She was obviously thrilled to have something new to wear. While we had been at our poetry, Rose's fingers had been busy. Now the garment was finished. Mainly white, with blue and red motifs, attractive against her skin - cut from a length of fabric sent by the Datchworth ladies, designed and stitched by her own hands..... a complete new outfit. Made from Ruby Jackson's kitchen curtains!

'Now my wife you are a queen,' had been Stephen's words to his wife, the day the parcels arrived. Today it was true. Rose looked pert enough to knock Julie Andrews off the convent wall.

Anne and I walked down to the river to look at the dinosaur footprints. Fred and the little girl came with us chanting their counting rhymes, running ahead of us and throwing dried cow dung at each other. Walter was explaining how much he loved his new job. The smart black jacket was a sign of improved status. He had already been invited to apply for the post of headmaster. He walked many miles every week to and from his school, sometimes not hitting his bed until late in the evening. The job was a challenge to his skills as a teacher and his energy, but he was happy. He had completely recovered from his illness. Not a vestige of depression remained.

The sun was high overhead and we should have worn hats. The ground next to the river was bone dry and our shoes were soon covered in dust. Small birds bathed in the shallows.

"Is it too hot for you?" I asked my friend who was beginning to appreciate the benefits of a souvenir suntan – Lesotho style.

"No, its lovely – by the way have you seen the group over there?"

Walter answered before I realised what Anne meant. Three youths were standing not far from us below the cliffs, one of them dressed in a skirt.

"It's a boy who has been to Initiation School. I know him. Do you want to talk to him?"

The indelicate subject of circumcision arose once again.

"Ask him if we may take his photograph Walter. We have some money....?" I suggested quickly.

"They don't usually mind."

Walter approached and spoke to the boy in Sotho, who was tall, physically fit but not feeling quite himself. He wore a red anorak, a skirt instead of trousers and a pair of black wellington boots. His own clothing would have been left in the *mophato*, which would have been set alight and burnt after his period of training, symbolically leaving his childhood behind. Round his waist hung various symbols of his new status (*makoloane*). Leaning on his stick, he grinned at Walter and nodded. The boy spoke to us, slowly and deliberately, raising his hand in acceptance of the money.

"My name is Michael. I am from a traditional initiation school. You will know I am a proud Mosotho......"

The camera clicked. He did not move and we walked on towards the flat stones. He seemed to be suspended between the cliffs and the river. In fact, he was hardly able to walk.

"This part of our tradition is hard for you to understand isn't it?" Walter asked.

"In western culture it is not acceptable - to ask people to suffer is not natural," I answered at the risk of sounding flippant. "We are in the wilderness when it comes to understanding initiation schools. What does your father believe Walter?"

"In our family we choose not to follow this tradition."

Not realising the significance of the hollows in the stones by the river where they played, Fred and his young friend danced up and down on the rocks. They knew that white people often came here and then paid them coins for looking. The remarkable five-toed fossil trackway known as the *Pentasauropus incredibilis*, discovered in the bed of the Subeng River near Leribe in 1953, was a far-reaching source of interest. The children stood beside us poking their bare toes into the footsteps of the giant creatures of the Upper Triassic period. Paul Ellenberger, an ordained Protestant minister who came to Leribe as a missionary, had discovered these fossil remains on the bend of the Subeng River. Combining his parish work with an interest in palaeontological studies, Ellenberger discovered these and other dinosaur remains at Maphutseng. Local people hereabouts know that this site attracts foreign visitors but few of them will have realized that the stones beside their river are important enough to be written down in record books, of crucial interest to scholars of the history of evolution.

Evidence of dinosaurs was first discovered in the 19th century by scientists searching for a landmark in Lesotho's palaeontological history and today we were standing at the very point where the feet of these creatures had rested three hundred million years ago. It appears that Lesotho was the first country in sub-Saharan Africa in which fossil footprints were discovered. Professor David Ambrose of the National University of Lesotho writes:

'There is little doubt that Lesotho can provide in the future as in the past, fossil material leading to discoveries of international significance. It is a challenge to Lesotho scientists to ensure that they play a significant role in this work.'

As we walked back up to the church we could hear the congregation singing 'Lead us Heavenly Father Lead us' in Sesotho. The tune was the one Anne and I recognised. The ladies in their blue and white uniforms were just coming out of the service. On Thursdays it was Ladies' Day, the time a little after three o'clock.

"Come and see the tree!" they shouted when they saw us, "it already has the leaves!"

Already our skinny sapling near the church was causing interest. It had leaned a little over to one side, but Walter had rescued it with a prop so that it would grow straight. We would be able to monitor its growth in years to come in Kodak gloss print.

Rose suddenly called from across the yard.

"Nettie can you take the ladies home tonight, it will save the taxi fare for them?"

"Yes I can. How many Rose?"

313

"Four ladies."

"My car will only take three in the back seat."

It was useless trying to explain this to Elizabeth and her three friends. Four bodies climbed into the Silver Fox. As the fourth one got in, the first one fell out. We started to laugh. We could not believe that they had not understood.The pantomime of four large ladies getting into my car has been told many times; a dinner party story of gigantic proportions!

"Elizabeth I'm afraid I can't get you all in."

"It is okay '*M'e,* we will all come home with you."

You cannot convince the Basotho that a volume of space has limits. To them, space is limitless, it just changes shape. They are used to squashing into corners.

"But look, we can't close the door!"

I might as well save my breath. Elbows, bottoms and bosoms folded themselves into a human ball and the one lady at each end hung onto a door handle. Slowly I put the engine into gear and more slowly, we laboured up the grass track which lead to the tarmac road. When we reached the dip, there was no chance we would make the upward slope.

"Two must get out please."

"Yes '*M'e.* We understand, but we will get in again at the other side."

Both doors flew open. Barrie would have had a fit if he could see me now. He would have confiscated my car for ever. Passing Albert's toilet factory on the way caused another ripple of hysterics from the squashed cargo.

"Why would you want to go and see his toilets '*M'e*? They are the same as many toilets."

"Whereabouts can I drop you in St Monica's, Elizabeth?" I questioned, once we were chugging along the main road at ox-cart speed.

"Oh it's not far. We will show you," came a muffled bleat. "My mother-in-law will be pleased to meet you and your friend from England."

Just after the Caltex Garage at Leribe crossroads, the hymns started. 'Lead us Heavenly Father Lead us' was never more appropriate. I prayed for two things - my springs and my brakes. Foot flat down on the accelerator, we were moving slightly faster than walking traffic. Only four or five kilometres before we reached their village, where by now, we had been invited for tea.

"My mother-in-law will be so pleased to meet you, she has never met English people before. And my husband will be there at home from the mines."

"What do you think they will give us?" whispered my slightly worried English guest.

"Not sure. Might be mealie or sorghum porridge. Don't worry, they'll understand if you don't like it."

"Not far now, turn right when you reach the mission." Elizabeth directed, as we crossed the river."It's up a slope when you leave the road." My heart sank. The singing had stopped. Bottoms and bags were shifting. "Three will descend here," came a voice. "You're an angel from Heaven, God will bless you."

They waltzed off up the road carrying large bags, looking pleased and not a little crumpled. Elizabeth's directions to her own house did not take into account distance or time. She pointed vaguely in the direction of the sun.

"Up there please 'M'e, a little way." The road was wide, the bumps were deep, the craters numerous. After about fifteen minutes we were still driving up and down river beds, negotiating rumps of cows with swatting tails and curly horned goats, fields of asparagus and rows of waving children. "Look 'M'e, here is my little church." There was a small mud hut. "It is where we hold our services when it is bad weather and we can't get to Ha Simone. We have three candles on the altar, like Stephen's service and sometimes the rain drips on us...... oh please stop now."

Before we were invited into Elizabeth's house, we must go and call on mother-in-law. The walk was not far. I began to realise that by African standards, 'not far' can mean 'a lot further than you think plus a bit more' On past the mealie patch, the cabbages and another field of asparagus. As we rounded the corner of a house, we were set upon by scores of children, a dog and Grandmama herself, who immediately asked us inside.

"This is where I live," she announced, with arms akimbo across large chest, not in the least fazed by two ladies from England, who had arrived out of the blue. Several children seemed to appear from the shadows. Grandma was very pleased to see us. She wore a faded yellow dress, with blanket tied round large middle, a woolly hat and a very big smile. I really liked her. She was a respected elder of the family and her attitude to God was that he was an okay bloke. When you see what they do not have inside a house with mud floors, it is so very humbling. Anne and I must please stay and watch traditional dancing.

The highest compliment a lady can offer another lady is a seat – usually wobbly and usually plastic, but it's always in the front row. For some reason this made me like Grandma even more. A young woman who may have been a daughter-in-law came to join us. Her albino child was slung on her hip - its arm encased in plaster-of-Paris. The baby's curly locks were blond and the skin was pink, yet the features were African. Curiosity consumed me, but questions seemed rude.

A gaggle of excited children realised they had an audience of two. Music was improvised by an upside-down plastic bucket placed on the ground. As soon as the beat started, hopping skipping feet turned the bare red earth into a dance floor, arms flying, bottoms wriggling, colourful skirts making patterns against the blue sky. Despite the fact that Grandma's upper body lacked a little underpinning, she grinned toothlessly, slapped her thighs and danced. Elizabeth and the other women sang and clapped.

I was constantly amazed by the grace and courtesy of local people, their wonderful manners and the desire to please. They have nothing to offer but their hospitality. No glasses of alcohol, no party plates....no table decorations, no cups of tea and no entrance ticket. Our appreciation in claps was no match for their talent. The sheer energy and legwork of the children, grandma and daughter-in-law (*with* sucking baby on breast) as well as their singing, was a memorable party.

Our adventure was not yet over. Returning to Elizabeth's house, we were offered a meal of sorghum porridge and fresh peaches, washed down with Coca Cola (no tea) a tour of their three-roomed house with breeze block walls and an introduction to the neighbours.

Recently home from the gold mines, her husband Solomon, made us welcome. He was dressed casual smart with heavy chain necklace. He was worldly and confident. His knowledge of England showed he was well travelled and well informed. Solomon would not have been out of place at an international travel desk. There was nothing parochial about this man. He knew what to say and he knew how to say it. The final surprise was when he sent one of the girls to bring a present for us to take home. The gift of a live chicken was a great compliment.

"*Tsamaea hantle 'M'e,* take the chicken for your husband. He will like..." began Solomon interrupted by loud squawk from inside cardboard box..

Thoughts of my navigator holding onto a hen while I manoeuvred up and down the steep sides of a dry river bed was too much.

"Thank you again Solomon, but I'm afraid we can't."

Much shrieking and laughter. The ladies thought this hilarious. Why did we not want a good meal and why could we not put Henny Penny on the back seat. True to Basotho gatherings, the farewell was a noisy affair.....ululating ladies and clapping children, not to mention the odd cluck from the cardboard box.

It was almost six o'clock and in Lesotho, all large four legged animals were on the move, prodded forward by skinny boys with sticks, hungry for their supper. At the place where we had come across the dry river bed earlier, a constant flow of frisky cows was lolloping home along the grassy bottom. It was almost a stampede at this time of the evening. The chances of the car making the steep bank opposite were slim, unless I took a run at it without a passenger. Anne must get out and walk across.

"Wait until there's a good long gap between them. Right - now run!"

"Okay – wait for me on the other side," she yelled loudly, "I'll choose my time."

The sun was a red ball in a wide red sky. I revved hard and zoomed off, leaving my friend standing on the upper slopes of a river valley, faced by herds of oncoming trotting cows...bulls?

After her leap between flicking tails, curly horns and buzzing flies, Anne shot back inside the car. We coasted back to the main road, counting our heat bumps. I was bitten in tandem as usual, every insect for miles around knew my Grade II listed blood supply. Praise be for Calamine Lotion. There was rather a lot of legless laughter on the way home, as my friend and I re-lived our walkabout at Ha Mathata village.

"We should have accepted the chicken, we could have given it to Thabo, he would have been pleased."

Back in the camp, Barrie had arrived home early from work and was already starting the supper. As we walked in the house a voice called out, "have you had a good day girls....by the way, thought we'd have chicken tonight."

Chapter 26

Zimbabwe Journey

Zimbabwe - the land of spectacular waterfalls, mountains, wild animals, colourful birds and baobab trees; the Great Zimbabwe Ruins, Chinhoyi Caves, Victoria Falls and Lake Kariba. Barrie and I felt we couldn't leave Africa without experiencing this country for ourselves. It would be a dream come true; elephant and zebra drinking from a water hole, an overnight sail on the Kariba, sight of the Great Zambezi River – to stand in a rainbow over the thunderous Victoria Falls where Dr David Livingstone stood in 1855, to visit Bulawayo, Hwange National Park..... we made up our minds to drive Zimbabwe in two weeks.

The planning was meticulous. Not a sqeak from our tuned-up vehicle with air-conditioning and just enough space for three people's luggage. Anne was coming with us. After several days of preparing documents, completing health checks and organising triple mosquito protection, we were ready. The local Chief of Police came to inspect our vehicle. We left Lesotho on February 26th. It would be the end of the rainy season and although Zimbabwe was in the tropics, daytime temperatures would be moderate. At night it would be cool. The condition of the roads was generally good, but we would take repair kits for all eventualities.

It was a 960 kilometres (six hundred miles) from Lesotho to the Zimbabwe Border and the plan was to go through Beitbridge early morning, which meant a one night stopover with Priscilla, at her farm near Pretoria and another night in Messina, South Africa's Northern Province. Beitbridge is the main port of entry into Zimbabwe, spanning the Limpopo River.

Approaching the driveway to Ilana Lodge near Messina, we saw our first Daddy Warthog, Mummy Warthog and three babies. They appeared in front of us having run out of the *bushveld*. It was so exciting.

I stopped at a roadside phone and rang my daughter – couldn't believe that the phones were so efficient (after Lesotho) to tell her we were leaving Africa on 29th March. Spoke to Abigail and she blew kisses from home....it was magic.

Silhouettes of acacia trees against the red sky looked awesome as we arrived at Ilana chalet site. That evening we cooked our own supper and Barrie collapsed with tiredness after a glass of gin and tonic and had to be poured into bed. He had driven 480 kilometres in one day.

The lodge was owned by an elderly white man with no legs, who was changing the engine on his Landrover when we arrived. From his wheelchair he could reach into his car engine with tools and take it all to bits. His house was beautiful – full of antique paintings and old victorian furniture, the garden full of mopane trees, mahogany trees and lemon trees – and one huge wonderful baobab tree, hundreds of years old. When we asked about troubles in Zimbabwe, he shrugged his shoulders.

"There are troubles all over the world. Zimbabwe is no different. Don't stay around Harare too long – otherwise just go and enjoy yourself. It's a beautiful country."

By seven o'clock we were at Beitbridge Passport Control on the South Africa side. It was already too hot. We were invited to park between two high-sided vehicles. Gangs of youths soon made themselves known to us. They offered to get us through the control office in quick time, for a small return. Their tireless attempts to become master criminals were obvious when we saw them reaching into the car to grab our passports. In hindsight, we should have been more careful, so moved our parking bay very quickly.

The place was bursting with bona fide tourists. My track record of queuing at Sainsburys is appalling, so Barrie chose the lane. It was the last control point at the end of the hallway, with an official who seemed to be working extremely efficiently and his queue looked about half an hour long. After forty five minutes and only another five passengers to go through, he closed his position down to go and have breakfast. The cornflake bell must have rung because several queues fell into disarray, while everyone tried to regroup.....displaying not quite road rage, but certainly queue rage. The sweat from my hands had formed a greasy smear across my plastic folder and my pen refused to write in the heat.

We had just married but I wasn't going to admit to my new surname, nor change my passport until I reached England, so I was having to remain single for the sake of immigration. Just before we got to the head of the queue I forgot who I was and blurted out my new name. Anne was busy taking her camera to bits as you have to give all serial numbers of hand luggage on your form and Barrie had taken the precaution of insuring the company car to the hilt – which seemed to cause a whole row of penalties and made us wish we hadn't bothered. The whole affair was tense and unfriendly.

The last expressionless official wanted to know how much money we had, just in case we didn't have enough to support ourselves while we were there. Opening my purse and handbag in front of a queue of people and throwing my cash, plus travellers cheques onto the counter was very disconcerting. There was no honesty box on the official form so that you could write in the amount. Only seeing is believing in Zimbabwe. Maybe I'm a prude, but there must be a nicer way.

"Have you any more money?" the man asked directly as I laid my fortune bare for all to see.

What he meant was had I got any stashed away in my knickers? I wanted to say that British women have finally discarded navy blue bloomers, once the only proper preparation for being run over by a bus. But I didn't.

"No, that is all I have and my credit card."

"Fine. What is your address while you are in Zimbabwe?"

The questions went on ad infinitum. We just wanted to get out of that building and on the road. It had taken us almost three hours to go through.

After passing through Customs and Immigration, you are not allowed to dally across the murky brown waters of the Limpopo. Your vehicle must keep moving. First they don't want to accept you and then they can't wait to get rid of you. The new bridge, built in 1929, is almost 500 metres long and on the other side is a vast expanse of *bushveld* where wild game is prolific. The bridge was nicely decorated with rows of razor wire - to stop you jumping overboard into the crocodiles......it has been known! After achieving passage through the border officials, even they seemed friendly.

The Limpopo - another reminder of my school days! I could remember standing up to recite a line of Kipling in front of my English class, about the age of twelve...... '*The banks of the great grey-green greasy Limpopo River, all set about with fever trees.*' Now I was seeing it for myself. My excitement level rose several notches.

We were now heading for the great Zimbabwe National Monument at Masvingo. Great Zimbabwe is the ruined remains of an ancient city and the capital of a large empire controlled by several Shona dynasties.

After many miles of unpeopled roads through the bush, we stopped for petrol about midday and spoke to Jeremiah, the friendly garage owner, who wished us well and gave us fair exchange for our money in Zim Dollars. He gave us directions ahead, to a reserve full of baobab trees.

Through Lutumba, Chimolo, Bubi, Rutenga then to Ngundu on long straight roads - passing through Shona villages of thatched rondavels built in family units, donkeys and cows tethered nearby with their carts. The heat-red earth between the huts seemed to be polished under the glare of the sun. Everyone sleeps at midday under cool thatch or slouches on the back of a donkey between the trees. Pretty white goats with brown patches moved in small herds through the terra cotta landscape and at times, you could imagine you were in Italy without the geraniums. No boundary fences, no signs saying 'keep out' just rolling hills flecked with wild flowers, stone monuments and those peaceful cattle with humps, standing four square on the horizon, looking well fed and watered. The foliage looked ravishingly green and healthy after recent good rains

We stopped for a break, some eighty kilometres from Msvingo at a roadside stall owned by a very handsome fellow who was lazing under his straw thatch. Strong poles supported the roof of the long low shelter and immediately behind grew thick bush. It didn't cross my mind until later that replicas of the animals on sale, could be living and breathing only a few feet away!

Zimbabweans are excellent craftsmen.Their carvings are superb and tourists were few along this stretch of road. The carver, whose name we

320

learned was Charles Zendera, surrounded by dozens of soapstone and wooden hippos, giraffes and eagles, greeted us pleasantly. Alarmingly good-looking in a kind of Tarzanian way, with bare feet and tousled hair, he recognised a good audience when he had one. We browsed for long enough in the intense heat. Charles had always wanted to come to England. (how often had we heard that) He said he was a teacher at Zifunzi Secondary School and was trying to sell his animals to pay for his studies. Anne and I were just wondering how we could send him a cheque for his flight from Victoria Falls to Heathrow, when Barrie stepped in.

"Don't even think about it...and I don't want a four foot giraffe in the back seat for the next two weeks. Come on girls we've got to move."

Everyone had told us if we don't see anything else in Zimbabwe, we must include the Great Zimbabwe Ruins in our itinerary. The word Zimbabwe has its plural in *madzimbabwe* which comes from the Shona words *dzimba dza mabwe* which means 'house of stone'. On the second day we were on our way to find The Iron Age site, Zimbabwe's most famous National Monument.

The Great Enclosure has evolved over many years, establishing that it was at one time a huge walled city which housed up to twenty thousand people. It provides evidence that ancient Africa reached a level of civilisation not suspected by earlier scholars. This may have been the Capital which dominated a realm which stretched across Eastern Zimbabwe and into Botswana, Mozambique and South Africa.

The lichen-grey walls, up to nineteen feet thick, are built of granite blocks without the use of mortar. Almost a million granite blocks were used in its construction. The amazing straight-sided stones like God's own bricks - almost identical in size - were actually discovered in the Valley of Granite several miles to the south. The bricks were a pure natural product of the earth and were brought one by one, over many years, by travellers who came this way from all points of the compass. In those days the King decreed that no traveller should pass this way without lugging two or three blocks in addition to his own load, to the great city. They were not machine crafted or fashioned by tools, they had been perfectly formed by nature herself - to be used in the construction of the Great City of Zimbabwe, now regarded as the earliest and largest single ancient structure in sub-Saharan Africa.

We saw the ancient curved walls of the elliptical Great Enclosure, which formed towers, corridors, domes, passages with narrow entrances – a large complex, which entirely covered the side of a hill. The largest hill enclosure was the Western Enclosure with a main perimeter wall of twenty six feet high and sixteen feet thick, all made with God's bricks placed there seven centuries ago. A thirty three foot high conical tower, a solid and apparently ceremonial structure, probably has a phallic significance.

The site has been the subject of extensive archaeological research. Recent excavations since the 1960s has suggested that the dates range from 13th to the early part of 15th centuries and it represents the spiritual and religious headquarters of the Shona dynasties, and that its structure is unique to this part of Africa. It was fully occupied for living and trading for approximately three hundred years, which is not long in the history of a civilisation. Therefore the question remains - what was the cause of its decline?

In this part of Africa, gold and ivory trading had formed part of its story of wealth. Treasures were brought from the Far East, Asia, India and China – the best there was in the world, to trade with the Great King of Zimbabwe - yet it seems that the professional history gatherers cannot agree on the original purpose of this establishment.

Nonetheless, for us it proved a fascinating walk between silent maze-like passages where centuries of suns had risen and set - between narrow stone corridors open to the rain and wind - imagining the lives of the people who lived here centuries ago. We found ourselves being easily drawn into the mysteries of this awesome place. Suddenly, to our utter astonishment, we heard singing. It was the sound of many voices – humming in chorus, too real to be ignored. We stared at one another.

"Listen - there are people here...."

Silence. Then it started again. This time not far away, in fact at the other side of the wall where we stood. It continued - quite lovely - echoing along the ancient hollow ruins. Anne and I discreetly tried to look through a gap in the stones and as our heads appeared, realised we were being watched by hundreds of people. We must have been a strange sight to them; two pale faces peeping through a hole

A gathering of women dressed all in white, seated in a kind of amphitheatre – stretched as far as the eye could see; men in uniforms with braids, ribbons and decorations, each displaying a wide cross sash. As we stood there, hundreds of black faces grinned – spreading along the rows until the white teeth became one huge smile. At the last few chords of music, two men left the group and walked over. They shook our hands and greeted us in English. The splash of red across their khaki uniforms were embroidered with large letters GPJ and each man and boy was wearing one. All the young boys had shaved heads.

"My name is Blessings. Welcome to our ceremony," said one man in a booming voice. He was huge in size and wore shorts and long socks, like a venture scout. His face crinkled into a dazzling smile.

"Our special service takes place on the anniversary of the day when our Prophet had a vision. We return to Great Zimbabwe every year. Please come and join us."

A bible was brought for us to read, written in Shona. Soon Blessings was pointing to the pages of the gospel and began translating the words. The ladies came with their little girls, beautifully dressed in pure white dresses – stunning against their blackness. Brown eyes, stared. We must have looked like intruders, caught in the act.

The crowds began drifting away from the amphitheatre. Anne and I were left feeling as though we had been part of a stage drama. My husband had fled. How he disliked being part of a large crowd, especially where religion was involved. We found him at the exit, leaning against a wall, laughing to himself.

"I knew you'd get involved…."

At the top of a long hill, a compound of conical Shona huts showed against the sky. A small group of entertainers were waiting for someone to entertain. A drum beat throbbed invitingly. A few dancers swayed to the beat, wearing animal skin skirts and calabashes filled with seeds, strapped to their feet and ankles, to add to the rhythm. A guy on a drum gave out a continuous hypnotic beat as he sat on the ground.

Before I left South Africa a friend had told me about Shona dancing, and it appeared this was what she meant. Anne was busy recording for posterity, so the following incident was crucial evidence that I had not wasted a moment in taking part in their culture. It would also prove beyond a doubt to my kids, that their mother had lost her marbles. I don't know what possessed me.

Picking up a bundle of firewood which was lying on the ground, I lifted it onto my head and started dancing towards the group of entertainers. Barrie, fearing the worst, was trying to keep a low profile in the background pretending he wasn't with me.

The t-shirt of the drummer was plainer to me now. It read *'Drugs and Alcohol can make you lose control'* – a riveting message for the fainthearted. It was obvious by his boyish flirtations that he was a crusader of peace and a carefree philanderer in his more lucid moments.

I fondly assumed he didn't mind me joining in. Encouraged by an extra member of the chorus, the Shona ladies took up their pots which they placed on their heads and launched seriously into the barefoot line-dancing, crocodile tails swinging around their legs. My sticks were thrown to the ground. The next moment, someone was attaching a rope to my knees fastening a set of marimbas to each of my legs. Lashed with ropes, I was then dressed with bits of the same crocodile and tied into it by way of a cow hide belt. Barrie was creased double with laughter and Anne was panning on full batteries in case she missed any of the live performance.

Energetically, the ladies pitched into their 'Happy Hour' routine and handed me a spear for good measure. The footwork was simple and my feet followed theirs.

"We're moving Mama….keep the rhythm Mama….."

It was hot - so hot - and we were all sweating……another roll of drums and a witch doctor character, dressed in cowtail headgear and frondy earrings, appeared from a hut nearby shouting loudly and gesticulating with a spear of his own. Nothing could stop me now. The guy with the t-shirt was pounding with glee and there was obviously a climax coming up. The friendly witch doctor took a flying leap and landed in front of me. Whistling and wailing, the girls encouraged me to leap also. Not the best high-jumper in my athletics team, I managed a sideways leap onto his foot. He winced to alleviate the symptons of a steamroller landing on his toe, laughed uproariously and came back for more. The ground shook. The sun beat down. My husband was now rolling on the ground some distance away, unable to believe his eyes.

Lest we both became casualties, the witchdoctor and I stopped war-dancing and with relief, he put down his spear and shook my hand. The drum beat ceased and everyone started to clap.

"Thank you lady, it was an honour to know you."

Post euphoric, I was able to thank him for teaching me part of his tradition which I could take with me to England. What fazed me completely was when he spoke English with the ease of an Oxford scholar. If only to prove that the incident really happened I bought a set of African marimbas to take home.

That night we slept in another beautiful lodge on the edge of the *bushveld*. Greeted by a lovely lady called Sue who introduced us to her peacocks on the lawn outside, before bringing in the most appetizing supper with lashings of wine and coffee. After catching sight of my insect bites, she regailed us with stories of mosquito-eating spiders which lived in her roof. Barrie wanted to trap one and take it home with us.

In conversation after dinner, she reported that things were getting more than a little tense in Harare and she was thinking of emigrating to another country, even though her family had lived there for more than fifty years. She wanted to know about England. Her family had lived through the Bush War; the fearful journeys taking their children to school with guns beside them on car seats.

"Why do you want to leave? This is such a beautiful country. Your children were born here – how can you leave?"

"I have always said that if ever there were food riots again, I would go. That is a sure sign that things will get worse. Recent maize prices are incredible. Agriculture is becoming a tool to whip us with. We're in for a tough time ahead, our services are awful and our money goes nowhere. Our children - well it's their home – they have not known anything else. They will stay no matter how bad it is."

After watching a display of finery on the lawn by a pair of colourful hoopoe birds, we said our reluctant uneasy farewells to Sue. On instruction, we drove straight though Harare without stopping, noticing empty streets and piles of litter, that was all.

Distances were a rolling sea of euphorbias, thorn bushes and bright birds fluttering into view, especially near waterholes. Monkeys with long tails screeched our approach from high branches while springbok stood like brown and yellow totems, marking the way. The road surfaces were excellent and with no other traffic, we thundered along at a good speed with air conditioning full on.

Beyond Harare, we came upon tiny villages with neat tidy compounds, their huts beautifully crafted with thatch. Children sat on the ground in groups, beaded women with their cooking pots smiled, men worked at their carving. Cows and goats grazed on fertile soil with healthy maize patch nearby. We all agreed that bush-village lives without water laid on, without Sainsburys round the corner, would knock us for six. We three alien city-bred tourists, ignorant when it came to survival in the bush, flattered ourselves that the cellphone-and-plastic-card syndrome was the right way to live though enjoyed seeing the real Zimbabwe. Rarely does one have to make the mental jump between such diversities. Would they choose our kind of life, even if they could?

I would love to have known more about the children. What kind of games did they play? Did they know what a jigsaw was or how to play with Lego? Did the girls knit or play hopscotch or cats cradle? The little ones sitting barefoot in the dirt, probably discovered earth worms and spiders long before English toddlers who slept inside prams under persil-washed blankets. Did goat's milk taste nice on maize breakfast? My children lived on Weetabix and marmite sandwiches for five years and survived. Perhaps the equivalent here was sugar cane dipped in mashed banana with mango syrup. And then again, how does a mother give birth? Is the baby born in a hut.... what if it's a difficult labour? As mile upon mile swished by, each new question burned a place in my thoughts until at last we came to the place of the baobab trees.

African legend has it that in a light hearted moment the gods planted the baobab tree upside down The mighty trunk looks more like the root of a tree, several feet across with stick-like ends on the branches. Its bizarre shape is more important to the natural kingdom than we think. The fibrous bark enables it to store plenty of water and can be chewed by animals in a drought. We discovered one with a hole down the middle, which housed a hive of weaver birds – the untidy sort who don't pay attention to the neat shape of their nest and drop sticks all over the place. The baobab, home to other birds such as hornbills and barbets, can be redeployed again and again by different families. It resembles a block of flats where the tenants are constantly changing. Snakes sometimes move in, with lizards or bees, so we didn't investigate too closely.

A small boy came to share our picnic and accepted fruit cake and crisps with a polite bow; a bold figure by the side of the road, watching our car pull away while waving the unopened packet of crisps.

No degree of attitude towards tourists was obvious. We stopped to buy petrol and fruit and they were courteous, yet suspicious. Smiles only came after you paid - not before.

'*Tatenda*' we had learned to say. They were okay with that. It meant thank you. They stared at the car with South African number plates and smiled some more. We gave dollar tips and they waved.

At   petrol stops, refrigerators provided by Coca Cola meant you drank plenty of it. A fridge makes or breaks a business. The space inside is rentable. White people appearing on the forecourt always caused a stir. First they looked at us with half friendly, half nervous smiles. Then the trading ladies would appear; intelligent handsome women with easy smiles, with none of the imploring pavement-level desperation. Beautiful well fed children with dimples in their cheeks. Crochet bedspreads, quality cotton garments decorated with colourful stitching, shawls and scarves hung with bright beads, fell from their hand woven baskets. Bartering in zim dollars was easy for us – and good fun.

One girl brought me a monkey paw for twenty dollars. I paid, then took one look at it and decided I couldn't hold a dead monkey's hand. She smiled and held it to her cheek.

Approaching Chinhoyi National Park, one immediately senses an aura of mystery. We had been told there was a deep water lake, known as the 'Sleeping Pool' in a labyrinth of underground caverns, known as the 'Blue Caves'. Inhabitants used to take refuge from marauding tribes, and it is said that human sacrifices used to be thrown in. No one really knows how deep it is.

After signing in at the Parks Board, we were invited to see the lake, which was at the bottom of a sinkhole .....similar to a pothole. A guide explained that we would see water of such a deep blue, but we must not go too near the edge.

"In the 19thCentury the tribes who fought against each other threw the bodies of their enemies into this cave and their bones still lie at the bottom of the pool. Local people say the walls of the cave have a powerful spiritual presence."

A nod and a wink from the guide and we were caught up in the excitement. It was a steep drop and the steps were narrow. Graceful maidenhair ferns and moonwort covered the rocks. Moisture dripped from mossy walls. The hidden lights made everything glisten and shine like a scene from fairyland. Anne took a moving film of our descent. The intense colour of the pool when we eventually reached the bottom was the most magnificent sight – a sort of mouldy penny colour. The reflections threw a greeny blue light all around us. Standing at the edge of the lake - not a ripple or a murmur broke its surface. Nothing moved. Only bats which dived around our heads, disappearing into crevasses up high.

"You can imagine people hiding down here, can't you," I whispered, feeling as if I daren't speak out loud.

"…and being dropped into the pool, never to be seen again."

"Oh don't ," said Anne, zooming the lens onto the water.

Barrie's owl impersonations echoed eerily round the chamber.

"Legend has it that tourists regularly disappear...."

"If you say bad things down here, you will disappear. It says so in the guide book. Listen."

'Many bones lie fathoms deep in these waters. It is thought to be part of a bigger underground waterway but has never been fully explored as the dangers are too great for divers. It is rumoured that if anyone says anything evil in the caves, the person will simply disappear or wither and die.'

"Ugh....it feels creepy, let's go back up."

It was refreshing to be above ground once more. We followed a tall lady in a magnificent African kaftan dress along a walkway, leading to a stall which sold handmade goods to tourists. Carved bowls of local hardwood - polished and finished; jade jewellery and other trinkets for excellent prices; walking sticks incorporating traditional symbols of their culture like totem poles. Anne and I were good tourists. We both bought souvenirs to take home. Barrie was still following the African dress.....

Our next stopover was Kariba-upon-Zambezi, 150 miles north of Chinhoyi.We filled up water bottles and set off. It was extremely hot and the air conditioning was having to work hard to stay cool. Our well packed suitcases had fallen into that untidy stage, where nothing was where we thought it was. Barrie couldn't find his sunglasses and my feet refused to slide into any of the shoes I had with me. You would have thought we had shares in Elastoplast judging by the state of our blisters. A jungle of dead insects had chosen our windscreen to die on and nobody could remember where the clean kitchen roll was – in actual fact, this was day one of heat-stroke entering the brain. A few more days of this and total amnesia would surely follow.

Our wheels sliced through the red dust and Anne and I drifted into semi sleep.

"I must admit I'm a bit disappointed," commented our driver after a particularly lonely stretch, with only miles of empty bush for company.

"Why, what's the matter?"

"No lions, no elephants, no giraffes. Where is everybody?"

"Barrie, most sensible animals are asleep! Only mad dogs and Englishmen ...." we replied drowsily from the rear seat.

"Anyway Annette would panic if a real elephant turned the corner," joked my friend.

"Look at that!" I shrieked, pointing a finger to a large notice nailed to a tree. 'This is dangerous country. Wild animals. Do not get out of the car' .

I sat up. Panic gripped me. I wasn't sleepy any more.

"What if we break down? What if we have to spend the night here...?"

Far from reducing my fear of large animals, a rhino incident at Hluhluwe Reserve last year in Qwa Zulu Natal had made matters worse. A rhino and I had shared the same bit of bush – me on foot. He was far too big for my liking and I had decided there and then that wildlife spotting was not my favourite thing! My eyes stayed open all the way to the Caribbea Bay Hotel – just in case. I was quietly terrified. If a pride of lions crossed the road in front of us this very minute, I would have needed smelling salts. We pressed on and the acacia trees thinned out as we approached the beautiful inland waterways meandering through the forests along the banks of Lake Kariba.

The hotel was divinely air-conditioned; a rather North African complex of impersonal corridors and archways. The rooms were huge with potted palms – and big beds. We swam at eleven o'clock, then fell into bed. I was so tired I never found Barrie! Noise from the Casino went on unabated through the night.

The smell of coffee woke us. The temperature was bearable and breakfast was a feast. Stepping outside into the carpark was like falling into a sauna. After the sun-cream application on all exposed parts, we made our way to the pick-up point to board the overnight ferry from Kariba Harbour to Victoria Falls.

It was a pretty morning. Reflections of houseboats with white deck rails, bobbing up and down on prisms of sunlight at the edge of the lake, made an attractive scene. Some were equipped with a glass swimming cages underneath, where tourists might cool down and view the passing tigerfish. Rent-a-boat holidays were flourishing.

We joined a queue. The smell of the river, the steamy heat which lifted from the creek, the colourful crowd waiting for the ferry boat, children and wide-hipped Shona women in bright dresses balancing baskets on their heads, jostled together. You couldn't tell which were passengers and which were crew. Aromas of tobacco, mangos, ripe bananas and perspiration filled the air.

Our small steamer held about fifty passengers. The uniformed captain stood on the quayside making the acquaintance of his newly arrived travellers. He read out our names in a dialect so foreign that at first we didn't recognise ourselves. His white peaked cap nodded as he welcomed us aboard. "This will be your bed and your seat for the journey. Sleep on the upper deck if you wish. You may use the showers day or night. Drinks are available round the clock and you can pay your bill when you disembark. If you don't pay, we throw you to the crocodiles."

Cars were loaded into the hold and passengers decanted into the main lounge which boasted a bar at one end. Descending onto the lower deck, everyone was allocated a chaise-longue with pillows/cushions. On the bar was a notice which said: 'Passengers are invited to take a swim off the boat once we reach the centre of the lake. A safe swim will be enjoyed by all. We have never lost a passenger yet! Please sign your name.on the list.'

My husband (unknown to me) signed up. Age is no guide to good common sense. The only breeze was up on deck. Our journey across Lake Kariba would take twenty two hours. This was the perfect invitation to relax. For Barrie it was a relief not to sit behind the wheel of a car. Happily, we celebrated our arrival on board with ice-cold rock shandies and prawn sandwiches. This journey was a totally new experience for us all and we must have looked like three excited children going on a picnic. We hung over the deck rail and stared across the calm waters of one of the world's largest dams, convinced that the old man of the river would be showing his scaly head above the water at any moment. Apparently these creatures don't live in deep water, their playground is in the shallows around the edge of the lake – all thirty thousand of them.

Kariba Dam was constructed between 1955-59 along the border between Zambia and Zimbabwe. An unprecedented flood in 1957, thought to be the work of Nyaminyami, the serpent river god, stormed down the gorge and washed away the foundations of the coffer dam and the newly constructed pontoon bridge, built by the Italian engineers appointed to do the work. Some groups of people living along the banks still opted to stay, even though rising water had carried off hundreds of their homes. Villages and forests turned into swamps and many people died. The building of the dam continued.

The enforced resettlement of fifty-seven thousand people and six thousand large animals along the reservoir basin became an agonising dispute for many years. In 1960-61 'Operation Noah' captured and removed animals threatened by the lake's rising waters. It was one of the biggest wildlife rescue missions since the Ark; a feat of both engineering and human endeavor.

In December1958 the scheme to produce hydro-electricity to both Zimbabwe and Zambia was officially opened by the Queen Mother. The final construction was disrupted until 1977, due largely to political problems in the two governments, exacerbated by the huge problems concerning the peace-loving Tonga people, whose homes were lost along both sides of the Zambezi. The resettlement problems of the riverside tribes were enormous.

A number of species of animals and birds have benefited by the new reservoir with a boom in fish life (forty two identified species at the present time). Mammals were initially released to the nearest shore, but later many were relocated to other areas. The disruption of wildlife has led to the creation of large sanctuaries, which over the years has created tourism; hence the flourishing ferry boat service allowing us the opportunity to make this crossing up to Victoria Falls which was the highlight of our trip.

Not long after leaving port, someone shouted, 'elephants on shore,' and sure enough by the edge of the lake, female elephants with their young were coming to drink. This was my first sight since I had been in Africa, of elephants in the wild. Somehow I couldn't believe they were real. Through binoculars we could see them meandering down to the shallows. There is no instrument dedicated to measuring pure thrill. The appeal to see more was very strong. Soon my eyes became accustomed to their gentle ambling shapes along the shore. The distance between us was appropriately desirable.

Life on board ship was comfortable enough. We fell into conversation with interesting strangers, two of whom were originally from Croydon - the buzz-town that everyone in the south of England loves to hate (how strange to be talking about it in the middle of Lake Kariba).Their families had migrated to Rhodesia in post-war years, looking forward to a better life. The new promised land of white Rhodesia, the British settler state north of the Limpopo, was then regarded as the envy of the world.

Their story followed well known landmarks. The mess that was U.D.I., then seven years of guerrilla warfare and the repugnant aftermath of killings between black tribes. Independence and the hope of peace with the new regime. Southern Rhodesia, the last of the British colonies in Africa to gain independence, the elections bringing in Mugabe, a hero for a brief spell. Times changed....the worsening economy, lack of jobs and lack of money until people wanted to escape the downward spiral. The exodus of white trades and professions to South Africa known as the 'chicken run' began. It was an obvious way out for thousands of families until the laws prevented them from taking their fortunes with them.

"None of us knows where to go from here," said one passenger, "it's the most difficult decision of our lives....we've been through so much....and it's our home."

The temperature on board was forty degrees with a slight breeze. The only requirements - armchairs, bottles of sunblock and long-stemmed glasses filled with ice and something. The waiter became a plate-laden blur through sun cream and moisture dripping from one's forehead.. An announcement from the captain came about two o'clock. Those who had signed up for the mid-lake swim were invited down to the engine room, post haste. Picking up swimming shorts and goggles, Barrie confessed to his secret desire to dive off the back of the boat and disappeared below, along with several other nervous volunteers. I was alarmed but it was not for me to persuade him otherwise.

Others travellers shared our deckspace. The individual recliners were superb and could be moved around the boat. The only decision one had to make was what to drink and which way to point the binoculars. Fragments of conversation floated by as snooze after snooze elapsed. A distraction came to my ears. The ready-to-leap passengers had returned to the upper deck. Apparently, the adventure had been cancelled due to the late start of our trip and not enough time to stop engines before reaching our destination. Smiling to himself, my other half returned to horizontal deck-chair mode – having lost neither limb nor reputation.

Later we watched the glorious sunset. An apron of luminous purple cloud, tinged with soft yellow, lay over the dazzling rays of the setting sun Every few minutes the patterns changed. Earth and sky melted into ribbons of light.

For two hours, diaphanous formations came and went until they formed a massive silvery birthday cake, slowly weeping into the lake.

It fell to Anne to keep up with the filming. To convince our friends at home how staggeringly beautiful dusk over Lake Kariba was, she had to keep her hand on the button. Behind us, other tourists were engaged in looking skywards; an American, a Scot, several South Africans, Zimbabweans, Zulus. Sunset became the sole subject of conversation in the entire party; everyone was entranced by the last rays of daylight.

After a late evening shower, I emerged from the bathroom feeling as hot and sticky as the well-oiled Christmas goose. The air smelled of cigars and wine. A giant pearl moon sailed high above the inky waters of the lake. The bow of the boat was silver in the moonlight - cutting smoothly through the blackness.

Midnight came and went. Snatches of conversation drifted and whispered across the boat. Passengers snored gently. We had all decided to sleep below deck to avoid being bitten by night flying insects. The number of bites on my arms had been known to reach double figures by morning. The bunks were comfortable and we slept to the lilt of the ship and purr of the engines.

By five o'clock a rosy glow like pink champagne, had alighted on the lake. Dawn-tipped waves rippled between stern and shore, rhythmically – almost musically. We ventured up on deck, to find more than half the passengers already awake watching the sunrise. The air was cool and fresh again. Someone said they had seen hippo swimming along the banks through binoculars….(I was reminded that hippopotamuses kill more people in Africa than anything except road accidents) Swallows dived around the boat and out of the sky came a formation of geese with pink-tipped wings. My spirit was impaled on the beauty of this African morning.

A very real sense of *being* descended on me at that moment. That I was here at all, seemed a miracle. Voices around me faded….the gentle waters of Lake Zambezi, (twenty miles across at this point) the anticipation at what we were about to witness at Victoria Falls, our lives in Africa coming swiftly to a close, the experience of watching night turn into day, came sharply into focus for a brief moment.

My uncle's stories about Africa that I had heard as a child. Meeting Barrie at the right time in my life. That day in July1996 when I leapt on board a flight to South Africa….then Lesotho. Our wedding, going home to England, exploring Zimbabwe…..was it all real? Had I dreamt this would happen to me…no, I couldn't have. Every detail of the last two years had left a mark The imprint was there inside me….creating lasting memories of my own inner journey. Suddenly, I heard someone say my name..

"Nettie, why don't we go below and have breakfast?"

Anne and I, hanging over the deckrail as usual, commented on the presence of waterweed in the lake which clouded its reflection. A near

331

passenger, not the best informed person in the world, nor the most scintillating, told everyone within ten decibels that the invasive weed was water hyacinth and there was no way to get rid of it. It's funny how one recognises the proverbial bore who knows the answers to the world's most difficult ecological problems. Other listeners moved sideways when the speaker introduced another wriggly subject – eels.

"*Ja* – look man, it takes twenty years for them to become mature and then they migrate to the sea....."

It was obvious *Meneer* had completely missed the point....soon he was busy telling nobody that eels were about to become extinct.

Victoria Falls are without doubt one of nature's most spectacular wonders. The Zambezi River plunges more than a hundred metres vertically into a deep gorge. We had read about them, heard about them – but nothing really prepares you for this mammoth spectacle. Our little boat pulled into the quayside at Milibizi, a short distance from the Zambezi National Park, the gateway to the falls.

First the cars shackled below deck must be driven onto dry land. The jetty was extremely narrow and very steep. Each vehicle, manned by a crew member, had to be negotiated off the landing board, driven slowly upwards in a curve with hardly an inch to spare - and no warning rail where the jetty dropped over the edge into the reservoir. It seemed a haphazard system – more hazard than hap!

The last few cars came out backwards. Rarely could one imagine a worse scenario to set nerves a-jangling. The lynchpin of the operation was the boat's chief engineer, who had obviously practised driving up Everest in a Toyota Corolla in another life. He squeezed inches off corners as nearside wheels teetered perilously close to the sheer drop.

Holding our breath and not daring to look, we filed off the boat and stood ready to receive our own four wheels again. Our waiting time coincided with a posse of ladies selling their wares. They descended on us like locusts, giggling and laughing at our attempts to fight them off. They knew we had money for travel so they knew we had money for their goods. Barrie's blank refusal to let me buy anything else to store in the car boot, fell on deaf ears. Shona women are capable of exquisite handwork. I bought three bedspreads and a tablecloth – hand-crocheted in unbleached cotton. Anne and I had similar tastes, so the ladies did well and our purchases were quickly stored under seats and in tight corners of Ali Pazuki's car.

After spending the night at a small lodge near the main falls, we rose early. Another adventure was soon to be added to Barrie's wish list. It transpired that there was no age restriction on volunteers who wanted to ride the dangerous Zambezi rapids. Senior engineers were as welcome as young fitness freaks. After once leaping from an aeroplane in a parachute jump for 5th Caterham

Scouts, he felt qualified to tie himself to a raft, and tackle eleven gorges in raging torrents. Anne and I awoke at six in the morning to send him off to his chosen fate. Shearwater Centre for kamikaze candidates was in Victoria Falls. Set up to supply rafts and training guides, it also issued flood levels, timetables, climatic changes, life jackets and hard hats. We said our farewells.

"In case we never meet again Barrie, I would like to thank you for bringing me to Zimbabwe," Anne joked as he disappeared into the building with a muscular Swede, who looked young enough to be his grandson. Several young Dutch and Scandinavian tourists had already sworn in.

"Do you think he'll go?" she asked as he waved from the doorway.

"Oh yes, he never breaks a promise."

"But nobody asked him to do it"

"….the promise to *himself* Anne, it's a protest. This is his mid-life crisis talking."

Victoria Falls town didn't have a lot to offer, except a glut of 'Sunset Cruises' booking offices, cheap bars and souvenir shops. A youth stopped us to say, 'I look after your camera for few dollars' and ' give me your rings' with more than a little persuasion, so we left in a hurry.

They tell you at the entrance gate of the Victoria National Park that you need waterproof clothing. That is not true. What they should say is that you get absolutely drenched to the skin. As we stood in the early sun at the viewing point, looking down at the sheet of water falling over the edge of the gorge, we heard for the first time, the mighty roar of thunder. My heartbeat quickened. The knot in my throat tightened. From the sheer sides of the chasm below, a curtain of spray rose a hundred feet into the air. It fell on our faces and soaked our hair, but it felt warm. A gash of rainbow sparkled through the haze, shrouded in purple and orange light.

"Magnificent!" we shouted through a veil of spray. The entire volume of the Zambezi River flows over these rocks, which defines the border between Zambia and Zimbabwe. In terms of sounds it was Wagnerian. It draws you. It elates you. You drown in your own excitement. The locals call it, '*the smoke that thunders*'. Anne and I ran with soaking hair and soaking clothes along the edge of each chasm, drenched in hot steaming rain. Each gorge was wider, deeper, louder, than the last.

Approximately twice as wide and twice as deep as Niagara Falls, the river plunges over a sheer precipice to a drop of 355 feet. In times past, there have been attempts by individuals who, in sheer madness, have hurled themselves over in a barrel – but unsurprisingly, none survived. At the end of the gorge is a deep pool, known as the Boiling Pot, where the waters churn and foam. Just below there, the gorge is spanned by the Victoria Falls Bridge which carries pedestrians and vehicles between Zimbabwe and Zambia. At a point on the bridge, bungee jumpers leap off and come hurtling down to the level of the river, tied by their feet. The tension of the rope pulls them back up about fifty feet into the air. We arrived when some poor sod was mid-flight and heard a tortured cry from the watching crowd.

"Rather you than me, cobber," shouted a young Australian.

The rope moved and suddenly there was another person sliding down from the bridge to bring the lad – now hanging by his feet – back up to the top on a winch. It was stirring stuff. The crowd moved off and we saw that others - like ourselves - were soaked to the skin. Congenial laughter erupted at our mutually ridiculous plight. It was at this point I realized my camera didn't work any more.

"Shall we go on and find Livingstone's statue?" I suggested, "we can't get any more wet – we might even dry."

Striding out through forest glades, the air smelled heavenly with eucalyptus and palms. Euphorbia as high as trees shading our way, we fell into step with other tourists. The slippery zigzag paths wound through hot dripping ferns and wet-black tropical jungle where vines hung low and where families of baboons roamed. Then, a few feet away from us, a tiny deer hopped out in front – straight from the soundtrack of a Disney film. He was exquisite. Patches of sunlight fell on him and the white marks on his back made him look like Bambi himself. Blue butterflies hovered over him and I quite expected Snow White to appear from behind a tree.

It was said that the famous African explorer had been so transfixed when he came across the gorge in 1855, that he named the waterfalls after his Queen. He was the first European to come across the mighty Zambezi and fall in love with it. The impressive bronze figure loomed high above us, we just about came up to the knees. The massive jowls gazed in rapture upon the scene which history tells us, had so moved him. Thousands now flock to see Victoria Falls every year and it has been acclaimed a World Heritage site.

Suddenly a familiar voice spoke behind us.

"Goeiemiddag dame - do you remember we met on the boat?"

Anne and I exchanged glances, turned and saw our friend of the waterweed, larger than life and poised to give a Livingstone lecture to anyone within earshot. Never had we moved so fast. As we looked back, the gentleman's chin moved up and down as he burbled merrily out of control. Our hurried departure was a matter of undisguised bad manners, which we would have to learn to live with and may even have been inscribed as a sin in God's little notebook.

Later that afternoon, Barrie emerged smiling through the doors of the White Water Rafting Centre, wearing what only could be described as the 'halo look'.

"Wow," was all he could say at first…..then, "fantastic. Really fantastic!"

"Was it worth it being frightened to death?" we wanted to know, goading him into telling every detail.

"They were all so young!" he replied, "I was the oldest person there. They try to put you off going – people actually get killed." He swallowed hard, more from relief than anything. "The river is in full flood now and that makes things easier. February is a good month to go. All I can remember is a pool called the 'Washing Machine'.... the instructor told us if we went overboard, not to fight it, but that we would come up like a cork – and it's true." His eyes blazed blue and his mouth smiled uncontrollably. "There's a seven hundred and fifty foot gorge at the end. Some of the lads are still fighting their way up. Right! Now I want to see the falls, come on girls, there's just time."

"But Barrie – we're just dry – we'll get wet again….."

"Too bad, you'll have to get wet twice."

For the second time that day, we stood by the edge of the gorges, the air now hotter than before, the rainbows sparkling like diamonds round every bend. We went right to the edge this time, feeling braver…that distinctive roar making the blood pound in our ears again.The morning visit had been fabulous. The afternoon was sensational. The skies were more radiant, the curtain of water shone iredescent and we had to shade our eyes.

Barrie insisted on doing the whole circuit. All three of us were soaked to the skin. It was late in the afternoon when we came across a company of baboons, sitting on the path. They stared at us; some huge males, many smaller females and babies. A huge fella on all fours was standing near and making noises that sounded threatening. Beady eyes glowed yellow.

"I think we'd better go the other way round. They don't like us," I said in a quiet voice.

The growling and spitting went on. Baboons can bite and I didn't fancy our chances. We backed into a clearing. There was a primeval agenda going on. It would take us at least forty minutes to return to the entrance gate ….and closing time was in fifteen minutes. Then the park would be shut. We would have to spend the night with the baboons. The most we could hope for was a friendly leopard who wanted to reduce the primate population. Suddenly Anne made the decision for us. She skipped into the middle of them and quickly disappeared from view.

We prayed that the guards at the big gate would fall for the charms of a lady in distress, as she pleaded for them to wait for two stranded tourists who had not made it back to base on time….

335

Chapter 27

The End of the Rainbow

Driving through the bush on a tarmac road, fifty miles from the nearest town, our car came to a grinding halt. In Zimbabwe there are few vehicle recovery services. In fact, in Northern Matabeleland, there are very few vehicles. We had pulled off the bush road to take photographs and had stopped to speak to the driver of a two wheeled cart, pulled by a span of four trotting donkeys - a lovely sight.Two little boy passengers and Daddy Matebele were on their way to find water, eight kilometres away. We were amazed at their ability to understand and speak English with us; trendy mud-hutters without a doubt.

A few miles after that, the silencer dropped off the car – and nobody could have mistaken us for well-mannered tourists. The sound emitting from the exhaust after that was appalling. At a tiny crossroads called Dete, a self-styled big-hearted welder took pity on us. Laying on his back underneath the car with a gas pipe and blow lamp (circa 1940), he effortlessly welded metal to metal. All we could see was a pair of bare feet sticking out from the underbelly of the car. Every few inches along the pipe, a blue flame burned, as it was full of holes and we were worried that melted tyres would be worse than a hole in the exhaust. The mechanic seemed unperturbed. He blew out one jet of flame and it re-lit itself further down the pipe.

"Okay man… de car will take you to heaven and back," he said, emerging from underneath our vehicle with an oily smile. Barrie paid him over the odds and shook his hand. We hoped our gratitude got throught to him.

Wild animals…... we saw plenty. Elephants are huge when you're standing next to them. In Hwange Park, rounding a bend in the track, without warning, they suddenly appeared in front of us…..we stopped the engine and waited. They were friendly, if a little curious. After a munch and a stare – they left quietly…..but they are big.

One hot still afternoon, we melted inside a 'hide' with millions of buzzing flies which can have an alarming effect on your brain. Our patience was rewarded by the arrival of several graceful giraffe with their babies at a water hole. Watching close by, a wildebeest. He was a rather ugly creature with the front of an ox, the rear of an antelope and the tail of a horse. This fellow was a bit jittery and gave the impression he was thinking of running away, but wasn't quite sure when.

Giraffe have a delightful way of bending necks through splayed legs to drink - and the zebras – well they are just so polite. Then came a tense moment. A passing crocodile started stalking the novices at the water's edge.

We were afraid the hungry jaws would lunge out of the water, but mother superior giraffe gave the babies a nudge and they moved off. The patriarchal one glanced approvingly and went on chewing. The croc disappeared.

Following miles of bush through the reserve, we came across snorkling hippos, antennae- ears cocked above the water, like microphones on red alert. Further on, a flock of long-legged birds, fully plumed with bridesmaid headdresses, strutting on a grass verge – and monkeys among the leafy branches of mopane trees, screeching our arrival to their mates up the road. All this in serious tropical heat. We decided to push on.

Bulawayo was fascinating, in particular the city's art gallery, where we were stirred by modern African paintings, sculpture, wood carving and etching in leather. Bushman paintings and symbols of animals, taken from cave dwellings had been recreated using modern dyes and colouring techniques. There could be no forgetting the primitive tribes, whose symbols had originally been smeared on the walls of caves under the influence of hallucinatory drugs which produced in them, a trance-like state. Amazingly, over thousands of years, the colours of vegetable dyes, mixed with ochre, lime and blood had faded - yet enough remained to please the human eye.

Bulawayo's raucous market showed how alive the town was; papayas and mangoes, glowing bright yellow, red and green, sweet potatoes, gourds, corn and maize in plenty. We stopped to admire hand-crafted leather goods made from ostrich, buffalo, elephant and crocodile. Witchdoctor powders came in psychedelic packets. Burning joss-sticks filled the air with jasmine and frangipani. Necklaces, made from special roots for when the wearer wanted to protect himself from dangerous animals, hung from snake-skin thongs. Medicines came in the form of wild olive for treatment of sore throats, bladder and kidney infections, weeping wattle to cure colds and chest infections. Sweet-scented flowers of the sweet thorn to be used as a poultice to draw abscesses or boils and to soothe sprains; the seeds – dried, crushed and roasted – can be used as a coffee substitute. In some parts of Africa, the thorns are used as needles. The concoctions were as fascinating as the sellers; tall bearded men in bright shirts – white teeth smiling, Matabele women, hard-working and friendly, shouting across the tide of market-place litter.

"Come on Mamma – try de medicine - make you feel heppy."

Thirty kilometres from Bulawayo (City of the Kings) we reached the Motopos Hills, an area of spectacular beauty and historical significance. The age old caves where the san left behind their legacy of rock paintings, are home to the rare white rhino and leopard. Cruel claws and animal spirits live side by side, where black eagles swoop and the air is sometimes foul with rotting carcasses. Primitive tribes, once the only hunters in this awesome valley of ancient granite, have been replaced by modern man, whose weapons are no longer poison arrows - but weapons, cleverly barbed with points of

337

steel - and guns which fire bullets into the head of an elephant, so that it dies quickly. The slaughter of wildlife in Zimbabwe has left its mark.

Volcanoes erupted in these parts millions of years ago, leaving Motopos a place of dramatic terrain. Ancient house-sized volcanic boulders perched above and below us on every peak and precipice. These granite *whalebacks*, as they are known, are a feature of the landscape as far as the eye can see. It is the part of Africa that Cecil Rhodes chose as his burial ground. His grave lies close by.

It was our last night in Zimbabwe. Matopo Ingwe Lodge was the perfect place to say farewell, providing us with a lasting memory of its wild beauty. Walking out on that warm evening, just before dusk, we watched dozens of darting lizards playing hide-and-seek between the boulders – miniature dinosaurs in their own playground. Avocado and lemon trees, heavy with fruit, scented the air outside our *rondavel* and as night fell, the sky was full of insects and beating wings. The three of us drank to our homeward journey.

Goodbye to magnificent Victoria Falls, goodbye to Kipling's fever trees on either side of the Limpopo River, goodbye to the great ruined citadel - where once, black slaves searched for gold. We had bathed in hot springs, danced with the Shona people, sailed across Lake Kariba. Now our time was running out. We must return to Lesotho to say more goodbyes. With the skies over the Zambezi still fresh in our minds and an assortment of Zimbabwean gear stashed aboard the car with its welded-together undercarriage, we set off on our remaining journey, which would take us across the Tropic of Capricorn and back into South Africa.

On reaching the gate of Priscilla and Guido's farm in Leeuwkloof Valley, we had proved that you could 'do Zimbabwe' in just over two weeks ...at a gallop....over two thousand kilometres on the clock. Priscilla was building a sawdust kiln in the garden when we arrived, in readiness for firing her numerous clay pots. Behind her on the parking lot stood an open-topped station waggon, with a newly painted picture of a cute-looking turtle on the rear tailgate. In shiny gloss paint the dynamic words, 'Please Go Slow, Tortoise Crossing' was a stern warning to drivers attempting to overtake. Her dear old truck, which rejoiced in the name of 'Betsie' had recently been stolen. She came out to greet us, hands covered in clay and hair crusted in paint, wearing the familiar bush hat. We could tell where Guido was by the curl of smoke from the *braai*, up near the house.

"Well, how was Zimbabwe....tell me, tell me – did you see any wild animals?"

We were given a rapturous welcome, a bed (under the pillow was a ridiculous rubber head with matted hair) and a fine meal. The next morning, after a delicious hot shower, this time without Norman hovering behind the wash basin (he had obviously gone off to find Mrs green lizard), I went out to swoon over the frangipani blossom - the fragrance more pungent than ever. In the kitchen, Priscilla was busy scraping cold food from the cooker into a large enamel bowl. The wild dog who lived in the outback had finally dared to come into their kitchen to feed. With a nod towards the porch and a vanishing sandy-haired mongrel, she drawled, "he *likes* my burnt casseroles, Guido won't eat them - so Charlie gets to eat these days."

Priscilla's culinary attempts were impulsive and short lived. Painting and potting were her great talents, cooking was a disaster. She would boil up an ox tongue for a day or so, then fling in a great quantity of garlic, which produced a grey gelatinous stew the consistency of wallpaper paste, mop it up with bread and slurp it down with vodka before sunrise. Guido did most of the cooking - Italian style.Today she had invited neighbours in for breakfast to meet us. Introductions followed. Anne poured coffee for us Brits and Priscilla poured something from a bottle for the visitors.

"I've decided to make my home into a sanctuary for sick animals.....I'd like a small zoo..."she said with an innocent smile. Guido carried on eating and didn't comment. He was used to Priscilla's passionate attempts to foster stray animals Grey louries, pairs of which hovered in nearby trees, came to breakfast on ripe bananas put out by Priscilla every morning and warthogs who foraged on the hillside were already coming closer to the house. It was only a matter of time before one appeared in the kitchen.

"You could have wall-to-wall straw, it would be cheaper than carpets," said Barrie.

We all laughed In this house - the idea might not be so far from reality.

"One of the garden boys brought in a spitting cobra – dead...thought I'd like to skin it," said the lady of the house, quite unperturbed, "they have wonderful markings, you know…"

Barrie and I exchanged glances. How would our lives ever return to normality when we returned to London? I tried to picture our suburban flat in des.res.Beckenham and couldn't. How would I cope with a Tesco trolley again? No Priscilla jokes which bordered on the ridiculous, no wildlife reserves to get lost in, no rollercoaster rides through the mounains, no electric storms, nor stars to go to bed with….and no snakes. I thought of our families and how they would view our homecoming – and wondered if Abigail would remember me….

First, we must say goodbye to our ever-cheerful fellow traveller. Anne caught the flight from Johannesburg to London Heathrow the following day, overloaded with extra luggage she had amassed while in Zimbabwe. We would meet again very soon. Three weeks to be exact. Barrie and I prepared for the journey back from Pretoria to Lesotho and tried not to think about our final goodbyes, which we would soon have to face at Ha Simone. Priscilla bought me a parting gift, typical of her nature – a plume of ostrich feathers on a pole – a sort of giant feather duster five feet long, enough to cause a modest riot at airport immigration. We departed their valley – with laughter still inside us.

*   *   *   *

By the following week, our overseas trunks had been collected from Leribe Camp and taken to Johannesburg Cargo International. All that was left in our house was the furniture which belonged to LHPC, our everyday cooking equipment and a temperamental house phone, which seemed to operate according to the weather. A cellphone call from the top of a hill near St Monica's Mount, was almost the only link with our country of origin. Barrie's contract with the joint venture was finished and his next assignment would be in England.

Butha-Buthe Camp was like a ghost town. The French school had closed. The English school had performed their end of term concert and the huge iron gates were locked for ever. Staff had been transferred overseas or taken jobs in other parts of Africa. A few had applied for posts up at Mohale, where a new school was due to be opened and a community would grow over the next six years. Pupils went their separate ways, African school days faded.... perhaps they would meet again - perhaps not.

Hundreds of local contract workers were repatriated. For five years they had earned good wages, now there was no more work. Perhaps the men would go back into the mines, the ladies into the domestic melting pot.The Butha-Buthe Clinic doors were closed and ambulances no longer roared past the guard hut with bells ringing, spewing clouds of dust. Medical staff were looking for new jobs but in this part of the world, nobody could afford to pay them. One of the lady doctors planned to open a centre for visitors at Mohale. She had ideas of a classy hotel - in essence, an enterprising idea.

Our friends the Pazukis went back to France. We had grown close during our time as neighbours. In the beginning, we were like settlers in a new land; knowing nothing about the people or their traditions. Stirred by the beauty and grandeur of Lesotho, exhilarated by its climate and stirred by the simplicity of its culture, we longed to explore and discover, wanted to know the country deeply, intimately. Gradually, we realised we shared a love of South Africa that was deep and long lasting. Our families had trekked together, climbed together, searched for cave paintings in South Africa, fallen in love with the night skies of the Karoo desert and gazed in awe upon dinosaur bones in Graaff Reinet. *Au revoir* was easier to say than goodbye.....and Paris isn't a million miles away from London. Horse rides at Bokpoort Reserve would not easily be forgotten and evenings at the Guinea Feather in Clarens – drinking rock shandies and devouring tandori chickens roasted in a clay pot, after our strenuous Sunday hikes......so many good memories.

I hated saying goodbye to Ficksburg, the brave little town near the border, where I spent my first South African Christmas teaching at Kindi Nursery School. With a cast of nations, I had helped to push miniature kings and shepherds onto the stage in a nativity play, in which a black baby doll acted the part of Jesus. Ficksburg was where I had taught the kids of Thotlisong High School, during the time they were housed in a squatter building which had been scheduled for demolition. I remember my first day there when I asked someone when the coffee-break was, only to be told there was no such thing as a break and they had no coffee. Then that memorable day in June last year, when Solomon and I had taken the kids over the border (without passports) to sing in that extraordinary concert, by special permission from the border authorities, as long as we brought them back on the same night - would we ever forget the moment our bus broke down.

Ficksburg was where Barrie and I were married in an April afternoon, during a special ceremony officiated by Ena Swanopoel, the magistrate, who sang gospel music at our wedding table. Ficksburg was where I spent housekeeping money, found telephones that worked, frequented the coffee shop with my friend Grace from Maputsoe, searched for the best supplies of fresh vegetables, visited the only 'hole in the wall' cash machine and had long arguments with bank managers. On a trip into town, Barrie and I would indulge ourselves by buying that rare thing called a newspaper to find out what the rest of the world was doing - then have a moan about the new British Labour Government. Brand Street Ficksburg had become as familiar as old slippers and it was where I felt as much at home as my own Beckenham High Sreet. And Judi's bar on Friday nights …..

From England, postbags of correspondence arrived, in anticipation of domestic engagements; the solicitor, the tax-man and the bank manager - all of them curried our favour. How dull, after life on camp without any administrative attachments. The old British officialdom had clawed us back into the system. A man came to collect my computer and I parcelled up my batches of diaries and scribblings. My oil paints and brushes were stacked inside my paintbox. Cerilean blue and magenta, I would not be using again on English skies.

Every week, staff numbers at Leribe were reducing and the canteen was one of the last bastions to go. When the last engineer had eaten the last thickly-crusted meat pie, Sophie would hang up her apron and douse the huge iron stove, scrubbed and polished as never before. These days you could hear her balefully singing from the cookhouse, where Thabo hung around for his meals. There was not much for him to do now as the gardens didn't have to be kept and his beloved swimming pool had no bodies in it, so he didn't have to clean it every day, as he used to. He seemed to spend most of his time washing cars for the last few residents, or appearing in the garden with a spade in his hand, ready to dig a trench, more from habit than neccessity. His spirits were flagging because he knew he would never have another job like this one and shortly Mrs Thabo would reclaim him for marital duties. Barrie gave him an armful of shirts and he remained speechless for a few seconds, then ran round the garden like a mechanical toy – kissing them and throwing them in the air.

341

Petros was ever campaigning the last few families for donations towards his new roof and showing pictures of his baby daughter to the ladies in the offices. I felt sorry that we were leaving him. Such resourcefulness I had never come across and probably never would again. My washing machine had already disappeared – no doubt into Petros's secret factory for extinct gadgets and sold to the highest bidder. I gave him our house radio and my book on the life of Princess Diana, as he admired her. Later he knocked on the back door and handed us a miniature Basotho rondavel, made from clay and grasses, which he had made himself.

Betty was distraught. She worked right up to the last week and brought Oliver and Margaret to say goodbye. She took the contents of my kitchen cupboards and as many pairs of my shoes as she could carry. The cardboard box on her head almost collapsed with the weight and I prayed it didn't rain before she reached home. We paid her six months wages. She had plans to become a student in Maseru and hoped her mother would take care of the children. She had decided it was time to further her career and we hoped it didn't include more babies. The money would help her to achieve some qualifications. She wore her best dress when she came to say goodbye - the brown version of the traditional attire for Basotho women. My hands were shaking. Sadly I hugged her. She had tears in her eyes.

"I always remember you Mrs Glenn, I will not forget you and Mr Glenn, you were kind to me and my family. God is always with you."

I could not watch her go, but sat on the bed with a heavy heart and thought how much my house would miss her. She had cleaned every inch of it for a year and a half – and now it would become empty and full of dust. These places would be towed up to Mohale on a trailer, to be used as homes for other engineers. Through swollen ankles, a broken arm, a pregnancy, the 'chick pox', and beetles in her leg, Betty had turned up for work, lest some-one else took her job. We had kept the wolf from her door for a short while. She would always think that white people were privileged and blacks were not.

Even Hercule had gone quiet . Most mornings he lay in his dug-out below the house and sulked. He could smell departure in the air and his breakfast was often left unlicked by the back door. His eyes, when he did put in an appearance, were dull and lifeless and he sure as eggs knew that we were all leaving. Where would he go? Someone would surely keep him when his master and mistress left – we hoped his new owner would love him despite his racist bark, even appreciate his fascination with smelly cow dung.

I drove to Ha Simone for the last time. It was raining stair rods. The mist rolled across the hilltops and clung in strands to the upper slopes, where cows went on hoovering dark green pasture. The mealie fields were high and full of ripeness. The sunflowers were leaning on the wind with their heads down and a black cloud sat above the hillside on both sides of the road. The weather was downcast and so was I. My windscreen was dirty and I would ask Walter if he could wash it - one last time. Barrie and Stephen had already said their farewells the previous Sunday. The two shook hands and blinked their goodbyes in gruff man-like tones.

The priest had given us an occasion to remember with an all-singing all dancing morning service. They wanted Barrie and I to wear traditional Basotho clothes. We felt rather awkward sitting at the front of the congregation wearing blankets and hats, but the people were overjoyed that we were dressed as one of them. We all knew it would be the last time. Presents poured in, home-made gifts from the children, a rug from the ladies, poems from Petros, Walter and Augustinus. Emily sang unaccompanied and my tears flowed. I couldn't bear the thought of not hearing her beautiful contralto voice again. She was an undiscovered gem, tailor-made for a soloist spot in a London concert hall- if only things were different.

Walter made a speech in English. Rose translated. Fervently, Stephen gave us a prayerful blessing in both languages, then as a farewell gesture, bid the assembled company sing us the familiar hymn they loved. The seated congregation sprang to their feet and stepping out to a rhythm, went 'Marching over to Jerusalem' in harmony fortissimo. Forming a human chain, we danced, chorus after chorus, round the church, wailing loudly to the Almighty to deliver us safely to our homeland. Pearly teeth smiled and dark eyes shone, young men eager to leap and shout, threw decorum to the winds. Stephen rallied the troops with his priest stick, and the congregation clapped us back to our seats. What would it have been like with an organist at full throttle!

Gospel Rock is part of the African soul; he must dance, he must sing – even if the heavens open or the roof is caving in. It corrects the imbalance between bliss and absolute hell. Impossible equations of food distribution, pain, hunger or cold – given that the African suffers from one or all of these most of the time – are temporarily banished by the rhythm of a dance. It would take a lifetime of living here to completely understand them. They have their own logic and one has to accept it. Faith is about believing in something bigger than yourself. And now the time had come to take our leave of Ha Simone, my belief was that God would make our transition from Lesotho to England bearable…with the help of Rose's prayers, Emily's singing and Stephen's Holy Water. Water had been the reason for us coming to Lesotho, now it was a symbol of our parting.

Walter wasn't even at home when I arrived, he had gone out with the cows, as Petros had gone to school. Justice and Bernice were also away at their lessons. Puddles on the clay-red earth made slippery steps to the front door and I noticed the glass angel hanging in the window threw out a few specks of purple light where the rain had splashed it. Stephen had gone to Teyateyaneng to an important church service. Only Rose and Emily were at home.

There were no words of greeting. Just embraces. The table in the living room smelt of wax polish as usual and the back of the chair was draped with a half finished garment. Rose had been up most of the night sewing. I placed a small plastic bottle on the side.

"Water from our fridge - *with ice,*" I said quietly. "It's not Holy…"

With a swift movement, Rose pushed something into my hand. It was a small blue envelope. On it she had written, 'Not to be opened until you reach England'.

"Nettie, I do not like goodbyes. Especially to you and Barrie." Her head lowered and I could hardly hear the words. "Stephen and me - we want to say many things,"she hesitated…..“we have given you a Basotho name – as a gift."

"But Rose, you gave us many gifts."

I was holding onto Emily's hand and squeezing it. My mouth was dry. I dare not let the tears come. They might not stop. Rose, the epicentre of this family – had already given me the most wonderful prize - the opportunity *to belong* in the lives of a Basotho family. The fine dignity she showed to everyone who knew her, the love she wove around the walls of this house, had reached me the day I first met Walter, when I was stranded outside their village. He had offered friendship. Rose was the reason I was here now.

"We have given you the name *'Malimakatso',* Nettie ……. it means *'Mother of Miracles'.*

I felt as though someone had put hot needles on my eyelids….. I stared at her, not quite knowing what to say next. "We want you to know that we feel a miracle has happened to our family since you came to our village." The serious assurance of my friend Rose, whom I admired so much, was saying this to me. She did not falter, as she bestowed this traditional privilege upon my leaving. "You and Barrie have been parents to us and we would like this to be our last word to you before you leave….so that one day you will come back"

She turned so that I should not see the large tears roll down her cheeks. Emily walked with me to the car and put her head on my shoulder……a moment to be by ourselves

"Nettie, before you go, I wanted to tell you. I've met someone….he is nice….. he wants to look after me and…..I will have someone I can turn to when you've gone to England. …only Walter knows about him - no one else."

She stopped. Her large eyes glowed like deep pools and her hand went over her mouth as if she was trying to stem the feelings which flowed from her heart. Dear Emily. It was time she had someone special. She was very pretty. Now this secret, held tight inside her.

I held both her hands in mine. "Goodbye Em, write to me….and keep singing."

The tyres of the Silver Fox slithered through craters of mud along the well worn path away from the house, my eyes were streaming with tears. The rain had stopped and a curtain of light glared on my windscreen, making me blink even more. I caught only a blur of landscape where the path went down to the river. Then on the main track, I met Augustinus on foot. Slipping on the wet ground, I left the car to find his warm handshake waiting for me. His coat was wet from the rain and he put his arm round my shoulder.

"Nettie, I will not forget you. Please tell Barrie I shall greatly miss his wisdom. England must have you back. I will write many letters to you. And when I am an architect ....one day, I will come and visit you."

We murmured our farewells and smiled a lot, though not wanting to smile. Behind him I could see someone hurrying towards us.

It seemed an age until Walter caught up The misted mountains beyond framed his youthful head, hair cropped short. He held out his arms. The smile that had *always* greeted me was missing. A veil of sadness hung over his whole body.

There would never be another time like this. His face was a mask of deep sorrow. His arms encircled me. I wiped my teary face on his coat. A million worlds apart, Walter and I hugged our goodbyes.

This familiar road leading to the Subeng River, with its donkeys and lazy wandering cows, where my wheels crunched on the stones and fell into the muddy hollows, would not come again into my gaze. My time was up.

"Keep looking at the stars Walter," I whispered hoarsly, "we will look at them too – from the northern hemisphere. Your moon will be our moon....and remember my tree will grow and you will grow too." Without a word, he let me walk away towards the car. Like a figure cast in stone, he let me slip from his embrace.

"Goodbye Walter..... look after the others....and write to me. One day I will come back."

In slow motion, I saw the mountain disappear through my storm-beaten rear view mirror. A smudged half rainbow lit the horizon, as the Basotho boy on the hillside wept.

I wish I could remember every sky , every rainbow,
every laugh, every tear, every journey,
every African child's face.

Reverend Makibi and Emily, with Annette and Barrie in a Service of Farewell at St John's Church, Ha Simone.

Bibliography for 'Born Singing'
In alphabetical order of Author's Surname

John Addison
Apartheid - Published by B.T. Batsford Ltd 1981

APA Publications
South Africa Insight Guide. Third edition 1998

Professor David Ambrose MBE
Maseru an Illustrated History - Published Morija Museum and Archives 1993
Journal of Research, a Tentative History of Lesotho Paleontology - published by
National University of Lesotho, Roma, Lesotho, 1991

Thomas Arbousset
Missionary Excursion – King Moshoshoe's Expedition from Thaba- Bosiu to the
Sources of the Malibamatso River in the year 1840, published 1991, edited and
translated by David Ambrose and Albert Brutsch

Gavin Bell,
Somewhere over the Rainbow - published by Little, Brown and Company, 2000

Shirley du Boulay
Tutu – Voice of the Voiceless – Published by Hodder & Stoughton 1988

John Briley
Cry Freedom - A true Story of Friendship - Published by Penguin Group, 1987

Charlotte Cameron
A woman's Winter in Africa – a 26,000 Mile Journey - Published by Stanley Paul & Co
, London 1913.

Spencer Chapman
Lightest Africa – Chatto and Windus 1955

Canon R.Dove,
Anglican Pioneers in Lesotho 1876-1930 - written 1975

Kate Fagalde
Lambs, Love and Laughter - published 1998 by Kate Fagalde

Athol Fugard
Sorrows and Rejoicings – a play about Apartheid set in the Karoo Desert S.Africa.

Kuki Gallman
I dreamed of Africa – Published by Penguin Books 1991
African Nights – published by Penguin Books 1994

John Gay and David Hall
Poverty and Livelihoods in Lesotho,2000 – published by Sechaba Consultants, Maseru

Stephen Gill
A Short History of Lesotho - published by Morija Museum & Archives, Lesotho 1993

Peter Goodwin
Mukiwa - A White Boy in Africa - Published by Macmillan 1996

John Gunther
Inside Africa – published by The Reprint Society Ltd /Hamish Hamilton, London 1957

Father Trevor Huddleston
Naught for your Comfort - by Collins, London 1956

Peter Joyce
South Africa in the 20TH Century – Chronicles of an era - first published in 2000 by
Struik Publishers (Pty) Ltd a member of the Struik New Holland Publishing Pty Ltd

Christina Lamb
Africa House – published by Penguin Books 1999.

Lesotho Highlands Water Project
Engineering Booklets, published by Pensord Press, Wales, Volumes 1 – 5, 1992 yearly.
Representing companies involved in Highland Water Scheme.

Lonely Planet
South Africa, Lesotho and Swaziland, March 2000

Dr Kenneth Luckman
Place of Compassion - published by Authorsonline Ltd, 2002

Peter Magubane
Vanishing Cultures of South Africa
First Published in USA by Rizzoli International Publications 1998
First Published Great Britain New Holland Publishers Ltd 1998

Nelson Mandela
Long Walk to Freedom – published by Little, Brown and Company 1994
No Easy Walk to Freedom - published by Heinemann

James Mc Gann
Green Land, Brown Land, Black Land. - An Environmental History of Africa 1800 -
1990,
Published by Heineman1999

Mpho 'M'atsepo Nthunya
Singing Away the Hunger - Souvenir Press, Edited by K Limakatso Kendall 1998

James Mitchener
The Covenant – Published by Random House, New York 1979

Aubrey D.Mokoena
SESOTHO Made Easy, part of 'African Languages Made Easy' series, published
1998 by JL van Schaik Publishers, Pretoria.

Dervla Murphy
Cameroon with Egbert – John Murray Publishers 1989
The Ukimwi Road – John Murray Publishers 1993
South from the Limpopo – John Murray Publishers 1997

National Environment Secretariat 2000, Ministry of Environment,
Lesotho Government
Biological Diversity in Lesotho - A Country Study - published Maseru 2000

J.M. Orpen
History of the Basutus of South Africa – Published by Mazenod Book Centre, Lesotho
National Environment Secretariat 2000.

Michael Palin
Pole to Pole with Michael Palin - published by BBC Books 1992

Margaret Phillips
Do Not Unsaddle your Horse - A Report on Leprosy in Uganda and Lesotho 2002.
Published by Mathabo Press, Swan Street, West Malling, Kent.

Gisela Prasad.
LESOTHO: WHERE TO?
Printed by Morija Printing Works, Morija, Lesotho 1991

Peter Saunders
The Last of the Queen's Men , A Lesotho Experience - Published by Witwatersrand University Press 2000

Olive Schreiner
The Story of an African Farm – published by by AD Donker (PTY) Ltd 1975

Dirk Schwager
LESOTHO - published by Schwager publications 1987

Russell Suchet
A Backpackers Guide to Lesotho 1997

Pauline Smith
The Beadle – published by Jonathan Cape Ltd, 1926

Colin Smith
Green Mountain Doctor – published by Colin Smith, Beaminster, Dorset 2001

Stephen Taylor
Livingstone's Tribe - published Harper Collins 1999

Jan and Fiona Teede
The Zambezi - River of the Gods - published by Andre Deutsch Ltd 1990

Laurens Van der Post
The Lost World of the Kalahari - published by Chatto and Windus 1958
Testament to the Bushmen and Witness to a Last Will of Man – With Jane Taylor 1984

Donald Woods
Rainbow Nation Revisited - published by Andre Deutsch in 2000.
This book is dedicated to STEVE BIKO who died for the dream and NELSON MANDELA who made the dream come true.

Martin West and Jean Morris
Abantu - Published by C Struik, Cape Town and Johannesburg 1976

Glossary

Sesotho – in plain Text
Afrikaans – in Italics

Bakkie – an open truck
Balimo - ancestral spirits
Bana secola – school children
Biltong – dried strips of meat
Bobotie – a meat dish served with sweet chutney
Boerewors – large meaty sausages
Bohobe - bread
Braai – to grill on an open fire, usually with charcoal
Cicadas – a cricket-like insect
Combi – a mini-bus style vehicle
Donga – a deep gully in the land formed by erosion.
Goeiemiddag Mevrou – Good afternoon, Madam
Goeiemiddag dame - *Good afternoon, ladies*
Goeie nag - Goodnight
Hantle haholo, Ntate - I am very well thank you, father
Highveld – open pasture of the highlands
Initiate – a person who has been through the ceremony of circumcision
Ja - yes
joala – homebrewed beer
Ke a kula - I am sick.
Kea Leboha – thank you
Ke hantle - okay
Ke nako mang - what time is it
Khoi Khoi- semi nomadic tribes who once inhabited what is now South Africa
Khoiti – Mole Rat
Khotso – Peace
Khotso 'M'e. Ke le boha – Peace and Blessings to you Madam.
Kobo – traditional blanket
Kombi – minibus
Kopjes – a small hillock
Kumbah (Indian word) – a throng
Kraal – small enclosure for animals, surrounded by a stone wall or thorns
Landdrost - tax collector
Lebitso la hau u mang? - what is your name?
Lihobe – a kind of porridge made from wheat and peas.
Litapole - potatoes
Litolobonya – a dance performed by women

351

Lobola – bride price paid by the groom's family

Lowveld – open pasture of the lowlands

Lumela 'M'e – hello Mother (a respectful greeting to women) pronounced 'dumela'

Lumela Ntate – hello Father (a respectful greeting to men) pronounced 'dumela'

Lumelang – hello everyone, when spoken to a group.

Lumelang bana secola - hello kids

Makoenya - fat cakes, made with yeast.

Makoloane - an initiate after completing his training

Mamokhorong – a traditional instrument made with a petrol can, twigs and string.

marabaraba – a game played by herd boys carved on the rocks similar to chess.

'M'e - Mother or Mrs

Mealie – corn

Metsi - water

Modimo - God

Mohlolo – a miracle

Mohobelo – a dance performed by men

Mokhibo – a dance performed by women on the knees.

Mokorotlo – a dance in praise of the ancestors

Molilietsane – ululations by the women

Moloti   - Lesotho currency – equivalent value of the South African Rand

Mophato - the makeshift shelter which initiates occupy during their training

Moroho – vegetables

Mosotho – singular of Basotho (one person)

Motebo – a simple hut in the mountains, where the herd boy sleeps.

Ngaka - doctor

Nkhono - grandmother

Ntate – father or Mr

O a phela? – are you all right?

Re a le lumedisa – we are greeting you

Rondavel- small round hut

Rooibos - *tea made from a Rooibos plant*

Sala hantle – stay well

Sangoma – witch doctor

Sepinichi - spinach

Sesotho – language spoken by the Basotho people

Setibeng – place of water

Shambas – groups of houses and animals

Shosholosa – a dance which miners perform in the gold mines.

Snoek – a fish, eaten as a delicacy

Stoep – verandah

Ttakkies – sports shoes or trainers

Tamati - tomatoes

Tatenda - thank you (Zulu)

Thaba Bosiu – the mountain where the Kings are buried

Theepe – a weed, sometimes cooked and eaten as a vegetable
Thokolosi – an evil spirit.
Topgehalte teesakkies - teabags
Tsamaea hantle - go well
Tsamaeang – go well (plural)
Tubu - a woman's scarf or headgear.
Uitlander – a foreigner
Ululations – high pitched appreciative noises generally used by women.
Veld – open pasture
Wat is dit? - What is this?

Other Titles by the same author

'Innocent in Africa'

ISBN: 0 7552 0009 8

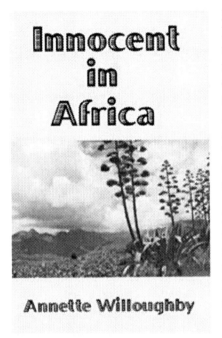

Innocent in Africa' is a tribute to the people of Lesotho. It came about through the writer's unexpected journey, at a time when she regarded England as the only home she would ever know. The prospect of cosy retirement in a suburban town near the North Downs in Kent, was beginning to appear an attractive choice, when suddenly she and her partner were catapulted into the Mountain Kingdom of Lesotho in Southern Africa - a land of electric storms and brilliant rainbows.

Instead of working with special needs children in outer suburbia, she came to know families with even greater needs, who lived in the foothills of the Maluti Mountains. Looking at life from both sides of the border, she observes contrasting attitudes of this Third World Kingdom with South Africa, two years after the end of apartheid.

She was totally unprepared and had no knowledge of Lesotho, not even where it was on the map of Africa. Her only preparation was a valid passport, four aggressive doses of vaccine and clothes suitable for meeting mosquitoes and elephants. Her partner, a civil engineer, had been contracted to work on a construction site in the Maluti Mountains - the last thing he expected was the arrival of his lady.

After leaving London in a stifling English summer, she arrived in a South African winter during their worst snowfall for twenty seven years. Nothing in her life could have prepared her for this extraordinary adventure.

Authors OnLine

Visit us online at www.authorsonline.co.uk

Lightning Source UK Ltd.
Milton Keynes UK
22 April 2010

153161UK00001B/16/A